Discourse Analysis and Austerity

In the immediate aftermath of the global financial crisis of 2008, governments around the developed world coordinated policy moves to stimulate economic activity and avert a depression. In subsequent years, however, cuts to public expenditure, or austerity, have become the dominant narrative in public debate on economic policy.

This unique collaboration between economists and linguists examines manifestations of the discourses of austerity as these have played out in media, policy and academic settings across Europe and the Americas. Adopting a critical perspective, it seeks to elucidate the discursive and argumentation strategies used to consolidate austerity as the dominant economic policy narrative of the twenty-first century.

Kate Power is a lecturer in Management Communication at the University of Queensland Business School, Australia. A critical discourse analyst with particular interest in interdisciplinarity, she has published linguistic analyses of both religious and economic discourses.

Tanweer Ali is a lecturer in finance and economics with Empire State College, SUNY. His research interests are in corporate governance and the application of linguistic methods to economic questions. He has guest edited two special editions of *On the Horizon*, focused on language and economics.

Eva Lebdušková is a PhD candidate at the J.E. Purkyně University in Ústí nad Labem. In addition, she holds a senior administrative position with the Charles University in Prague. Her main field of research is in linguistics, and she has published a number of articles on the use of language in economic discourse.

Routledge Frontiers of Political Economy

248 Ethics and Economic Theory
Khalid Mir

249 Economics for an Information Age
Money-Bargaining, Support-Bargaining and the Information Interface
Patrick Spread

250 The Pedagogy of Economic, Political and Social Crises
Dynamics, Construals and Lessons
Edited by Bob Jessop and Karim Knio

251 Commodity
The Global Commodity System in the 21st Century
Photis Lysandrou

252 Uncertainty and Economics
A Paradigmatic Perspective
Christian Müller-Kademann

253 Discourse Analysis and Austerity
Critical Studies from Economics and Linguistics
Edited by Kate Power, Tanweer Ali and Eva Lebdušková

For more information about this series, please visit:
www.routledge.com/books/series/SE0345

Discourse Analysis and Austerity

Critical Studies from Economics and Linguistics

Edited by Kate Power, Tanweer Ali and Eva Lebdušková

Routledge
Taylor & Francis Group
LONDON AND NEW YORK

First published 2019
by Routledge

2 Park Square, Milton Park, Abingdon, Oxfordshire OX14 4RN
52 Vanderbilt Avenue, New York, NY 10017

Routledge is an imprint of the Taylor & Francis Group, an informa business

First issued in paperback 2020

British Library Cataloguing-in-Publication Data
A catalogue record for this book is available from the British Library

Library of Congress Cataloging-in-Publication Data
A catalog record has been requested for this book

ISBN: 978-1-138-63254-7 (hbk)
ISBN: 978-0-367-67158-7 (pbk)

Typeset in Bembo
by Newgen Publishing UK

Contents

Figures

Tables

Contributors

Tanweer Ali is a lecturer in finance and economics with Empire State College, SUNY. His research interests are in corporate governance and the application of linguistic methods to economic questions. He has guest edited two special editions of *On The Horizon*, focused on language and economics.

Alina Bârgăoanu is a Romanian communication scholar and Dean of the College of Communication and Public Relations at the National University of Political Studies and Public Administration (Bucharest). She is also both a member of the High-Level Expert Group on Fake News and Digital Disinformation (European Commission), and Jean Monnet chair holder "EU Communication and the Public Sphere" and "Communicating Europe: Policies for Increasing EU's Visibility among Member States."

Emanuele Brambilla is Adjunct Professor at the University of Milan, Italy, where he teaches English for Specific Purposes in the Departments of Language Mediation and Intercultural Communication, Political Sciences, Economics and International Studies. He holds a PhD in Interpreting and Translation Studies from the Department of Legal, Language, Interpreting and Translation Studies (IUSLIT) of the University of Trieste. His research interests include interpreting and translation, LSPs, corpus linguistics, political and judicial argumentation.

Piedad Fernández Toledo, as part of the academic staff in the English Philology department, lectures English for Specific Academic Purposes (ESAP) and Discourse Analysis at the College of Information and Communication Sciences, University of Murcia (Spain). Her interests include Discourse and Genre analysis, Critical Discourse Analysis (CDA), and multiple literacies in relation to foreign language pedagogies.

Antonis Galanopoulos is a PhD Candidate in the School of Political Sciences, at the Aristotle University of Thessaloniki, Greece. He holds a master's degree in political theory and philosophy. His research is financially supported by the General Secretariat for Research and Technology (GSRT) and the Hellenic Foundation for Research and Innovation (HFRI) (Scholarship Code: 2552)

Nuria Giniger is an anthropologist, has a PhD from the Universidad de Buenos Aires, and is a researcher in the National Scientific and Technical Research Council (CONICET), in Argentina. Her research is based on labor conditions, corporate policies in big transnational companies, and workers' resistance inside and outside labor places. She is a Fellow of the World Social Science Fellowship program.

Bob Hodge is Emeritus Professor at the Institute for Culture and Society, Western Sydney University, Australia. Bob has published extensively in social semiotics and discourse analysis, with special interest in interdisciplinary connections with organization studies and economics.

Lesley Jeffries is Professor of English Language and Linguistics at the University of Huddersfield, UK, and specializes in stylistics, including the stylistics of non-literary texts (news and political texts) as well as literary texts (contemporary poetry). Her recent work has been concerned with combining corpus methods with her critical stylistics framework.

Darren Kelsey is Head of Media, Culture, Heritage and co-convener of the Newcastle Critical Discourse Group at Newcastle University, UK. Darren's publications have focused on media mythologies and ideology, war and terrorism, moral storytelling, the banking crisis, right wing populism, journalism ethics, social media, and surveillance and affect theory.

Eva Lebdušková is a PhD candidate at the J.E. Purkyně University in Ústí nad Labem. In addition she holds a senior administrative position with the Charles University in Prague. Her main field of research is in linguistics, and she has published a number of articles on the use of language in economic discourse.

Antonella Luporini holds a PhD in English Linguistics and is currently a researcher with the University of Bologna (Department of Modern Languages, Literatures and Cultures), Italy. Her research interests include corpus-assisted metaphor studies and computer-mediated communication in EFL teaching.

Christina Lykou is Research Associate at the Research Centre for Language Teaching, Testing and Assessment and the National and Kapodistrian University of Athens, Greece. Her research interests are in the areas of critical discourse analysis, systemic functional linguistics, social semiotics, and also literacy and language education.

Giuseppe Mastromatteo is Full Professor of Economics at the Catholic University of Milan, Italy. He has published several articles in the fields of monetary and public economics.

Naoise McDonagh is a political economist and PhD candidate in the Sociology Department at the University of Auckland. His research focuses on the cultural and institutional evolution of economic life.

Bessie Mitsikopoulou is Associate Professor in the Department of Language and Linguistics, Faculty of English Language and Literature, at the National and Kapodistrian University of Athens, Greece. Her research interests are in the areas of critical discourse analysis, educational linguistics, literacy studies and digital media in language education.

Ann Pettifor is the director of Policy Research in Macroeconomics (PRIME), and is a member of the Council of the Progressive Economy Forum (PEF) in the UK. She was one of a few to predict the Great Financial Crisis, in 2006.

Kate Power is a lecturer in Management Communication at the University of Queensland Business School, Australia. A critical discourse analyst with particular interest in interdisciplinarity, she has published linguistic analyses of both religious and economic discourses.

Stephan Pühringer is a post-doctoral researcher at the *Institute* for Comprehensive Analysis of the Economy at the Johannes Kepler University of Linz, Austria, and the Cusanus-University Bernkastel-Kues, Germany. His main research interests include the history of economic thought, political and societal consequences of economics, and the role of economists in neoliberal economic think tanks.

Loredana Radu is Associate Professor, Head of the Communication Department and the Director of the Center for EU Communication Studies at the College of Communication and Public Relations, National University of Political studies and Public Administration, Romania. Her research and professional interests focus on Europeanization (i.e., discursive/narrative construction of Europe), attitudes towards the EU (i.e., euro-scepticism, extremism, euro-populism), evidence-based policy making, and development models.

Catherine Resche is Professor Emerita, Panthéon-Assas – Paris 2 University / CeLiSo Paris Sorbonne. Her research interests, ranging from terminology, neology and metaphor to genre and discourse analysis, pertain to applied linguistics, with a focus on the language and culture of specialized communities in the fields of economics, finance and management. The author of over fifty articles and books, she is also a Knight of the French National Order of Merit.

Sergio Rossi is Full Professor of Economics at the University of Fribourg, Switzerland. He has a long record of academic publications in monetary macroeconomics, and is frequently invited to talk-shows on Swiss television discussing macroeconomic issues at national and international levels.

Ellen D. Russell is interested in economic discourses as they interact with struggles for social justice. She received her PhD in economics from the University of Massachusetts Amherst, and is currently Associate Professor at Wilfrid Laurier University, Canada, cross-appointed to Digital Media and Journalism and Social and Environmental Justice.

Inês Signorini is Full Professor of Applied Linguistics at the State University of Campinas (Unicamp), Brazil. She is also Researcher of the Brazilian National Council for Scientific and Technologic Development. She has published on intercultural communication, identity and language, multiliteracies and metapragmatics.

Irene Sotiropoulou is a Fellow of the GEM-IWG/GEM-Europe and World Social Science Fellowship programs. She is based in Greece, and her research specialty is heterodox economics, particularly theories about money and finance, feminist economics, solidarity economics, non-capitalist economic structures, grassroots economics, small production modes, ecological economics, and economics of the commons.

Yannis Stavrakakis is Professor of Political Discourse Analysis at the Aristotle University of Thessaloniki, Greece, where he directs the POPULISMUS Observatory of populist discourse (www.populismus.gr).

Eduardo Strachman is Associate Professor of Economics at the São Paulo State University (Unesp), Brazil. He is also Researcher of the Brazilian National Council for Scientific and Technologic Development. He has published on macroeconomics, monetary economics, industrial economics, and institutional economics.

Virginia Villaplana-Ruiz is a member of the Information Science department at the University of Murcia, Spain. As a lecturer at the College of Information and Communication Sciences in this centre, she has focused on Media and Gender Studies. Her research interests range from writing as a negotiation between memory and history to the interrelations among gender narratives, identity and community.

Brian Walker is a visiting research fellow in the department of Linguistics and Modern Languages at the University of Huddersfield, UK. His research interests focus on the combination of (critical) stylistics and corpus linguistics in the analysis of political discourse and news texts.

Foreword

By Ann Pettifor

As a non-academic of lifelong duration, I am honored to be invited to provide an introduction to this ground-breaking (agricultural metaphor!) set of essays on *Discourse Analysis and Austerity: Critical Studies from Economics and Linguistics.*

I have been a long-time admirer of George Lakoff and his colleagues, and try to find Metaphors We Can Live By. But in the modern world (perhaps in the ancient world too) metaphors cannot live by words alone—it is the deeper associations and linkages of tone, image, and cultural assumption—as well as the exercise of dominance and power—that make metaphors work, or not work, as tools of persuasion, or (too often) propaganda.

One area of contested discourse and metaphor with which I am fully conversant relates to international debt. When I was director of Jubilee 2000 in the late 1990s, our task was to persuade the 'international community' to cancel the unpayable debts of the poorest countries (in the event, around $100 billion owed by 35 countries was written off by the official institutions). In developing our global advocacy campaign, we had to decide on the images and metaphors to adopt, and chose—as our dominant image—the chains of debt. This both echoed the chains of slavery, and also in a practical sense helped to mobilize millions through the active task of forming 'human chains' at G7 meetings.

But the image of debt as bondage or slavery was in opposition to the dominant metaphor even of those in the 'international community' (work on the deeper meaning of that phrase is overdue!), who far prefer to speak of 'debt forgiveness' or 'debt relief'. Both of these terms locate the role of the 'forgiver' within the frame of charity, the first as an individual act, the latter as a more collective approach. The first—'forgiveness' —in fact still echoes, though from a different perspective, the frame of both sinfulness on the part of the debtor, and debt as bondage; in this case the 'good' slave-owner who manumits his loyal long-standing personal slave.

In his 1991 book *Rhetoric of Reaction*, Alfed O. Hirschman proposes that conservative thinkers and rhetoricians tend to use three techniques of persuasion—'perversity, futility, jeopardy.'

Perversity here means that any intended progressive reform can only have adverse consequences. You try to improve the lot of the poor, but in so doing, you make things worse. In the words of a nineteenth century English essayist,

> The Poor-laws were intended to prevent mendicants; they have made mendicancy a legal profession; they were established in the spirit of a noble and sublime provision, which contained all the theory of Virtue; they have produced all the consequences of Vice.... The Poor-laws, formed to relieve the distress, have been the arch creators of distress.
>
> (Hirschman, 1991, p.29)

This Hirschmann compares with Charles Murray's similarly-angled attack on the Welfare State in 1984 (*Losing Ground*):

> We tried to provide more for the poor and produced more poor instead.
>
> (p.29)

Closely aligned to perversity is 'futility.' Here, any action to promote progressive change is pointless, because it will have no lasting effect. As Hirschmann (1991) points out,

> The claims of the futility thesis seem more moderate than those of the perverse effect, but they are in reality *more insulting* to the change agents... The demonstration or discovery that such action is incapable of 'making a dent' at all leaves the promoters of change humiliated, demoralized, in doubt about the meaning and true motive of their endeavors.
>
> (p. 45)

As an example of this, he draws on the work of the Italian economist Vilfredo Pareto, who claimed there to be a 'natural law'—Pareto's Law—on the fixity of the distribution of income across societies. Pareto was a far-right Italian nationalist, and it does not seem to me to be a coincidence that he is still associated, in contemporary mainstream economics, with reactionary economic concepts that bear his name:

> Pareto efficiency or Pareto optimality is a state of allocation of resources from which it is impossible to reallocate so as to make any one individual or preference criterion better off without making at least one individual or preference criterion worse off.
>
> (Wikipedia's short definition)

The text-books go out of their way to say that Pareto optimality is not the same as equitable or productive optimality, but what on earth is the point in having such a sub-optimal definition of optimality, if not to implant ideas that any negative impact on the economic interests of the very rich is somehow inefficient or suboptimal?

And so to 'jeopardy,' which is surely the most common rhetorical flourish in support of 'austerity.'

Conservative Jeopardists, as Catherine Resche exemplifies in her essay in this book, commonly use three metaphors of potential doom—meteorological, seismological, and medical—when arguing for austerity:

> In both the institutional and the academic corpora analyzed here, the crises are first presented in terms of natural catastrophes or fast spreading contagious diseases. The ship 'Economy' is caught in extraordinary storms and winds at sea; the economic structure, like that of a building, is threatened by devastating earthquakes or fire, and economies must be protected from a deadly epidemic.

As Eduardo Strachman and Inês Signorini identify in their chapter on Brazil, there is in fact a fourth, the runaway train model, where only a brave train driver and his friend are able to first slow the train down, then reverse it back to safety, getting it 'back on the right track.'

And we must not forget the fifth, the most enduring, metaphor—the national economy is a household that needs prudent management—if the householder is a spendthrift, the Debtor's Prison and the Workhouse face the whole family.

In his 2009 speech to the Conservative Party's spring Conference, David Cameron (then UK Leader of the Opposition) announced the coming of the Age of Austerity, which is the title of the speech:

> There are deep, dark clouds over our economy, our society, and our whole political system.
>
> Steering our country through this storm; reaching the sunshine on the far side cannot mean sticking to the same, wrong course.

Ah yes, the Great Helmsman steers the nation safely through the Storm to the Sunshine far beyond. George Osborne, when Chancellor of the Exchequer, much favored the meteorological approach, with his frequent references to Mending the Roof While the Sun Shines, though this is more about seizing the moment (the sun will maybe soon stop shining) than Cameron's vision of Steering through the Storm.

Now, another favorite metaphor—there is no more money!:

> Labour's Debt Crisis. The highest borrowing in peacetime history. The deepest recession since the war. Labour are spent. The money has run out.

The spendthrift—the incompetent patriarch, or head of the household. Time for a new patriarch to take control of the family's finances, and restore the confidence of the local tradesmen who have extended credit but have Frankly Had Enough. (This metaphor is closely associated with the central bankers' favored trope of Taking Away the Punchbowl; "governments are too undisciplined and profligate to be trusted with the family finances").

But what's this?

> Unless we deal with this debt crisis, we risk becoming once again the sick man of Europe.

Ah, that old favorite, the sick man of Europe—so it's time for the medical metaphor and medical men to step in and take back control, cure the disease (by blood-letting?), stop the infection from spreading.

And finally, back to debt as unjust burden—

> Our recovery will be held back, and our children will be weighed down, by a millstone of debt.

A "millstone of debt"? This is an odd choice, since a millstone (or rather, two millstones working together) forms the basis for grinding grain to make our daily bread. It does not, if used properly, hold anyone back, or weigh anyone down. In the Old Testament (Deuteronomy 24:6) of the Bible, we are forbidden to take a single millstone as a pledge for a debt, since that deprives a man and his family of their means of living. Maybe Cameron meant to imply a millstone round the neck—a metaphor to be found in Saint Mark's Gospel in the New Testament. Perhaps Cameron was back to his Great Helmsman metaphor, since according to Saint Mark Jesus said,

> Whosoever shall offend one of these little ones that believe in me, it is better for him that a millstone were hanged about his neck, and he were cast into the sea.
>
> (Mark 9:42)

Thus, so far from our children, 'these little ones,' being weighed down, the millstone is to be a punishment of death round the neck of the offender. But to place a millstone round a person's neck, however guilty you claim them to be, would involve dismantling a functioning pair of millstones, thereby reducing the economic capacity and productivity of the economy. So maybe this is a more telling metaphor than Cameron imagined.

In fact, I'm inspired to take Cameron's metaphor one step further. If we take the upper millstone to represent *private* credit and debt, and the lower to represent *public* credit and debt, working and adjusting together they grind the 'grain' of the economy—the raw products—into economically useful and digestible commodities; they ensure us our daily bread. But if one wheel stops working, the whole mill 'grinds' to a halt. The local community may starve, unless the expense of a new mill or major repair is incurred. Through public spending, in all probability.

Maybe it's easy game to mock the use of metaphors by politicians. It is their task to create images and narratives—'discourses'—that touch on their listeners' emotions and inspire (I nearly wrote 'trigger') a shared supportive response.

But economics claims to be neutral and scientific, free from political bias. This is of course pure fantasy. It is impossible to separate economics from politics. All economics is political. The two are inextricably intertwined. Often, the preference or bias is unconscious, but at other times, it is quite deliberate. The 'father' of economics as science, Alfred Marshall, was in many respects fairly progressive for the age, but occasionally displayed his prejudices in open form. This was surely without awareness that they were deep prejudices, as when he says—in a chapter of his 'Principles' on 'Industrial Organisation':

> For, though biology and social science alike show that parasites sometimes benefit in unexpected ways the race on which they thrive; yet in many cases they turn the peculiarities of that race to good account for their own purposes without giving any good return. The fact that there is an economic demand for the services of Jewish and Armenian money-dealers in Eastern Europe and Asia, or for Chinese labour in California, is not by itself a proof, nor even a very strong ground for believing, that such arrangements tend to raise the quality of human life as a whole.
>
> (Marshall, 1920, p. 22)

Or again,

> The wages of women are for similar reasons rising fast relatively to those of men. And this is a great gain in so far as it tends to develop their faculties; but an injury in so far as it tempts them to neglect their duty of building up a true home, and of investing their efforts in the personal capital of their children's character and abilities.
>
> (Marshall, 1920, pp. 685)

(I am struck by the reference to the 'personal capital' of children—an early forerunner of Gary Becker and the 'human capital' school).

It is less common for modern economists to display their bias so openly, but one of our favorite examples relates to 'financial repression,' a term much beloved by economists and commentators alike to represent any policy that controls or regulates the finance sector, including the alleged use of inflation as a deliberate tactic for reducing public debt as a proportion of GDP. One of the most egregious users of the term is Carmen Reinhart, who with Kenneth Rogoff claimed to find that if debt as a percentage of GDP rises above 90%, economic activity tends to be adversely affected. More specifically, with M. Belen Sbrancia she wrote *The Liquidation of Government Debt* in which they claim:

> A subtle type of debt restructuring takes the form of 'financial repression.' Financial repression includes directed lending to government by captive domestic audiences (such as pension funds), explicit or implicit caps on interest rates, regulation of cross-border capital movements, and (generally) a tighter connection between government and banks. In the heavily regulated financial markets of the Bretton Woods system, several restrictions facilitated a sharp and rapid reduction in public debt/GDP ratios from the

> late 1940s to the 1970s. Low nominal interest rates help reduce debt servicing costs while a high incidence of negative real interest rates liquidates or erodes the real value of government debt.
>
> (www.bis.org/publ/work363.pdf)

Professor Alan Taylor of the University of California at Davis responded:

> We must be wary of confusing financial repression (which sounds like a terrible thing) with financial regulation (which sounds a good deal more wholesome). In the context of current debate on how better to regulate the financial sector after the recent debacle, it is entirely understandable that the authorities have decided that banks and other entities were given far too much leeway to pursue activities that were not only self-destructive, but also destructive of the wider economy...
>
> Whether we call it financial repression, lack of competition, tough regulation, the fact remains that the 1945 to 1975 era was a glorious period of economic growth in the advanced countries, as well as in many emerging economies. It was a time of rapid economic growth with the allocation and mobilization of large amounts of capital, generalized macroeconomic and financial stability, sustained real wage growth and low unemployment.
>
> (www.bis.org/publ/work363.pdf)

The term 'financial repression' was invented in 1973 by two Stanford University economists, Ronald McKinnon and Edward Shaw, who worked in the field of LDCs ('less developed countries'). McKinnon argued, in the first instance, that it was the rural poor in poor countries who were financially repressed—a reasonable argument. His remedy, however, was to remove all maximum interest rates, and let banks lend at 15 to 25% interest. He swiftly moved on to argue that in most LDCs it is the whole monetary system that is 'repressed'—and others swiftly applied the metaphor to any limitations of the finance sector. The term found almost universal—and positive—acceptance among the economists' profession, infused as it was by the 1980s with hard neoliberal ideology, and appears in learned paper after learned paper. In a more recent interview with *Der Spiegel*, Reinhart described financial repression as a 'technical term.'

Not long before his death in 2014, McKinnon, a respected conservative economist, explained the origin of the term—it was to make a political point.

> In the 1970s, the term financial repression originated with McKinnon and Shaw when inflation was a problem in a number of less developed countries (LDCs). In the 1960s and 1970s, governments in many LDCs intervened to put ceilings on nominal interest rates and impose high reserve requirements on their banks, along with other techniques to direct the flow of credit in the economy... Wanting to find a pejorative term—akin to

> political repression—to describe this syndrome, McKinnon and Shaw first used the term financial repression in 1973.
>
> (www.adb.org/sites/default/files/publication/30133/hot-money-flows-commodity-price-cycles-zero-interest-rates.pdf)

So here we have a 'pejorative term' invented to make a political point on behalf of neoliberal policies, using the analogy of political repression with all of its mental associations, propagated to stand against any management or regulation of the finance sector, and later transmuted by Carmen Reinhart into a purely 'technical term'!

It is of course not my purpose to criticize the use of metaphor or other rhetorical techniques in economic discourse—especially since, as we have known at least since Lakoff and Johnson opened our eyes to the metaphors we live by, our whole human world is structured by metaphor. But what is important is (a) to work to identify and make public the means of conceptual manipulation used by the powerful to maintain control or denigrate any policy of a progressive character, and (b) ensure that the hidden, or not so hidden, biases or assumptions of economists are made explicit. After all, as Keynes remarked in the General Theory:

> The ideas of economists and political philosophers, both when they are right and when they are wrong, are more powerful than is commonly understood. Indeed the world is ruled by little else. Practical men, who believe themselves to be quite exempt from any intellectual influence, are usually the slaves of some defunct economist.

Foreword

By Darren Kelsey

We live in a world where human beings have created social structures, economic systems and entire civilizations based on the ideas we have and the stories we tell about the world. These ideas become so ingrained in the way we live that they sometimes appear to be natural. One of those ideas is money. Despite the fact that money is our creation, it often feels impossible to picture a world without it. Alternative stories seem implausible, unrealistic and irrational. With money we have created systems of exchange that enable us to buy and sell things. But when those systems we have designed go wrong, money causes us problems. How we deal with those money problems poses political questions. But what questions do we ask and how do we answer them? How do we decide that 'an age of austerity' is the answer to our money problems? Who tells that story and how do they convince people that it is the right thing to do? These questions show why critical attention to the stories we tell about money is necessary if we are to understand who benefits and who suffers from the stories we tell.

From the micro structures of language to the macro social practices of political ideologies and global economics, discourse is fundamental to the stories we tell, receive and share about money. This timely edited collection addresses one of the most pressing issues in contemporary politics and economics. The topic of austerity is interdiscursively and intertextually linked to multiple socio-economic and cultural contexts concerning power, exploitation and other social relations that discourse analysts are often concerned with. Hence, this book provides a significant intervention that reminds us of the importance of studying language and communication due to their ideological function in society.

Kate Power, Tanweer Ali and Eva Lebdušková have successfully combined approaches to economics and linguistics to provide a rigorous compilation of chapters that critically analyze the role of language and communication in austerity politics. Metaphor, argumentation, and concepts of 'crisis' all feature as key components throughout these analyses, which are supplemented with other chapters providing historical and theoretical critiques of austerity in both economic and communicative contexts.

The editors of this collection deserve enormous credit for this compilation. This book demonstrates not only the value of interdisciplinary collaboration but also the necessity of these fields working together to understand the economic and communicative practices that shape the world we live in. This collection is decorated by distinguished scholars and rising stars who will continue to innovate the field of discourse studies through interdisciplinary innovations.

The stories we tell and the myths we create define us as societies and civilizations. We must become increasingly well equipped to scrutinize our collective stories and social structures. As the late mythologist, Joseph Campbell once said, "If you want to understand what's most important to a society, don't examine its art or literature, simply look at its biggest buildings."

Comedian and political activist, Russell Brand has taken Campbell's words further in his contemporary criticism of austerity and financial elites: "In modern Western cities, the biggest buildings are the banks—bloody great towers that dominate the docklands—and the shopping centers, which architecturally ape the cathedrals they've replaced: domes, spires, eerie, celestial calm, fountains for fonts, food courts for pews." Whether it's the language we use, the stories we tell or the buildings we build, the mythology of money is central to the lives we live and the ideological conventions of our society.

Acknowledgements

The editors wish to thank all of the contributors to this volume for their hard work, patience, and willingness to step outside their disciplinary comfort zones to make this innovative project possible. In particular, we are grateful to all of the authors who, in addition to producing their own chapters, acted as reviewers for chapters from other disciplines—economists for linguists, and linguists for economists—thereby ensuring the genuinely interdisciplinary nature of this effort.

We acknowledge and thank Andres Rábago García—award-winning Spanish satirical cartoonist—for permission to reprint some of his work, previously published under the pseudonym El Roto, in Chapter 15.

We would also like to thank those friends and colleagues who discussed this project with us, or reviewed parts of this book, and whose comments and advice have been extremely valuable: Sheila Dow, Alan Freeman, Claes Ohlsson, Marc Pilkington, and Tess Slavíčková.

Last but by no means least we would like to thank staff within both the economics and the linguistics portfolios at Routledge for their interest in this project and for guiding us through the process of bringing this interdisciplinary volume to publication. Special thanks in this regard are due to Emily Kindleysides, Laura Johnson, Lisa Lavelle, Ruth-Anne Hurst, and Peter Hall.

We believe that this book presents a fresh look at the austerity debate, at an interesting juncture in the history of the idea, and we hope it will inspire ongoing interdisciplinary collaboration between economists and linguists.

Introduction

Interdisciplinary* approaches to austerity discourses: A case study in why and how economists and discourse analysts should work together

Kate Power, Tanweer Ali and Eva Lebdušková

In May 2010, the incoming Chief Secretary to the UK Treasury (deputy finance minister) in David Cameron's new Conservative government found the shortest of notes from his Labour Party predecessor, Liam Byrne. The note read: "Dear Chief Secretary, I'm afraid there is no money."

This brief sentence, which Byrne was to regret bitterly for years (Byrne, 2015), seemed neatly to summarize the common sense argument for the set of government policies that have come to be known under the collective term of 'austerity' (by which we will understand a program of spending cuts aimed at reducing public sector borrowing in the hope of reducing overall levels of government debt). Surely, if the government runs out of money, what else can it do but cut spending? This came to be the underlying rationale for the austerity program implemented in the years following the 2010 UK election. Similar programs of cuts were introduced at around the same time in many other countries, with differing degrees of severity.

Austerity was to become one of the defining political themes of the period following the immediate aftermath of the 2008 global financial crisis. Once it was clear that a second Great Depression had been averted in the immediate wake of the fall of Lehman Brothers, policy makers around the world turned to addressing rising public debt levels, which became their most pressing concern—and arguably remain so. It might be tempting for members of the public to regard austerity as an inevitability: a simple matter of technocratic economic management, better left to economic experts and seasoned central bankers. This would be a mistake, however, for three important reasons.

First, austerity is not a simple decision, a straightforward matter of accounting necessity. In reality, the policy package covered by the all-encompassing label of 'austerity' has involved making myriad choices. There is, at the outset, one basic major fiscal choice: public sector deficits can be reduced in two ways, either by raising taxes or by cutting expenditure, and in most cases the overwhelming focus has been on cutting expenditure. In the United Kingdom, for instance, around 89% of the projected savings for the 2010–2020 period will have been made through spending cuts (Reed & de Henau, 2016). And once this ratio has been decided, a multitude of individual decisions follow on all manner of budgetary line items.

The second main reason is that the consequences of all of these decisions have been far reaching and have affected all aspects of social life. The impact of austerity on different communities and demographic segments varies enormously. And women and men are not affected equally. A study for the Women's Budget Group indicated, for example, that some 81% of the overall burden of austerity policies (including cuts to services, changes to the tax and benefit system, and reductions in public sector employment) in the UK implemented since 2010 and planned before 2020 will fall on women (Reed & de Henau, 2016). An important element of this is public sector employment. In the UK, for instance, a majority of the public-sector jobs that were axed under austerity policies had been performed by women. Moreover women, being overwhelmingly more likely than men to be primary carers, have been more severely affected by the reductions in the provision of social transfers and services that followed the implementation of austerity.

The political repercussions of austerity have also been severely disruptive. It is hardly surprising, for example, that years of grinding cuts—borne by some communities and social groups more than by others, whilst leaving a privileged minority barely touched—would disrupt the balance of political power and the political culture of affected countries. The election of Donald Trump in the United States and the UK vote to leave the European Union may well have resulted from souring national moods, at least in part exacerbated by years of declining living standards and deteriorating public services.

The third major reason for rejecting the argument that austerity is simply a technocratic question of economics is the level of controversy amongst experts surrounding its efficacy and desirability. Austerity has been presented to the wider public as 'common sense,' that is, as the only sensible option if public finances were to be put in order and future well-being secured. This was the main view presented in the media and across the political spectrum—indeed, even opponents of austerity in the political arena took care to emphasize their commitment to 'fiscal responsibility.' Yet there was no consensus on austerity amongst professional economists, inside or outside academia. Prominent economists such as Joseph Stiglitz and Paul Krugman led the charge against austerity, along with a host of other major figures in the field, arguing that implementing austerity in times of recession or weak economic growth would be counterproductive. Even institutions such as the IMF—which has long been an advocate of small-state neoliberalism—have been more nuanced in their positions than many might have expected.

The economist Simon Wren-Lewis has used the term 'mediamacro' to describe the dominant media narrative on the economy and the need for austerity. Mediamacro is presented as a system of beliefs which feed the view that austerity is a common sense response to the economic crisis. Wren-Lewis (2015) argues that these beliefs are incorrect, essentially representing ignorance and negligent journalism: "A formal definition [of 'mediamacro'] could be a set of ideas about macroeconomics promulgated by the media that seem very different to the macro taught to economics students." The role of the media in creating and propagating narratives about the economy that fail to reflect either the scholarly debate or the popular controversy around the issues involved is also behind Paul Krugman's (2012) characterization of the "Very Serious People" who dominate public debate. This is, of course, not to suggest that expert opinion was exclusively or even predominantly anti-austerity. Numerous academics supported and contributed towards the basic premises behind the rationale for cutting public spending and were (selectively) given ample media airtime. For instance, an influential paper by Carmen Reinhart and Kenneth Rogoff (2010), which claimed that economic growth generally suffers when the public debt-to-GDP ratio rises above a critical level of 90%, was widely cited by politicians and journalists alike. Their findings were at least partially debunked, however, when a PhD student at the University of Massachusetts Amherst discovered errors in the dataset used by Reinhart and Rogoff (Herndon, Ash, & Pollin, 2014).

With no clear consensus on the best set of economic policies in a post-crisis environment, even amongst economists who might be considered mainstream (two of the three critics of austerity mentioned in the above paragraphs are Nobel laureates), a narrative emerged which came to dominate the public debate. This narrative was predicated upon viewing the State as an individual person, or as a household, and this metaphor of the State as a private individual is foundational to the theoretical rationale for austerity. To use the economist's language, it is a basic assumption behind the model of public finance which leads us to austerity as a logical conclusion.

Running out of money is a fear that most of us have experienced at some point or other in our lives. At least one of the co-editors of this volume can recall experiencing (as a student, and thanks to embarrassingly poor financial planning) being unable to withdraw money at an ATM. There was simply no money left. And when the money runs out there are not many options. One can look for ways to increase one's income (the stark advice given to that student, all those years ago, was 'get a job') or cut down on one's expenses—preferably both at the same time. Apply the common sense lessons of this situation at the level of the State, and the conclusion is clear. And this is especially plausible at a time of recession, during which people are generally feeling the pressure on incomes (or reeling under the burden of debt). When the money runs out, it's time to 'tighten one's belt.' And what applies to the man and woman on the street must surely apply to the government. Hence, we have a narrative of past profligacy leading to a need to cut back and bear the inevitable pain—the logic is clear.

But this raises a number of questions: How did the particular set of views, expressed in this narrative, come to be so influential? How were they reinforced and by whom? What ideological principles support this dominant perspective? What vision of society underpins this position? Who benefits from the resulting policy choices? What power relations are preserved by austerity? These questions are not purely a matter of technical detail, comparable, for instance, with deliberations amongst dentists on the latest extraction techniques. These are questions that go to the heart of discussions about the kind of society we wish to live in. And these are exactly the type of questions critical discourse analysis explores, engaging—as per its mandate—with "the most pressing social problems of the day: those aspects of the structure, organization and functioning of human societies that cause suffering, injustice, danger, inequality, insecurity, and self-doubt" (Fairclough, Graham, Lemke, & Wodak, 2004, p. 1).

Despite his general pessimism about interdisciplinary economics, Nobel Prize winning economist, Robert M. Solow (1970) pointed out some decades ago that "[t]here really are some problems outstanding that seem to call for an interdisciplinary approach" (p. 102). More recently, Vitor Neves (2017) similarly argued that "the economy [...] is far too complex [...] to leave the economy only to economists or to some sort of self-sufficient 'economistic' approach" (p. 359). Thus, a study of the causes and impacts of such a complex phenomenon as austerity will require the analytical tools of several disciplines, including economics, political science, sociology, psychology, philosophy, and history. And we believe there is also a vital place here for (critical) discourse analysis, not only due to its mandate (see Fairclough et al., 2004, mentioned above), but also because of the unique insights it offers into *how* it is that specific narratives (e.g., Labov & Waletzky, 1967; Labov, 1997), arguments (e.g., Iectu, 2006), and stances (e.g., Biber & Finegan, 1989; Englebretson, 2007) are constructed and gain influence.

One of the key platforms of critical discourse analysis (Gill, 2000)—which resonates throughout critical social analysis more generally (Fairclough, 2013)—is the observation that language not only communicates, but also contributes to creating thoughts, ideas and, even at times, material realities. This is not to suggest "that creativity or 'construction' can occur out of nothing, and regardless of the properties of the materials used in construction" (Sayer, 2003, p. 10). But theories, policies, and platforms are arguably realized—in the first instance—through language, and (potentially) gain both weight and power as they are documented, disseminated, and enacted. The genius of critical discourse analysis lies, first, in identifying and explaining how *construal* is recruited for *construction*—that is, how certain depictions of reality are used to actualize particular conceptions of reality, whether through persuasion and/or enforcement—in specific situations and for specific ends; and, second, in thereby girding resistance.

Critical Discourse Analysis—or "Critical Discourse Studies" (CDS) as the field has increasingly come to be known (as noted by Hart & Cap, 2014)—has been an interdisciplinary project since its inception. In 1999, for example, Lili Chouliaraki and Norman Fairclough observed that "the logic of one discipline (for example, sociology) can be 'put to work' in the development of another (for example, linguistics)" (p. 16). Since then, this prospect has been borne out in countless studies, through the theories and methods CDS has borrowed from other disciplines, as well as in the diverse questions and contexts to which CDS has been applied. However, leading critical discourse analysts have also repeatedly lamented, first, that interdisciplinarity has been the goal, more than the accomplishment, of much discourse analytic work (van Dijk, 1995, p. 459);

second, that the 'interdisciplinarity' observable in CDS research often amounts to little more than "unjustified eclecticism and superficiality" (Wodak, 2005, p. 170; for notable exceptions, see Kotwal & Power, 2015; Sum & Jessop, 2013; Whitehouse & Perrin, 2017); and, third, that the "inter- and transdisciplinary nature [of CDS] still needs to be carried forward before it yields fruit" (Hidalgo-Tenorio, 2011, p. 206). Indeed, Johnny Unger (2016) has recently noted two broad orientations current within CDS: on the one hand, **a centrifugal force,** which pushes away from detailed linguistic analysis, allowing other disciplines to open up and enrich CDS (this is clearly the orientation Unger prefers); and, on the other hand, **a centripetal force,** which pulls back towards the discipline, focusing on linguistic and semiotic analysis—which Unger suggests runs the risk of consolidating 'disciplinary silos' (p. 4), particularly as CDS matures as a discipline in its own right (Hidalgo-Tenorio, 2011, p. 206).

Economic theories and questions have been of central interest to some critical discourse analysts, particularly as they relate to and have found expression in the realms of politics (e.g., Fairclough, 2016; Fairclough, 2000) and the media (e.g., Kelsey, 2012). Yet, economic issues have appeared more often as *ground* than as *figure* in CDS research (Rubin, [1915] 1958). In Christopher Hart and Piotr Cap's (2014) comprehensive survey of *Contemporary Critical Discourse Studies*, for example, economic questions and theories are detectable throughout the volume, but 'economics' per se does not receive its own chapter as a 'domain of discourse' with which CDS is centrally concerned. In short: CDS has only barely begun to scratch the surface of economic issues which have discourse at their heart.

It is important to note at this point that, since the late twentieth century, the term 'discourse' has come to be used so widely—in so many different contexts, to refer to so many different phenomena—that there is now considerable confusion around its meaning (as criticized by Fairclough, 2005, p. 58). In this volume, we use *discourse* to refer to "the language used in representing a given social practice from a particular point of view" (Fairclough, 1995, p. 56). In other words, 'discourse' here is a count noun—one that can take a plural form ('discourses')—with the plural form pointing to the multiplicity of views that might be adopted.

Like CDS, economics has long displayed interdisciplinary inclinations (as noted by Arena, Dow, & Klaes, 2009; Neves, 2017), but has also resisted interdisciplinarity (as noted by Boswell & Mueser, 2008; see also Sozstak, 2008, 2013)—particularly collaboration with the so-called 'soft' social science and humanities disciplines (Zilberman, 1994, p. 38). Distinguishing between **'absorptive'** (i.e., defining problems typically addressed by other disciplines as 'economic' problems) and **'insertive'** interdisciplinarity (i.e., supplementing the work of other disciplines with economic theories and reasoning), Bradford (2013) observes that the former has been adopted by mainstream (but not Post-Keynesian) economists, while the latter has occurred between economics and numerous other disciplines, "as if by osmosis" (p. 147), but could still be further explored by economists.

In both cases, however, the interdisciplinarity in question is a form of **'colonization,'** in which one discipline imposes its "preferred disciplinary methods" on another (Price, 2014, p. 53); "economic[s] imperialism" is perhaps the most well-known example, which has been the subject of much debate amongst economists (Mäki, 2009; Marchionatti & Cedrini, 2017). Much less common has been **'interdisciplinarity*'**—marked with an asterisk by Huutoniemi, Thompson Klein, Bruun, and Hukkinen (2010) to distinguish it from more generic usage of the same word (p. 80)—which Moran describes as "always transformative in some way, producing new forms of knowledge in its engagement with discrete disciplines" (p. 16).

This checkered history of interdisciplinary engagement notwithstanding, some economists have borrowed research questions, theories, and methods from other disciplines in order to explore the discursive practices of their own discipline (e.g., Maesse, 2018; McCloskey, 1988; Rubinstein, 2000; Samuels, 1990; see also Royce, 1995 for a review of additional literature pre-dating 1994). Much of this work draws on rhetorical and literary theory (e.g., Woodmansee & Osteen, 2005), but CDS has also begun to feature in such studies (e.g., Erreygers & Jacobs, 2005; Ginsburgh & Weber, 2016; Mooney & Sifaki, 2017; Kelsey, Mueller, Whittle, & KhosraviNik, 2016, 2017; see also the 2015 "Language and economics" special issue of *On the Horizon*, and the 2016 "The discourse of crisis and austerity" special issue of *Critical Discourse Studies*).

We believe CDS is well-suited to this task because *discourses* are realized in *texts*—whether written, visual, or multi-modal (Johnstone, 2008; Kress & van Leeuwen, 2001; Machin, 2013)—which in turn are produced, disseminated, and received in specific, multi-levelled *contexts*, comprising 'text internal co-text,' relationships between 'texts, genres, and discourses,' "extralinguistic social/sociological variables and institutional frames," and "broader socio-political[, economic] and historical contexts" (Wodak, 2001, pp. 66–67). CDS addresses each of these concerns (i.e., discourse, text, context) through its combination of highly-situated and fine-grained linguistic/semiotic and contextual analysis. Consequently, we view interdisciplinary* collaboration between economists and discourse analysts as a highly productive way of expanding the range of questions explored, diversifying and sharpening the analytical tools used in each discipline, and enriching the analyses that flow therefrom.

In their study of new management ideology, for example, economic sociologist Eve Chiapello and leading critical discourse analyst Norman Fairclough (2002) adopted this approach—albeit under the label **'transdisciplinary research'** (p. 185)—laying bare the internal workings of an influential book by management 'guru' Rosabeth Moss Kanter of Harvard Business School. In reporting on their work, Chiapello and Fairclough specified not only the results of their analysis but also what each of their disciplines had gained from the collaboration, namely: theoretical insights to complement and develop those already in use within CDS, and a means by which economists can see in more detail how it is that discourse generates meaning, identity, power, and legitimation. In doing so, Chiapello and Fairclough modelled a level of critical self-awareness that is seldom evident in interdisciplinary research; and, by working together in this way, we believe both economists and discourse analysts will be better able to address not only a more fulsome range of 'economic' issues but also the economic dimensions of 'other' issues, that find expression in and gain real-world significance from the strategic use of language.

In this volume, therefore, we have brought together economists and discourse analysts around the question of austerity, recognizing of course the considerable attention this topic has already received (e.g., Blyth, 2013; Krugman, 2013; Skidelsky & Fraccaroli, 2017; Varoufakis, 2017). We hope here to do more than simply generating new insights about austerity discourses, however (although, of course, we do hope to do that). By intentionally 'joining forces'—so to speak—we aim both to model and to foster 'a dialogue' between economics and discourse analysis in which each discipline can develop by engaging with "the logic of the other" (Chiapello & Fairclough, 2002, p. 185), whilst exploring a question of mutual interest. In doing so, we believe that both economists and discourse analysts will gain self-critical awareness and expand our disciplinary horizons and tool-boxes.

Drawing on a typology from Huutoniemi et al. (2010), we will now briefly outline the *goals*, *scope*, and *type* of interdisciplinarity we have aimed for in this volume. In their terms, our goals have been chiefly 'epistemological' (p. 85); that is, we have aimed to generate new knowledge about how austerity discourses became the preeminent policy response to financial 'crisis.' Our subsidiary but related goals were twofold. First, as previously mentioned, we sought to respond to critiques of CDS by realizing its interdisciplinary agenda in a robust way; we have also sought to respond to the growing number of economists interested in working across disciplinary boundaries to explore the discursive dimensions of their own discipline. To these ends, we have piloted a form of collaboration that we believe will be both feasible for individuals and small groups of scholars with limited funding or institutional support, and applicable to diverse research questions and sites. Second, in introducing and modeling how various discourse analytic approaches can be applied to economic questions, while inviting economic theory and findings to inform CDS, we have aimed to demonstrate both the relevance of close linguistic analysis to economics and the benefit of collaboration between economists and discourse analysts. In this respect, we were inspired by Marzano, Carss, and Bell (2006), along with other commentators, who observe that many scholars find "the knowledge demands of other disciplines daunting" (p. 189); and we hope that this volume will overcome at least some of the impediments to 'genuine' interdisciplinarity* (Huutoniemi et al., 2010, p. 84) by both explaining and demonstrating the use of various discourse analytic approaches.

The second dimension of Huutoniemi et al.'s (2010) typology relates to interdisciplinary scope—that is, what it is that gets integrated. They distinguish between 'narrow' and 'broad' interdisciplinarity, where the former integrates "fields [that] are conceptually close to each other" such as the "natural sciences, engineering fields, biological and life sciences, social sciences, and humanities"

(p. 82). Broad interdisciplinarity, by contrast, integrates "conceptually diverse fields" that operate in different intellectual domains such as "law and engineering, cultural studies and medicine, philology and neurology" (p. 82). In these terms, the present volume represents 'narrow' interdisciplinarity: Economics and CDS are both social sciences with overlapping interests and commitments. As Lélé and Norgard (2005) point out, however, social science disciplines can be even more deeply divided than are the natural sciences and some social sciences. They argue, for example, that mainstream economists are separated from other "interpretive social scientists" not only by significant epistemological and methodological differences but also by "[t]he higher social standing of economics vis-à-vis other social science disciplines" which often results in "tensions between these disciplines" (p. 973). We posit, therefore, that the interdisciplinarity* attempted in this volume is best described as being 'mid-range' in scope.

Finally, Huutoniemi et al. (2010) categorize interdisciplinarity according to various types of interaction that take place between collaborators. We will not review their complex typology here, but we believe that the present volume straddles their categories of "methodological" and "theoretical interdisciplinarity*" (p. 84). In the former, methods from participating disciplines are "not merely juxtaposed or borrowed from one field to another, but also developed to suit the interdisciplinary context" (p. 84); in the latter, participating disciplines "develop new theoretical tools for interdisciplinary analysis" by sharing "concepts, models, [and] theories" (p. 84). Unlike some other conceptions of transdisciplinarity, we have not sought fully to unify participating disciplines, but rather to allow each to inform and extend the other, both methodologically and theoretically. With this in mind, we framed our project, first, by adopting an interdisciplinary approach from the outset (Campbell, 2005), at both the editorial and the contributor levels: our editorial team comprises two linguists and an economist, and we invited contributions through both economics and discourse analytic networks, selecting contributors from each discipline as well as authors working across both fields. Second, we chose to focus on *situated representations* of austerity, rather than austerity policies per se, as a question to which both disciplines could meaningfully contribute. Third, we arranged for each chapter to be peer-reviewed by at least one of the economists and one of linguists contributing to this project, so that perspectives from both disciplines would inform the entire volume.

What value did this process add to economics and/or to CDS? Clearly, this is the question most readers will need answered before venturing into the rugged terrain of interdisciplinary collaboration (Marzano et al., 2006, p. 192). In reviewing the feedback given and received between our contributors, we noticed that nearly all comments involved substantive critique bringing to bear on one another's work our contributors' respective disciplinary and genre expectations, specialist knowledge, methods and modes of argument, as well as literature recommendations, queries about terminology, and requests for both more background and contextual information, and—surprisingly—less theory.

Reviewers also contested specific concepts, claims and causal relationships posited by co-contributors; they preferred differing levels of theoretical grounding and empirical analysis; they questioned the relevance of certain types of analysis; and they noted the relative inaccessibility of each other's work to readers outside the author's discipline. And, in each case, our authors "returned to the drawing board," challenged to rethink their work via the critical gaze of another discipline.

As a result, this volume can be read not only for the new insights it offers into austerity discourses, but also as a case study in how and why economists and discourse analysts should work together. On the one hand, it invites **economists** to interrogate their "illusions of value neutrality" and reliance on "quantitative methods and mathematical models" (Lélé & Norgard, 2005, p. 972), as well as "their status as conveyors of disinterested knowledge" (Moran, 2002, p. 184). At the same time, it points them towards new questions and prompts them to approach well-worn questions, such as austerity, from new angles. On the other hand, this volume raises the bar for **discourse analysts**, pushing them to become more thoroughly "conversant in the theories, methods and materials" of economics (Moran 2002, p. 184); or—better yet—to collaborate directly with economists, as critical partners mutually sharpening one another's iron. We believe the analyses presented in this volume have benefited from precisely that kind of sharpening, and—drawing on Platt's ([1988] 1999) work about the value of case studies—we propose that similar benefits are likely to flow from other collaborative and interdisciplinary* projects involving economists and discourse analysts.

This volume has six sections, each of which addresses austerity discourses from a different perspective. Part I provides a foundation for approaching austerity through discourse: leading critical linguist Bob Hodge (Chapter 1) illustrates the relationship between Critical Discourse Analysis, social semiotics, and economics via the twin themes of 'crisis' and 'austerity'; and economist Ellen D. Russell (Chapter 2) reviews the case made by economists in favor of austerity, observing that it rested on the discursive construal that the confidence of economic elites was paramount to general economic well-being.

Part II adopts an historical lens, beginning with linguists Lesley Jeffries and Brian Walker (Chapter 3) combining two discourse analytic tools (corpus linguistics and critical stylistics) to compare uses of the term 'austerity' in UK political debates in the 1940s and post-2008. Economist Irene Sotiropoulou and anthropologist Nuria Giniger (Chapter 4) then demonstrate that economic and social history can be rethought through discourse, examining how the 'less State' argument has been employed and/or realized in Argentina and Greece since 1975; and linguists Bessie Mitsikopoulou and Christina Lykou use two discourse analytic tools (corpus linguistics and Systemic Functional Linguistics) to discuss media representations of austerity in relation to three key moments of change in the Greek economic 'crisis.'

Part III picks up and explores further this notion of 'crisis.' Economist Eduardo Strachman and linguist Inês Signorini (Chapter 6) trace Brazil's financial policy U-turn and the discursive construction of crisis with which it was legitimated. Political economist Naoise McDonagh (Chapter 7) uses Cultural Political Economy—an interdisciplinary approach that marries critical semiotic analysis and critical political economy (Sum & Jessop, 2013)—to analyze discursive representations of 'crisis' by the Irish media which contributed to fixing a narrative in terms of which austerity policies were legitimated. Drawing on methodological tools from the Essex School of Discourse Analysis, Yannis Stavrikakis and Antonis Galanopoulos (Chapter 8) provide a genealogy of normalizing economic and political discourses used to support austerity policies in Greece.

Perhaps the most widely studied characteristic of economic language is its fundamental reliance on metaphors: *The Body Economic* (Stuckler & Basu, 2013, 2014), for example, is a classic economic metaphor. In Part IV, two linguists bring new depth to this discussion by exploring the metaphorical dimensions of austerity discourse via Conceptual Metaphor Theory (also known as Cognitive Metaphor Theory): Catherine Resche (Chapter 9) uses corpus-informed Cognitive Metaphor Theory to explore the extent to which metaphor usage by European institutions and academics can be predictive of their stances on austerity; and Antonella Luporini (Chapter 10) combines Conceptual Metaphor Theory with the Systemic Functional Linguistics framework of grammatical metaphor to describe how metaphorical framing by British and Italian specialized financial newspapers contributed to legitimating austerity policies.

Part V focuses on this question of legitimacy, studying the arguments used to promote and validate austerity. Economist Stephan Pühringer (Chapter 11) uses corpus-informed Critical Discourse Analysis and conceptual metaphor theory to identify dominant discursive patterns in Austria's public debate over the European Fiscal Compact. In Chapter 12, economists Giuseppe Mastromatteo and Sergio Rossi use methods from critical political economy to explain the hypotheses upon which arguments in favor of austerity have been based, and who benefits from their uptake. Linguist Emanuele Brambilla (Chapter 13) combines Pragma-dialectics and the Discourse Historical Approach to describe the argumentative strategies used to justify austerity measures in American, British, and French political speeches.

Finally, Part VI explores discursive—including multimodal—responses to austerity. Communications experts Alina Bârgăoanu and Loredanu Radu (Chapter 14) use Fairclough and Fairclough's (2012) crisis narratives typology to examine public statements about austerity made by Romanian political and economic elites; and, in Chapter 15, visual artist Virginia Villaplana-Ruiz and discourse analyst Piedad Fernández use genre and discourse analytic tools, working from a cognitive functional angle, to examine the combination of iconic and protesting narratives in the satirical cartoons of Andres Rábago (better known as "el Roto").

The volume concludes with a summary of the main findings from each of our contributors which highlights both distinct characteristics and areas of common ground across geographical boundaries, different types of source material, and different methodological approaches. We also explain where we see potentially fruitful areas for further investigation, especially since we view this book as the start of a longer-term collaboration between the fields of economics and critical discourse studies.

The phenomenon of austerity and its discursive characteristics merits considerably more analysis in order to understand its power and effect, in all of the different contexts in which it appears. This volume aims to be a timely contribution to this process. Besides contributing to the scholarship, we have also adopted an innovative approach to interdisciplinarity, which we hope others will consider taking up. First, we believe that our approach could usefully be applied to other discourses explicitly related to economics. Second, we see applications to other themes, with less obvious economic dimensions, but where economic theory might contribute to more fully analyzing public debates. The study of the language of economics is a field that is still young, but it is coming of age.

References

Arena, R., Dow, S., & Klaes, M. (Eds.). (2009). *Open economics: Economics in relation to other disciplines*. Abingdon, UK: Routledge.

Biber, D., & Finegan, E. (1989). Styles of stance in English: Lexical and grammatical marking of evidentiality and affect. *Text, 9*(1), 93–124.

Blyth, M. (2013). *Austerity: The history of a dangerous idea*. Oxford: Oxford University Press.

Boswell, C., & Mueser, P. R. (2008). Introduction: Economics and interdisciplinary approaches in migration research. *Journal of Ethnic and Migration Studies, 34*(4), 519–529.

Bradford, W. (2013). Interdisciplinary applications of post-Keynesian economics. In G. C. Harcourt, & P. Kriesler (Eds.), *The Oxford handbook of post-Keynesian economics* (Vol. 2: *Critiques and Methodology*, pp. 143–161). Oxford: Oxford University Press.

Byrne, L. (2015, May 9). "I'm afraid there is no money." The letter I will regret forever. Retrieved from *The Guardian* (online edition): www.theguardian.com/commentisfree/2015/may/09/liam-byrne-apology-letter-there-is-no-money-labour-general-election

Campbell, L. M. (2005). Overcoming obstacles to interdisciplinary research. *Conservation Biology, 19*(2), 574–577.

Chiapello, E., & Fairclough, N. (2002). Understanding the new management ideology: A transdisciplinary contribution from critical discourse analysis and new sociology of capitalism. *Discourse & Society, 13*(2), 185–208.

van Dijk, T. A. (1995). Interdisciplinarity. *Discourse & Society, 6*(4), 459–460.

Englebretson, R. (Ed.) (2007). *Stancetaking in discourse: Subjectivity, evaluation, interaction*. Amsterdam, Netherlands/Philadelphia: John Benjamins.

Erreygers, G., & Jacobs, G. (Eds.). (2005). *Language, communication and the economy*. Amsterdam, Netherlands: John Benjamins.

Fairclough, I. (2016). Evaluating policy as argument: The public debate over the first UK austerity budget. *Critical Discourse Studies, 13*(1), 57–77.

Fairclough, I., & Fairclough, N. (2012). *Political Discourse Analysis: A method for advanced students*. London: Routledge.

Fairclough, N. (1995). *Critical Discourse Analysis: The critical study of language*. London: Longman.

Fairclough, N. (2000). *New Labour, new language?* London: Routledge.

Fairclough, N. (2005). Critical discourse analysis in transdisciplinary research. In R. Wodak, & P. Chilton (Eds.), *A new agenda in (Critical) Discourse Analysis* (pp. 53–70). Amsterdam, Netherlands/Philadelphia: John Benjamins.

Fairclough, N. (2013). Critical discourse analysis and critical policy studies. *Critical Policy Studies, 7*(2), 1777–1197.

Fairclough, N., Graham, P., Lemke, J. L., & Wodak, R. (2004). Introduction. *Critical Discourse Studies, 1*(1), 1–6.

Gill, R. (2000). Discourse Analysis. In M. W. Bauer, & G. Gaskell (Eds.), *Qualitative researching with text, image and sound: A practical handbook* (pp. 172–190). London: Sage.

Ginsburgh, V., & Weber, S. (Eds.). (2016). *The Palgrave handbook of economics and language.* Houndmills, Basingstoke, UK: Palgrave Macmillan.

Hart, C., & Cap, P. (Eds.). (2014). *Contemporary critical discourse studies.* London/New York: Bloomsbury.

Herndon, T., Ash, M., & Pollin, R. (2014). *Does high public debt consistently stifle economic growth? A critique of Reinhart and Rogoff.* Amhurst, MA: Political Economy Research Institute, University of Massachusetts Amherst.

Hidalgo-Tenorio, E. (2011). Critical discourse analysis: An overview. *NJES: Nordic Journal of English Studies, 10*(1), 183–210.

Hirschman, A. O. (1991). *The rhetoric of reaction: Perversity, futility, jeopardy.* Cambridge, MA: Belknap Press.

Huutoniemi, K., Thompson Klein, J., Bruun, H., & Hukkinen, J. (2010). Analyzing interdisciplinarity: Typology and indicators. *Research Policy, 39*, 79–88. Iectu, I. (2006). *Discourse analysis and argumentation theory: Analytical frameworks and applications.* Bucureşti: Editura Universităţii din Bucureşti.

Johnstone, B. (2008). *Discourse analysis* (2nd ed.). Malden: Blackwell Publishing.

Kotwal, A., & Power, K. (2015). Eating words: A discourse historical analysis of the public debate over India's 2013 National Food Security Act. *On the Horizon, 23*(3), 174–189.

Kelsey, D. (2012). Pound for pound champions: The myth of the Blitz Spirit in British newspaper discourses of the City and Economy after the July 7th bombings. *Critical Discourse Studies, 9*(3), 285–299.

Kelsey, D., Mueller, F., Whittle, A., & KhosraviNik, M. (2016). Financial crisis and austerity: Interdisciplinary concerns in critical discourse studies. *Critical Discourse Studies, 13*(1), 1–19.

Kelsey, D., Mueller, F., Whittle, A., & KhosraviNik, M. (Eds.). (2017). *The discourse of financial crisis and austerity: Critical analyses of business and economics across disciplines.* London: Routledge.

Kress, G., & van Leeuwen, T. (2001). *Multimodal discourse: The modes and media of contemporary communication.* London: Arnold.

Krugman, P. (2012, September 27). Europe's austerity madness. Retrieved from *The New York Times* (online edition): www.nytimes.com/2012/09/28/opinion/krugman-europes-austerity-madness.html?ref=opinion

Krugman, P. (2013). *End this Depression now!* New York: W.W. Norton & Company, Inc.

Labov, W. (1997). Some further steps in narrative analysis. *Journal of Narrative and Life History, 7*, 395–415.

Labov, W., & Waletzky, J. (1967). Narrative analysis: Oral versions of personal experience. In J. Helm (Ed.), *Essays on the verbal and visual arts* (pp. 12–44). Seattle: University of Washington Press.

Lélé, S., & Norgaard, R. B. (2005). Practicing interdisciplinarity. *Bioscience, 55*(11), 967–975.

McCloskey, D. (1988). *The rhetoric of economics* (2nd ed.). Madison, Wis.: University of Wisconsin Press.

Machin, D. (2013). What is multimodal critical discourse studies? *Critical Discourse Studies, 10*(4), 347–355.

Maesse, J. (2018). Austerity discourses in Europe: How economic experts create identity projects. *Innovation: The European Journal of Social Science Research, 31*(1), 8–24.

Mäki, U. (2009). Economics imperialism. *Philosophy of the Social Sciences, 39*(3), 351–380.

Marchionatti, R., & Cedrini, M. (2017). *Economics as social science: Economics imperialism and the challenge of interdisciplinarity*. Abingdon, UK: Routledge.

Marshall, A. (1920). *Principles of economics: An introductory volume* (8th ed.). London: Macmillan.

Marzano, M., Carss, D. N., & Bell, S. (2006). Working to make interdisciplinarity work: Investing in communication and interpersonal relationships. *Journal of Agricultural Economics, 57*(2), 185–197.

Mooney, A., & Sifaki, E. (2017). *The lanuage of money and debt*. Houndmills, Basingstoke, UK: Palgrave Macmillan.

Moran, J. (2002). *Interdisciplinarity*. London, New York: Routledge.

Neves, V. (2017). Economics and interdisciplinarity: An open-systems approach. *Brazilian Journal of Political Economy, 37*(2), 343–362.

Platt, J. ([1988] 1999). What can case studies do? In A. Bryman & R. Burgess (Eds.), *Qualitative Research* (Vol. 1, pp. 1–23). London: Sage.

Price, L. (2014). Critical realist versus mainstream interdisciplinarity. *Journal of Critical Realism, 13*(1), 52–76.

Reed, H., & de Henau, J. (2016). *A cumulative gender impact assessment of ten years of austerity policies*. London: Women's Budget Group.

Reinhart, C., & Rogoff, K. (2010). Growth in a time of debt. *American Economic Review, 100*(2), 573–578.

Royce, T. (1995). The analysis of economics discourse. *Australian Review of Applied Linguistics, 18*(2), 137–159.

Rubin, E. ([1915] 1958). Figure and ground. In D. C. Beardslee, & M. Wertheimer (Eds.), *Readings in perception* (pp. 194–203). Princeton, NJ: Van Nostrand.

Rubinstein, A. (2000). *Economics and language: Five essays*. Cambridge, UK: Cambridge University Press.

Samuels, W. J. (Ed.) (1990). *Economics as discourse: An analysis of the language of economists*. New York: Springer.

Sayer, A. (2003). *Restoring the moral dimension in social scientific accounts: A qualified ethical naturalist approach*. Paper presented at the International Association for Critical Realism Annual Conference, Amsterdam. Retrieved from www.lancaster.ac.uk/fass/resources/sociology-online-papers/papers/sayer-restoring-the-moral-dimension.pdf

Skidelsky, R., & Fraccaroli, N. (2017). *Austerity v. stimulus: The political future of economic recovery*. London: Palgrave Macmillan.

Szostak, R. (2008). Classifying heterodoxy. *The Journal of Philosophical Economics, 1*(2), 97–126.

Szostak, R. (2013). The state of the field: Interdisciplinary research. *Issues in Interdisciplinary Studies, 31*, 44–65.
Stuckler, D., & Basu, S. (2013). *The body economic: Why austerity kills*. London: Allen Lane.
Stuckler, D., & Basu, S. (2014). *The body economic: Eight experiments in economic recovery, from Iceland to Greece*. Philadelphia, PA: Perseus Books.
Sum, N., & Jessop, B. (2013). *Towards a cultural political economy: Putting culture in its place in political economy*. Cheltenham, UK: Edward Elgar.
Varoufakis, Y. (2017). *And the weak suffer what they must? Europe, austerity and the threat to global stability*. New York: Nation Books.
Whitehouse, M., & Perrin, D. (2017). *Schrieben in der financial community [Writing in the financial community]*. Wiesbaden, Germany: Springer.
Wodak, R. (2001). The discourse-historical approach. In R. Wodak, & M. Meyer (Eds.), *Methods of Critical Discourse Analysis* (pp. 63–94). London: Sage.
Wodak, R. (2005). Inter/trans/post-disciplinarity and the study of language and/in politics. *Journal of Language and Politics, 4*(2), 169–171.
Woodmansee, M., & Osteen, M. (Eds.). (2005). *The new economic criticism: Studies at the intersection of literature and economics*. London: Taylor & Francis.
Wren-Lewis, S. (2015, May 1). *On mediamacro*. Retrieved from Mainly Macro: https://mainlymacro.blogspot.cz/2015/05/on-mediamacro.html
Zilberman, D. (1994). Economics and interdisciplinary collaborative efforts. *Journal of Agriculture and Applied Economics, 26*(1), 35–42.

Part I

Approaching austerity through discourse

Together, the two chapters in this part set the scene for, and model, the interdisciplinary* approach promoted in this book. Each begins with basic questions about the crisis of 2008, and austerity as part of the response to that crisis; each then also draws on economic and discursive insights—highlighting both the discursive underpinnings of economics and the economic underpinnings of discourse—to explain key moments in the ascendance of austerity as the dominant policy response to the financial crisis of the early twenty-first century.

In Chapter 1, Bob Hodge revisits the question posed by Queen Elizabeth II in the immediate aftermath of the crisis: How was it that the economics profession, which included so many distinguished minds, failed to see it coming? Hodge shows, first, that at least a large part of this failure lies in an inability to view the economy as a whole system, susceptible to instability on a systemic level; and, second, that in order to view the economy as such, one must approach it armed with insights from multiple fields of study, in particular economics and semiotics. Analyzing several short texts related to austerity measures in Australia and the UK,

Hodge convincingly argues for—and clearly illustrates—the kind of critical literacy needed by ordinary citizens everywhere, to evaluate and counter unjust financial and economic policies. In Chapter 2, Ellen D. Russell asks why the 2008 financial crisis did not lead to a more fundamental revision of the consensus view of economic policy, but instead to even more neoliberalism. Russell examines how Keynesian analytics were countered by the 'Expansionary Fiscal Contraction' hypothesis, whose theory about and narrative framing of crisis enabled the mainstream economics profession to resist not only views that threatened the neoliberal agenda (and, along with it, the perceived prestige of economics as a technical discipline), but also alternate analyses which would have exposed choices that were fundamentally political in nature.

Both chapters bring a critical and interdisciplinary* perspective to the consideration of austerity discourses, which is replicated throughout this volume and which we hope readers will consider taking up.

1 Deep interdisciplinarity and responses to crisis

Bob Hodge

Among its many merits this book demonstrates the value, even the necessity, of interdisciplinarity in any adequate response to crises, of all kinds, of all scales, in all times. Its topic, Austerity and the Global Financial Crisis (GFC), affected everyone, but it is usually seen as the special province of economists. This book has a majority of chapters by authors from linguistic disciplines, but they all assume they have something valuable to say about economic issues. I believe they are right. The other authors use their economic expertise, but they also include the role that discourse played in shaping events. They are all interdisciplinary, and that benefits the book.

In this early framing chapter, I explain why this de facto interdisciplinarity is so essential, and how deeply it is grounded. According to Ashby's (1956) cybernetic Law of Requisite Variety, control systems must include all factors in the systems to be controlled. In all financial crises, economic, discursive and political factors interweave so inseparably that, for those who would understand and control them—from politicians to effective citizens—interdisciplinarity is prerequisite. I also argue that links between the two major disciplines, economics and linguistics/semiotics, go deeper. In this chapter I emphasis this broader framework, as my main contribution to the project of the book.

I use an economist to set the scene for this discussion. Yanis Varoufakis's (2011) beautifully written popular book *The Global Minotaur* presents a controversial case, as popular books do, but he argues it against a consensus account of the background. His first explanation of what happened comes from a response by the British Academy to a letter from the Queen: "Why had you not seen it happen?" Varoufakis paraphrases the answer: "Principally a failure of the collective imagination of many bright people… to understand the risks to the system as a whole" (Varoufakis, 2011, p. 4).

No one argues with this judgement by these expert economists on their own discipline. There are some notable exceptions amongst economists, including Varoufakis himself. No one doubts their brightness. They were the 'smartest guys in the room' to quote a best-selling account of the Enron scandal (McLean & Elkind, 2003). That shifts attention to the basis of their expertise, their disciplinary formation. The GFC in Varoufakis's diagnosis demonstrates the failure of a discipline, whose fatal flaw is that it does not understand systems as wholes.

In this chapter, I argue that this is the crucial problem for the experts who should have flagged warnings long before they did. It is not disciplinarity as such that is the problem so much as tightly-framed disciplinarity. Varoufakis for instance is an economist but he takes a broader view. He includes novelists and philosophers in his bibliography, and takes a long view on the origins of the crisis. He includes the politics of the system over time, because he understands the problem as systemic. In my terms, he is interdisciplinary without having to emphasize the fact.

This book focuses especially on neoliberal austerity as an inadequate and damaging response to the GFC. I use 'neoliberal' to cover the ideological framework associated with policies often described as the 'Washington consensus,' which I unpack and discuss below.

Varoufakis is fully aware of how damaging these policies were in Greece, the nation he was born in and whose finance minister he was for six months in 2015:

> In a never-ending circle, the imposed austerity worsens the recession afflicting these deficit states.
>
> (2011, p. 208)

Economic analysis alone is enough to show that these policies do not work. But more important questions remain, demanding a more complex interdisciplinary response. How is neoliberal austerity part of the larger system which includes the factors leading to the GFC? Why did the proponents of austerity think it would work, and why did they persist when it didn't? What could or did opponents do as they talked and reasoned about events, and why could they not prevent or mitigate it?

Our object of analysis is constituted by discursive and economic forces which link the two moments, crisis and austerity, into a minimal object, needing analysts minimally to combine linguistic and economic analysis. That analysis is not only interdisciplinary. It must reframe these disciplines to deal with hybrid facts normally seen as outside their scope: economic processes as linguistic forms, linguistic processes as economic facts.

Systems

A core integrating idea for this process of interdisciplinification is 'system.' Varoufakis (2011) diagnosed its absence as a fundamental flaw he saw in academic economists. This concept appears in different forms in both fields, so the idea is itself interdisciplinary. The idea becomes richer and more explanatory when enriched by many perspectives, including economics and linguistics. A system is an arrangement of parts which has outcomes other than the products of those parts. It is a whole which is other than the sum of its parts, and those parts have other effects and meanings in a system than when they are alone.

I draw on the two disciplines to examine an instance apparently so minor and undramatic it would usually be ignored by both disciplines. I am motivated by an idea from social semiotics (Hodge, 2017), multiscalar analysis. In terms of this concept social reality is not made up of two distinct levels, micro- and macro-. It consists of many levels, each of equivalent complexity. Even a smaller-scale analysis can include the inherent complexity found at every level. In this case, it can allow hypotheses about the interaction of economic and discursive facts in empirical reality.

In early 2017, a small scandal briefly erupted in Australia. The Government Department of Human Services used a computer system to generate letters to some welfare recipients claiming that they had a debt arising from discrepancies found between their welfare claims and the tax returns. One article on the scandal was headlined:

> Centrelink debt letter scandal worsens.
>
> (Kachor, 2017)

I selected this text because of a political economy interest, but the sentence also illustrates the complex way linguistic systems work, in general and in this instance. Each word is an element in a five-term structure whose meaning is greater than the sum of its parts. The same is true of every sentence in every language.

In this case, four words make up the complex subject of the sentence. Each word corresponds to a different social and semantic system. Centrelink is the trademark name of the Human Services, part of the system of government. 'Debt' belongs to the financial system. 'Letter' refers to systems of communication, in this case a printed letter generated by a computer system.

'Scandal' comes last but not least. This is the subject of the verb, the reason the item has become news. It belongs to the media system, the system the author of the article belongs to, which gives her power, and which governments respect and try to control. Government 'scandals' are sites where the agenda has escaped their control, where what has happened and how it is reported have political effects

A political analysis of this incident could come up with the analysis that the incident is driven by the intersection of these four systems. Analysis of the headline not only comes up with this analysis, it provides evidence that the author of the article is conscious of this analysis, and frames the story in its terms.

I chose the story to analyze because it illustrated neoliberal austerity and its consequences, in a small scale. The Government had announced in its budget that it intended to claw back $A350m in excess payments from the welfare budget, in order to deliver on their claim to move the budget into surplus. They blamed the previous Government for creating this debt, and in a typical example of austerity discourses they made budget rectitude a primary goal.

A later story used budget documents that had been available for six months to reveal that the government planned to extend this policy to more welfare recipients. 'Elderly, disabled next on Centrelink hit list' said one headline. It used tables published by the Government to say the government

> Has booked savings of $A1.1billion from clawing back overpayments of the aged pension, and another $A400million from the disability support pension.
>
> (Towell, 2017, p. 1)

'Hit list' comes from another discourse, this time fictional, referring to criminals. Its basis is in economics, a set of figures that had been hiding in plain sight, buried under the masses of figures in the document. It needed a well-motivated expert in finances to bring it out, but the journalist used discourse to give it the impact it had.

But the austerity policies on their own would not have made a news story. They were compounded by the 'debt letter.' Defending the policy, Minister Alan Tudge objected to the term 'debt.' He showed his concern for semantic precision, or betrayed the point of his discomfort, by insisting that the letter only pointed out the discrepancy between Centrelink applications and Tax Information. Tudge drew on his Harvard MBA to design the policy, but became a discourse analyst to implement it. His response to criticism was not to withdraw the letter, but to rephrase it.

Behind this error was a problem he refused to acknowledge with the information system he relied on. It came up with a high number of false positives, cases sent letters as a result of computer error. Those letters had the force of commodities, demanding payment for a product generated only by a computer. In effect, the faulty computer program was printing money.

Tudge's defence continued that, although the system was working, people who objected to the calculation could contact Centrelink staff. When told that the waiting time for calls was impossibly long, he merely appealed for 'patience' (McIlroy, 2017). This added to the impression that he lacked empathy, a minister presiding over a dysfunctional system, in denial over its defects.

The long waiting times, and indeed the whole fiasco, came from the consequences of another systemic plank of austerity policies. The government had slashed numbers of public servants in that and other welfare-related departments in order to make budget savings. Those no longer employed would have checked the calculations before they were sent out and corrected egregious errors.

The role of IT systems in this scandal is no accident. Part of the claim that cuts can be made with no reduction of service relies on a widespread collective delusion that IT systems can do everything their salespersons say. In a concurrent news item, one journalist reported on the development of a software program called 'Roxy.'

> Roxy supplies answers that used to be given by public servants who have now been freed up to handle very complex problems that still require a human touch.
>
> (Towell, 2017, p. 4)

This comes in a media report, but to a discourse analyst it has unmistakable signs of a department media release. It contains the two parts of the dominant ideology, that these systems can be given a slightly cheeky name and feminine voice and perform most of the complex decisions and responsibilities of expert humans. Meanwhile, no one loses his or her job. They are merely 'freed up' to operate at an even higher level. Win-win, as the favorite management term says. A clear case of discursive inflation, discourse analysts might reply.

As other commentators noted, the effect of this scandal was compounded by a concurrent scandal. A government minister had had to resign over a controversy over excessive entitlements she claimed. This controversy threw a spotlight on excessive claims by many Members of Parliament, including the opposition.

The minister's defence was that the rules for this system were so vague that no one knew what they were or how to interpret them. The government had admitted this a year before, promising to clarify the rules. They still had not done so, moving much slower on these lax entitlements than on the sums involved in the welfare system. But the minister resigned rather than the government.

One headline captured the connection:

> Coalition slips further amid Centrelink furore: poll.
>
> (Remeikis, 2017, p. 6)

The article reported the latest poll, which showed the government trailing the opposition 54 to 46. This draws the causal link. This link is not in itself a fact except as mediated by discourse like this. Because the media report the connection, it becomes a fact in the situation. A chain of discourses becomes a political force.

In drawing lessons from this analysis, I do not over-claim the contribution of either linguistic or economic analysis. On the contrary, the dialectic between the two is what makes the analysis so productive. Without the versions of reality provided by economic analysis it would not be easy to understand the point of the discursive moves. Without the discourse analysis asking questions of the context, the economic description would be thin and unilluminating.

This incident like many others could be aggregated into numbers that show the ineffectiveness of neoliberal austerity policies. This case analysis complements quantitative analysis by seeing the complex ways different elements interacted in a real-life instance, and showing how far the various agents were conscious of these structures and meanings.

In this case, participants were aware of the role IT systems played in the causal chains that constituted the scandal. An equally important outcome of the analysis was the role of the category of 'scandal.' The catalyst for opening up the system was the role of the discursive force of 'scandal.' Behind that small scandal was a small crisis. There is an analogy between scandals in political discourses and crises in the political economy. To explore them, we need a deeper analysis of the two disciplinary areas

Deep interdisciplinarity

Thus far I have presented disciplines as transparent contemporary social facts without a history. In practice, modern disciplines are far from transparent and they all have complex histories. That lack of homogeneity and transparency and the silence about contested histories within disciplines make the task of interdisciplinary research far harder. In this section, I step back from immediate concerns with austerity and financial crises to provide some background for the kind of interdisciplinarity the broad project needs.

To begin, I take my cue from Varoufakis (2011) again, from the myth of the Minotaur. In that myth, the hero Theseus uses a single thread given him by Ariadne to guide him in the labyrinth which contains the monstrous Minotaur, half man, half bull.

I interpret this hybrid form in my own way, as the irreducibly interdisciplinary monster at the heart of the labyrinth: the secret of global capitalism, according to Varoufakis. I therefore use two disciplinary threads, not one: economics tracked back to Marx, and semiotics back to Saussure. My aim is to build up a dynamic, usable version of the two strands, not offer a comprehensive account of either or both. I explain the two bodies of theory in a single text which can be read, in different ways, by different categories of discipline. The same text will explain too much for some and too little for others, but that is the price for interdisciplinary, intercultural communication. It requires a form of critical literacy that ordinary citizens could use, to dismantle toxic theory and cope with dangerous economic discourses.

Semiotics: Saussure

Modern semiotics and linguistics of course have taken many forms in the 100 years since Ferdinand de Saussure wrote his seminal work. Yet for someone coming to this disciplinary area, critical citizens from off the streets or from the opulent financial centers where economists ply their trade, Saussure's concepts lead directly to key developments that are still illuminating tools. I call my own approach Social Semiotics (Hodge, 2017), which includes Critical Discourse Analysis and other branches of linguistics, with a materialist base drawing on Marxism.

I use one piece of text to illustrate the concepts and connect the discussion with the topic of the book. In the 2015 British election, David Cameron won a surprise victory using the slogan: "Britain: living within our means." He proclaimed:

> Nothing we achieve will be possible unless we eliminate our deficit and deal with our debts.
>
> The security of your family depends on the stability of our public finances.
>
> (Cameron, 2015)

I take two main concepts from Saussure. One we have already touched on, the importance of system: "language is a system of signs" (1974, p. 15). The other is his founding of semiotics, a general theory of signs: "a science that studies the life of signs within society" (1974, p. 16).

Others have developed the idea of 'systems.' Saussure had some distinctive things to say on the theme. His ideas were more ambiguous than most of his followers realized. For instance, his semiotics included society as part of the object of the science, yet he also carefully separated linguistics as an autonomous discipline from all other disciplines, including sociology and economics. Seemingly the two kinds of system, language and society, operate together yet the disciplines do not. Saussure's dualism is curiously ambiguous.

Academic linguistics followed the separatist line, and attempted to analyze language as isolated from the study of society. In this, it was like purist forms of economics that propose abstract models of markets and economic life. But within linguistics there developed a critical form of linguistics (Kress & Hodge, 1979; Fairclough, 1992; Lakoff, 2004) which followed the other option within Saussure's dualism: to see the two systems, language and society, inter-related as a system of systems.

In Cameron's speech each sentence makes sense to English-speakers, with the system of the sentence ordering the elements into simple sense. Yet overlaying this sense are the effects of the social system, in which Cameron was the current Prime Minister of the UK and leader of the party in an election. The hearer/reader is understood as an average voter, like a standard consumer in market analysis.

This relationship is part of the meaning in a direct sense. 'We' is an ambiguously inclusive collective: Cameron and his party, Cameron and the British people, and/or Cameron and the individual voter listening to him. Meanwhile 'you' is ambiguously singular or plural: one voter eye-ball to eye-ball with the Prime Minister, or an abstract individual replicated 30 million times. The social meaning and effect of the statement is distinct from its linguistic meaning. It either persuades or turns off voters.

Saussure's ambiguous dualism appears in many places in his theory. He proposed two fundamental planes or axes in language and thought. One was syntagmatic, how meaning is made by combining elements (like *eliminate* plus *deficit*, *Cameron* plus *PM*). All discourse is made of syntagmatic strings on different scales. The other, he called the 'associative plane.' This plane contained the classification systems that give meaning to utterances (e.g., *debt* opposed to *surplus*). But Saussure included non-logical systems usually seen as associations, hence his name for this plane. The association plane contains multiple systems, some logical but others more random.

Saussure gave a significant role for another non-logical quality, analogy. Analogy is a more general term for metaphor-like processes, where one structure is transformed into another. Saussure (1974) saw these processes as both generative and conservative: "Forms are preserved because they are constantly renewed by analogy" (p. 172).

These ideas come together in Lakoff's form of critical discourse analysis. Lakoff emphasized the importance of metaphors in language and thought (Lakoff & Johnson, 1980). Metaphors and associative thinking are basic to language and thought. Among metaphors a special role is performed by what he called 'frames.' Frames in this view are like Saussure's analogue structures. They underpin a range of metaphors in discourse which are organized by deep analogue forms, models.

Lakoff (2004) applied his theory to US politics. He argued that two underlying frames lay behind the respective policies of Republicans and Democrats. The Democrats favored the Nurturant Parent model, while the Republicans preferred the Stern Father model. In this framework, austerity programs are a direct expression of the Stern Father framework.

Lakoff's theory is clearly a relevant model for discourse analysis that tracks such policies through the discourses that sustain them and that have made them so politically strong. It is no accident that several authors in this collection use the concept of metaphors as a guiding thread. Cameron's text rests on the Stern Father frame, which holds together the two levels of society, government and (patriarchal) family.

Saussure's greatest innovation was his brief, suggestive invention of the meta-discipline semiotics. He emphasized the importance of verbal languages, and his first great influence was on linguistics as the science of verbal language. But semioticians followed his suggestion to study other signifying systems, visual and behavioral, as languages.

In some instances, a claimed language seems metaphorical, such as the language of commerce or the common phrase 'money talks.' But what for some people is a metaphor, for others is a model. In the case of economics, I believe that it is productive to consider phenomena in economics in a double way: including verbal language as part of the total communication, while also seeing some systems in economic life as kinds of language in the semiotic sense.

Saussure did not specifically call economics a language, but his use of the term 'value' suggests a deep commonality. Value is his key term to describe and analyze systems. He illustrates it with an example from economics which could come from a discussion by Marx:

> To determine what a five-franc piece is worth one must therefore know: 1) that it can be exchanged for a fixed quantity of a different thing, e.g. bread; and 2) that it can be compared with a similar value of the same system, e.g. a one-franc piece, or with coins of another system (a dollar etc.).
>
> (1974, p. 115)

I suggest this analogy between this aspect of money and a fundamental property of language according to Saussure is so close that we can legitimately argue that Saussure saw money as an exemplary semiotic system. If so, then economics is as much part of semiotics as linguistics.

Some modern semioticians have developed Saussure's claim about multiple kinds of language co-existing into a theory of multimodality (Kress, 2010). These theorists showed that not only are there different semiotic modes in language, but even languages that were regarded as single systems have many modes functionally interweaving. So writing uses spatial signifiers as well as words. Speech includes gestures and expressions, sub-language systems.

Cameron's speech in its print form—the text itself—initially seems monomodal, but it was delivered in a richly semiotic context, a policy launch with many signifiers of power. When we drill down we can see some interesting aspects of the text's modality. The whole speech is almost entirely in verbal language, but it includes another major semiotic mode, numbers.

This discourse of power is multimodal, including mathematics as well as words. The balance of modes is strategically asymmetrical. In the whole speech there are only six figures quoted, all in billions of pounds. This text is about budgets but it is directed at the numerically illiterate, who are not expected to drill down into the figures. The manifesto seems addressed to economically-oriented leaders of a household, but the numerical mode constructs them as all-powerful, dealing with billions of pounds in a sentence, yet also economically illiterate, not to be trusted with the real details. This contradiction contains the key to one of the great mysteries of austerity discourses: how so many voters gave power to politicians to implement policies those voters did not understand and which were not in their interests.

Critics of economic policies like austerity need to be able to analyze all forms of discourse that carry the meanings and effects of those policies, and provide evidence of what happened on the ground. They need flexible forms of what is called 'discourse analysis.' They need to integrate these methods of analysis with economics' modalities, including the languages of diagrams and mathematics. Semiotics underpins the idea of a comprehensive critical literacy which experts across economics and social sciences mostly lack, which society needs everyone to have.

Political economy disciplines and Marx

Marx has a similarly ambiguous position in economics as Saussure has in semiotics, making them both especially useful as starting points to unravel the complex dynamics of their disciplines. The death of Marxism was announced regularly throughout the twentieth century, but the stake apparently never reached this monster's heart. Varoufakis rejects a purely Marxist analysis, but Marx is the only nineteenth-century economist he refers to (2011, p. 19). Marx is the major economist who has crises as structural in capitalism, and with each crisis that hits an unprepared capitalist system he returns as a relevant figure. It happened again with the GFC.

I do not want to bring Marx back unchanged. He got many things wrong, as is inevitable when theories are tested in different complex situations over a long time. More important for my purposes is the model of interdisciplinarity implicit in his methods. As is well known, his economic theories were irreducibly part of his political theories, and the interweaving of these strands took him to political-economic history. What is less often emphasized is that Marx began as a discourse analyst, with a critique of ideology (1976) and his day job was as a journalist.

Ideology is an organizing category for the analysis of texts and other systems of meaning, as well as basic in his analysis of political economic systems. This gives an interdisciplinary scope that is still part of his legacy. He describes ideology in a famous passage:

> If in all ideology men and their relations appear upside down as in a *camera obscura*, this phenomenon arises just as much from their historical life process as the inversion of objects on the retina does from their physical life-process.
>
> (Marx & Engels, 1976)

Lakoff's theory (2004) reminds us that this statement is simultaneously a metaphor and a model. The picture-like form of the metaphor makes it easily comprehensible by ordinary citizens, while its force as model gives it massive explanatory power. A critical perspective adds that it is also itself ideology, a distorted image of reality.

Marx has two images for the process, not just one, which have different implications. If ideology is like the mechanical device of a *camera obscura* then it gives an inverted image, though only within the space of the *camera*. But as a physiological process, the process follows the same geometry within the eyeball for normal perception, but it is then corrected automatically in the mind.

This gives rise to two versions of ideology and two analytic strategies. In the one, texts can mostly be trusted once the bias has been removed. In the other, the processes of distortion are part of interpretation. But for both strategies, reality is the key, at the beginning or end of the analysis. Some forms of discourse analysis maintain what is called constructivism, the idea that all reality is socially constructed through discourse. The Marxist theory I support agrees with one part of this position, that no one's account of reality can be entirely trusted, while seeking energetically and confidently to get at what discourses are trying to conceal.

Joseph Stiglitz won the Nobel Prize for economics in 2001 for his critique of globalism, especially of the role of the three pillars of the global economic order: the World Bank, whose Chief Economist he was from 1997 to 2000; the International Monetary Fund (IMF); and the US Treasury. His critique (2002) emphasizes the role of what he terms 'ideology,' especially in the IMF, he claims. In this case, he writes, "ideology guided policy prescription and countries were expected to follow the IMF guidelines without debate" (Stiglitz, 2002, p. xiv). This views ideology as an effective force in the economic and policy landscape, not to be ignored in purely economic analysis.

Globalization between 1980 and 2000 is outside the time frame of the GFC and post-GFC policies of austerity, but this is a single system that can only be understood through its changes over time. According to Varoufakis, the Minotaur of US budget and trade deficits began to deliberately increase from 1971 (Varoufakis, 2011, p. 22), yet instead of having a negative effect on growth it powered the global economic system, as capital flowed from the periphery to the center in a debt-driven economy. It is the first inversion created by ideology: debt is profit.

Meanwhile the three central institutions of global capitalism, the World Bank, the IMF and the US Treasury, lent money following the prescriptions of what came to be called 'the Washington Consensus' (Williamson, 1989; Chomsky, 1999). The Washington Consensus consisted of 10 principles, the first of which was fiscal policy discipline. These principles continued barely changed into the post-GFC era, becoming the basis of policies of austerity whose failure was already known and had contributed to the crash. As Williamson, author of this document noted wryly, this discipline was notably absent from the policies of the dominant nations. Some critics call this hypocrisy. In terms of the Ideological Complex in a Marxist framework, contradiction and asymmetry constitute the system.

Marx's ideas of contradiction bring out complications in such analyses. Stiglitz remembered his first day as Chief Economist for the World Bank in 1997. As he entered the majestic building on 19th Street in Washington, he was struck by the institution's motto: "*Our dream is a world without poverty*" (2002, p. 23). Stiglitz contrasts the World Bank with another opulent monument of neoliberalism, the IMF: "One is devoted to eradicating poverty, the other to maintaining stability" (2002, p. 23).

How could so acute a critic as Stiglitz be blinded by so obvious an ideological device as the World Bank slogan? But Stiglitz acted as though he believed it. He was inspired by the World Bank ideology to become a fierce critic of the IMF and its toxic role in using austerity as a main tool whose effect was stagnant economies and spiralling debt. Ideology is not simply wrong or bad. Meanwhile those policies, proven not to work in the two decades of neoliberal dominance, returned as the new default response to the GFC.

In social semiotics, Marx's ideas have been extended in the concept of the Ideological Complex (Hodge & Kress, 1988; Hodge, 2017). This incorporates Marx's ideas on contradiction in a theory of ideology to guide analytic practice. The ideological complex is

> A functional set of contradictory versions of the world, coercively imposed by one social group on another on behalf of its distinctive interests or subversively offered by another social group in attempts at resistance in its own interests.
>
> (Hodge, 2017, p. 169)

In this view, the contradictions are not between ideology and reality, as many analysts assume. They are contradictory versions of reality within the ideology itself. Moreover, these contradictions are not a weakness in the ideology but are functional. Economic discourse analysis in these circumstances does not need to find which half of a contradiction to select and which to ignore. Analysts instead accept the contradiction and ask why it is there, what functions it serves, and what tactics might work.

In the Centrelink/Expenses pair of scandals, the government was caught in a contradiction, between the austerity it was enforcing on the poor and disadvantaged and the austerity it conspicuously did not enforce on Members of Parliament. In the scandal, the contradiction alone was not the problem for the government. It was the conditions which brought the two parts into visibility that laid them open to scrutiny.

In each of these cases, the government tried to maintain both parts of a similar contradiction. The minister and others on his side repeatedly claimed that they even-handedly acted on underpayments as well as overpayments. In practice, the computer was not programmed to write to those who had been underpaid. The trick with Ideological Complexes is the ways the dominant manage asymmetries in favor of their class. These asymmetries are then built into financial processes which have real effects, paying less to the poor, imposing austerity on them.

Ideology is primarily a semiotic theory yet it plays a central role in Marxism. His theory of money and commodities is a complementary case. It is a basic premise in his economic theories. It can be treated equally usefully as semiotic theory. In this form it is illuminating about complex economic processes, as well as excellent semiotics.

Marx's economics starts with his theory of commodities. Crucial here is the concept of the dual nature of commodities. A commodity like a table, he says, has a physical existence and social history which give it value, but it also has a value in exchange:

> As soon as it emerges as a commodity, it changes into a thing which transcends sensuousness. It not only stands with its feet on the ground, but in relation to all other commodities, it stands on its head.
>
> (1977, p. 163)

This is the same inverse image as is given by ideology. It gives rise to an inverted world whose connection with the material world is essential for understanding it, yet is mystified. This is like Saussure's doctrine of dual functions, which his followers did not understand. Fifty years earlier Marx understood it well.

Marx proposes a semiotic chain which goes between reality to signifiers that are increasingly remote, yet he insists they are always essential to the functioning of the system. So the financial system is anchored to gold as a signifier or symbol of other commodities, and these are signifiers of real values, the material goods and the labor that created them.

Marx's theory supports the economic policy of the gold standard, whereby monetary values are anchored by the idea of an imaginary exchange into gold bullion. The twentieth century saw many attempts to follow this principle, with damaging lack of success. Even John Maynard Keynes (1920) argued that it had a deflationary pressure, as proved the case in the Great Depression of the 1930s. Marx's theory on this point was wrong.

What Marx needed was the idea of 'slippage.' In Lacan's development of Saussure (1977), slippage is the generative movement of meaning allowed when signifiers slide over signifieds. In finance, it means the gap between computer-fixed prices and actual prices, available to be exploited by shrewd traders (Taleb, 1997). Slippage can be seen as a general, often productive quality of semiotic and economic systems alike, gaps within specific margins between all elements of the system.

I claim Marx's theory of money is essentially semiotic, but I should mention that Marx specifically rejected the analogy: "To compare money with language is not less erroneous [than to compare it to blood]" (Marx, 1973, p.162).

I feel uncomfortable disagreeing directly with Marx. But I am not committed to the truth of everything Marx wrote. Besides, this was just a parenthetical note in an unpublished manuscript. At this time, Marx did not know about Saussure's semiotics and its new definition of language. I am using that reframing to offer a new perspective on Marx's theories of money.

Marx's discussion of paper money illustrates the strengths and weaknesses of his theory. He sees its natural role in the contemporary economic system, as a necessary convenience, but does not recognize that it marks a new stage, semiotically and economically. He argues that paper money only means what it signifies, its value in money, which in turn signifies material commodities. He notes that when governments print money they do not increase value, they simply decrease the value of the money.

With this argument, Marx proposed the insight that won neoliberal guru Milton Friedman a Nobel prize in 1976, 100 years later: that printing too much money produces inflation (Friedman, 1980). The same reasoning can be applied to the development which has dominated the last 50 years and underpinned the GFC, the development of electronic money.

Marx understood the differences between different stages and forms of money systems, but he did not fully appreciate the difference made by the later semiotic change to paper money. He might have made the same mistake with the electronic revolution. Marx's semiotic realism was too fixed. He needed a concept something like 'slippage' to adequately describe how the economic systems work. But his concern for controls that rely on real links to material realities remains an essential premise for critical economic analysis, today as when he wrote.

As might be expected, Marx is at his most original, in economics and semiotics alike, in discussing crisis. Crisis in traditional economic theory is outside the scope of what it seeks to explain. As Stiglitz observed in the wake of the GFC, there had been more than 100 crises in the past three decades, and still mainstream economics did not treat them as a natural part of the system (2014, p. 337). Nor is 'crisis' well represented as a concept in mainstream semiotics.

Marx wrote: "In a crisis, the antithesis between commodities and their value-form, money, is raised to the level of absolute contradiction" (1977, p. 236). This can be reframed as a semiotic principle, as illustrated by the GFC, where money no longer coded the state of affairs in the material world and the crisis in this key signifying system drove what was called a financial crisis.

This analysis of the effect of crisis on money-systems also applies to systems of meaning which accompany and reinforce or counteract those crises and the measures that arise against them. In the Centrelink crisis, the confident semiotic chain which linked the generation of debt by a computer to actions by the welfare agency was broken, and the real suffering and injustice became public knowledge.

What is said and seen at these moments of crisis reveals the basic mechanism of the system, and the slippages it relies on. That is one reason governments like Cameron's seek to seem realists as they talk of real debt and the need for austerity. Given the asymmetry that constitutes the dominant system, however, it is the poor who have 'realism' imposed on them, while the members of the dominant in business and government still have access to the fantastic wealth generated on their behalf.

Stiglitz mostly ignored Marx. However, the work that won him the Nobel Prize for economics in 2001 combines one premise which ultimately comes from Marx, crisis as inherent in capitalism, and another which connects with semiotics, the role of information and its asymmetries in economic processes. He demonstrates the value of the disciplinary hybridity I advocate in this chapter.

The recurrent crises Stiglitz observed in America and the developing world drove him to reject the key premise of the dominant system: that the dominant system basically worked well, with minor perturbations that would correct themselves if they were left alone. The omnipresence of crisis drove him to challenge the paradigm that coped with crisis by ignoring its existence.

This led him to oppose one major premise of the traditional paradigm, the assumption that the market is perfect and self-correcting. This assumption was hidden from attack by being made the premise in the dominant model, taken for granted, and then made visible again as argued in support of policies by right-wing, pro-market governments.

The trick the neoliberal economics paradigm pulled was to exclude political discourse from their economic models and reintroduce it into their discourse with political leaders. Milton Friedman did this with Reagan and Thatcher, and more controversially with General Pinochet the Chilean dictator. Its other trick was to include information and everything that semiotics might contribute to economics, and then effectively say it could be ignored. Neoliberal economists assumed that information was effectively perfect, so they did not need to study the supposedly minor imperfections in practice.

Stiglitz's basic principle, the asymmetry of information flows in real-life communication, is capable of richer development in semiotics, where it is a basic principle for the new paradigm in linguistics, critical discourse analysis.

'Asymmetry' is a revolutionary premise in economics. But it has an even stronger, more structural role in Marx, in the underlying antagonisms which pervaded and formed all of social life.

Semiotics and discourse analysis have a structural place in Stiglitz's new paradigm. His published research mainly focused on information and discourse relevant to the behavior of markets, but he also made more wide-ranging observations on the semiotic practices of institutions:

> The truth is subtler. Often it's a tone of voice, or a meeting behind closed doors, or a memo that determines the outcome of discussions.
>
> (Stiglitz, 2002, p. xv)

Stiglitz did not carry out explicit semiotic-economic research himself, but he established a broad field in which it could be done, in which the effects of inequalities of power on meaning and action should be studied in all policy areas, from small-scale crises like Australia's Centrelink scandal to the GFC, and the crises precipitated by austerity programs in Europe and elsewhere.

Conclusion

I do not claim that Marx and Saussure, economics and semiotics are equally important. Saussure is influential but Marx was a founding father of both economics and sociology, with social semiotics his bastard child. But issues of priority are less important than a better understanding of the complex products of their interweaving. As Marx memorably wrote:

> Humans make their own history, but they do not make it just as they please... The tradition of all the past generations weighs like a nightmare on the brains of the living.
>
> (Marx & Engels, 1970, p. 96)

These traditions act through language of all kinds. Money systems inherited from the past impose their own logic and create their own insane worlds of meaning. Other forms of talk about money make this insanity seem like the new normal.

Varoufakis diagnoses toxic theory as a major driver of the crisis and the austerity policies that were effectively sold to voters in many jurisdictions as a necessary remedy. Society was unwise trusting so key a discipline to be autonomous and regulate itself. There needed to be some form of oversight, with interdisciplinary expertise and input from concerned citizens.

This chapter has built up some ideas on what that critical literacy should include. Basic principles of discourse analysis should be part of it. So should multimodal expertise in the special languages of the financial world, in a critical framework. Too many exponents of critical discourse analysis shy away from the languages of mathematics which are interwoven with verbal modes in running the world today.

With that kind of shared basis, critical economists would have found many more allies outside economics, and many more critical discourse analysts would have realized that these issues touch on everyone, and everyone has a duty to contribute to social understanding. Academics talking to each other in this deeper way will be better able to talk with ordinary citizens, and learn from them.

In this climate, asymmetrical austerity talk like Cameron's would have less of a hold. When he launched a hoary slogan like 'living within our means,' everyone should have been able to perform the first level of economic discourse analysis, checking it out against reality and exposing its manipulations. 'Who is living within what means?' And where has that debt come from that 'we' must pay? These questions lead into economics and return to the discourse, and to the complex unrealities it has constructed over time.

That leads to the main value I see reason for the project of this book: to combine expertise from economics and discourse to enable fairer and more productive markets, fairer and more productive societies. Is a market still a market if it is subject to continual tricks and frauds? Yes, Stiglitz would say. They are all like that. That is good reason for societies as collectives to find ways of intervening. Is a democracy subject to tricks and frauds, still a democracy? I echo Stiglitz: Yes, they are all like that in differing degrees. They all need academics like the authors of this book, free to draw on their disciplinary expertise and transcend it.

References

Ashby, W. R. (1956). *Introduction to cybernetics.* New York: Chapman Hall.

Cameron, D. (2015). *Britain: Living within our means.* Conservative Election Manifesto.

Chomsky, N. (1999). *Neoliberalism and the global order* New York: Seven Stories Press.

de Saussure, F. (1974). *Course in general linguistics.* London: Fontana.

Fairclough, N. (Ed.). (1992). *Critical Language Awareness.* London: Longmans.

Friedman, M. (1980). *Free to choose.* Harmondsworth, UK: Penguin Books.

Hodge, B. (2017). *Social Semiotics for a complex world.* Cambridge, UK: Polity.

Hodge, B., & Kress, G. (1988). *Social Semiotics.* Cambridge, UK: Polity.

Kachor, K. (2017, January 5). Centrelink debt letter scandal worsens. *9 Finance.* Retrieved from https://finance.nine.com.au/2017/01/05/16/25/centrelink-debt-letter-scandal-worsens

Kress, G. (2010). *Multimodality: A social semiotic approach to contemporary communication.* London, New York: Routledge.

Kress, G., & Hodge, B. (1979). *Language as ideology.* London: Routledge.

Lacan, J. (1977). *Écrits: A selection.* New York: W.W. Norton & Company, Inc.

Lakoff, G. (2004). *Don't think of an elephant.* VT: Chelsea Green.

Lakoff, G., & Johnson, M. (1980). *Metaphors we live by.* Chicago, IL: Chicago UP.

Marx, K. (1973). *Grundrisse.* London: Penguin.

Marx, K. (1977) *Capital.* New York: Vintage.

Marx, K., & Engels, F. (1970). *Selected works*. London: Lawrence Wishart.
Marx, K., & Engels, F. (1976). *The German ideology*. Moscow: Progress Publishers.
McIlroy, T. (2017, January 12) Controversial debt recovery letters still on. *Sydney Morning Herald*, p. 7.
McLean, B., & Elkind, P. (2003). *The smartest guys in the room*. Harmondsworth, UK: Penguin Books.
Remeikis, A. (2017, January 16). Coalition slump further amid Centrelink furore: poll. *Sydney Morning Herald*, p. 6.
Stiglitz, J. (2002). *Globalization and its discontents*. New York: W.W. Norton & Company, Inc.
Stiglitz, J. (2014). The lessons of the North Atlantic Crisis for economic theory and policy, in G. Akerlof, M. Blanchard, D. Romer, & G. Stiglitz (Eds.), *What have we learned?* (pp. 335–347). Cambridge, MA: MIT Press.
Taleb, N. (1997). *Dynamic hedging*. New York: John Wiley & Sons.
Towell, N. (2017, January 18). Elderly, disabled, next on Centrelink hit list. *Sydney Morning Herald*, p. 4.
Varoufakis, Y. (2011). *The global Minotaur*. London: Zed Books.
Williamson, J. (1989). *Latin American readjustment: What has happened?* Washington, DC: Institute for International Economics.

2 Austerity and the eclipse of economic alternatives

The theoretical terrain of neoliberal economic crisis narratives

Ellen D. Russell

Austerity prevailed over other potential responses in the aftermath of the economic crisis of 2008, yet this return to neoliberal economic policies was far from inevitable. Economic crises are particularly volatile junctures in the prevailing 'sensemaking,'[1] thus crises may provide an opportunity to expand debates about what is economically necessary, possible, and desirable. Economic crises do not inevitably generate new economic imaginaries; whether an economic crisis will provoke a rethinking of existing economic arrangements will depend on the interplay of a panoply of factors that shape struggles for social change and the defensive reactions to such struggles. But economic crises do present an auspicious occasion to promote critical scrutiny of the hegemonic economic paradigm amidst widespread perceptions of an unsustainable, difficult and/or dangerous situation that demands urgent action. Ideas may be entertained that might have seemed unthinkable amidst the inhibiting momentum of "governance as usual" (Boin, t'Hart, & McConnell, 2009, p. 82). As an advisor to the Obama administration famously instructed, "You never let a serious crisis go to waste. And what I mean by that it's an opportunity to do things you think you could not do before" (*Wall Street Journal*, November 19, 2008).

Crises offer the opportunity for a contest of "crisis exploitation" (Boin et al., 2009, p. 83) as various social actors seek to parlay this aleatory discursive terrain into a political opportunity to advance their respective agendas. Since every crisis narrative is permeated with diagnostic, evaluative, and prescriptive implications, this struggle over "sensegiving" (Gioia & Chittipeddi, 1991, p. 434) is never politically neutral. Defenders of the status quo marshal their forces to interpret and remediate the crisis in ways they find favorable, while new or previously marginalized vantage points seek to gain traction in the public debate. Crises pose a particular peril to defenders of the status quo: at precisely the moment that the legitimating capacities of the prevailing justificatory discourses are most destabilized, there is urgent need to defend the status quo against the potential gains of its critics. Thus it is remarkable that the hegemonic neoliberal economic paradigm managed to regain sufficient legitimacy in the aftermath of the 2008 crisis that policy-makers in the OECD countries succeeded in taking concerted action to impose an aggressive neoliberal austerity agenda by the 2010s. Despite the popular and intellectual appeal of arguments that implicated neoliberalism in generating and deepening the crisis, the solution to the crisis of neoliberalism was further neoliberalism.

This chapter analyzes the struggle over crisis narratives that followed the economic crisis of 2008 to understand how a neoliberal paradigm in considerable disrepute advocated for a project of neoliberal economic recovery that foreclosed other rival narratives and economic alternatives. As an economic doctrine, neoliberalism heavily supports conditions that maximize the latitude of capital to pursue profit (thus venerating such policy agendas as promoting 'free markets' and deregulation, lowering taxes, and reducing trade and investment barriers across jurisdictions). Neoliberals celebrate a minimalist role of the State, which is understood as enabling the State to engage in activities that support capital but compelling the State to renounce activities that run afoul of the agendas of capital. Neoliberalism typically advocates for the reduction of social programs, privatization, and constraints on governments' abilities to run deficits and accumulate debt. Yet in the aftermath of the 2008 crisis, many neoliberal tenets were in dispute. Trends attributed to the neoliberal agenda (such as rising inequality, rampant deregulation, the growing influence of corporations, and the eroding democratic attributes of political processes) stood accused of having fueled the economic crisis itself. Thus the neoliberal interventions in economic discourses following 2008 are notable in that they not only undermined the momentum of those critiques that might have facilitated the pursuit of alternative economic options, they also managed to legitimate austerity initiatives with close affiliations to the economic logics and arrangements that stood accused of helping to generate the crisis.

In order to understand the capacity of neoliberal advocates to parlay a crisis of neoliberalism into an opportunity to intensify neoliberalism, we approach the analysis of crisis exploitation as a framing contest, where "[t]o frame is to select some aspects of a perceived reality and make them more salient [...], in such a way as to promote a particular problem definition, causal interpretation, moral evaluation, and/or treatment recommendation" (Entman, 1993, p. 52). Various crisis narratives seeking to gain influence will present diverse (and often contradictory) perspectives on pressing questions such as: what is deemed to be 'in crisis'; to what degree is the crisis understood as significant, systemic, normatively and/or morally problematic; to whom/what is the blame for the crisis attributed; what should be 'fixed' to avert future crisis; how should these 'fixes' be accomplished; and who should bear the cost of 'fixes.' Those considerations focused upon by a crisis narrative will attract critical scrutiny and challenge, while the omission of other aspects tends to reinforce the perception that they are correct, natural, or otherwise not implicated in the crisis. Thus what is obscured and what is accorded prominence will orient the prescriptive and normative implications of a crisis narrative.

In the aftermath of an economic crisis, contestants in crisis exploitation are obliged to engage with extant theoretical and popular debates and historical precedents concerning economic crisis as they seek to promote their preferred crisis narrative. Both in its implications for economic theory, and its resonance in popular dystopian economic imaginaries, the Great Depression looms large as the archetypical economic crisis. The 1929 stock market crash and the ensuing decade of profound economic depression "delegitimized the capitalist system itself" (Birdsall & Fukuyama, 2011, p. 45), thus creating space for widespread economic rethinking. Under these extraordinary conditions, a wide range of theories competed for public and intellectual attention—including ideas culled from progressivist, socialist, communist, anarchist, and other typically marginalized traditions. Ultimately, the economic ideas of Keynes gained ascendency in the interpretation of the Great Depression, thus precipitating a paradigm shift from the neoclassical veneration of free market capitalism to post-war Keynesian welfare state capitalism. While the Keynesianism that buttressed post-war capitalism was drained of many of its more radical possibilities, it nevertheless has remained a theoretical anathema to neoliberals long after Keynesian ideas and public policies had been overshadowed by the rise of neoliberalism. In the midst of an economic crisis evocative of the Great Depression, neoliberals in the late 2000s sought to avoid a resurgence of Keynesian (or even more radical) crisis narratives. The focusing of public attention on the case for austerity, and the imposition of austerity measures themselves, did much to avert these possibilities.

To examine the contest to rethink (and deter rethinking of) economic possibilities in the late 2000s, this chapter focuses on the contribution of economists who arose from the tradition of neoclassical economic theory to provide a rationale for implementing austerity at a time of profound global economic fragility. Their 'Expansionary Fiscal Contraction' (EFC) hypothesis (also referred to as 'Expansionary Fiscal Consolidation') both reaffirmed and extended neoliberalism and foreclosed more radical economic reimaginings. The EFC hypothesis's most prominent spokesman, Alberto Alesina, cooperated with other coauthors[2] to diametrically contradict the Keynesian proposition that government economic stimulus encourages economic recovery and growth in the aftermath of an economic crisis. Instead he argued that austerity (under some conditions[3]) could promote economic recovery. While Alesina and his colleagues had conducted research into this proposition prior to 2008, in the immediate aftermath of the 2008 crisis their EFC hypothesis shot to immense prominence. By 2010, *The Economist* proclaimed that it was "Alesina's hour" as the "new favorite of fiscal hawks" who provided the "theoretical ammunition that fiscal conservatives want" (Coy, 2010). Alesina's widely cited research, together with his appearance before the European Union's Economic and Finance Ministers, provided the rationale for the turn towards austerity embodied in the G20's 2010 commitment to shrink budget deficits.

This chapter examines the theoretical case offered to legitimate the turn towards austerity in the early 2010s by situating the EFC hypothesis as a crisis narrative that advocated on behalf of a particular framing of the problem of economic recovery. To understand the evolution of this crisis narrative, Section 1 begins with an analysis of the rival crisis narrative that the EFC was designed to counter: the Keynesian analysis of economic crisis and recovery that emerged from the Great Depression. In particular, we will examine the Keynesian analytics that both facilitated the pursuit of certain types of redistributive economic change, and buttressed the proposition that austerity is contraindicated in times of economic weakness and instability. Section 2 discusses the argument presented by proponents of the EFC hypothesis to counter this Keynesian crisis narrative and its condemnation of austerity. Based on the particular problem definition and argumentation espoused by the EFC hypothesis, austerity advocates sought to deter any Keynesian (or more radical) reconsideration of economic possibilities and to expand the implementation of the neoliberal paradigm via austerity measures.

The legacy of the Great Depression: Framing austerity and economic possibility

Times of (comparative) economic stability and prosperity tend to enhance the legitimacy of the economic status quo. If consent to the prevailing economic arrangements becomes destabilized during an economic crisis, a "window of opportunity" (Keeler, 1993) may open to question hegemonic economic ideas. Whether a given economic crisis will provoke critique and mobilization to promote substantive change in existing economic arrangements depends on a host of factors, including the particular crisis narratives that rise to prominence to make sense of the crisis. Some crisis narratives may tend to support radical critique, popular mobilization, and systemic change, while other crisis narratives encourage only relatively modest and systemically-validating responses. Thus the struggle to promote particular crisis narratives is immensely consequential, as every crisis narrative will tend to facilitate and legitimate some possibilities and dissuade and delegitimate others.

While crisis narratives are shaped by the confluence of many discursive and contextual influences, our focus is the struggle to assemble and propagate more technical accounts that interpret the crisis in the terrain of economic theory. As a hegemonic economic theory, neoclassical economic theory assiduously cultivates its positivist mystique (buttressed by elaborate mathematics and vigilantly guarded disciplinary prestige), and it exerts immense normative influence in debates about economic possibility by (among other things) its portrayal of certain economic arrangements as optimal, inevitable, or otherwise impervious to dispute. Yet in the aftermath of an economic crisis, the economic theory underpinning the economic status quo is vulnerable to critique. Its failure to predict or prevent the economic crisis, and its complicity in perpetuating whatever economic dysfunction is seen to have contributed to the crisis, encourages the critical scrutiny of prevailing economic theory. This offers an opportunity for oppositional knowledge production as advocates of new or typically marginalized economic ideas benefit from the visible disarray of the hegemonic economic paradigm. Potentially, a theoretical interregnum ensues as previously hegemonic narratives are in disarray but rival narratives are not yet consolidated and popularized. Struggles to promote analyses derived from various theoretical traditions (and even the debates among proponents of particular theoretical orientations) will influence which economic understandings and arrangements come under criticism and what actions are proposed to address these criticisms. A theoretical interregnum presents an ominous challenge to those seeking to avoid more radical possibilities. Proponents of the status quo must scramble to address the fault lines apparent in the theoretical infrastructure through which prevailing economic arrangements have been legitimated, while seeking to deter or defend against rival theoretical interventions conducive to other (and potentially more radical) possibilities.

The Great Depression is arguably the archetypical instance of a dramatic and prolonged economic crisis that provoked an extensive reconsideration of economic thinking. While Keynesian economic theory ultimately prevailed as a new theoretical consensus to make possible the continued embrace of capitalism (although under circumstances of a dramatically reimagined role for government), the ultimate ascendency of Keynesianism was not a tidy or prompt teleological necessity. In a context in which many radical possibilities were in circulation, even governments explicitly committed to preserving capitalism[4] and fearful of anti-capitalist alternatives[5] were uncertain about how to understand and respond to the calamitous economic context. For example, while Roosevelt's 'New Deal' is often retrospectively regarded as the embryonic expression of post-war Keynesian welfare state capitalism,[6] a melange of diverse (and sometimes mutually inconsistent) theoretical perspectives were evident in New Deal policies.[7] In his *Designs within Disorder*, Barber (1996) depicts the fluidity of economic theories in circulation in the Roosevelt administration:

> Roosevelt inherited a disorderly economy whose behavior was at odds with textbook teaching. At his death he bequeathed a restructured economy—in which the role of government had been redefined—that would inspire a rewriting of the textbooks. Along the way, he was to execute more than one 'U-turn' in his economic strategies. It is small wonder that this apparent disorder induced his critics to question whether Roosevelt's economic thinking was rooted in any coherent analytic perspective.
>
> (p. 1)

While discursive ambiguity and instability in both theoretical and public policy contexts creates opportunities for more radical economic critique and action, the ability of these radical possibilities to gain traction will be influenced by (among other factors) the struggle over problem definition in crisis narratives. By establishing 'what went wrong,' a crisis narrative selectively attempts to establish one (or a subset) of economic attributes as the focus of examination. The problem definition embraced by any crisis narrative is necessarily selective—since no theory can account for all of social totality. But by establishing what is taken to be 'the problem,' other economic attributes are shielded from causal attention, thus establishing the boundaries of what is posited (by the crisis narrative) as the relevant terrain of debate. At various points during the

Great Depression, the economic crisis was attributed to one (or more) issues, including dysfunctions in 'free' markets, inequality in power, wealth and/or income, questions of property (such as ownership of the means of production), capital/labor struggles (including the concept of exploitation), domestic and/or international governmental regulatory or policy failures, as well as various (and perennial) ad hoc favorites (bad luck and/or lack of appropriate moral rectitude, nationalistic arguments, etc.). From this mêlée, a particular Keynesianism emerged as the hegemonic theoretical perspective of the post-war era,[8] but this development was not inevitable.

The Keynesian theory that became hegemonic in the post-war era of "Keynesian welfare state capitalism" focused on one particular problem afflicting laissez-faire capitalism: the possibility that the profit-motivated investment behavior of private capitalist firms may provoke and exacerbate economic recession. By refraining from critiquing private, for-profit capitalism per se, this entry point largely endorses private capitalist firms as engines of economic growth owing to their role in orchestrating productive investment (thus foreclosing other alternative economic arrangements). Instead, this Keynesian crisis narrative regards the problem posed by capitalist investment behavior as manageable so long as government economic intervention is orchestrated so as to secure business confidence. From this analysis emerged the justification for a profound reconsideration of the role of the State in capitalism, in order that it might create conditions that would stabilize business confidence and thereby ameliorate the dysfunctional aspects of business investment.

Keynes's analysis highlights the uncertainty plaguing business investment. Capitalist enterprises must make investments without knowing whether conditions will unfold such that an investment will be profitable in the future. Thus Keynes viewed investment as being highly influenced by business confidence. If businesses fear that they will not be able to sell their output, they will reduce their investment, which may start or prolong an economic downturn (Crotty, 1992; Dow, 2012). A vicious cycle can ensue as weak business investment reduces employment, which in turn reduces purchases by both workers and other businesses. Weak demand among purchasers further reduces businesses' confidence in their ability to sell their output, thereby intensifying the downward cycle. Thus the profit incentive of capitalist firms leads them to exacerbate the economic crisis by refraining from investing precisely when investment is most urgently required.

From this analysis emerged a theoretical justification for government policy to reverse this downward cycle. Businesses lack confidence because they fear insufficient aggregate demand, meaning the lack of purchasers capable of buying their products. Who might reverse this unwillingness of businesses to invest? Consumers were unlikely to increase their purchases amidst the widespread unemployment during economic crises. Nor were international sources likely to increase their purchases during a global depression. Thus only government remained as an entity capable of stimulating aggregate demand. Keynesian countercyclical aggregate demand management argues that government should spend money during an economic downturn to step into this breach. Increased government spending might enhance businesses' confidence in their ability to find purchasers of their products, which might entice them to expand investment and production, thereby increasing employment and economic activity. Since other actors could not (workers/consumers) or would not (businesses) step up, only government could intervene to save capitalist firms from the systemic threat posed by their own profit-motivated investment decisions that provoke and exacerbate economic recessions. Government spending thus became the salvation that might alleviate the instabilities emanating from capitalist investment behavior.

The Keynesian economic theory that emerged from the Great Depression to undergird post-war welfare state capitalism transformed subsequent understandings of austerity. The previous laissez-faire economic orthodoxy condemned government budget deficits.[9] In an economic slowdown budget deficits are all but inevitable, since tax revenues suffer when economic activity declines, while government expenses are likely to rise.[10] Thus the pre-Keynesian theoretical consensus advocated making cuts to government spending during depressed economic conditions to minimize government budget deficits. From a Keynesian perspective, austerity as a response to economic crisis is a pathological intensification of an economic downturn. Just when government coffers are being squeezed by an economic slow-down, Keynesian theory indicates that governments should further *increase* their deficits so as to enhance aggregate demand. This stimulation of aggregate demand will enhance business confidence and abbreviate or avoid the economic downturn, thus setting the stage for improved government finances as tax revenue recovers (and government expenses diminish).

The implications of this reversal of previous economic logic can hardly be understated. Contrary to the directives of the previous economic orthodoxy, Keynesianism presented budget deficits as the advisable and prudent response to economic crisis. Indeed, much of the Keynesian-informed critique of New Deal policies argued that the government unnecessarily prolonged the depression because it wasn't sufficiently aggressive in its stimulus measures (Hansen, 1941; Brown, 1956) and that the government's premature attempt to return to balanced budgets ultimately provoked the 'Roosevelt Recession' of 1937/38 (Keynes, 1938).

This version of Keynesianism averted attention from other potentially objectionable attributes of the economic status quo. For example, it left unchallenged the control of private capitalist firms over the investment process, thereby conferring on them the capacity to sabotage economic recovery should they conclude that conditions were such that they lacked confidence to invest. So long as private capitalist firms hold this economic veto power, governments are compelled to design public policy to secure business confidence, thus insulating them from responding to democratic pressures if such pressures might contribute to pessimism among capitalist firms. But in other respects, Keynesian analysis facilitated the pursuit of other economic alternatives. While

Keynesianism prescribed government spending to avoid or lessen an economic downturn, it did not dictate what sorts of spending governments should undertake. The overall stimulatory impacts of government spending might be achieved whether the government spent money on social programs for the economically marginalized, subsidies to businesses, public works, or military endeavors. Thus Keynesianism provided a theoretical terrain on which political struggles over the characteristics of government fiscal policy might be fought.

While military, business, and other constituencies might frame their agendas via Keynesian logics, labor unions and social justice advocates enjoyed some important advantages in using Keynesian arguments to promote redistributive government policies. The Keynesian concept of 'marginal propensity to consume' suggested that supporting the incomes of the unemployed and lower income citizens is a preferred way of stimulating aggregate demand, since they are more likely to spend any additional money they receive than are business or more affluent individuals. Moreover, the Keynesian concept of an 'automatic stabilizer' suggested that any programs (such as unemployment insurance) that automatically channel money to those hurt in an economic downturn were a particularly effective means of smoothing economic cycles. Thus Keynesian logic could be readily invoked to argue that the preferred path to securing economic growth and stability should be government support for the marginalized and/or unemployed. In this manner, Keynesianism lends itself to social justice agendas arguing that economic prosperity and stability for all is enhanced via government initiatives that promote greater equity, support workers' incomes, reduce poverty, and target support to historically marginalized groups.

The theoretical terrain opened by Keynesianism also segued into larger topics of economic justice. For example, the preoccupation with the economic suffering endured during the Great Depression created a political climate in which governments were compelled to demonstrate that capitalism could be 'better" in some important ways. This led many national governments to espouse formal commitments to 'full employment.' As full employment public policies contributed to the reduction in unemployment, worker bargaining power was enhanced, which tended to enable workers to secure rising real wages and also contributed to moderating income inequality (Russell & Dufour, 2016; Dufour & Russell, 2015). Roosevelt's 1944 agenda for his 'Economic Bill of Rights' (Rosenman, 1950, pp. 40–42)—which asserted the right to employment, health care, and decent housing, among other things—illustrates this aspiration to enlarging the economic entitlements of citizens in the context of vigorous government economic policy.

Crisis discourse reprise: Austerity in the wake of the economic and financial crisis of 2008

Since the Great Depression, neoclassical economic theory has mounted a sustained and successful campaign to supplant Keynesianism as the hegemonic economic paradigm. On the level of both theory and policy, this battle has been centrally focused on the role of government. In particular, we focus on neoclassical economics's condemnation of government budget deficits together with their depiction of many social programs as unsustainably expensive and/or 'bad' for the economy.[11] This demonization of social programs alongside the relentless promotion of a moral panic concerning the perils of budget deficits have been particularly effective in securing public acquiescence to the evisceration of the progressive dimensions of Keynesian public policy, such as the elimination or reduction of social programs with redistributive attributes. By provoking public anxiety about government finances, and by holding social programs responsible for government deficits and detrimental economic conditions, neoliberals have had considerable success in depicting attacks on social programs as a fiscal and economic necessity rather than a political choice. (Ironically, even government deficits exacerbated by neoliberal policies themselves have been seized upon to legitimate further austerity.[12])

While neoclassical economic theory has been remarkably successful in creating the theoretical environment conducive to dismantling the social programs characteristic of Keynesian welfare state capitalism, Keynesian ideas continue to regain prominence during times of acute economic crisis. This Keynesian resurgence was evident in the response to the economic crisis in 2008 and beyond. Despite their previous opposition to budget deficits, even stalwart neoliberal governments pursued emergency Keynesian stabilization and stimulus measures in the face of the largest crisis of neoliberal capitalism to date. Predictably large budget deficits ensued, thanks to the confluence of shrinking tax revenues in the economic downturn, the expenses of economic stabilization measures, and the bailouts of prominent financial and industrial firms. Nor were these Keynesian-style stimulus measures (and their concomitant budget deficits) a momentary lapse from neoliberal government as usual; the persistence of these Keynesian policies in the face of prolonged economic weakness and instability invited the perception that a sustained turn away from neoliberal economic doctrine was plausible. A potential 'window of opportunity' for resurgent economic critique and mobilization was discernable. Contra the neoliberal mantra that governments must refrain from intervening in the economy, widespread and often unprecedented government economic initiatives were demonstrating that economic options existed beyond the typical neoliberal playbook.

As governments demonstrated their willingness to act counter to neoliberal dictates in a crisis, neoliberalism was also being accused of having fueled the economic crisis itself. Various critiques focused on neoliberal attributes such as lax regulation, permissiveness towards capital (particularly financial capital), and the disavowal of the many government initiatives that might have promoted greater stability. In this environment, the possibility and validity of alternatives to neoliberalism gained traction in public debate. Certainly a compelling case could be made that governments should support those who benefited least from neoliberal capitalism yet suffered most acutely from its crisis. These demands for economic change might take many forms, reflecting the influence of many theoretical traditions. But in light of a resurgent implementation of Keynesian-style stimulative deficits, it was possible that momentum might build to couple the Keynesian case for government spending on social programs with broader social and environmental justice agendas, as is illustrated by the growing prominence of demands for a "green new deal" (Barbier, 2010).

A convergence between Keynesian stimulus measures and various social justice agendas would threaten to reverse the dismantling of social programs assiduously pursued by neoliberal advocates for decades. Typically, the neoliberal strategy to pre-empt demands for expanded social programs was to depict them as fiscally unsustainable. Yet the budget deficits of 2008 and beyond were manifestly not provoked by overly generous social programs, but rather were the product of government actions designed to save capitalism from a crisis that many regarded as a manifestation of the pathologies of neoliberal capitalism itself. Thus the perennial staple of austerity discourses—that social programs are fiscally unfeasible—was implausible in a context in which social programs could not be blamed for either provoking the economic crisis or the budgetary fallout of measures intended to contain the crisis. Moreover, the fact that government actions during the crisis demonstrated that it is quite possible for governments to run large deficits when they so choose revealed that budgetary constraints are not as inflexible as neoliberals tend to portray. If money could be found to bail out those responsible for the crisis, why could there not be resources to support those suffering the most from the crisis?

The EFC hypothesis emerged to both avert renewed demands to enhance social programs (or even more radical possibilities) and legitimate a return to austerity despite continued economic weakness and instability. Its central concern was to dispute the Keynesian proposition that government deficits could stimulate economic recovery and growth in the present circumstances. In casting doubt on the benefits of government economic stimulus, the EFC shifted focus away from firms' investment behavior in the context of uncertainty over future demand conditions,[13] which in turn deterred critical scrutiny of the role of capitalist firms in provoking and/or exacerbating economic crisis. Instead, the EFC hypothesis built a theoretical foundation from which to argue that continued government deficit spending might prolong economic weakness, while austerity measures might promote economic recovery.

Advocates of the EFC hypothesis constructed their theoretical interventions by returning to the concept of Ricardian equivalence in order to shift causal attention towards the behavior of households as they react to government deficit spending. Ricardo (as updated by Barro and others)[14] proposed that rational consumers who optimize their lifetime savings and consumption choices view current government deficit spending as necessitating future tax increases to service and repay debt. If consumers expect that government deficit spending implies future tax increases, they may react to government deficits incurred to generate economic stimulus by reducing their spending. Despite the many theoretical concerns regarding these Ricardian equivalence models,[15] advocates of the EFC hypothesis were remarkably successful in arguing that government deficits might sabotage their intended goal of stimulating the economy because of their chastening impact on consumer spending.

The EFC hypothesis expanded this analytic trajectory to depict the confidence of businesses and affluent consumers[16] as crucially turning on their expectations related to future government finances. If businesses and the affluent fear that future tax increases will be the consequence of current government deficit spending, they will restrain their consumption and investment expenditures and thereby intensify an economic downturn. If they are confident that taxes will not increase (or be cut) this will induce them to enhance economic growth by increasing their spending. Based on this analysis, the EFC hypothesis argues that Keynesian-style deficit spending may backfire in its quest to stimulate the economy. While conceding that government deficit spending may enhance aggregate demand conditions and thereby buttress the confidence of the private sector, advocates of the EFC hypothesis argue that this expansionary impact of Keynesian policies must be weighed against the contractionary implications that ensue if the fear of future tax increases causes business and affluent consumers to lose confidence and thus restrain their spending. If the impact of feared taxation overwhelms the stimulative effect of deficit spending, the EFC hypothesis argues that Keynesian economic stimulus will perversely undermine the economic growth it seeks to promote. Under these circumstances, EFC proponents argue that austerity policies would promote economic growth.

In addition to discrediting Keynesian stimulus measures, the EFC hypothesis argued that those who benefited most from the ascendency of neoliberal capitalism—businesses and affluent consumers—were the groups to whom government must be accountable in order to secure economic recovery. Since businesses and the affluent were understood as focusing on future tax expectations, governments' anti-tax credentials were essential to the promotion of economic recovery. This conveniently insulated business and the affluent from any popular demands that they should be taxed more heavily to reflect the benefits they reaped under neoliberalism, as well as to recompense society for both the role that these groups (such as financial institutions and their highly-remunerated leadership) played in generating the economic crisis, and the benefits these groups received from publicly-financed bailouts and stabilization measures.

By making the consent of business and the affluent so central in its argument, the EFC hypothesis encouraged the proposition that the most harsh neoliberal governments stood the best chances of promoting economic recovery. Governments were advised to boost their reputation for fiscal restraint by making spending cuts "large, credible and decisive" (Alesina, 2010). Such wholesale spending reductions implied a direct attack on social programs that had thus far resisted neoliberal attack, for EFC adherents acknowledged that it is "increasingly apparent that cuts in the 'welfare state' will have to be a critical part of the necessary fiscal adjustments" (Alesina & Perotti, 1995, p. 1).

Conclusion

For decades, the public has become habituated to neoliberal public policy responses to virtually any concern. Thanks in large part to the hegemony of neoclassical economic theory and its astute strategy of crisis exploitation, the ubiquitous neoliberal tool kit—tax cuts, privatization, reduced social spending, the redesign of social programs so as to reduce their accessibility and efficacy, deregulation, attacks on workers, etc.—has enjoyed legitimacy as the required response to (seemingly) any problem. Government budget deficits (or even the provocation of fears about purported trouble in government finances) have typically offered auspicious opportunities to advance neoliberal agendas (Russell, 2014). A rhetorical canon has been routinized in which all problems are framed as the absence of sufficient neoliberalism, thus further neoliberalization is the answer to all problems. Indeed, neoliberal public policy might well be understood from the vantage point of 'garbage can theory,' an approach to the study of public policy that views actors as scanning the horizon for plausible problems in order to promote their preferred solutions (Boin et al., 2009, p. 83).

The situation unfolding in the late 2000s might have upended this relentless dominance of neoliberal framing and its advocacy of austerity as the solution whatever the problem. With alternative crisis narratives enjoying considerable success in implicating neoliberalism itself in the economic crisis, it was a much more challenging proposition to persuade the public that neoliberal prescriptions must carry the day. Thus the neoclassical theoretical tradition sought a response to deter anti-neoliberal crisis narratives and defend and extend the neoliberal project. As proponents of the EFC hypothesis rose to meet this challenge, they were obliged to engage with the Keynesian-inspired crisis narratives that might have been parlayed into a renaissance of welfare state Keynesianism, or perhaps even more radical economic alternatives. By elevating the confidence of businesses and affluent consumers to analytic prominence, and by positing that their confidence rested on their expectations concerning future taxation, the EFC hypothesis presented an elegant rationale for the implementation of austerity as a means of reassuring businesses and the affluent of governments' neoliberal credentials regarding lower future taxes. Thus the beneficiaries of neoliberal capitalism—the affluent and businesses—were accorded a veto power over the implementation of any alternatives to neoliberalism.

Seen as an exercise in selectively marshalling certain evidence to reach certain conclusions and thwart other interpretations, the creation and dissemination of crisis narratives can be understood as a contest of ideas rather than the revelation of incontestable 'truths.' Perhaps uniquely among the various academic disciplines, economists have been hostile to scrutiny of the discursive and normative attributes of their interventions. For to regard an economic theory as a selective project of problem definition, interpretation, and recommendation is to undermine the disciplinary prestige of economics as a positive 'science' investigating objective economic reality. To scrutinize economic theory to discern how importance is attributed and withdrawn, how certain logics are foregrounded or eclipsed, and to see how these elements are marshalled to legitimate certain understandings of causality and corrective action over others, is to understand economic programs such as the imposition of austerity as a political choice that foreseeably favors some while imposing suffering on others. While economists enhance their authority by cloaking their policy recommendations with all of the legitimating trappings of 'evidence-based decision making,' their interventions are (consciously or unconsciously) constructed based on their preferred problem definition, causal interpretation, and evaluatory criteria. Those who are influenced by some form of 'argumentative turn' (Fischer & Forester, 1993) in their approach to crisis narratives and their policy implications can appreciate that these theoretical interventions are deeply contestable exercises in knowledge production. By understanding the contestability of these discourses, terrain is opened to re-examine the construction and advocacy of rival theoretical orientations which might advance other alternatives that will imply differing winners and losers.

Notes

1 Diverse organizational studies and crisis communications literatures build on Weick's view that "the basic idea of sensemaking is that reality is an ongoing accomplishment that emerges from efforts to create order and make retrospective sense of what occurs" (Weick, 1993, p. 635).

2 Prominent contributions to the expansionary fiscal contraction literature include Alesina & Perotti (1995), Alesina, Perotti, & Tavares (1998), Giavazzi & Pagano (1990), Alesina & Ardagna (1998), Alesina & Ardagna (2009), Alesi, Favero, and Giazvazzi (2014), Alesina, Barbiero, Favero, Giavazzi, & Paradisi (2015), Perotti (2013), & Alesina (2012).

3 While the advocates of the EFC hypothesis initially admitted that their case was 'weak' and dependent on certain contextual factors, these caveats became much less prominent in their later writings immediately preceding the imposition of austerity measures in the early 2010s (see Blyth, 2013, pp. 173–175).

4 See Humphrey (1970) on Roosevelt's explicit commitment to "private business, private property and private profit" (pp. 11–12).

5 Marriner Eccles, depression-era chairman of the US Federal Reserve, illustrated the serious possibility of more radical alternatives in his comment that "We shall either adopt a plan that will meet the problem of unemployment under capitalism, or a plan will be adopted for us which will operate without capitalism" (as cited in Hyman, 1976, p. 106).

6 Keynes published his influential 'General Theory' in 1936, three years after the New Deal began pioneering some of the policy innovations that would retrospectively be understood as characteristic of Keynesian fiscal policy. However some ideas now associated with Keynesianism were in circulation prior to the publication of the General Theory (see Russell, 2007, p. 6).

7 Several economic and political theoretical traditions influential among the New Deal 'Brains Trust' include the advocacy of 'administered pricing,' enhanced government planning, opposition to trusts, underconsumption theory, etc.

8 There are a variety of Keynesianisms, some of which depart substantially from the so-called 'bastard' Keynesianism more closely associated with welfare state capitalism.

9 For an overview of the pre-depression consensus against budget deficits to support countercyclical fiscal policy, see Delong (1998). Examples of fiscally conservative influences in the Roosevelt administration can be found in Zelizer (2000).

10 Where so-called countercyclical government programs exist, such as support the unemployed or poor, government expenses will increase during an economic downturn.

11 While not discussed below, neoclassicals often argue that social programs are economically damaging because they create perverse economic incentives, as when unemployment insurance is theorized as a disincentive to work.

12 The Reagan Administration's 'starve the beast' strategy is a useful example. Fearful that it was politically unfeasible to cut popular social programs directly, Reagan boosted defence spending while cutting taxes, thus exacerbating budget deficits that it subsequently portrayed as evidence of the necessity of cuts to social programs.

13 This builds on the neoclassical invocation of Say's Law (supply creates its own demand) to dispute the relevance of demand constraints on economic growth.

14 Ricardo's tentative comments in his *Essay on the Funding System* (1820) was applied by Barro (1974) and others, including in recent policy studies (Nickel & Vansteenkiste, 2008).

15 Models in the Ricardian equivalence tradition tend to employ rather strenuous assumptions regarding the proposition that government deficits are serviced solely via future tax revenue, the capacity of consumers to save and borrow so as to alter the timing of their expenditures over their lifetimes, as well as assumptions that address the problem that consumers do not know the timing of a future tax increase (or even if the tax increase will occur in their lifetime). Nor do these models tend to accord much importance to the possibility that current deficit spending in such areas as education, transportation, infrastructure, etc. might produce economic benefits that support increased tax revenues in the future.

16 Presumably the only consumers able to have discretion over spending on non-essentials—and who have the access to borrowing to alter their consumption over time—are higher income consumers.

References

Alesina, A. (2010, April). Fiscal adjustments: Lessons from recent history. In *ECOFIN meeting, Madrid, April* (Vol. 15, pp. 1909–1940).

Alesina, A. (2012). Fiscal policy after the Great Recession. *Atlantic Economic Journal, 40*(4), 429–435.

Alesina, A., & Ardagna, S. (1998). Tales of fiscal adjustment. *Economic Policy, 13*(27), 487–545.

Alesina, A., & Ardagna, S. (2009). *Large changes in fiscal policy: Taxes versus spending.* (Working Paper No. 15438). Washington, DC: NBER. Retrieved from www.nber.org/papers/w15438

Alesina, A., Barbiero, O., Favero, C., Giavazzi, F., & Paradisi, M. (2015). Austerity in 2009–13. *Economic Policy, 30*(83), 383–437.

Alesina, A., & Perotti, R. (1995). Fiscal expansions and adjustments in OECD countries. *Economic Policy, 10*(21), 205–248.

Alesina, A., Perotti, R., & Tavares, J. (1998). The political economy of fiscal adjustments. *Brookings Papers on Economic Activity, 29*(1), 197–266.

Barber, W. (1996). *Designs within disorder.* Cambridge, UK: Cambridge University Press.

Barbier, E. B. (2010). *A global Green New Deal: Rethinking the economic recovery.* Cambridge, UK: Cambridge University Press.

Barro, R. (1974). Are government bonds net wealth? *Journal of Political Economy, 82*(6), 1095–1117.

Birdsall, N., & Fukuyama, F. (2011). The post-Washington consensus: Development after the crisis. *Foreign Affairs, 90*(2), 45–53.

Blyth, M. (2013). *Austerity: The history of a dangerous idea.* Oxford: Oxford University Press.

Boin, A., t'Hart P., & McConnell, A. (2009). Crisis exploitation: Political and policy impacts of framing contests. *Journal of European Public Policy,* 16(1), 81–106.

Brown, E. C. (1956). Fiscal policies in the 1930s: A reappraisal. *American Economic Review, 46*(5), 857–879.

Coy, P. (2010, July 1). Keynes vs. Alesina. Alesina who? *Bloomberg Businessweek.* Retrieved from www.bloomberg.com/news/articles/2010-06-29/keynes-vs-dot-alesina- dot-alesina-who

Crotty, J. (1992). Neoclassical and Keynesian approaches to the theory of investment. *Journal of Post Keynesian Economics, 14*(4), 483–496.

DeLong, J. B. (1998). Fiscal policy in the shadow of the Great Depression. In M. Bordo, C. Goldin, & E. White (Eds.), *The defining moment: The Great Depression and the American economy in the twentieth century* (pp. 67–86). Chicago, IL: The University of Chicago Press.

Dow, S. (2012). Keynes on knowledge, expectations and rationality. In R. Frydman & S. Phelps (Eds.), *Rethinking expectations: The way forward for macroeconomics* (pp. 112–129). Princeton, NJ: Princeton University Press.

Dufour, M., & Russell, E. (2015). Why isn't productivity more popular? *International Productivity Monitor, 28,* 47–62.

Entman, R. (1993). Framing: Toward clarification of a fractured paradigm. *Journal of Communication, 43*(4), 51–58.

Fischer, F., & Forester, J. (Eds.). (1993). *The argumentative turn in policy analysis and planning.* Durham, NC: Duke University Press.

Giavazzi, F., & Pagano, M. (1990). Can severe fiscal contractions be expansionary? Tales of two small European countries. *National Bureau of Economic Research Macroeconomics Annual, 5,* 75–111.

Gioia, D. A., & Chittipeddi, K. (1991). Sensemaking and sensegiving in strategic change initiation. *Strategic Management Journal, 12*(6), 433–448.

Hansen, A. (1941). *Fiscal policy and business cycles.* New York: W.W. Norton & Company, Inc.

Humphrey, H. H. (1970). *The political philosophy of the New Deal.* LSU Press.

Hyman, S. (1976). *Marriner S. Eccles: Private entrepreneur and public servant.* Stanford, CA: Graduate School of Business, Stanford University.

Keynes, J. M. (1938). Letter of February 1 to Franklin Delano Roosevelt. In *Collected works.* (Vol. 21: Activities, 1931–1939). London: Macmillan.

Keeler, J. T. (1993). Opening the window for reform: Mandates, crises, and extraordinary policy-making. *Comparative Political Studies, 25*(4), 433–486.

Nickel, C., & Vansteenkiste, I. (2008). *Fiscal policies, the current account and Ricardian equivalence.* (Working Paper Series no. 935, September 2008). Frankfurt: European Central

Bank. Retrieved from www.ecb.europa.eu/pub/pdf/scpwps/ecbwp935.pdf?515569e1de059679c15457ac5ed6b3dd

Perotti, R. (2013). The 'austerity myth': Gain without pain? In A. Alesina & F. Giavazzi (Eds.), *Fiscal policy after the Financial Crisis* (pp. 307–354). Chicago, IL: University of Chicago Press.

Ricardo, D. (1820). Essay on the funding system. In J. R. McCulloch (Ed.), *The works of David Ricardo: With a notice of the life and writings of the author* (pp. 515–549). London: John Murray.

Rosenman, S. (1950). (Ed.). *Roosevelt, Franklin: The public papers & addresses of Franklin D. Roosevelt* (Vol. 8). New York: Harper.

Russell, E. (2007). *New Deal banking reforms and Keynesian welfare state capitalism*. London: Routledge.

Russell, E. (2014). The strategic uses of budget crisis. In D. Baines & S. McBride (Eds.), *Orchestrating austerity: Impacts and resistance* (pp. 34–49). Halifax: Fernwood.

Russell, E., & Dufour, M. (2016). Why the rising tide doesn't lift all boats: Wages and bargaining power in neoliberal Canada. *Studies in Political Economy*, *97*(1), 37–55.

Soares da Silva, A. (2016). The persuasive (and manipulative) power of metaphor in 'austerity' discourse: A corpus-based analysis of embodied and moral metaphors of austerity in the Portuguese press. In M. Romano & M. D. Porto (Eds.), *Exploring discourse strategies in social and cognitive interaction: Multimodal and cross-linguistic perspectives* (pp. 79–108). Amsterdam, Netherlands: John Benjamins.

Weick, K. E. (1993). The collapse of sensemaking in organizations: The Mann Gulch disaster. *Administrative Science Quarterly*, *38*(4), 628–652.

Zelizer, J. E. (2000). The forgotten legacy of the New Deal: Fiscal conservatism and the Roosevelt administration, 1933–1938. *Presidential Studies Quarterly*, *30*(2), 331–358.

Part II

Historical perspective

This part of the book examines *austerity* in its historical context, with analyses stretching back to the pre-Second World War era. This is an indispensable exercise as the concept has meant different things at different times. The three chapters in this part focus on the United Kingdom, Greece and Argentina, all important showcases in terms of the way austerity has been legitimized and implemented.

A common thread that runs through these chapters relates to how the proponents of austerity have been able to evoke different associations in support of their policy package; associations that have questionable relevance to contemporary reality and which have more often than not served to cause confusion. In the United Kingdom, as Lesley Jeffries and Brian Walker (Chapter 3) show, the use of the word 'austerity' in the twenty-first century was intended to rekindle a spirit of wartime and post-war community and collective purpose, with a view thereby to garnering support for quite a different set of policies in a very different political and economic context. Nuria Giniger and Irene Sotiropoulou (Chapter 4) have conducted a wide-ranging comparative study of austerity discourses, according to which in both Argentina and Greece much of the case for cutting public spending rested on hostility to State interference in private business, despite the fact that public policy actually strengthened the role of the State in many areas. Lastly, in a detailed and focused study of portrayals of Greece in the British media, Bessie Mitsikopoulou and Christina Lykou (Chapter 5) explain how austerity has been legitimized and institutionalized by foregrounding technical and non-political aspects of the debate.

The authors in this part use various discourse analytic methods, each of which makes a unique contribution to our understanding of austerity discourses. Lesley Jeffries and Brian Walker combine corpus linguistics and critical stylistics to provide a detailed study of the word 'austerity,' drawing on a large-scale corpus—that is, a computer-searchable electronic database of texts—covering parliamentary debate in the United Kingdom, where *austerity* originated as a term. Given the importance of *austerity* as a sociopolitical keyword, characterizing a large part of contemporary public discourse on a global level, this is as important as it was revealing.

Nuria Giniger and Irene Sotiropoulou draw on the Discourse Historical Approach (DHA), which pays considerable attention to the sociopolitical, economic and historical context in which discourses are produced and received. We believe the DHA is a potentially very fruitful avenue for collaboration between economists and linguists, to which each discipline can make a substantive contribution, and we hope that some readers will consider exploring it further.

The chapter by Bessie Mitsikopoulou and Christina Lykou involves much closer linguistic analysis, drawing on the highly-respected and widely-used paradigm of Systemic Functional Linguistics (SFL), also known as Systemic Functional Grammar. Unlike traditional grammar, which focuses on the form of words, phrases and sentences—and rules about their combination—SFL views language as a process of culturally-contextualized meaning-making and, consequently, attends to the linkages between grammatical form and function: the *ideational* function involves representations of reality; the *interpersonal* function entails relationships between text producer(s) and consumer(s); and the *textual* function refers to the organization of texts into coherent and recognizable genres. SFL uses an intricate and highly specialized vocabulary, which can be off-putting to the non-initiated, but its value lies in explaining very precisely where and how it is that ideology is encoded in language.

Readers familiar with pro-austerity discourses will find much in all three chapters that is relevant and applicable elsewhere.

3 Austerity in the Commons

A corpus critical analysis of austerity and its surrounding grammatical context in Hansard (1803–2015)

Lesley Jeffries and Brian Walker

June 2015 saw thousands of UK citizens join 'anti-austerity' protests after the surprise election of the Conservative Party as the party of government at the Westminster parliament. People in other European countries have also campaigned against the prevailing political ideology that asserts that 'we' need to 'balance the books.' The very existence of a protest movement defining itself by opposition to austerity[1] supports the status of *austerity* as a sociopolitical keyword summarizing a complex political process.

Our research explores the ways in which the word *austerity* is used in a corpus of Hansard reports (1803–2015) and, using a combination of corpus tools and critical stylistics (Jeffries, 2015), considers its co-textual-driven meaning in a sociopolitical context.

In this chapter, we will outline our methodology for data collection and analysis, report frequencies of use across our data, describe patterns of usage in our data, and finish by drawing conclusions about the potential impact and/or effect of *austerity* as a sociopolitical keyword. We start by introducing the concept of the sociopolitical keyword.

1. Sociopolitical keywords

The notion of sociopolitical keyword is inspired by *Keywords* (Williams, 1983 [1976]), which listed words characterizing and sometimes challenging the ideology of the post-war years. Significant power can be wielded in political discourse by individual words which may connote a whole complex of meaning subtly different from the everyday usage of the same word and work as a kind of shorthand for a whole ideological stance.

Whilst Williams's concept of keywords was a cultural one, drawing on his wide knowledge and expertise in the area of sociocultural history, we have been concerned in our research (Jeffries & Walker, 2012, 2017) to use computer tools to establish both the popularity and the specialized meaning of such keywords in corpora reflecting the political or cultural views of the period in which they are used. The current study, however, depends on an *a priori* judgement that *austerity* is indeed a sociocultural keyword of the kind we have been examining. As in the case of Jeffries and Evans (2015), which looked at the word *choice* in political manifestos, the keyword we are interested in here is not in dispute from the outset, so our focus is on the use and emergent meaning (see Jeffries, 2003, 2010b) of that particular word at different periods in the Hansard data.

2. Methods, frameworks and theoretical considerations

The kind of meaning development that we are interested in can be traced to the co-textual surroundings of keywords in larges bodies of data consisting of many texts. Such investigations require a combination of tools that facilitate detailed linguistic analysis across large amounts of data. This section introduces and explains how we combine the methodological strengths of corpus linguistics (see also Jeffries & Walker, 2012, 2017) with insights from the critical stylistic framework (Jeffries, 2010a).

Corpus Linguistics

A corpus (pl. corpora) is a collection of electronically stored language data representing a particular language or language variety (see McEnery & Wilson, 2001, p. 73). Typically, corpus linguistics is the investigation of language phenomena using a corpus, assisted by the outputs of computer software designed to process large quantities of data in various ways. For example, corpus tools are typically able to calculate (absolute and relative) word frequencies and display every instance of a given word in a corpus with some of its surrounding co-text in a list known as a concordance. Such outputs can help to discover patterns of usage that may otherwise go unnoticed.

To assess patterns of usage of *austerity* in our data, we use word frequencies and concordances, as well as the notion of collocation, by which we mean the tendency for words to co-occur. It was J. R. Firth (1957) who first suggested that such co-occurrence can affect word meaning, and famously said "you shall know a word by the company it keeps" (Firth, 1957, p. 179). Collocation can thus contribute to what might be termed the textual meaning of a word derived through usage. In corpus studies, collocates are usually identified automatically within a fixed span (e.g., within four words each side) of the word under investigation (see Sinclair, Jones, Daley, & Krishnamurthy, 2004, p. 35), irrespective of punctuation or grammatical boundaries. Whilst there may be some effect from co-text beyond the immediate clause in which an item occurs, we consider the clausal co-text as most likely to influence the development of meaning. Our analysis will show that both the collocates of *austerity* and its syntactic context, which we analyze manually using concordances, are important in gaining an understanding of the textually constructed meaning of the word.

Critical stylistics

Stylistics is the study of the meaning of texts, and applies the models and insights of modern linguistics to explore how texts create meaning and how they are understood by readers. The development of a specifically 'critical' stylistics (see Jeffries, 2010a, 2015) aimed to create a framework for discussing those aspects of ideological meaning which could be identified as non-propositional, but are nevertheless present in the text. These elements of textual meaning, together, form a layer of meaning which can be identified in the choices of language used, and give the reader a sense of the ideational world that the text is taking for granted, including the shape, size and nature of that world, and its values (ideologies). The critical stylistics framework draws on well-established theories of language, including, for example, Hallidayan (Halliday, 1994) Systemic Functional Grammar, which is based on the notion that structural aspects of language are intrinsically linked to their function in interaction. Critical stylistics combines this and other insights with some original concepts of its own in a larger overarching model of language which identifies a set of 'textual-conceptual' features which can be traced in texts (see Jeffries, 2014a, 2014b, 2015). This textual-conceptual level differs from the purely linguistic on the one hand, which is where propositional meaning is constructed, and the interactional or pragmatic on the other hand, which is where interpersonal meaning is found.

In this study, we first focus on two of the main textual-conceptual functions, relating to how *austerity* is used in naming in the Hansard data (Section 6) and how it interacts with verbs, or processes (Section 7). These analyses of our keywords' behaviour are followed by analysis of how *austerity* is equated and contrasted with other political concepts (Section 8). The advantage of the critical stylistic model for the current study is that it examines textual features which, although variable in form, can largely be identified (and if helpful, counted) to characterize the world being created by textual means.

Combining corpus linguistics and critical stylistics

Combining corpus linguistics with critical approaches to the meaning of discourse is becoming established as a way of identifying and analyzing ideologically important language patterns in large sets of data. Work such as Baker, Gabrielatos, KhosraviNik, Krzyzanowski, McEnery, and Wodak (2008, 2013), Gabrielatos and Baker (2008), Gabrielatos, McEnery, Diggle, and Baker (2012), Baker, Gabrielatos and McEnery (2013), and KhosraviNik (2009) has enriched our understanding of the way groups of people in society are constructed in texts, through the examination of particular terms including *refugee* and *immigrant*. Jeffries (2003) has also demonstrated that inanimate entities can be linguistically constructed for political ends by analyzing the emergent meaning of *water* during the 1995 water crisis in Yorkshire, England.

More recently, corpus techniques have facilitated rigorous linguistic research into sociopolitical keywords (Jeffries & Walker, 2012, 2017) and shown that they acquire a specific meaning within a (historically) short space of time, often simultaneously developing an associated evaluation. This process allocates a specific set of semantic features to the word and paradoxically also empties the word of meaning. It is often evidenced by an increased use of the keyword as an unmodified noun (i.e., a noun with no adjectives or other modifiers) which the recipient is expected to understand without further elaboration. The potential effects of this process include the danger that the electorate may be persuaded to accept an ideologically controversial concept (e.g., choice in public services) as benign and naturalized (Fairclough, 2001, p. 76); as an absolute good. Fairclough (2001) notes that the process of naturalization—turning ideologies into common sense—is "the most formidable weapon in the armoury of power" (p. 87). The importance of individual lexical choices in political data should, in our view, not be underestimated.

3. Data and methodology

Our analysis of *austerity* focuses on its usage in parliamentary debates, as recorded in Hansard, the official record of the House of Commons and House of Lords (hansard.parliament.uk/). Hansard archives go back to 1803 and for part of our investigation we used a pre-existing 1.6 billion word electronic collection of the transcribed UK parliamentary debates 1803 to 2005, known as the Hansard Corpus (1803–2005). The corpus was constructed by Marc Alexander and Jean Anderson (Glasgow University) in 2011 during the JISC Parliamentary Discourse project[2] and later, as part of the SAMUELS project,[3] the corpus was enhanced with word-level metadata about grammar and semantic categories. The particular version of the Hansard Corpus (1803–2005) that we use for this chapter is that prepared by Mark Davies and is available at corpus.byu.edu (www.hansard-corpus.org/). Davies's web-based front-end to the corpus enables complex searches of Hansard at the word level, the grammatical level, and the semantic level. The discussion of *austerity* presented in this chapter considers only the word level (Demmen, Jeffries, & Walker, 2018, utilizes the semantic tagging of the Hansard Corpus).

The historic Hansard Corpus (1803–2005) falls short of the recent period in UK and other European politics when *austerity* returned to the national debate. So, to bring the data up-to-date, we created our own supplementary corpus of Hansard data for the period 2006–2015 using the data repository at the *TheyWorkForYou* website.[4] Though we started out with the aim of investigating *austerity* across the whole of the historic Hansard corpus, the relatively low occurrence in earlier decades, except for the war years, means that our additional 2006–2015 Hansard data became the main focus of this investigation. We compare our results, however, with 1940s usage where this is enlightening.

Our investigation uses the concordancing facilities of *AntConc* (Anthony, 2014) to facilitate a detailed co-textual analysis of the word *austerity* and find salient patterns of occurrence in the data. While many studies of this kind rely very heavily on collocational patterning (i.e., co-occurrence) to produce an analysis of a word's meaning (see for example Baker, 2016), this approach can miss important features of usage that are evident from the co-textual data. Our approach thus considers the individual concordance lines of *austerity* to see how the word functions syntactically (i.e., in terms of its grammatical function and relationships) and semantically (i.e., in terms of its meaning and meaning relationships). We manipulated the concordance lines using *AntConc's* sort function which allows sorting up to three places each side of the search term (*austerity*). Repeated sorting on different patterns was our first step in considering the local textual context of *austerity* in detail because it enabled us to consider large numbers of examples fairly rapidly and observe regular patterns of co-occurrence where they existed.

Once we had a picture of the co-textual surroundings of *austerity*, we also considered the potential effect of its close and frequent collocates. This facilitated our analysis of how *austerity* makes meaning in relation to textual-conceptual features as defined by critical stylistics; specifically how it contributed to naming practices, how it interacts with verbs and whether it was constructed as equivalent or opposite to any particular concepts.

4. Austerity, its roots and revivals

Before we consider the development of *austerity*'s meaning in our Hansard data (Sections 5–8 of this chapter), we review the background to its rise as a sociopolitical keyword during and after the Second World War and its recent revival as a political descriptor of economic policy. As a starting point, it is interesting to see what senses of the word have been defined by the professional lexicographers at Oxford English Dictionaries (OED), in order to contextualize the political usage of the word against its more general background senses.

According to the online version of the *Oxford English Dictionary* (OUP, 2010), *austerity* is a noun with four senses:

1. a. Sternness of manner, appearance, or disposition; severity in judgement; (esp. of a law or judgement) harshness, severity.
   b. With reference to taste: astringent sourness or bitterness; harshness. *Obs.*
   c. With reference to the weather, landscape, etc.: harshness; ruggedness; bleakness.
2. a. Severe self-denial or self-restraint; moral strictness; rigorous abstinence, asceticism. Chiefly in religious contexts.
   b. In pl. Severely abstinent or ascetic practices; mortifications.
3. Severe simplicity; lack of luxury or adornment.
4. Restraint in public spending; spec. a programme of government measures designed to reduce public spending and conserve resources, esp. during a time of economic hardship; the conditions resulting from such measures.

The OED describes the fourth sense as becoming common in 1942, and says that it was "frequently used in the context of rationing and other measures introduced by governments in the period during and after the Second World War (1939–1945)." A number of compound forms involving *austerity* are recorded in the OED, all relating to the fourth sense: *austerity budget*; *austerity clothing*; *austerity measures*; *austerity programme*. As we will see in Section 6, these descriptions of the wartime sense of *austerity* and its common collocates are supported by the 1940s Hansard data, though the more recent usage (2006–2015) diverges from these patterns.

Austerity, then, has strong connections with 1940s Britain, being linked historically with the Attlee government of 1945–1951 and the economic policies of the Chancellor of the Exchequer at that time, Stafford Cripps (Tomlinson, 2013). During these years, the consumption of food, clothing and other goods was regulated and reduced by the Government via rationing and controls on pricing (Zweiniger-Bargielowska, 2000, p. 9). During the war, this was deemed necessary in order to "reduce personal consumption" so that "a balanced redistribution of resources between military and civilian requirements" (Zweiniger-Bargielowska, 2000, p. 9) could be achieved. After the war, the Attlee government continued with the rationing and regulation in order to suppress personal consumption and channel the still fairly limited resources into exports and investment (Tomlinson, 2013). Domestic consumption was held stable, while production and exports were steadily rising to improve the balance of payments (see Cairncross, 1985, p. 24). While the consumption of food and goods was restricted, the Attlee government was simultaneously investing in infrastructure and the new welfare state, amongst other things.

Although we are writing 70 years on from the end of the war, the sense that everyone was suffering and that it was for a 'greater good' (i.e., winning the war against Hitler, and then rebuilding Britain) and that we were all 'in it together' remains strong in the cultural memory of UK citizens over 50. During the build-up to the 2010 general election, the UK leader of the Opposition, David Cameron, attempted to evoke those days of national unity during the war-years by repeatedly using the word *austerity*. In a speech titled 'The age of austerity' that he gave on April 26, 2009 at the Conservative Party spring conference, Cameron said:

> In this new world comes the reckoning for Labour's economic incompetence. The age of irresponsibility is giving way to the age of austerity.

Cameron offers austerity as a positive alternative to Labour's handling of the UK economy. Similarly, in speeches at around the same time, the Shadow Chancellor of the Exchequer, George Osborne, stated, for example, that "the politics of prosperity is giving way to the politics of austerity" (April 8, 2009) and "we have moved from the age of prosperity to an age of austerity" (April 23, 2009). Osborne (and Cameron) continued to use *austerity* in a vague evocation of 1940s–1950s Britain with everyone pulling together, stating that their strategy of cutting public spending was "the only sustainable route from austerity to prosperity" (Osborne, September 15, 2009).

5. Frequencies of austerity across Hansard 1803–2015

In investigating the use of *austerity* in parliamentary debates, one question we wanted to answer was how frequently it was used over the period 1803–2015.

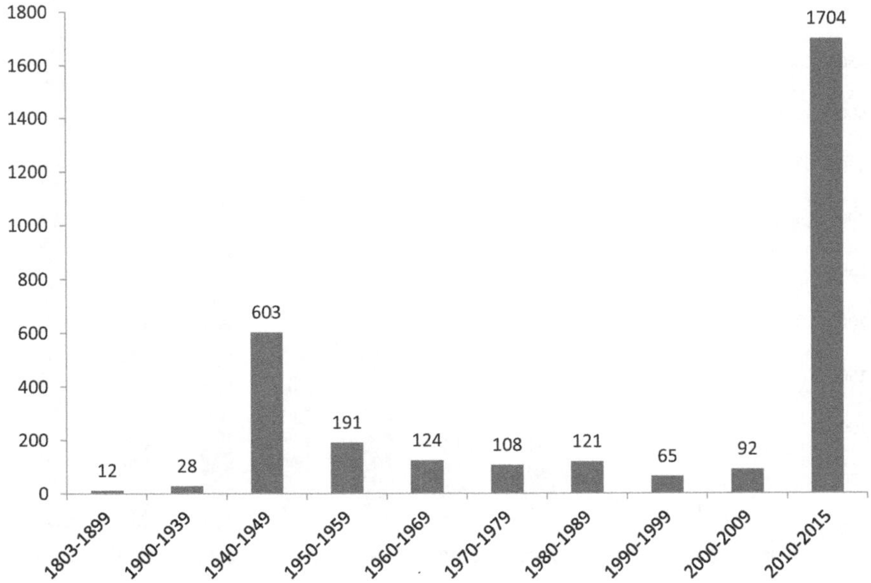

Figure 3.1 Number of times *austerity* is mentioned in Parliament by decade (1803–2015)

The Hansard Corpus (1803–2005) shows *austerity* being used 1,261 times and if we add in the results from our additional corpus (2006–2015), its usage rises to 3,171. Figure 3.1 shows how this total number is spread over the whole period (1803–2015) by decade.

There is a spike in occurrence of *austerity* in the 1940s which lends support to the idea that there was a specific use of the word at that time (OED sense 4) which reflected the measures taken by governments to survive the Second World War and its economic aftermath. Thereafter, the only other striking increase in occurrence is to be found after the financial crash of 2008. Figure 3.2 shows in more detail how the increase in occurrence of *austerity* in this later period is spread out, year by year.

There is a steady rise in occurrence of *austerity* from 2008 through to 2012, followed by a dip in 2013/2014 and a further rise in 2015 to numbers higher than ever before.[5] These rising frequencies of *austerity* reflect its role as one of the keywords of the recent political crises.

The earliest instances of *austerity* in Hansard are found during the 1800s where the word is used only 12 times, in senses 1 and 2 from the OED, as the co-text in the following examples shows:

1815 the austerity of a Russian climate
1825 without any thing of austerity or moroseness in his manners

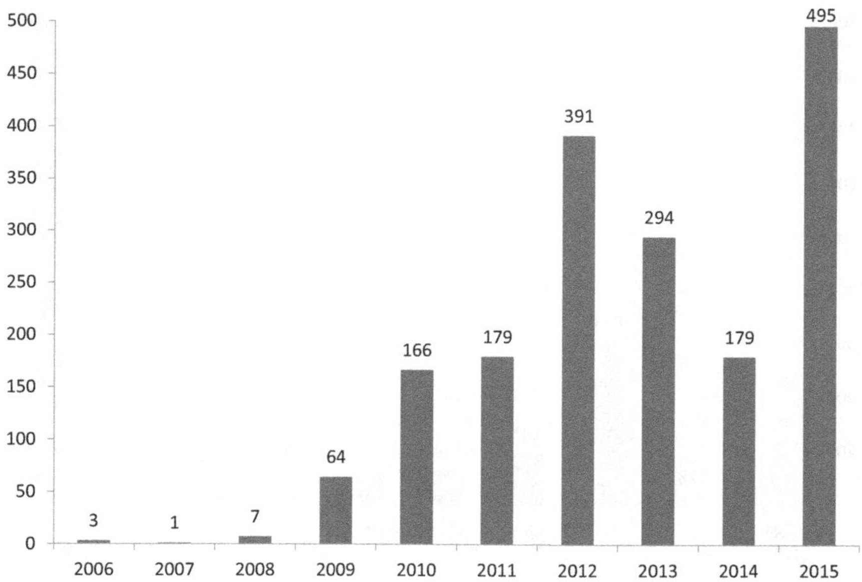

Figure 3.2 Frequencies of *austerity* in Hansard (2006–2015)

1831 they should lead a life of chastity and austerity,
1889 this display of force, this austerity, this cruelty in Ireland

The first mention of *austerity* connected to finance is in 1919, and more notably in 1930, where the phrase *financial austerity* first appears (emphasis added):

1919 That least emotional of all Government Departments has not only scrutinised with its accustomed **austerity** the finances of this measure, but, as will be seen from the Bill
1930 nor is there any need in the present, for such a pretence of **financial austerity** and virtue, which nobody else has shown before:

During the 1940s, its meaning becomes tied to rationing and shortages, relating to sense (4) from the OED, for example (emphasis added):

1946 We are told that we have to have this appalling **austerity** to develop the export market which is essential to this country
1947 and indeed we have often been criticised for too much **austerity**, for diverting goods from the home market for export

In Sections 6–8 of this chapter, we analyze *austerity* in its context to see how its usage contributes to its meaning in the two periods of significant occurrence, the 1940s and 2006–2015.

6. How *austerity* is named

The first textual feature we were interested in was the immediate noun phrase in which *austerity* occurs, either as the main noun or as a modifier. This established a sense of how *austerity* is used as—or in—a name, and what kind of a referent it is linked to. If we take a noun phrase as being made up of the main noun (i.e., the head noun, e.g. ***cat***) with various potential pre-modifiers, such as articles and adjectives (e.g., ***the black*** *cat*) or post-modifiers, such as prepositional phrases (e.g., *the black cat* ***in the garden***), we can group together the different patterns of usage of *austerity* and see how such patterns influence the meaning that it takes on. We divided the instances of *austerity* in our 2005–2016 corpus into six broad categories, based on their syntactic roles, as shown in Table 3.1.

The most frequent categories at just over 30% each are *austerity* as a pre-/post-modifier, followed by *austerity* when it is unmodified. It is worth noting that when *austerity* is itself postmodifying other nouns (e.g., *age of austerity*) or when it is a nominal premodifier of another head noun (e.g., *austerity plan*), it is technically still unmodified itself, which means that the unmodified usage is by far the most common usage overall in this data.

We carried out a similar analysis with the 1940s data; Figure 3.3 below shows a comparison between the percentage totals of the patterns we found.

In the following sections, we offer a short discussion of each of the categories in Table 3.1 and the associated differences in the data from the two time periods.

NP + preposition + austerity

A large proportion (31%) of the instances of *austerity* in the 2005–2016 data form part of a prepositional phrase post-modifying a noun phrase. The most frequent (302 out of 549) noun phrases that are post-modified in this way are those relating to a unit of time (e.g., *age, time*), as seen in Table 3.2.

Table 3.1 *Austerity* patterns in the 2006–2015 data

No.	*Pattern*	*Freq. (%)*	*Examples*
1	NP + preposition + *austerity*	545 (30.6)	an age of **austerity**
2	[pre-modifier+] *austerity* + noun	542 (30.5)	**austerity** agenda; failing **austerity** programme
3	unmodified	365 (20.5)	Europe is facing **austerity**; **austerity** has failed
4	pre-modifier + *austerity*	230 (12.9)	fiscal **austerity**; Westminster **austerity**
5	*austerity* + post-modifier	60 (3.3)	**austerity** for the many; **austerity** alone
6	hyphenated *austerity*	37 (2.1)	anti-**austerity**; **austerity**-driven
	Total	**1779 (100)**	

Figure 3.3 Comparison of percentage frequencies of patterns on *austerity* in the 2006–2015 data and the 1940s data

Table 3.2 Nouns phrases relating to time post-modified by a prepositional phrase containing *austerity*

Pattern	*Freq.*
in (a/this) **time of austerity**	94
[in] [a/an/the/this/his] [new/possible/forthcoming/current/post-recessionary] **age of austerity**	77
(in|at) [these] [troubling/difficult/straitened] **times of austerity**	58
[the] [more/extra/three/five/seven/ten] **years of austerity**	31
(in/during) (a/this) **period of austerity**	25
a **decade of austerity**	10
in an **era of austerity**	6
these **days of austerity**	1
Total	**302**

These patterns *an/the age of austerity* suggest inevitability, where the definite article presupposes that such an age exists and the indefinite article, while not presupposing, strongly suggests the existence of such an age, alongside other types of ages (what Hawkins 1978, calls the 'exclusiveness' condition). The packaging of these temporal states into a noun phrase also makes the existence of such an age less contestable and gives it gravitas, which for O'Hara (2014) is unwarranted, as she notes, "awarding it such an epochal epithet serves to imbue it with an undeserved legitimacy" (p. 2).

Within this category of *austerity* as post-modifier, there is also a minor pattern, occurring 31 times, where *austerity* modifies a noun that has negative associations, for example:

> *the (burden/challenge/beast/scourge/onslaught/rut/punch/madness/cult) of austerity.*
> *a (fixation/obsession) with austerity.*

These patterns suggest that austerity is not desirable, demonstrating that anti-austerity language could be found in parliament as well as in the street.

There are also 24 instances where austerity modifies more neutral nouns, for example:

> *the (economics/policy/policies/politics) of austerity.*

These nouns are preceded by the definite article, which create presuppositions that such phenomena exist. Such phrases help to legitimize policy decisions made by government by suggesting that they are grounded in an actual discipline/science, or part of a planned set of policies.

In the 1940s data, there are proportionally fewer occurrences of the NP+prep+*austerity* pattern, accounting for 19% of total instances. While some sort of unit of time (days/period/time(s)/years) is also the most prevalent pattern here, accounting for a similar proportion of occurrences, there are no examples of *age of austerity*. The most common pattern is *these days of austerity*, occurring eight times. The other common patterns are *period of* and *conditions of austerity*. These results suggest that *austerity* in the 1940s does not have same level of negative association as in the later period and has not acquired epochal status since *days of austerity* seems to be shorter and more temporary than *age of austerity*.

[pre-modifier +] austerity *+ noun (Table 3.3)*

This category of usage in the 2005–2016 data shows *austerity* pre-modifying another noun, either alone (for example, *austerity measures*) or itself pre-modified (for example, *fiscal austerity programme*). (See Table 3.3.)

Table 3.4 shows the nouns that are (co-)pre-modified by *austerity* (i.e., occur to the right of *austerity*) with the majority being *measure(s)* and *programme(s)*.

Table 3.3 Breakdown of [pre-modifier +] *austerity* + noun pattern

Pattern	*Freq.*	*Examples*
austerity + noun	321	**austerity** measures; **austerity** programme; **austerity** cuts
pre-mod + *austerity* + noun	221	disastrous **austerity** policies; Tory **austerity** cuts; crazy **austerity** budget

Table 3.4 Breakdown of *austerity* + noun (2006–2015)

Noun	*Freq.*	*%*
measure/s	178	32.90
programme/s	100	18.48
cuts	37	6.84
agenda	35	6.47
policy/ies	34	6.28
plan/s	28	5.18
budget/s	26	4.81
package/s	11	2.03
economics	6	1.11
government	6	1.11
period	6	1.11
Other	74	13.68
Total	**541**	**100**

(% = the total as a percentage of the number of instances of *austerity* + noun, i.e., 541)

These patterns show that *austerity* is tied to words that add an air of legitimacy or sense of planning to the concept. Persistent co-occurrence of *austerity* with technical sounding words, such as *fiscal*, create an association, in the sense described by Firth (1957), that furnishes *austerity* with a meaning on the one hand more precise, and on the other more euphemistic and oblique. Other words, such as *cuts*, seem to benefit from being attached to *austerity*, because the latter helps to justify the former.

The most frequent nouns modified by *austerity* in 1940s Hansard are shown in Table 3.5 and show a different pattern. The most frequent items *suit*, *suits*, *clothing*, *clothes* and *garments*, give 1940s debates on *austerity* a sartorial focus (the 'other' category also contains one instance each of *dresses*, *frocks*, *socks* and *overcoat*). This suggests more emphasis on material items and other visible manifestations of 1940s *austerity*, and rather less on the more abstract concepts that are prevalent in the 2006–2015 debates.

Unmodified austerity

This category consists of instances of *austerity* where the word is neither modifying other nouns, nor itself modified in any way (e.g., *ranting against austerity*, *pursuing austerity*, *austerity will continue*, *austerity is a zombie economic process*). In such cases, *austerity* is being used to reference a complex meaning with nothing in the immediate context to give clues to the reader as to the nature of this meaning. The word is being used as if its meaning were transparent and readers/listeners are assumed to know this meaning. The tendency for *austerity* to be used in this way is clear, with 21% of the occurrences in the 2006–2015 data being unmodified nouns in their own right.

Table 3.5 Breakdown of *austerity* + noun (1940s)

Noun	*Freq.*	*%*
suit/s	44	27.67
style/s	14	8.80
clothing/clothes	10	6.29
garments	7	4.40
conditions	6	3.77
design	6	3.77
basis	4	2.52
measures	4	2.52
programme	4	2.52
standard	4	2.52
Budget	3	1.89
Other	53	33.33
Total	**159**	**100**

(% = the total as a percentage of the number of instances of *austerity* + noun, i.e., 159)

In the 1940s data, a higher proportion (26%) of cases was similarly unmodified. As with other sociopolitical keywords we have investigated elsewhere (Jeffries & Walker, 2012, 2017), there appears to be a tendency to use these words unmodified as a kind of political shorthand, and this was happening in the 1940s when austerity first became sociopolitically key. As we will see below, however, the question of what it is shorthand for can change over time.

pre-modifier + austerity

Although unmodified *austerity* is common in both corpora, there is also a considerable amount of modification which can help us understand the intended meaning of the word in the periods concerned. In the 2006–2015 corpus, there are 247 instances of pre-modified *austerity* and a total of 125 different pre-modifiers. Table 3.6 shows the 12 that occur at least 10 times.

The most frequent pre-modifier (*Government's*) shows that some speakers are keen to identify who is responsible for the policy. Indeed, collected together, the pre-modifiers that identify to whom the *austerity* belongs (e.g., *Government's*, *Tory*, *Chancellor's*, *coalition's*) is the largest grouping. In the 1940s data, there are no instances where individuals or groups of people are singled out as owning *austerity*, perhaps suggesting that *austerity* was seen less as a political choice and more an inevitable consequence of the world war and its economic aftermath.

Other pre-modifiers in the data identify the type of *austerity* (e.g., *fiscal*; *economic*; *financial*; *public-sector*; *orthodox*; *ideological*). This seems to suggest that different types of *austerity* exist for the politicians debating this issue. One might ask whether the apparent differences between *fiscal*, *economic* and *financial austerity* relate to actual differences in policy and note that *fiscal* is most frequent, lending *austerity* legitimacy due to the official and technical tone of the word.

Table 3.6 Top 12 pre-modifiers of *austerity* (2006–2015)

No.	*Word*	*Freq.*
1	government's	63
2	fiscal	31
3	tory	18
4	more	16
5	further	14
6	economic	14
7	extreme	13
8	chancellor's	13
9	great	12
10	severe	11
11	failed	11
12	failing	10

Other pre-modifiers (e.g., *more*; *further*; *great*; *prolonged*; *greater*; *sizeable*; *less*; *deep/er*; *additional*; *massive*; *extended*; *considerable*) suggest that one component of *austerity*'s meaning is gradability in size, extent or duration, mostly emphasizing greater amounts with only *less* indicating reduction rather than increase. Also, *prolonged* and *extended* are suggestive of a temporal meaning not acknowledged in the dictionary definition. *Prolonged* also links quantity with negative associations (see Louw, 1993), because it collocates significantly frequently with negative concepts such as *drought*, *illness*, *recession* and *struggle* (British National Corpus[6]). Other negatively evaluated pre-modifiers of *austerity* in the data include for example: *failed*; *harsh*; *appalling*; *misguided*; *crippling*; *painful*; *disastrous*; *unfair*; *reckless*; *punitive*; *horrendous*; *futile*; *excessive*; *catastrophic*; *brutal*. There is no equivalent list of positive pre-modifiers.

In the 1940s data, where a similar proportion of instances of *austerity* (13%) are pre-modified, there are none relating to economics or finances and no recurrent patterns, with most pre-modifiers occurring just once. The most frequent pre-modifiers are *continued*, *greater*, *grim* and *spartan*, the last two indicating that negative evaluation was also common in this period. Other pre-modifiers also evaluate *austerity* negatively (*appalling*; *terrible*; *awful*; *harsh*), others comment of the level of *austerity* with associated negativity (e.g., *drastic; extreme; excessive; rigid; sternest*), while just two instances (*purposeless*; *unnecessary*) suggest disagreement with the policy. Again, there are no instances of pre-modification which evaluate austerity positively.

austerity + *post-modifier*

As well as the pre-modification we saw in Section 6.4, *austerity* in the 2006–2015 corpus is also sometimes post-modified (3.3% of cases). In 24 instances the post-modification is a relative clause, for example *the austerity that exists in Britain today*. There are, however, no further patterns of meaning within these subordinated clauses.

The next largest grouping is where *austerity* is post-modified by *alone* (×18), *by itself* (×2) and *on its own* (×3), emphasizing the inadequacy of *austerity* as the only strategy to solve the perceived problems. Most instances are characterized by stating what austerity *alone/by itself/on its own* cannot do:

> *austerity alone will not (create jobs/reduce the budget deficit without/fix the Eurozone);*
> *austerity [alone/by itself] (is not/will not be) enough;*
> *austerity [by itself/on its own/alone] (does/will) not work.*

These examples presuppose that there are other policies that could solve the economic problems in conjunction with *austerity*. This usage also suggests that the complex phenomenon of political austerity is actually a single, simple concept. This is useful rhetorically since it allows a simple concept to be dismissed or argued against with equally simplistic arguments. When we see arguments in the chambers of Parliament which rely on such assertions (e.g., *austerity alone is not enough*), it may indicate that our legislators are talking in shorthand rather than examining a complex situation in detail. As we have seen with *Brexit*, distilling complex issues down to simple one-word labels can be a powerful tool for creating persuasive arguments for or against a concept or policy (Jeffries & McIntyre, 2018).

In the 1940s data, there are 14 cases of *austerity for austerity's sake* or *austerity for its own sake*. This pattern, which does not occur at all in the 2006–2015 data, indicates austerity lacks any point in relation to anything else; it doesn't help the economic situation or people living under it, and people sign up to it as a kind of principle rather than thinking of it as a practical solution to the problems of the day. Rather like unmodified *austerity*, these phrases do not tell the hearer/reader anything about the meaning of *austerity* and are being used as if its meaning were transparent.

Another pattern in the 1940s data that does not occur in 2006–2015 Hansard is *austerity* modified by a prepositional phrase with *in* at the head, for example:

> *austerity in (consumption/food supplies/living/motor cars/the cinema/the public house).*

Aside from the examples showing that austerity affected many different specific aspects of life, within this pattern *austerity* seems ambiguous in meaning, incorporating the OED sense (3)—described in Section 4—relating to a lack of luxury, and the sociopolitical meaning relating to economic policy.

Hyphenated austerity

The hyphenated instances of *austerity* make up the smallest category in the 2006–2015 data. Some of these forms are similar to examples we have examined elsewhere (e.g., *austerity-alone*, *austerity-only* are similar to *austerity alone* or *austerity by itself*) and can be considered in the same way as challenging the idea that *austerity* is opposed to other measures (e.g., public spending).

The two other main groups of hyphenated examples are those where *austerity* seems to belong in the semantic field of ideological or political programmes (e.g. *anti-austerity; austerity-driven; austerity-based*) and those where there is a sense of quantity, usually with connotations of negative evaluation. For example, *austerity-riddled*, which occurs four times, evokes other negative collocates such as *riddled with woodworm*. A similar effect is found in the one case of *austerity-choked UK economy* (Jeffries & McIntyre, 2018).

7. How *austerity* behaves

In this section we shift our focus to the verb choices in the co-text of *austerity* and explore how our keyword functions syntactically in the clauses it occurs in. Essentially, adopting Halliday's (1994) transitivity system, we are interested in what *austerity* is doing (actions), what is happening (events) and what *austerity* is like (states). We are therefore interested in what role *austerity* has in clauses, for example, whether it is actor (doing something), or is being described in some way.

This line of investigation requires detailed, manual analysis of the concordance data that needs to consider whole clauses or sentences; an approach that becomes rather impractical, even with the relatively small number of results we are dealing with here. For this reason, we limited ourselves to two relatively straightforward searches. The first searched for those instances of *austerity* where it is the subject of a verb phrase that contains a form of the verb *be*. Our search detected 112 such instances of *austerity* (6.3% of the 1,779 total in the 2006–2015 data set). We divided this subset of data into cases where *austerity* is:

- being described, when a form of *be* connects *austerity* with a word or phrase that is or acts adjectively (known as a complement) as in *austerity is a bad idea* (see 7.1 below), and
- doing something, when a form of *be* precedes a main verb as in *austerity is working well* (see 7.2 below).

Our second search sorted the data immediately to the right of the keyword in order to consider main verbs that co-occurred with the remaining instances of unmodified *austerity* (see 7.3 below).

Cases where **austerity** *is being described*

In the 2006–2015 data, there are 52 instances (around 3% of all instances) where *austerity* is followed by a form of the verb *be* and either a nominal, adjectival, clausal, or prepositional complement. We hypothesized that these syntactic locations might be places where *austerity* is defined. However, rather than finding definitions, we observed overwhelmingly negative evaluations, as the examples show below.

> *a zombie economic idea; a gamble which Britain can ill afford; a failed policy; a mistake; not a good idea; a very bad idea; not the right thing to do; not the only way forward; socially destructive; worse for growth; 'fundamentally mad'; 'seriously bad for our health'; unacceptable; painful.*

A further seven examples evaluate *austerity* more neutrally but nevertheless cast doubt over the legitimacy of *austerity* as a policy or mode of governing by, for example, suggesting that *austerity* is a political choice, rather than an economic one.

> *not an economic necessity; a political choice; a good catch-phrase; a buzz word; an ideological fixation; their choice.*

Even the ten complements that appear to be more positive are quoting someone's opinion or claim before offering an opposing position. For example, one speaker[7] states that *[t]he Chancellor's claim is very specific: that his plan of fiscal austerity is the best route to economic expansion* before going on to discredit this claim over an extended statement. Similarly, where *austerity* is said to be *the best route to economic expansion, the reason for low interest rates, the only way* and *the answer*, these are preludes to opposing views that evaluate *austerity* negatively.

By contrast, in the 1940s data we found only four (0.6%) examples of *austerity* followed by a form of *be* and a complement. These were either only mildly negative (*austerity is too hard to bear*) or more positive (*austerity is absolutely essential*).

Cases where **austerity** *is doing something*

There are 33 instances in the 2006–2015 data where *austerity* is followed by a form of *be* and a main verb (*-ing* form). Many of these denote violence and damage, as the following examples show.

> *hitting the poorest and innocent taxpayers; hurting the most vulnerable in our society; hurting across the board; biting very hard for many of our constituents; crucifying the public and private sectors; striking at every local authority.*

Other instances focus on the impact on health, on particular sections of society, or on the economy.

> *having a devastating effect on health; costing lives; having an impact on life expectancy; impacting disproportionately on those living with disabilities; leading to social devastation.*
>
> *starving the economy; making the economy worse; sending us into bankruptcy; leading to record joblessness.*

There is also a small group that are more general, but assert that *austerity* is failing, not working, or just bad.

> *failing; making matters worse; causing hardship; going too far; going really, really badly; not working.*

When *austerity* is an actor, the things that it is doing could be described as Events—in the same way that *the sun is melting the snow* is an event—since *austerity* is abstract and inanimate. The effect is that, even though these examples are clearly criticizing *austerity*, human agency is missing or played down, and *austerity* becomes reified.

In the 1940s data, there are no such *be* + -ing forms which could indicate something of a change in style rather than relating to the meaning of the word.[8]

Cases where unmodified **austerity** *does something*

The second search considered other verbs in the data which were found immediately to the right of unmodified *austerity*. As in the previous section, most of these examples involve *austerity* as the subject of verbs where it is constructed in the role of actor. In a number of cases, the present form of the verb suggests an ongoing and iterative effect:

> *austerity (fails/hurts/kills/reigns/discourages makes things worse/reduces demand/does not boost short-term growth/does not work).*

Other verb forms that follow *austerity*, with different tenses/aspects, continue the negative assessment of *austerity* and its actions, for example:

> *austerity strangled the recovery; austerity has (wreaked havoc/failed/added to the problems/hit consumer confidence/hit the poor/caused this recession/never worked).*

With these verbs, many of which require objects, *austerity* is constructed as an agent that acts on other entities.

There is a different pattern in the 1940s data, where *austerity* does not act upon things, but has its own agency, for example:

> *austerity began some time ago; austerity must and will continue; austerity prevails; austerity tends to pall.*

The general acceptance of austerity as a force beyond even politicians' control seems to dominate in these wartime examples, whereas in the later data there is more of a suggestion that it is a political choice with consequences, though the nature and identity of the human agency is often left unspecified.

8. Equating and contrasting *austerity*

We have dealt in Sections 6 and 7 with the two main textual-conceptual features constructing a word's meaning, by looking at the noun phrases in which *austerity* occurs and at the verbs with which it collocates. In this section, we consider the more intermittent, but nevertheless powerful, ways in which a word can be characterized by being equated or contrasted with other concepts.

Constructing equivalence

Coordination is one way in which equivalences between entities can be textually created, as part of a particular world-view or ideology (see Jeffries, 2010a, p. 51). The sorts of things that *austerity* is coordinated with gives an indication of what *austerity* means for those using it.

Using sorted concordance lines, we systematically searched for all instances of *and* where it coordinates:

(i) two noun phrases (NPs), one of which contains *austerity*, e.g., *the Chancellor is using* <u>*the deficit and austerity*</u> *to reshape the role of the British state.*
(ii) two verb phrases (VPs), one of which contains *austerity*, e.g., *So we in the UK are* <u>*implementing austerity*</u> *and* <u>*limiting the pay rises for our public*</u>.

We found that 243 (14%) of the instances of *austerity* were involved in coordination as described above. We did not count the instances of *and* that join two independent clauses: e.g., *There is a responsible alternative to austerity, and this Bill is not it.*

We derived data-driven categories, summarized below:

(i) *Austerity* equated with cuts or reduced spending, e.g., *(public sector/spending/service/more/damaging/swingeing/billions of pounds of/savage/further) cuts*; *(general reductions in/strict control of/reduced) spending; spending restraint; cost-cutting; cutbacks.*
(ii) *Austerity* equated with pay, poverty and welfare, e.g., *low wages; welfare; access to housing; declining standards of living; mass unemployment; poverty.*
(iii) *Austerity* equated with negative emotional effects, e.g., *hardship; difficulty/ies; uncertainty; untold damage; the pain; the suffering; unending misery.*
(iv) *Austerity* equated with a lack of economic growth, e.g., *zero growth; low growth; economic downturn; the economic disaster; stagnation.*
(v) *Austerity* equated with financial concepts and processes, e.g., *the deficit; challenging financial times; ultra-loose monetary policy; more neo-liberal economics; massive debt; market-led economics; the recession; fiscal consolidation; balancing the books.*
(vi) Other, e.g., *responsible measures; public pressures; difficult choices; difficult national decisions; neglect.*

These categories indicate that *austerity* is mostly equated with negative experiences relating to state provision, unemployment, and reduced spending in the public sector. It is also equated with financial phenomena and economic problems. All this is perhaps not unexpected. However, in relation to sense (4) of the OED definition of *austerity*, a number of the coordinated phrases seem tautological since they explicitly restate or confirm the meaning of *austerity* (i.e., spending cuts, etc.). This suggests that the speakers in Hansard sometimes feel the need to emphasize the exact nature of what is being referred to.

In the 1940s data, there are fewer occurrences of coordination of this nature (54), accounting for 9% of the instances of *austerity*. These include examples which are similar to categories (ii) and (iii) above in the more recent data and evaluate *austerity* negatively (e.g., *misery*; *dullness*; *hardships*). Many of them also allude to the 'all in it together' ethos of these years (e.g., *willingness to work hard; restraint; personal self-sacrifice*). Other examples are more similar to the examples in the 2006–2015 data (e.g., *cuts*; *economic conditions; economic problems*) or are linked specifically to the war years thematically (e.g., *rationing*).

Constructing opposites

A powerful way of constructing meaning textually is to produce an opposite for a word which has no conventional opposite in the language. This type of opposition-construction by textual frames is a phenomenon which was first mentioned in Jeffries (1993) and has been noticed by scholars working on lexical opposition, most notably Mettinger (1994, p. 74) who called them "non-systemic opposites" and Murphy (2003, p. 11) who calls them "non-canonical antonyms." Jeffries (2010a, 201b) and Davies (2007, 2012, 2013) compiled a typology of the different types of contextual frames that produce opposition of this kind. Using these typologies, we manually searched the 2006–2015 data using the sorting facility in *AntConc* for contexts that put *austerity*, which has no conventional opposite, into an oppositional frame. We found 52 instances of *austerity* in a textually-constructed opposition, and these assisted us to draw conclusions about the current meaning of the word.

As we saw in the last section, *austerity* often falls in a pattern of coordination with other nouns. Not all of these create equivalence, however, and 11 cases followed the preposition *between* which combines with the coordinated structure to create an oppositional meaning relation. Of these 11 cases, 9 construct *austerity* as being opposite to *growth*. The remaining instances are *a greener world* or a longer phrase based on the headword *ambition*:

> *(balance/choice/trade-off) between austerity and (growth/a greener world)*
> *choice between ambition driven by the values of fairness and opportunity or austerity driven by an outdated dogma.*

Notice that the nouns preceding the prepositional phrases (*between austerity* and __) all appear to confirm that this oppositional relationship is mutually exclusive, rather than gradable (e.g., *hot/cold*) or mutually dependent (e.g., *buy/sell*). Thus there is a trade off or a choice between *austerity* and *growth* or *a greener world*; one cannot have both. There is a tendency for such textually-constructed opposites to be of this mutually-exclusive kind, known as 'complementaries' (see Cruse 1986 for more detail on linguistic opposition). The effects are to position *austerity* as the opposite of *growth*; the latter long having been seen as an absolute good in the (mostly) capitalist world, its opposite (conventionally *recession*) will therefore be negatively valued. Thus the result of seeing *austerity* repeatedly set up in opposition to *growth* will be its gradual naturalization as a) a bad thing, and b) the equivalent of *recession*. In the 1940s data, this constructed opposition does not occur, perhaps because *austerity* was a different concept then, economically, being used to stimulate growth, rather than limit it.

The same relationship is created by other frames too, where 14 instances of *austerity* are in opposition to *growth*. Of these 14 instances, there were 5 cases where it seemed that although *austerity* and *growth* were seen as opposites, they could nevertheless coexist:

> *now arguing for growth and job creation, not austerity alone*
> *and a greater emphasis on growth rather than austerity alone*
> *focus on growth and job creation, rather than austerity alone*
> *It is no good having austerity, austerity, austerity; we also need a growth strategy*
> *a desire to move away from nothing but austerity to an emphasis on growth.*

In all these cases, there is an argument being made for not relying on *austerity* without other measures, which seems to make the two potentially compatible and, rather than constructing them as mutually exclusive opposites, they are being presented as mutually dependent opposites (converses) whereby both coexist (e.g., *borrow/lend*), or even as gradable opposites with *austerity* at one end and *growth* strategies (i.e., spending) at the other, with a 'happy medium' position in the middle where you have some of each. We could argue that this returns the debate to a 1940s-style austerity whereby the sacrifices were made in order to build a better infrastructure. The difference here is that it is not infrastructure, but economic growth, which is being advocated. These are, of course, related in some fashion, as advocates of a 'Green New Deal' (see for example http://greennewdeal.eu/) and other similar state-sponsored schemes might argue.

The remaining ten cases where *growth* is the simple opposing term to *austerity* are more clearly complementary, as in *growth versus austerity* or *real growth for the many rather than failed austerity*. Note that the latter example demonstrates not only the textual process of constructing opposition, but also the strength of naming practices in our data. The two noun phrases in this clause incorporate the views of the speaker by characterizing growth as *real* and *for the many* whilst *austerity* is seen as *failed*, which by default is therefore also constructed as *unreal* and *for the few*. The placing of these adjectives within the noun phrase boundaries makes them part of the naming system of the text, and less susceptible to questioning by readers.

A different set of oppositional relationships are found in three other structures, leading to a slightly different emphasis:

> *all those who will oppose austerity and work for freedom, human rights and social justice*
> *They want an alternative to austerity and a fairer social security system*
> *support a real end to austerity and a real increase in public spending.*

Unlike the examples which look simply at economic *growth* as the opposite of *austerity*, what these structures do is to oppose *austerity* to a different set of absolute goods (*freedom, human rights; social justice; fairer social security*) and to an increase in public spending, which is constructed as a good thing in this context. There is a different feeling in these examples which, by making a connection to the human cost of *austerity*, also construct it as a negatively valued concept, with something more concrete and human-scale in the positive side of the equation, instead of the more abstract *growth*.

The other main group of examples in the data where *austerity* is constructed as an opposite is with *prosperity*. These include a number of examples where the trigger frame is of the *X not Y* type, and one example where the opposition is created by a parallel structure:

> *(we want/I believe in/I rise to speak for) prosperity, not austerity*
> *prosperity, not austerity: that is what we want*
> *Government Members do not favour austerity; we favour prosperity.*

These examples create mutually exclusive opposites which set *austerity* up as negatively evaluated (since *prosperity* is another absolute good) and also as equivalent to the conventional opposite of *prosperity*, which is *poverty*. Unlike the cases we saw above where it seemed as though *austerity* could coexist with *growth*, here the slogan-like nature of some of the contexts emphasizes the importance of not muddying the water when you are trying to argue the case for a particular political strategy. Most campaigning of this kind tends towards the mutually-exclusive type of opposition, and this underlines a problem in political debate; the need to exaggerate the negative features of what you are arguing against.

Another set of *austerity/prosperity* examples builds on a conceptual metaphor[9] of LIFE = JOURNEY (Lakoff, 1993; Lakoff & Johnson, 1980). In this case, 'life' means political life and the 'journey' is from the *austerity* of hard times towards the *prosperity* of the (imagined) future. Six of the seven examples we found in our data use a *from X to Y* frame, and one uses *out of X and into Y*:

> *(has taken Britain/and put the country on the path/one more big step on the road/ It is the only sustainable route/an economy taking another big step/We are on the path, therefore,) from austerity to prosperity*
> *we are getting out of austerity and into prosperity.*

Like the earlier gradable examples, these constructions of opposition, in particular *from X to Y*, also appear to envisage two ends of a spectrum, in this case a journey. What is not clear in such cases is what the journey would look like in the middle, where there is some *austerity*, and also some *prosperity*. The consequences of some textually constructed opposites are sometimes illogical or difficult to work out and yet these intermediate places are where the real political activity has to play out in practice.

Based on these data, we can say that *austerity* is not represented in Parliament as equivalent to *growth*, *job creation*, *fairness* or *opportunity*. Rather, *austerity* is mostly constructed as the opposite of *prosperity* and the opposite of *growth*.

In the 1940s data, by contrast, the oppositions into which *austerity* is placed have a different flavor. There is one example only in the earlier data which links *austerity* to *prosperity*:

> *We shall never get back to prosperity through austerity.*

This metaphorically sees *austerity* as an unlikely staging post on the route back to *prosperity*, contradicting the later journey metaphors we saw above and reflecting the policy of the time for stimulating growth (rather than being an alternative to *growth*) by constraining private consumption. Other examples draw on a religious vocabulary of pain and redemption:

> *escape from the wearisome toils of austerity and enter the promised land of freedom*
> *What sensible Hebrew would wish to transfer from austerity to purgatory?*
> *but do not let us convert that austerity into a chilling penury by unjust taxation.*

The 'from-to' construction (from *the wearisome toils of austerity* to *the promised land of freedom*) constructs *austerity* as the opposite of *freedom* and draws on the common LIFE = JOURNEY metaphor often used in the discourse of salvation and liberation. This representation ties in with the political and economic ideology of the 1940s whereby the government restrained people's freedom to spend via rationing and pricing controls. Note, however, that the second example, which also uses a *from-to* construction, views *austerity* from a different and more positive evaluative perspective, by opposing it to *purgatory*, suggesting that while *austerity* might be bad, the alternative is worse. The final example sees *austerity* as being different from *penury*, which suggests a meaning that differs from the more recent version of *austerity* where the two would be aligned.

The construction of opposition is particularly helpful in tracing the difference between *austerity* in the 1940s and more recent data. *Austerity* was seen in the post-war period as akin to a kind of self-denying Christian virtue that is unavoidably necessary at this period and ultimately better than the alternative. Whilst Cameron may have initially been attempting to use this sense of all being 'in it together' as a kind of tribute to the *austerity* of the war and post-war years, in the new context, when it appeared that governments had choice of action not open to the (post-)war government(s), *austerity* became seen as a stick with which to beat the electorate, rather than a general virtue shared by all.

9. Conclusions

This exploration of the use and meaning of *austerity* in Hansard has established a number of facts and raised some issues about both lexical meaning and corpus methodologies.

To deal with the methodological issues first, our analysis reveals that focusing uniquely on the automated analysis of words and their collocates can not only restrict our understanding of the data but also mislead us, whereas a wider context may provide evidence of opposite findings. This is true, for example, of the apparently positive comments about *austerity* examined above (Section 7), where the positive evaluation is in fact no more than a precursor to a more negative comment in the wider context.

Also, many of the more subtle constructions of meaning in texts cannot be searched for automatically. This includes the constructed opposites which have revealed some interesting tendencies in our data, but which would not have been discovered by a purely automated analysis. Collocate analysis can help us find some patterns, when we know what we are looking for, but may miss some of the less regular patterns and cannot provide information on textual-conceptual patterning that underlies the ideational structure of the data. Neither can unmodified uses of a keyword be located by automatic searching. For these reasons, and until there are further developments in corpus parsing and semantic tagging, the concordance feature of most software is the most useful facility available to researchers working on small to medium corpora.

As to the findings of this study, we have established some differences between the 1940s usage of *austerity* and its more recent use during the financial crisis. This is despite a clear intention on the part of some Conservative politicians to evoke the spirit of everyone playing their part and suffering together for the greater good. Though *austerity* in wartime was perhaps accepted more readily as unavoidable, our analysis shows that it was nevertheless negatively evaluated even then. It is perhaps surprising that Cameron and Osborne adopted it to describe their own agenda. Having done so, they found that since it was not linked to increased investment in infrastructure to stimulate growth, in the early twenty-first century it rapidly became seen as the opposite of growth and equivalent to poverty and recession. Although the financial crisis may have proved an excuse for those on the right-wing of the Conservative Party to drive towards a permanently smaller state, this sleight of hand was not accepted in Parliament as the largely negative construal of the word *austerity* in our data shows.

The rise in occurrence of *austerity* through the period that is covered by the historical Hansard corpus, plus our more recent data, shows that this lexical item not only came to prominence as a sociopolitical keyword in the post-war period, but also became increasingly popular shorthand for a different kind of political package in the early twenty-first century. The unmodified use of such keywords is a phenomenon that deserves greater attention in the discussion of both politics and economics, since they seem to carry a great deal of meaning without scrutiny in places where meaning should be clear and yet also open to debate, such as in the UK Parliament.

Notes

1 See, for example, The People's Assembly (www.thepeoplesassembly.org.uk/) for reports of anti-austerity marches such as the following: www.bbc.co.uk/news/uk-politics-33210014.
2 See www.gla.ac.uk/schools/critical/research/fundedresearchprojects/parliamentary discourse/
3 This project, based at the University of Glasgow, and funded by the AHRC (grant reference AH/L010062/1), developed new software to tag (i.e., label) all of the words in a corpus with semantic information, to distinguish the different senses of words. The sub-project at the University of Huddersfield tested the software on the historic Hansard corpus (1803–2005): www.gla.ac.uk/schools/critical/research/fundedresearchprojects/samuels/
4 (www.theyworkforyou.com/), built by *My Society* which is a not-for-profit social enterprise, based in the UK and working internationally. *MySociety* builds online technologies that give people the power to get things changed, and share these technologies so that they can be used anywhere. Their website is at www.mysociety.org/
5 We can speculate as to the reason for the fall and rise in austerity tokens during these years, but this would need more work looking at individual examples in context. Our hunch is that the early rise reflects Cameron's and Osborne's adoption of the term. The later rise may reflect the attacks on austerity from opposition politicians during the build up to the 2015 general election.
6 The British National Corpus (BNC) is a 100 million word corpus of written and spoken British English.
7 Although it is of some interest who said what in our data, we are more interested in the cumulative effect of usage on a word's meaning at this point than the question of individual contributions to its emergent meaning. We therefore choose not to disrupt our argument by including such details here or elsewhere.
8 A wider investigation would be needed to establish whether the continuous form of the verb (i.e., be + -ing) was used less at that period.
9 See Soares da Silva (2016) for detailed research into the metaphors used in the Portuguese press in relation to austerity.

References

Anthony, L. (2014). *AntConc* (Version 3.4.3) [Computer Software]. Tokyo, Japan: Waseda University. Retrieved from www.laurenceanthony.net/

Baker, P. (2016). The shapes of collocation. *International Journal of Corpus Linguistics*, *21*(2), 139–164.

Baker, P., Gabrielatos, C., KhosraviNik, M., Krzyzanowski, M., McEnery, T., & Wodak, R. (2008). A useful methodological synergy? Combining critical discourse analysis and corpus linguistics to examine discourses of refugees and asylum seekers in the UK press. *Discourse & Society*, *19*(3), 273–305.

Baker, P., Gabrielatos, C., & McEnery, T. (2013). *Discourse analysis and media attitudes: The representation of Islam in the British press*. Cambridge, UK: Cambridge University Press.

Cairncross, A. (1985). *Years of recovery: British economic policy 1945–55*. Oxford: Routledge.

Cruse, D. A. (1986). *Lexical semantics*. Cambridge, UK: Cambridge University Press.

Davies, M. (2007). The attraction of opposites: The ideological function of conventional and created oppositions in the construction of in-groups and out-groups in news texts. In D. Bousfield, L. Jeffries, & D. McIntyre (Eds.), *Stylistics and social cognition* (pp. 71–100). Amsterdam, Netherlands: Rodopi.

Davies, M. (2012). A new approach to oppositions in discourse: The role of syntactic frames in the triggering of non-canonical oppositions. *Journal of English Linguistics, 40*(1) 47–73.

Davies, M. (2013). *Oppositions and ideology in news discourse*. London: Bloomsbury Academic.

Demmen, J., Jeffries, L., & Walker, B. (2018). Charting the semantics of labour relations in House of Commons debates spanning two hundred years: A study of parliamentary language using corpus linguistic methods and automated semantic tagging. In M. Kranert & G. Horan (Eds.), *Political discourse: Multidisciplinary approaches* (pp. 82–104). Amsterdam, Netherlands: John Benjamins.

Fairclough, N. (2001). *Language and power* (2nd ed.). Harlow, UK: Pearson.

Firth, J. R. (1957). *Papers in linguistics 1934–1951*. London: Oxford University Press.

Gabrielatos, C., & Baker, P. (2008). Fleeing, sneaking, flooding: A corpus analysis of discursive constructions of refugees and asylum seekers in the UK Press 1996–2005. *Journal of English Linguistics, 36*(1), 5–38.

Gabrielatos, C., McEnery, T., Diggle, P. J., & Baker, P., (2012). The peaks and troughs of corpus-based contextual language. *International Journal of Corpus Linguistics, 17*(2), 151–175.

Halliday, M.A. K. (1994). *An introduction to Functional Grammar* (2nd ed.). London: Edward Arnold.

Hawkins, J. A. (1978). *Definiteness and indefiniteness*. Atlantic Highland, NJ: Humanities Press.

Jeffries, L. (1993). *The language of twentieth century poetry*. Houndmills, Basingstoke, UK: Palgrave Macmillan.

Jeffries, L. (2003). Not a drop to drink: Emerging meanings in local newspaper reporting of the 1995 water crisis in Yorkshire. *Text – Interdisciplinary Journal for the Study of Discourse, 23*(4), 513–538.

Jeffries, L. (2010a). *Critical stylistics*. London: Palgrave Macmillan.

Jeffries, L. (2010b). *Opposition in discourse*. London: Bloosmbury.

Jeffries, L. (2014a). Interpretation. In P. Stockwell & S. Whiteley (Eds.), *The Cambridge handbook of stylistics* (pp. 467–484). Cambridge, UK: Cambridge University Press.

Jeffries, L. (2014b). Critical stylistics. In M. Burke (Ed.), *The Routledge handbook of stylistics* (pp. 408–420). London: Routledge.

Jeffries, L. (2015). Critical stylistics. In V. Sotirova (Ed.), *The Continuum companion to stylistics* (pp. 157–176). London: Bloomsbury.

Jeffries, L., & McIntyre, D. (2018). The devil has all the best tunes: An investigation of the lexical phenomenon of Brexit. In Page, R., Busse, B., & Norgaard, N. (Eds.), *Rethinking language, text and context: Interdisciplinary research in stylistics in honour of Michael Toolan* (pp. 100–119). Abingdon: Routledge.

Jeffries, L., & Evans, M. (2015). The rise of choice as an absolute 'good': A study of British manifestos, (1900–2010). *Journal of Language and Politics, 14*(6), 751–777.
Jeffries, L., & Walker, B. (2012). Keywords in the press: A critical corpus-assisted analysis of ideology in the Blair years (1998–2007). *English Text Construction, 5*(2), 208–229.
Jeffries, L., & Walker, B. (2017). *Keywords in the press: The New Labour years*. London: Bloomsbury.
KhosraviNik, M. (2009). The representation of refugees, asylum seekers and immigrants in the British newspapers: A critical discourse analysis. *Journal of Language and Politics, 8*(3), 1–29.
Lakoff, G. (1993). The contemporary theory of metaphor. In A. Ortony (Ed.), *Metaphor and thought* (2nd ed.) (pp. 202–251). Cambridge, UK: Cambridge University Press.
Lakoff, G., & Johnson, M. (1980). *Metaphors we live by*. Chicago, IL: University of Chicago Press.
Louw, W. (1993). Irony in the text or insincerity in the writer? The diagnostic potential of semantic prosodies. In M. Baker, G. Francis, E. Tognini-Bonelli (Eds.) *Text and technology* (pp. 157–176). Amsterdam, Netherlands: John Benjamins.
McEnery, T., & Wilson, A. (2001). *Corpus linguistics* (2nd ed.). Edinburgh: Edinburgh University Press.
Mettinger, A. (1994). *Aspects of semantic opposition in English*. Oxford: Oxford University Press.
Murphy, M. L. (2003). *Semantic relations and the lexicon*. Cambridge, UK: Cambridge University Press.
O'Hara, M. (2014). *Austerity bites*. Bristol, UK: Policy Press.
Oxford University Press (2010). *Oxford English Dictionary*. Retrieved from www.oed.com/
Sinclair, J., Jones, S., Daley, R., & Krishnamurthy, R. (2004). *English collocational studies: The OSTI Report*. London: Continuum.
Soares da Silva, A. (2016). The persuasive (and manipulative) power of metaphor in 'austerity' discourse: A corpus-based analysis of embodied and moral metaphors of austerity in the Portuguese press. In M. Romano & M. D. Porto (Eds.), *Exploring discourse strategies in social and cognitive interaction: Multimodal and cross-linguistic perspectives* (pp. 79–108). Amsterdam, Netherlands: John Benjamins.
Tomlinson, J. (2013). The spirit of '45? Austerity then and now. *Renewal, 21*(2/3), 46–53.
Williams R. (1983 [1976]). *Keywords: A vocabulary of culture and society*. London: Fontana.
Zweiniger-Bargielowska, I. (2000). *Austerity in Britain: Rationing, controls, and consumption, 1939–1955*. Oxford: Oxford University Press.

4 'Less State' in austerity

A concept masking the central agent of neoliberal policies

Nuria Giniger and Irene Sotiropoulou

To Santiago Maldonado[1]

In this chapter, we aim to explore critically, and through the use of two case studies, the public discourse concerning the role of the State in structural adjustment programs and in the implementation of austerity policies. We use historical and contemporary information from two countries, Argentina and Greece, as case studies. Our purpose is to investigate, first, the ways in which the examined discourse about the role of the State supported austerity policies; and second, whether and to what extent the 'less State' argument was a method for changing or even expanding the role of the central government to directly benefit capitalist agents.

In contrast to the discourse that we examined in this chapter, when we examine what really happened with the roles of the State in Argentina and Greece, the State seems not to be 'reduced' but rather enhanced or expanded towards a different direction. Within this contradiction, we critically narrate the neoliberal policies in comparison for Argentina and Greece, using not only academic literature but also examples of discourse used in the two countries to reshape the role of the State.

In particular, our focus is on the section of neoliberal discourse that depicts the State as a wasteful and inefficient manager of resources. The solution proposed by the people who use this discourse is that the State should leave individuals and companies to pursue their own interests without legal or institutional constraints.

We focus on discourse because it is an important element of the neoliberal policies and it is used as one more policy implementation tool (Fairclough, 2015; Schmidt, 2002). Although we share the view that the material conditions of neoliberal policies create a nexus of economic and social conditions that systemically and physically 'persuade' individuals and communities to behave in a certain way, we focus on discourse. The first reason is that this type of anti-State discourse is extensively used by the neoliberal policy supporters. Second, this same discourse seems to be intertwined with the material conditions imposed on societies, constituting a material condition itself as it creates images, sounds and narratives that are necessary for the neoliberal cosmology.

The next section presents some basic definitions, the theoretical framework of our analysis and the methods we used to approach our research question. Section 2 presents the different time periods of neoliberal State intervention in chronological order. Section 3 discusses how the austerity discourse since 1990 capitalized on people's (existing) negative feelings towards the State and diverted those feelings to enhance the State's role. We present our conclusions in the fourth section, where we also point out topics for further research.

1. Definitions, theoretical background and method of analysis

Definitions

By the term 'austerity,' we mean the policies adopted mostly in the 1980s onwards within a neoliberal political economic context, where the market is considered to be a more efficient allocation mechanism than redistribution structures, particularly those run by State authorities, whether of central or local character. We understand 'austerity' as a policy whether it is named as such or not, because we identify it with the serious expenditure cuts in public services and provisions, the suppression of both wages and worker movements, and the support of capitalists by the State and by central authority institutions (like central banks) with a clear preference for big/concentrated capital. We follow the austerity-in-practice analysis of Mark Blyth (2013), who analyses the austerity mentality in modern economic thought as a core concept of liberal and then neoliberal economics, whether the term appears as such in an economic text or not.

We therefore, distinguish between 'austerity' as a policy and 'austerity' as a term, because from the analysis of our two case studies it seems that 'austerity' as a discourse is encountered in Greece, as part of the European neoliberal project, but not in the Argentinean public debate, despite the similarity of the policies and State practices during the years 1975–2017. In other words, we are fully aware that the regional experience of Europe and the use of 'austerity' as a term does not define as such the experience of Argentina and of countries outside Europe in general. We further examine this divergence of neoliberal discourse in Section 2.

Discourse is a human phenomenon involving complicated relationships between different dimensions or aspects. Discourse is, at the same time, a complex biological, sociological, linguistic, cognitive, and political phenomenon. Thus, the multiplicity of relationships between categories, levels or theories generates diverse foci of interest. According to Charaudeau (2000), the term 'discourse' is highly polysemic. Nevertheless, when we distinguish different meanings of 'austerity' and different *uses* of the word (in Argentina and Greece, that is), we take the contributions of Voloshinov (1973):

> Thus various different classes will use one and the same language. As a result, differently oriented accents intersect in every ideological sign. Sign

> becomes an arena of class struggle. This social multi-accentuality of the ideological sign is a very crucial aspect. By and large, it is thanks to this intersecting of accents that a sign maintains its vitality and dynamism and the capacity for further development. A sign that has been withdrawn from the pressures of the social struggle—which, so to speak, crosses beyond the pale of the class struggle—inevitably loses force, degenerating into allegory and becoming the object not of live social intelligibility but of philological comprehension.
>
> (p. 29)

Therefore, we understand 'discourse' as the verbal or non-verbal (whether oral, written, or image-based) communication between humans, that is constrained by a particular social relation of forces historically determined. 'Discourse' is being performed, sanctioned, and defied through action, whether in verbal or non-verbal ways, because the signs, the discourse, and all communications are being performed in a contested arena.

Still, the discourse about the State in Latin America was, during the 1990s, synthesized in the suggestive slogan in Argentina: "Shrink the State to enlarge the Nation."[2]

Today, after the last 15 years of tensions between progressive and revolutionary projects, the idea of 'austerity' has not become the flag with which the ruling classes, and especially right-wingers, are recovering their initiative, in Argentina. As Voloshinov said, the sign becomes an arena of class struggle, and the ruling class in Argentina, just like in other cases in South America, has had to present neoliberal policies with other words.

We also recover the discourse analysis presented by the Argentine philosopher Dagatti (2007), which posits that the notion of 'austerity' antagonized with 'frivolity,' at the end of the crisis of 2001: "As can be seen, frivolity is stated dysphorically on the pragmatic axis, which is *not necessary*, as such, it carries its negative charge to an ethical level: *the useless is immoral*" (p. 262, emphasis original). In 2001, Argentina had 25% unemployment and almost 50% poverty and for this reason the attitude that was spread had to see the idea of 'frivolity' as ostentation, as useless. The opposite—'austerity'—was the usual way of governance, during the crisis, but ruling classes could not talk explicitly about that. Therefore, in Latin America, the supporters of neoliberal policies have not reached consensus to carry on the offensive with an explicit 'austerity' slogan, as clearly happened in Europe.

Theoretical background

We critically explore neoliberal economic theory to understand the basic notions that turn a specialized discourse of economics into an everyday public discourse about 'austerity.' In many ways, 'austerity' is a difficult concept, because it describes an adjustment policy of certain choices under a notion positively connoted, and aims to set an antithetical dyad between Welfare and

Austerity, linked to other central notions like Spending/Consumption, Saving, and Investing. We also needed to critically assess the fact that 'austerity' is by no means a universal idea, as we explained in Section 1 above.

Second, 'austerity,' in the European and Anglo-Saxon register, is set from the main axis of the Protestant ethic for which 'austerity' (a positive sense) is the antithesis of both 'waste' (a negative sense) (Weber, 1904) and spending. This Protestant ethic articulates with other historical processes linked to hunger and war, which (particularly in Europe) configured meanings about waste, saving, and austerity. Moreover, the rise of capitalism and capitalist-favoring economics in Europe meant that the capitalist classes needed a discourse to explain not only the accumulation of capital in their hands but also the dispossession that was imposed on working classes, who were (and still are) depicted as not wise enough with money, and not working and saving enough (Blyth, 2013).

Therefore, justifying capitalist adjustment processes under the idea of 'austerity' is a procedure that has historical bases in Europe and in other cases where capitalist advancement is in process. The provisioning or redistributing State seems to be synonymous with waste and bad fiscal administration and, as such, becomes the antithesis of the Austerity State. This central moral argument against spending for public provision characterizes austerity policies, particularly those adopted in recent years in the European continent, that are explicitly promoting austerity (Clarke & Newman, 2012; Kelsey, Mueller, Whittle, & KhosraviNik, 2016; Blyth, 2013).

Therefore, 'austerity' as a concept does not help to understand the role of the State, either as an organizer of capitalist business, or as a producer of hegemony. Instead, the category of 'austerity' veils and hides the complex processes our societies are going through today and the role of the State in those processes. In this direction, we argue and show in the following sections that the policies implemented under the austerity argument in favor of the 'reduced State' are very different to what that argument actually proposes: the State is not in fact reduced, but, rather, changes its intervention center and direction of the resources under its control.

In this sense, we recover the meaning of 'the State' in its dual role: as a tool and as territory of dispute (Poulantzas, 1978). The State is not only an instrument of the ruling classes, but also the form and content in which the ruling classes develop hegemonic processes; and, at the same time, the State expresses the reaction of the ruling classes to resistance (organized and unorganized) of the people. Moreover, we recover the contributions of Antonio Gramsci (1975) who explains, by using the concept of 'hegemony,' how the interest of the ruling class is considered as identical to the general interest of society. To do this, the ruling class uses the State and the institutions of civil society; people end up producing and reproducing the hegemonic logic, and the social order is constructed, at least in part, through the discourse under the control of those in power (Mylonas, 2014).

In our analysis, we understand hegemony not as something that can be negotiated, as if colonialism and neocolonial practices never existed

(Theodossopoulos, 2014), but rather as a major setting where colonialism exists and is enhanced through neoliberal policies (Radice, 2005). The State, therefore, undertakes a central role in order to facilitate the transition between hegemonic projects while ensuring the survival and growth of capitalist agents and capitalist economy itself. It also participates in the construction of neoliberal discourse as hegemonic and it is active in silencing dissenting or counter-hegemonic discourses that challenge the neoliberal project. This is why we do not use the distinction between roll-back and roll-out neoliberalism, because we see in our case studies that the State never stopped being present and steering the neoliberal processes towards their deployment (Essex, 2008; Graefe, 2005; Munck, 2005; Peck, 2010, chapter 1; Peck & Tickell, 2002; Peet, 2009, chapter 1; Karaliotas, 2017).

Neoliberal policies in Europe under the named Austerity State have one more instrument for transferring wealth; that is, the privatization of common and public goods. This process crystallizes austerity discourses and policies in a subtle way, because in many cases of 'State reduction' the State abandons public enterprises and services. The social space for production that is left after this reduction or retreat of the State is made available to the market and to private capitalist interests. The privatization of common goods and public services means a huge loss of access to social, economic and cultural opportunities for those who do not have private means of production, and a decrease of income that was previously provided in kind through social services (Arestis & Sawyer, 2005; Clarke, 2005; Karaliotas, 2017; Konstantinidis & Vlachou, 2018).

Consistent with this process, the State increases patrolling and monitoring of the working classes, while State assistance and protection for those who expropriate public wealth increases. Repression then acquires its dual dimension: of protecting appropriated and privatized goods; and of containing and suppressing social struggles, discontent and protest, by implementing different and varied control techniques (Karaliotas, 2017; Konstantinidis & Vlachou, 2018).

We therefore share the view that the State is central to neoliberal policies and overall restructuring of capitalist economies, not only for supporting capitalist interests but also for taming resistances and intervening extensively in social life. The role of the State becomes aggressively central in turning social activities towards capitalization or at least towards frameworks that allow easier transfer of value into capital circuits (Johnston & Saad-Filho, 2005, pp. 1–6; Dumenil & Levy, 2005; Colas, 2005; Peck, 2010).

To understand both the meaning and the practical implications of the contradiction between the public discourse for 'less State' (or 'shrunken State') on the one hand, and the real, material State policies that become more and more interventionist in the economy and society on the other, we used the theory of 'double bind' by Gregory Bateson (1972).[3] By 'double bind,' we understand a situation in which a message receiver has to tackle two messages from the same sender; there is no need that both messages be explicit or verbal—they can definitely be non-verbal, but still messages that require the receiver to act, or they construct the receiver's relationship to the sender in a fundamental way.

In this situation, the double bind is based on the fact that the two messages are contradictory and the receiver has no practical chance to escape the communication field, because there is a material, ideological, emotional or even cultural dependence between sender and receiver. In other words, the receiver is trapped in at least one way in that same communication field (that can be any material field whatsoever, like a workplace, a devastated community, or a discriminated social group).

Bateson is clear on how the double bind communication technique is endemic in capitalist societies and has devastating effects on the ability of message receivers effectively both to counter-argue with the message sender and to construct an alternate communication strategy. The situation in which a message receiver is trapped in a field of communication where the messages are contradictory and lead to negative effects for the message receiver—no matter which message she/he chooses to follow—can be dangerous in itself (for example, by trivializing the expenditure cuts in food or healthcare). However, in terms of mental robustness, the perpetuation of such a situation places the personality of the (trapped) message receiver in severe danger of breakdown. Bateson suggests that the results of double bind situations are psychological and psychosomatic, and in some cases irreversible, in the sense that the message receiver might not recover mentally and psychologically after having been subjected to such behavior by the message sender who controls the communication field.

Method of analysis

We understand neoliberalism as a long-term project which had been developed well before 1971, when Keynesianism started to show its limitations. Although the usual impression given through mass media, and sometimes academic literature, is that neoliberalism becomes prominent in the late 1970s, that is only when it becomes directly visible as a policy option in Western Europe and in the USA—it gained academic momentum long before its policies started to make the news. We also recognize that the mainstream narration of neoliberalism is quite Euro-centric and possibly colonial enough to hide that the policies we name today as 'neoliberal' and 'hardcore monetarist' had been imposed outside Western Europe and the Anglo-Saxon world years, or even decades, before they became European or American path-breaking policies that attracted attention since the crisis of 2008. Even in the usual narration, the dictatorship of Pinochet in Chile—who, since 1973, implemented the Chicago School recipes by-the-book—is erased in the statement that contemporary monetarism and neoliberalism starts in the late 1970s in the USA and the UK. In the same way, the structural adjustment programs and heavy indebtedness imposed upon most countries outside Western Europe in the 1980s and 1990s (as well as the resistances since the mid-1970s outside Europe) are not considered the core story of austerity, but rather peripheral examples of 'failures and poverty' which have nothing to do with the rich capitalist core countries that, curiously, are submitted to similar policies after 2008 (Peck, 2010; Blyth,

2013; Peet, 2009). We do not concur with this Euro-centric narration, and we see clearly that erasing the economic histories outside Western Europe and the USA does not allow us to understand what happened either with neoliberalism in general or, in our case study countries in particular.

Starting from this historical perspective, we get inspiration from the decolonial and feminist-Marxist tradition, in order to compare two landmark cases (those of Greece and Argentina), which in the last 40 years have experienced various neoliberal adjustment processes. These contrasting experiences allow us to problematize both the justificatory arguments of dominant political-economic doctrine and the role of the State in neoliberal discourse and practice. We draw inspiration for our analysis from the Discourse Historical Approach (Reisigl & Wodak, 2009), although we preferred to focus mostly on the general historical background of our case studies because our main concern was to keep the long-term historical perspective in our analysis and avoid an analysis of political discourse that would end up to seem out of its time-space context (Block, 2012). After all, as Holborow (2012a) points out, "focus on a text leaves out any broader sense of history…Ideology can be better grasped through a general approach to the meanings" (pp. 23–24).

We would not like to replace linguists in their field, but we would like to see the recent economic history of the two countries as a comparative case, which allows re-narration of both policies implemented and discourse used to justify those policies. In that sense, we proceed within our disciplines but thinking from the point of view of the public audiences that receive the neoliberal discourse, and this discourse, even if it is contested, goes hand-in-hand with change in social and economic situations. Therefore, we show that we can critically rethink economic and social history in general through the discourses, and contrast policy and discourse as such, starting the critical analysis from the discourse and not from the policy or economic model.

In particular, although Greece and Argentina are two very different countries, we think that the differences allow us to see the two cases with a critical eye and seek commonalities only where those exist and to the extent that they might have any significant analytical power for each case. We do not aspire to create a mega-narration but we think that comparative analysis makes us aware of political economic contexts that elude our attention when we focus only on one case study. This is the reason we examined the case studies together and in a comparative manner, in order to understand where the experiences in the two countries intersect and where each economy is restructured under the neoliberal policies in a way that is either unique or linked to local particularities. Our intention is not to transform the terminology of 'austerity' as universal for all countries but to show the plasticity of the discourse used to make neoliberal policies simultaneously invisible as aggressive choices of capitalist groups that impose austerity on the majority of a society's population.

In terms of empirical data, we used published material, whether from everyday press and mass media or social movement documents and statements.

The material proved to be chaotic in character. This is why we opted to present only certain major examples that can be common or interrelated in the two case studies we examine. The incoherence of the material we gathered and the various practical limitations of this project at this stage did not allow us to have an organized corpus of discourse that could be also provided to other scholars for further analysis, although we aspire to continue towards this method of analysis in a future project.

2. The case studies: Austerity in the near past, in the recent past, and the more-or-less 'now'

One major finding of our analysis is that, as far as it concerns Argentina and Greece, the time periods we could identify in each case were coinciding with each other, even if the content of each period was different in each of the two countries. In other words, we could observe the political and economic cycles having the same time limits or turning points, although the content of the cycles was not similar during the same time period. However, we could see that the content had some similarities if taken outside its timeline, i.e., similar policies might have taken place in different time periods in both countries, although there might have been a time lag between the policies themselves. This made us accept that our analysis will not be as deep as we would like it to be at this stage, and that we will have some major questions for future research based on combining those contrasts of timeline placement of policies. As a consequence, we worked with some explanatory arguments, in order to compare and contrast neoliberal policies in Greece and Argentina with the hope that if we cannot reach definitive answers yet, we can at least raise more specific questions for further research.

1975–1983: Dictatorship, 'strong State,' and the silencing of alternatives

As Antunes (2005) proposes, around the oil crisis, we can locate the starting point of explicit neoliberal policies.

This has been the period with major difference between the two countries: Greece was just getting out of a dictatorship that lasted seven years (1967–1974), after several decades of persecution against communists and leftists, as well as a civil war (1945–1949) and post-civil war persecutions (1950–1967). The civil war had been won by the right wing with the support of the UK and USA governments, leading whole regions to slaughter, social dissolution, and displacement of populations.

By 1975, in Greece, effective resistance to capitalist advancement seems to have been appeased one way or another. The State was powerful in 1975: the Communist Party was legalized again, thereby the State institutions could claim that they were establishing a 'bourgeois democracy' after the 1967–1974 Junta. By 'bourgeois democracy,' we mean the connection of the country to the European neoliberal structure and the dissolution of any real anti-capitalist potential. We understand the European Communities and then European Community/European Union institutions as part of a neoliberal project that was established quite early in the European continent, despite the formal Keynesianism that was prevalent on the nation-state level after World War II. The European Community and then the common currency project had a lot to do with the early neoliberal or proto-neoliberal ideas that involved a rather strong role of the State as a coordinator and protector of the free market and the capitalist interests competing within it. We see, therefore, the European Community project as stemming from the local Ordoliberal traditions (based on writings by mostly German and Italian thinkers) and taking influences much later from the Anglo-Saxon tradition, in order to supersede or perhaps coordinate member-states to adapt to neoliberal restructuring (Blyth, 2013, esp. chapters 4–6; Milios, 2005; Peck, 2010, preface, chapters 1–2; Peck & Tickell, 2002; Varoufakis, 2016).

Within this framework, the dictatorship experience in Greece was used in support of the argument that being close to the European Community institutions would prevent a new dictatorship in the future. What changed in the late 1970s—the era in which neoliberal policies became more or less permanent in Greece (Mavroudeas, 2010)—was that neoliberalism was depicted as the alternative to the military dictatorship and a safe political economic solution given the international economic turbulences of the time (Pagoulatos, 2002; Ministry of Foreign Affairs, 2014; Varoufakis, 2016).

Argentina, on the other hand, in 1975, was just starting some violent political-cleansing policies. The Argentine genocide[4] perpetrated by the Army and right-wing civilians, paramilitaries, and the Catholic Church inaugurated a process of disciplining the Argentine working class. With the defeat of the popular emancipatory projects uprooted in the cultural and social relationships we had known until then, ended was a cultural premise that taught that life conditions were plausible to be improved via the path of struggle and collective projects. Genocide also began a process of transfer of wealth from the working-class sectors to national and international concentrated capital, which deepened with hyperinflation (1989–1990) and mass unemployment (1997–2003) (Giniger, 2014).

1983–1990: Inflation and monetary instability

The monetarist theory's success had a background in both Greece and Argentina: both experienced high inflation since the late 1970s and during the 1980s, as well as mostly downward instability in real wages and purchasing power for the working classes. At that time, there was no chance to make things easier, because the global restructuring of capitalism affected monetary reserves and trade terms in all countries, but especially those countries with less political and economic power on the global stage. It was very easy therefore for ruling classes in developing countries to construe inflation as the number one problem in public discourse and wage increases as the number one reason for inflation (Hondroyannis & Lazaretou, 2004).

It is during this period that the term 'austerity' enters the official Greek public discourse and becomes an axis of State policy. The devaluation of the drachma in order to save the (external) trade balance is just one aspect of the set of policies of 'thatcherian austerity' implemented with 'protestant ethic,' as comments the reporter Nikolaou (2008), who recounts personal discussions with the then governors and how they explicitly owned the austerity policies imposed on the Greek people by a socialist government in the 1980s. Wage labor was discursively criminalized as an agent exercising inflationary pressures upon the (national) economy, especially when workers asked for higher purchasing power. This position is also found in academic literature (Pappas, 2010; Alogoskoufis,[5] Giavazzi & Laroque, 1995) which does not take into serious account the oil peak and other international economic conditions that affected economies like Greece. Argentinian and Greek economies were at the same time in a process of opening, particularly given the latter's new membership in the European Community at that time (Dellepiane & Hardiman, 2015; Ladi, 2012, 2014; Hadjimichalis & Vaiou, 1990).

At the same time, hyperinflation ended this decade in Argentina: the process of capital concentration produced a monopolization of the national economy; the external debt crisis[6] developed a tremendous increase of prices (inflation in 1989 was 1.923%[7]), that increased the number of people forced into poverty; and the new administration (Menem 1989–1999) began with adopting policies for an effective privatization process (Azpiazu & Basualdo, 2004).

Also at the same time, huge changes were taking place in international capitalist production spaces and markets, with the international monetary system, especially the US dollar, to pass from regulated to de- or un-regulated regimes (Campbell, 2005; Varoufakis, 2016). In both case studies, pegging your currency to a more stable one (USD/DM/ECU) worked like a light version of the gold standard in the economy, i.e., the ability to run the local finances while maintaining some redistribution policies was severely reduced (Saad-Filho, 2005). The situation got worse for Argentina during the next period, with the peso being pegged to the US dollar, and for Greece, for which the pegging became a full change of currency. As Blyth (2013) comments, "you cannot run a gold standard in a democracy" (p. 197).

1990–2008: Financialization, deregulation, and central planning of the mess

For this time period, Argentina and Greece followed the monetarist flow,[8] initially with budgetary restrictions to decrease inflation and then with pegging the currency to either USD (as Argentina did), or the ECU/Deutschemark and then entering the Eurozone (as Greece did). This policy led to the collapse of the Argentine peso in 2001 and is nowadays leading to a possible collapse of the euro, as well as the Greek economy, which has been deprived of monetary liquidity. Even if one followed the neoliberal orthodoxy on optimum currency areas, one was expected to tolerate high unemployment for the deficit areas in order to save the main currency from inflation, making the poor regions or countries that use the single currency the depositories of the inequality created by the common currency (Blyth, 2013; Mundell, 1961; Hondroyannis & Lazaretou, 2004; Varoufakis, 2016).

During the 1990s, employment deregulation and deteriorating labor conditions were sanctioned through the adoption of legislation that not only allowed them but also encouraged them as a solution to persistent unemployment, an argument that still proliferates in both political and academic discourse concerning Greece. The new legislative frameworks created a chaotic context for labor in terms of employment statuses, even within the same sectors of production that gave opportunities to many employers to take further advantage of their employees or press them for even worse working conditions, legal or illegal (outsourcing, job insecurity, etc.). The most vulnerable workers—like women, immigrants, people with disabilities, and people belonging to discriminated minorities—had to cope with a declining working environment. In the end, precarious working conditions were generalized for everyone, or at least for vast parts of the work force that had to face a downward spiral of accepting worsening working conditions in a self-destructive effort to compete with the social groups that were under the least employment protection (Barbieri, 2009; Pouliakas & Theodossiou, 2007; Peck & Tickell, 2002; Kasimis, Papadopoulos, & Zacopoulou, 2003; Kougias, 2017; Hadjimichalis & Vaiou, 1990).

This led to long-term poverty, especially when the crisis of 2008 erupted because the capitalists had a legislative framework ready to use and deepen as institutional framework, as one can see from the changes in welfare state that took place well before the 2008 crisis. It also led to a segmented labor force that would be forced to compete with each other instead of protecting the most vulnerable worker groups to reach the working conditions of other, less exploited, parts of the working class. The discussion was transposed away from improving the working conditions of the many to reach the working conditions that some upper working-class members had ensured; instead, the employment and pension benefits of the few have been tagged as privileges that should be reduced in favor of the least advantaged worker groups. This thesis was prominent among the academic literature informing both the media and policy choices (Ferrera, 2000; Katrougalos & Lazaridis, 2003; Featherstone, 2005).

The share of the capitalist profit in the production sector was not discussed as an obstacle or issue of fairly redistributing employment and pension conditions to everyone. The State was considered both the main bad manager of this employment inequality and the agent that was responsible to redistribute the meagre benefits of some workers to other workers. However, that same State was not allowed (it was considered harmful) to intervene and transfer part of the capitalist profits to the most exploited part of the working classes, always respecting the anti-distribution demands of neoliberal efficiency. It is during this period (1990–2008) that the privatization discourse and policies start to become prominent in both Greece and Argentina (Johnston, 2005; Ladi, 2012, 2014; Spanou, 2008; Cifarelli, 2005).

Especially in relation to Greece (just like in other Southern European countries), one can see that the State was not really generous towards workers, because it was already too patriarchal and familial at the same time, transferring the main burden of social reproduction onto the unpaid labor of household members—a labor provided usually by women. Therefore, it seemed much easier to start changes in the European Union from Greece—not only because it was a 'peripheral' member state compared to the 'core' ones, but also because its welfare state was already limited compared to Central and Western European welfare states—with the result that effective poverty was endemic for an important part of worker classes, well before 2008 (MacGregor, 2005; Dumenil & Levy, 2005; Karamessini, 2007; Martin, 2015; Mingione, 2001; Papatheodorou & Petmesidou, 2006). It is very interesting to see authors with neoliberal approaches to the welfare state admit in their own writings the low level of social provision in Greece and in Southern Europe in general (Ferrera, 2000; Katrougalos & Lazaridis, 2003). The same patriarchal injustice about domestic, predominantly women's, labor takes place in Argentina. Inequality between genders is sustained even when labor employment indicators improve: wages are lower, job stability is lower, and living conditions even worsened with the proliferation of femicides (CEMyT, 2011).

It is indicative that "Operation Less State" is the term used with a thoroughly positive connotation by the reporter Hassapopoulos (1997)—writing in *To Vima* newspaper, one of the major ones in Greece at that time—to entitle his report about a plan by the government for 'the rationalization of the State.' The plan attempted to restructure the administrative mechanism through the elimination and merger of various State sections and entities for the provision of public services. It is not sure whether the reporter copies the press release or writes with his own words that "it is expected to be a 'revolution' in public administration, to directly affect the relationships between citizens and the State and to lead about 10,000 public servants to change of job positions."[9] In Greece, the State—within its transnational framework of European Union membership and with its dedication to apply monetarist and anti-labor policies—was arguably an important agent in aggravating the crisis of 2008. The possibilities of debt augmentation and monetary collapse increased due to both the reduction of State control over capital (especially through financial deregulation) and the increase of disciplining policies at the expense of the working classes (Ericsson & Sharma, 1998; Featherstone, 2005; Hondroyannis & Lazaretou, 2004; Kosmidou, 2008; Pagones, 2013; Hondroyannis, Lolos, & Papapetrou, 2005). It is interesting to see that the deterioration of employment conditions for working classes in Greece is hailed as "Substantial reduction of labor costs and more flexible labor markets" by the September 2017 Review of one of the four Greek banks, already bailed out several times by the citizens' taxes (Karamouzis, Monokroussos, & Anastasatos, 2017).

However, other sectors were also heavily affected during this same period. Argentina gives an important example as this process involved a general reconversion for agriculture. The colonization of soy has its origin in the 1990s, when 75% of the production units disappear and 'soybean production' unfolds, along with the disappearance of State regulation of exports and the assumption of this 'regulation' role by transnational corporations.[10] In addition, this reconversion exponentially increases the value of land, transforming family farms—small and medium non-performing tenants, who rent their land to sowing pools, formed by large transnational corporations or linked to transnational capital—with minimal risks. This attack on the production arrangements related to land is part of the primitive accumulation aspect of neoliberalism for which the State is the main agent (Neiman, 2011; Byres, 2005).

2008–2017: The debate on the neoliberal State

During the years 2008–2017, the public discourse on the role of the State in Greece and Argentina has been an expression of the intersection of economic language with class interests, under the severe circumstances of global economic crisis. Greece has been explicitly depicted as unable to manage its own finances, such that it should be put under international custody, with the State governors of other countries and international organization executives imposing policies to be adopted. The central aim of this custody arrangement was not only the direct transfer of State income to State debtors but also the transfer of public property[11] to private investors, whether local or international. In some cases, State-owned corporations from other countries have bought, as private investors, the public property of Greece, showing that the role of the State in neoliberal plundering can be prominent on both sides: seller and buyer.

After the international banking crisis of 2008, the Greek State paid a huge amount of money to bail out the Greek (private) banks, which had been quite profitable until that moment (Kosmidou, 2008; Hondroyannis, Lolos, & Papapetrou, 2005; Fratianni & Marchionne, 2010). Therefore, the public bailout of private banks increased the public deficit and debt in favor of the private banking sector, leading to further expenditure cuts—a policy that has been common in the European Union to varying extents. However, in the case of Greece, the stereotype of the "lazy Greeks who lived luxuriously and now should better live with austerity" became the ultimate story or boogeyman of neoliberal discourse to justify public expenditure cuts not only in Greece but also in many other countries. Erasing the bailout of Greek banks as a factor that seriously aggravated a public deficit creates a frame of discourse that assists the redirection of the State away from social provision, because the State that saves the private banks is then blamed for the bad finances that the bailout has created (Blyth, 2013; Laeven & Valencia, 2010; Toussaint, 2017; Fratianni & Marchionne, 2010).[12]

However, the term "Less State" has been promoted not only as the main axis of the policies adopted but also as the ideal target, which the country should make every 'effort' (external debt, reduction of State expenditures, privatizations, cuts in health and public education) to achieve. It means the reduction of expenditure and the implementation of adjustment changes in the economy ("'Less State' announced Ev. Venizelos," 2011), as well as a restructuring of the State itself to accommodate better support for neoliberal policies, with devastating effects for the lives of the majority (Ladi, 2012, 2014; Karanikolos, Kentikelenis, McKee, Reeves, & Stuckler, 2014; Karaliotas, 2017; Koratzanis & Pierros, 2017; Patergiannaki & Pembetzoglou, 2017).

It is indicative of the discourse that was used in the early stages of post-2008 austerity in Greece, to see how the Prime Minister saw the reduction of the State in September 2011:

> *The big target, however, now in the Budget of 2012 is the decrease of public expenditure, the decrease of the state. A state [that is] smaller, better, cheaper and smarter in the service of the citizen. We all want reduction of expenditures, everyone wants limitation of the state. This is our obligation, this is the voice of society and of the citizens. This [voice] we hear and we will implement it. Decrease of expenditure, decrease of state, which must be at the service of the citizen. Everybody wants this, and we will implement it.*[13] (emphasis original)

The same discourse continues, however, as one can see from the 2016 *To Vima* newspaper report ("N.D. Public consultation: Citizens demand less State") on a public consultation about the government policies that citizens want introduced by the right-wing party of Nea Dimokratia (New Democracy, main opposition party at that time). Allegedly, the participants in the consultation were supporters of the party. The report does not make clear whether the wording is a copy of the press release or the anonymous reporter's choice, but the results of the consultation are a reminder of the conservative discourse prominent in other countries too: decrease of public expenditure and taxation should somehow be coupled with an increase of availability of public services during the day; there should be zero tolerance of criminal behaviors; and migrant workers who do not have a residence permit should be expelled.

At the same time, the Greek State proceeded with lowering by law the minimum wages and reducing the chances that trade unions and employer associations have to negotiate collectively on the share of income made or output produced between capital and labor. In other words, the State did not allow trade unions to negotiate with employer unions for a better share of income or employment conditions, but imposed a minimum wage and other employment conditions that are in favor of the capitalist employers. The expenditure cuts in public services have had devastating effects on the survival and living conditions of the majority of the population, while the State makes sure that it invests enough in order to have the equipment and personnel for the repression of dissent (Anagnostopoulos & Siebert, 2015; Koratzanis & Pierros, 2017).

In short, 'Less State' in the Greece of recent years has arguably meant "less democratic control of the State" as manager and distributor of common property and income. Neoliberalism in general seems to be incompatible with democracy and this is related not only to monetarist policies but also to the entire neoliberal nexus of political and economic processes (MacEwan, 2005).

At the other side of the globe, during the global financial crisis of 2008–2009, Cristina Fernández de Kirchner was the President of Argentina (2007–2015) and a political-economic crisis developed in that country, linked to the export agricultural sector. The conflict was based on the need for the State to expand, via exports, taxes, and revenues. That is, the ruling party provided a portion of the differential agricultural income to continue and/or deepen their policies, benefiting the popular welfare.

After this crisis, the Fernández de Kirchner administration developed a pool of public policies such as notebooks for kids, dentists providing services free of charge at the poorer neighborhoods, benefits for newborn babies, programs to finish secondary school, opening of new public universities, increasing the budget for government-funded science and technology development, etc. There were almost four years in which there was an effort to develop wealth distribution, but the dominant sectors felt this as an affront (in an economic, political, and cultural sense).

In terms of discourse disputes, those were very stressed days for Argentina. The dominant sectors (external and internal industrialists and land tenants) were very aggressive in their claims: the pejorative idea of *populism*[14] to refer to Latin-American administrations added to some insults to the President (the most famous of these was 'yegua,'[15] which means 'mare' and is a very derogatory way to talk about a female). In this context, the government imposed a new media law (in 2009). In Argentina, a law had been enacted under the last Dictatorship that promoted the concentration of big media making "everyday news construction" the exclusive possibility of big corporations. However, both the administration and many popular organizations promoted a change of the law, and a much more democratic law was enacted in October 2009. From there to Mauricio Macri winning as President, the public discourse—particularly as it concerned the role of the State—was in the middle of a battle between popular sectors (sometimes including representatives of the administration) and the ruling/dominant sectors of capitalist markets.

Since spring 2013, when Hugo Chavez died and Francisco Bergoglio became the Pope, the situation in Latin America has changed. As García Linera (2016) says, Latin-American right-wingers have regained the initiative. In Argentina, CEOs of large companies[16] were voted to rule the country and one of their first steps was to deal with the new media law, by a presidential order.

3. 2008 onwards. A re-narration: Double bind tactic

In both countries, citizens and social movements are not necessarily happy with the State roles they have experienced since 1975, and certainly not in the decades prior to 1975. Sometimes it seems to have become a form of common sense to view the role of the State as supporting the ruling classes and attacking working classes whenever they are too demanding, or maybe too able to be demanding.

In Greece, despite the harsh neoliberal policies imposed on the country in recent decades—and perhaps exactly because of them—the discourse against the State by the neoliberal policy-makers and propagandists seems to be very popular and effective in terms of public appeasement and electoral voting. People recognize that the State is a major problem, if not *the* problem, in late, crumbling, and extremely aggressive capitalism. Capitalism-favoring experts rush to exploit this widespread understanding by proposing another type of State—that is, a 'reduced' one—by transferring political power to private corporations and banks.

Even the actual Greek government, self-identifying as leftist,[17] confuses people by releasing contradictory statements on how the income through selling public property is necessary. For example, in June 2017, the Minister of Finance, E. Tsakalotos stated the following about the privatization of public property:

> There was no mutation but compromise and within this compromise, we kept the baby and we threw away the washing water.
>
> We will try within this compromise to protect everything that is public.[18]
>
> (Newmoney.gr, 2017)

In May 2017, the Greek Minister of Economy and Development labeled the privatization programs "one of the biggest worldwide" ("Papadimitriou: one of the biggest worldwide programs of privatization 2016–2017," 2017), as if there were a worldwide contest of privatization, and Greece should be happy to be among the winners. In December 2017—while a new wave has started in Greece of auctioning off the residences of people who cannot pay their mortgages—the Greek Vice-Minister of Foreign Affairs, G. Katrougalos,[19] gave one more explicit example of double bind, with the occasion of the Greek government introducing special criminal legislation that criminalizes the social movements that try to stop the auctions in the court rooms ("G. Katrougalos: After 8 years of Memoranda, we want to choose our policy on our own," 2017):

> We do not want to criminalize the protest. We are a party who wants the society to have the right to resist power. On the other hand, the auctions must be done, because we must be able to balance the banking system, so that it stops being a 'zombie,' who just absorbs money and so that it can again give money to the market, for a poor man to be able to get again a loan, to buy a house, and for a small businessman to get a loan for his business.
>
> We want to protect the first, the popular residence, this is the precondition for the success of our effort. At the same time, however, we want the balance sheets of the banks to balance again.[20]

However, given that the major party of the coalition is the leftist Syriza, the Greek government has taken the multi-layered art of contradictory messages even further. A very eloquent example of this may be found in the speeches of

Vice Employment Minister, Th. Fotiou, who has repeatedly advised the Greek people on *how to survive in austerity*.[21] In reality, she admits that the State plans to administer the little money of the very poor, instead of allowing them to administer their own benefits. This is an outrageously intrusive policy, which claims that the very poor are unable to administer even a tiny amount of money and that they have to be controlled by the State when they buy their basic foodstuffs, like potatoes or milk. This case shows how the polysemic notion of *austerity* is becoming (or is manipulated to become) a form of common sense with which to articulate State policies and private life in ways that were unthinkable some decades ago, and in ways that show that—for the working classes, at least—there is actually more State. It is the State that exercises not only surveillance but also supervision of the working classes, treating them as cheaters, minors, and unable to make everyday decisions about the resources available to them.

In our analysis, we understand this double bind (Bateson, 1972) in current neoliberal discourse as a tool to bend resistance, in both discursive and practical terms. One edge of the double bind is that neoliberal discourse accepts the negative attitude towards the State, co-opting the majority's aversion to the State—an aversion that can originate in other ways of thinking, and not only in the neoliberal mentality that favors free markets (Anderson, 2015). Neoliberal discourse co-opts this negative attitude towards the State by channeling it towards specific activities (State welfare and services) instead of letting the aversion express itself in ways that might harm the capitalist accumulation processes. The other edge of the double bind is that both the discourse (for example, normalizing military expenditure[22]) and the practice of neoliberal policy-makers make the State even more powerful and even more class-biased than it was before; and the entire anti-State discourse becomes a tool to impose more numerous, violent, and intrusive State policies at the expense of the working classes.

This can be seen directly in Argentina, where, for the first time,[23] a right-wing party won elections in late 2015. Fifty one percent of the electoral roll voted for "Let's change,"[24] —the so-called 'Alliance'—which represents a classist, sexist, and elitist proposal. Just two years after the victory of this party, the transfer of wealth to the dominant sector (i.e., external and internal big industries and land tenants) implacably began: devaluation of the currency, removal of withholding taxes, rising interest rates, trade liberalization, demand adjustment, external debt, removal of subsidies for light and gas, exorbitant increases in food prices, rising fuel prices and public transport fares, openness to imports, and more than 250,000 formal layoffs among State and private workers (Carbone & Giniger, 2017). These measures have had a direct impact on the purchasing power of workers and have been accompanied by the stigmatization of workers,[25] the criminalization of protest, and the strengthening of police power. The confused information and the prosecution of political activists are part of the conservative restoration in Latin America, as Garcia Linera (2016) points out.

The current economic and social situation in Argentina is certainly complicated: it is going through a setback in economic, social, and cultural rights, which had been attained in the last decade, but popular movements resist. Since the Macri administration won, resistance has had significant street protest milestones: at least twice a month, there have been demonstrations that united at least a part of the union movement with the university movement, besides the participation of popular political organizations and territorial movements.[26] In this sense, the Macri administration holds to its ideology on free market and ideologically assigns a minimal role to the State, but it cannot run publicly, for lack of legitimacy: the Macri administration does not explicitly promote the neoliberal idea of *austerity*. In contrast to this, the discourse is ambiguous: the government does not say that the State should be reduced, but rather that it has to be more efficient.[27] The notion of *austerity* is not perceived well in Argentinian common sense, so—in order to implement cuts—the government has to talk about *efficiency*.

We see the two case studies as examples of how the political repression of popular dissent and economic violence against working classes rearticulate capitalist processes, where the State shifts its focus in a mobile manner to articulate the markets and the worker producers in ways that better fit the globalized needs of capital. Instead of providing social services and goods that create conditions of social consensus, or at least social tolerance, it invests in further control of resources and violence against protesters and dissident voices. The State becomes the protector of neoliberal advances by conflating them with security concerns, which in the two case studies are concerns oriented towards the internal politics of each country (Essex, 2008; Ong, 2007).

Finally, the major tool is the contradiction itself between an austerity that does not (and could not) bring positive results for the economy and the promotion of austerity as a good chance to reduce the State (Koratzanis & Pierros, 2017; Polychroniou, 2012)—which makes the majority spend time, effort, and intellectual capacity to balance the contradictory messages received everyday by the same senders, namely: neoliberal supporters and politicians, mass media, and experts-analysts. Contradictions in neoliberal discourse and policies are typical modes of handling the contradictions in the economic system itself and this is why they need to be deconstructed (Holborow, 2012b). In both Greece and Argentina, we understand the votes in favor of neoliberal policies as signs and results of this double bind tactic, at least for people who belong to the working classes.

4. Conclusion

In this chapter, we worked to contribute to the discussion about how the discourse of austerity turns the State into a major agent of capitalist restructuring, and how that same discourse takes advantage of the majority's aversion to the State to impose policies that, at the end of the day, enhance the State's role in society. We have seen the evolution of neoliberal policies and the discourse that promotes them during the last decades, using two case studies: Argentina and Greece. We have shown that *austerity policies* are distinct from *austerity discourses*, and that despite the similarity of policies in the two countries, discourse and neoliberal tactics can vary in order to impose aggressive capitalist practices over populations that—one way or another—may resist the loss of income and the deprivation of basic common goods, services, and resources. The contradictions between neoliberal discourse and practice concerning the role of the State have their material parallel in the merger of State and economic power through neoliberal policies (Mylonas, 2014; Karaliotas, 2017; Konstantinidis & Vlachou, 2018).

The important issue that emerges while viewing the deployment of discourse and policies through time is that both cannot last long as effective tools of policy imposition over societies, especially over working classes. That is a major question, in the sense that the double bind technique we identify via our analysis is a condition that can lead to results which, at some point in the near future, could be unpredictable. Bateson's theory shows how the double bind can lead to permanent breakdown of the mental ability of the receiver to construct a coherent perception of reality—or not, depending on the ability of the double bind captives to escape the communication field (Bateson, 1972, pp. 126–244). What we do not know, even by using this theoretical approach, is how and when one result happens instead of the other when the double bind refers to entire societies.

This can be a research path for the authors of this chapter or for other colleagues who would like to approach critically our findings or refine our analysis. We are also aware of the limitations of this chapter, that came up due to various practical constraints. Nevertheless, we feel that the discussion of the use of the anti-State discourse by neoliberalism is not just a trick, but rather a major policy instrument, and that we needed and still need to work more on this question in the future.

Acknowledgements

We are deeply grateful to the editors of this volume for the support, understanding, and comments they have provided us with in order to finalize this chapter, as well as to the three colleague referees who gave us great advice on improving this chapter, concerning both content, literature, and argument structures, as well as presentation of findings and language. All deficiencies remain the sole responsibility of the authors.

Notes

1 Santiago Maldonado was an activist who first was missing (abducted) and when his body was found, it was proven that he was killed by the Argentine State regular forces in a protest against Benetton, the owner of the clothing corporation, who has occupied the indigenous peoples' lands in Patagonia. Santiago's missing produced many demonstrations in Argentina and in other countries worldwide.

2 "Achicar el Estado para agrandar la Nación" was the slogan in Spanish.

3 Blyth (2013, chapter 7) depicts neoliberalism's position towards the State as schizophrenic, while Peck (2010, chapter 1) describes neoliberalism as a 'bipolar' project, with 'bipolar disorder' in its intellectual origins. We opted to avoid medical terms in our analysis, although the terms 'schizophrenia' and 'double bind' are directly linked in the work of Bateson (not so 'bipolar' as this is a much later term). One reason has been that, by describing the neoliberal policy-makers and experts as suffering from a mental condition, one depicts them as vulnerable and 'victims' of their own ideology. At the same time, the medical discourse in economics might create a discriminatory or even offensive framework against people who might truly have a medical condition, but who never tried to transfer wealth from the poor to the rich or to impose poverty over millions of people. We therefore, opted to stick with the technical language of Bateson about the 'double bind' and the communication violence it induces, in order to show the function of the discourse on the collective level without medicalizing our chapter and without making neoliberal discourse appear as inevitable or as random as a medical condition.

4 The judicial decisions closed the debate on whether or not there was a genocide in Argentina (EASQ, 2015). Legally, genocide is the systematic annihilation of a population group as such. Since the Second World War, this began to circulate as the definition of a new type of crime (see: UN Genocide Convention). From the sociological point of view, genocide is not only the annihilation of a social force but also the destruction of social relations in whole society. That is what the Argentinean dictatorship meant.

5 Alogoskoufis was the Greek Minister of the Economy and Finance during the years 2004–2009.

6 In 1975, Argentina's external debt was 7.875 billion dollars. In 1983, the indebtedness reached 42.319 billion dollars (www.ambito.com/748406-la-argentina-y-su-drama-con-la-inflacion-a-25-anos-de-la-hiper)

7 See: www.asteriscos.tv/dossier-23.html

8 The monetary policy of liberalism, in both theory and practice, wants the State not to interfere with the currency and the facilitation of transactions in the economy. The supposed reason is that the State and particularly government politicians are susceptible to pressure by the public—i.e., their voters—to undertake monetary policies that can favor the latter and leave the economy vulnerable to inflation and monetary instability. The solution proposed by neoliberal theory is that monetary policy should be determined by an independent central bank and not by the government, nor by a central bank under the control of elected politicians.

9 The text in Greek is "αναμένεται να αποτελέσει «επανάσταση» στη δημόσια διοίκηση, να επηρεάσει άμεσα τις σχέσεις του πολίτη με το κράτος και να οδηγήσει περίπου 10.000 δημοσίους υπαλλήλους σε μετατάξεις."

10 The main oil companies are Cargill, Dreyfus, Aceitera General Deheza, Bunge, Molinos Río de la Plata, etc.

11 Public property in Greece has various statuses. Therefore, it can be a 'common' (there are 'commons' designated as such in Greek law, e.g., the beaches are commons, even if they are part of a private island), or it can have a special status. The Greek State might own a forest, or a public place/building can be owned by a public entity that legally is distinct from the State but which performs a public role or service (e.g., a local authority or a public institution, like a university). A lot of commons are owned by the Greek Orthodox Church. There are also commons which are

privately owned—some of them by private individuals, some by the Greek State or other public entities which are private owners of a common, but which still perform a public role with them. Therefore, Greek State has property over commons as a State, but also has private property over lands, buildings or other commons, depending on the case.

12 It is interesting that Mark Blyth (2013) explains in detail how the mechanism of transferring a private capitalist debt and risk exposure to the State and the public treasury holds for all countries, but not for Greece. He appears oblivious to the fact that the then Greek government not only bailed out its private banks but some years afterwards also gave them public money to aggressively merge with other private banks or to buy the Bank of Cyprus, which was under severe bankruptcy risk.

13 The text in Greek (To Ethnos, 2011) is presented as the original speech of Venizelos: "Ο μεγάλος στόχος, όμως, τώρα μέσα από τον Προϋπολογισμό του 2012 είναι η μείωση της δημόσιας δαπάνης, η μείωση του κράτους. Ένα κράτος μικρότερο, καλύτερο, φθηνότερο και εξυπνότερο στην υπηρεσία του πολίτη. Όλοι θέλουμε μείωση δαπανών, όλοι θέλουν περιορισμό του κράτους. Αυτή είναι η υποχρέωσή μας, αυτή είναι η φωνή της κοινωνίας και των πολιτών. Αυτήν ακούμε, αυτό θα εφαρμόσουμε. Μείωση δαπανών, μείωσηκράτους, το οποίο πρέπει να είναι στην υπηρεσία του πολίτη. Ολοι αυτόθέλουν, αυτό θα εφαρμόσουμε."

14 Just as an example of this, it can be seen some of the bigger newspapers:
www.clarin.com/opinion/populismo-economia_latinoamericana-crecimiento-credito_externo-politicas_de_ajuste-inflacion_0_r1F-wg9P7l.html
www.clarin.com/opinion/energia-luz-populismo-derroche-cortes_0_Hkz_7GucvXx.html
www.lanacion.com.ar/1558248-un-populismo-de-exportacion
www.lanacion.com.ar/1627224-el-populismo-patologico-del-pais

15 For example: www.infonews.com/nota/307987/el-misogino-editorial-de-clarin-contra

16 Current president, Mauricio Macri, is a corporation owner; he and his family own many different companies (cars, postal services, real estate, etc.) and they have continually been doing business with the State: www.infobae.com/opinion/2017/02/17/los-negocios-de-la-familia-macri-la-transparencia-y-la-etica/

17 In reality, it is a leftist-right wing coalition. In the beginning, several analysts attributed the neoliberal choices of the government to the right-wing elements of the coalition or to the inexperience of the government (this has been the first time that a self-labelled leftist party effectively reached government). However, the discourse and action of the party members and now government members has revealed that those have been their ideas or core visions for their administration. This chapter has been very informative for both authors, that a self-named leftist government can adopt neoliberal policies and use the prevailing neoliberal discourse in a perverse way to justify their actions, either by using that discourse or by opposing it. In that sense, our approach to compare discourse with action was aiming to shield this analysis from the fact that self-identification is over-used in discourse analysis, and that we cannot limit ourselves to self-identification when we are critically assessing the action and discourse of those in power.

18 The statements in Greek are as follows: "Δεν έγινε μετάλλαξη, αλλά συμβιβασμός και μέσα σε αυτόν τον συμβιβασμό κρατήσαμε το μωρό και πετάξαμε το μπουγαδόνερο…Θα προσπαθήσουμε μέσα από αυτόν τον συμβιβασμό να προστατεύσουμε όσα είναι δημόσια."

19 He is the same author who writes with G. Lazaridis about the welfare state in Southern Europe (Katrougalos & Lazaridis 2003). He definitely applies neoliberal policies and uses neoliberal discourse, just like he did in his academic book.

20 The Greek text attributed directly to the Vice-Minister (G. Katrougalos: After 8 years of Memoranda, we want to choose our policy on our own, 2017) is as follows: "Δεν θέλουμε να ποινικοποιήσουμε τη διαμαρτυρία. Είμαστε κόμμα που θέλει την κοινωνία να έχει το δικαίωμα να αντιστέκεται στην εξουσία. Από την άλλη μεριά οι πλειστηριασμοί πρέπει να γίνουν, γιατί πρέπει να μπορέσουμε να ισορροπήσουμε το τραπεζικό σύστημα, για να πάψει να είναι «ζόμπι», που απλώς απορροφά χρήματα και να μπορεί να ξαναδώσει χρήματα στην αγορά, να μπορεί ένας φτωχός άνθρωπος να ξαναδανειστεί, για να πάρει σπίτι και για να ξαναμπορεί ένας μικρομεσαίος επιχειρηματίας να πάρει δάνειο για την επιχείρησή του." "Θέλουμε να προφυλάξουμε την πρώτη, τη λαϊκή κατοικία, αυτό είναι προϋπόθεση για την επιτυχία της προσπάθειάς μας. Ταυτόχρονα, όμως, θέλουμε να ξαναϊσορροπήσει το ενεργητικό και το παθητικό των τραπεζών."

21 Fotiou's statement was: "You must be a Harvard graduate to manage to survive on 200 euros per month. But if we give you a 70-euro card which is prepaid for food that you get from any shop, free electricity, that is what a family needs and if we give you, and if you have no home, 70-euro rent subsidy but always to the owner, not to you. That is a logic in kind and not in cash. When you arrive at such small levels in terms of benefit, like GMI (welfare benefits) currently is, 200 euros, the benefits in kind can make you survive. Cash benefits will destroy you. Because as I said before, it is impossible to survive on 200 euros, while those that I mentioned to you just before are 150 euros. And you can survive, in great difficulty, but you can." (902.gr, 2016). The original text in Greek: "Πρέπει να είσαι απόφοιτος του Χάρβαρντ για να καταφέρεις να επιβιώσεις με 200 ευρώ το μήνα. Αν σου δίνουμε όμως 70 ευρώ κάρτα η οποία είναι προπληρωμένη για τρόφιμα, που τα παίρνεις από οποιοδήποτε μαγαζί, δωρεάν ηλεκτρική ενέργεια, δηλαδή αυτό που έχει ανάγκη μια οικογένεια και σου δίνουμε, και εφόσον δεν έχεις σπίτι, 70 ευρώ επιδότηση ενοικίου αλλά πάντα στον ιδιοκτήτη όχι σε σένα. Δηλαδή μία λογική σε είδος και όχι σε χρήμα. Όταν φτάνεις σε τόσο μικρά επίπεδα επιδοματικά όπως είναι σήμερα το GMI (προνοιακό επίδομα), τα 200 ευρώ, οι παροχές σε είδος μπορούν να σεκάνουν να επιβιώσεις. Οι παροχές σε χρήμα θα σε καταστρέψουν. Γιατί όπως είπα και πριν είναι αδύνατον να επιβιώσεις με 200 ευρώ, ενώ αυτά που σας είπα μόλις πριν είναι 150 ευρώ. Και μπορείς να επιβιώσεις, πολύ δύσκολα, αλλά μπορείς." (902.gr, 2016).

22 www.businessinsider.com/why-greeces-military-budget-is-so-high-2015–6 www.eldestapeweb.com/exclusivo-la-escalofriante-lista-armamento-que-argentina-le-pidio-estados-unidos-n27058

23 In Argentina, the right-wing has led the government many times, but that has always been—and is still now—through coups d'état.

24 "Alianza Cambiemos" is the name of the right-wing party.

25 An example of this was the idea of "gnocchi" to talk about State employees. In Argentinian tradition, families eat gnocchi on the 29th of each month: thus, a "gnocchi employee" is one who works only one day per month. So, calling them "gnocchi" assumes both that State employees work only one day per month, and that the State is too "big" to be efficient. www.lanacion.com.ar/2024579-el-plan-de-macri-para-terminar-con-los-noquis-en-el-estado

26 Only in Buenos Aires and to name only those of national importance: On February 24, 50,000 people protested against government layoffs; on March 24,

250,000 people demonstrated on the 40th anniversary of the coup; on April 29, the four unions protested (350,000 people); on May 12, 40,000 people protested as part of the university movement against cuts to higher education; on June 2, two trade union confederations protested against layoffs (40,000 people); on July 2, the National March involved 250,000 people, etc. (Source: Diario Tiempo Argentino)

27 www.telam.com.ar/notas/201707/196320-modernizacion-desmentida-ola-despidos-estatales.html

References

902.gr (2016, September 13). Με παροχές 150 ευρώ «σεείδος» αντί προνοιακού επιδόματος μπορείς να επιβιώσεις! [With 'in kind' benefits of 150 euros instead of welfare benefits you can survive!]. *902.gr* [online news portal]. Retrieved from www.902.gr/eidisi/politiki/108126/vaftizei-exorthologismo-tin-perikopi-ton-pronoiakon-epidomaton

Alogoskoufis, G., Giavazzi, F., & Laroque, G. (1995). The two faces of Janus: Institutions, policy regimes and macroeconomic performance in Greece. *Economic Policy, 10*(20), 147–192.

Anagnostopoulos, A., & Siebert, S. (2015). The impact of Greek labour market regulation on temporary employment: Evidence from a survey in Thessaly, Greece. *The International Journal of Human Resource Management, 26*(18), 2366–2393.

Anderson, B. (2015). Neoliberal affects. *Progress in Human Geography, 40*(6), 1–20.

Antunes, R. (2005). *Los sentidos del trabajo. Ensayo sobre la afirmación y negación del trabajo.* [The senses of work. Essay on the affirmation and denial of work]. Buenos Aires, Argentina: Editorial Herramienta.

Arestis, P., & Sawyer, M. (2005). The neoliberal experience of the United Kingdom. In D. Johnston & A. Saad-Filho (Eds.), *Neoliberalism: A critical reader* (pp. 199–207). London/Ann Arbor, MI: Pluto Press.

Azpiazu, D., & Basualdo, E. (2004). Las privatizaciones en la Argentina: Génesis, desarrollo y principales impactos estructurales. [Privatizations in Argentina: Genesis, development and major structural impacts]. Retrieved from http://bibliotecavirtual.clacso.org.ar/ar/libros/argentina/flacso/azpiazu.pdf

Barbieri, P. (2009). Flexible employment and inequality in Europe. *European Sociological Review, 25*(6), 621–628.

Bateson, G. (1972). *Steps to an ecology of mind: Collected essays in anthropology, psychiatry, evolution and epistemology.* New Jersey/London: Jason Aronson Inc.

Block, D. (2012). Economising globalisation and identity in applied linguistics in neoliberal times. In D. Block, J. Gray, & M. Holborow (Eds.), *Neoliberalism and applied linguistics* (pp. 56–85). London: Routledge.

Blyth, M. (2013). *Austerity: The history of a dangerous idea.* Oxford: Oxford University Press.

Byres, T. (2005). Neoliberalism and primitive accumulation in less developed countries. In D. Johnston & A. Saad-Filho (Eds.), *Neoliberalism: A critical reader* (pp. 83–90). London/Ann Arbor, MI: Pluto Press.

Campbell, A. (2005). The birth of neoliberalism in the United States: A reorganization of capitalism. In D. Johnston & A. Saad-Filho (Eds.), *Neoliberalism: A critical reader* (pp. 187–199). London/Ann Arbor, MI: Pluto Press.

Carbone, R., & Giniger, N. (2017). *Cientificidio, soberanía y lucha de clases: Una agenda para el debate.* [*Scientificide*, sovereignty and class struggle: An agenda for debate]. Buenos Aires, Argentina: 8vo Loco Ediciones.

CEMyT (2011). *Situación laboral de las mujeres período 2009–2010*. [Women's labor situation, 2009–2010]. Retrieved from www.cta.org.ar/IMG/pdf/_informe_no3_definitivo_definitivo_.pdf

Charaudeau, P. (2000). Problématique discursive de l'émotion: A propos des effets de pathémisation à la télévision. In C. Plantin, M. Doury, & V. Traverso (Eds.), *Les émotions dans les interactions* (pp. 125–135). Lyon: Presses Universitaires de Lyon.

Cifarelli, V. (2005). *Las privatizaciones en Argentina*. [Privatizations in Argentina]. Retrieved from www.tel.org.ar/lectura/privarg.html

Clarke, J., & Newman, J. (2012). The alchemy of austerity. *Critical Social Policy*, *32*(3), 299–319.

Clarke, S. (2005). The neoliberal theory of society. In D. Johnston, & A. Saad-Filho (Eds.), *Neoliberalism: A critical reader* (pp. 50–59). London/Ann Arbor, MI: Pluto Press.

Colas, A. (2005). Neoliberalism, globalization and international relations. In D. Johnston & A. Saad-Filho (Eds.), *Neoliberalism: A critical reader* (pp. 70–80). London/Ann Arbor, MI: Pluto Press.

Dagatti, M. (2007). La Ostentación de la austeridad: Hacia una visibilidad del cambio. [The ostentation of austerity: Towards a visibility of change]. In *La Trama de la Comunicación* (Vol. 12, pp. 256–269). Rosario, Argentina: UNR Editora.

Dellepiane, S., & Hardiman, N. (2015). Fiscal politics in time: Pathways to fiscal consolidation in Ireland, Greece, Britain, and Spain, 1980–2012. *European Political Science Review*, 7(2), 189–219.

Dumenil, G., & Levy, D. (2005). The neoliberal (counter-) revolution. In D. Johnston & A. Saad-Filho (Eds.), *Neoliberalism: A critical reader* (pp. 9–19). London/Ann Arbor, MI: Pluto Press.

Ericsson, N., & Sharma, S. (1998). Broad money demand and financial liberalization in Greece. *Empirical Economics*, *23*(3), 417–436.

EASQ (2015). Informe sobre el juzgamiento del genocidio argentino. [Report on the trial of the Argentine genocide]. *Tela de Juicio*, *1*, 25–58.

Essex, J. (2008). The neoliberalization of development: Trade capacity building and security at the US Agency of International Development. *Antipode*, *40*(2), 229–251.

Fairclough, I. (2015). Evaluating policy as practical argumentation: The public debate over the first UK Austerity Budget. *Critical Discourse Studies*, *13*(1), 57–77.

Featherstone, K. (2005). 'Soft' co-ordination meets 'hard' politics: The European Union and pension reform in Greece. *Journal of European Public Policy*, *12*(4), 733–750.

Ferrera, M. (2000). Reconstructing the welfare state in Southern Europe. In S. Kuhnle (Ed.), *Survival of the European Welfare State* (pp. 166–181). London: Routledge.

Fratianni, M., & Marchionne, F. (2010, February 25). *Banks' Great Bailout of 2008–2009*. Retrieved from http://dx.doi.org/10.2139/ssrn.1559413

"G. Katrougalos: After 8 years of Memoranda, we want to choose our policy on our own" (2017, December 22). Γ.Κατρούγκαλος: Μετά από 8 χρόνια Μνημόνια, θέλουμε να επιλέγουμε την π ολιτική μας μόνοι μας, *Left* [online newspaper]. Retrieved from https://left.gr/news/g-katroygkalos-epeita-apo-8-hronia-mnimonion-theloymena-epilegoyme-tin-politiki-mas-monoi-mas

Giniger, N. (2014). Doctrina Social de la Iglesia y Responsabilidad Social Empresaria: Ética y política del neoliberalismo. [Social doctrine of the church and corporate social responsibility: Ethics and politics of neoliberalism]. *Sociedad y Religion*, *24*(42), 34–66.

Gramsci, A. (1975). *Quaderni del Carcere*. [Jail notebooks] Roma: Einaudi Editore.

Graefe, P. (2005). *Roll-out neoliberalism and the social economy*. Paper presented at the Annual Meeting of the Canadian Political Science Association, University of Western Ontario.

Hadjimichalis, C., & Vaiou, D. (1990). Flexible labour markets and regional development in northern Greece. *International Journal of Urban and Regional Research, 14*(1), 1–24.

Hassapopoulos, N. (1997, October 26).Επιχείρηση «Λιγότερο κράτος» Καταργούνται υπουργεία, νομαρχίες και δημόσιοι οργανισμοί. ["Operation Less State": Ministries, counties and public organizations get eliminated]. *To Vima* [online newspaper]. Retrieved from www.tovima.gr/politics/article/?aid=92393

Holborow, M. (2012a). What is neoliberalism? Discourse, ideology and the real world. In D. Block, J., Gray, & M. Holborow (Eds.), *Neoliberalism and applied linguistics* (pp. 14–32). London: Routledge.

Holborow, M. (2012b). Neoliberal keywords and the contradictions of an ideology. In D. Block, J., Gray, & M. Holborow (Eds.), *Neoliberalism and applied linguistics* (pp. 33–55). London: Routledge.

Hondroyannis, G., & Lazaretou, S. (2004). *Inflation persistence during periods of structural change: An assessment using Greek data*. (Working Paper No. 370). Frankfurt am Main: European Central Bank. Retrieved from www.ecb.europa.eu/pub/pdf/scpwps/ecbwp370.pdf?86c0b580d6f22025f59eebe7b29e255c

Hondroyannis, G., Lolos, S., & Papapetrou, E. (2005). Financial markets and economic growth in Greece, 1986–1999. *Journal of International Financial Markets, Institutions & Money, 15*(2), 173–188.

Infobae (2016, July 28). Marcos Peña: "Tarde o temprano se van a tener que pagar las facturas de gas." [Marcos Peña: "Soon or later they will have to pay gas bills"]. Retrieved from www.infobae.com/politica/2016/07/28/marcos-pena-tarde-o-temprano-se-van-a-tener-que-pagar-las-facturas-de-gas/

Johnston, D. (2005). Poverty and distribution: Back on the neoliberal agenda? In D. Johnston & A. Saad-Filho (Eds.), *Neoliberalism: A critical reader* (pp. 135–141). London/Ann Arbor, MI: Pluto Press.

Johnston, D., & Saad-Filho, A. (Eds.). (2005). *Neoliberalism: A critical reader*. London/Ann Arbor, MI: Pluto Press.

Karaliotas, L. (2017). Performing neoliberalization through urban infrastructure: Twenty years of privatization policies around Thessaloniki's port. *Environment and Planning A, 49*(7), 1556–1574.

Karamessini, M. (2007). *The Southern European social model: Changes and continuities in recent decades*. (Discussion Paper Series No. 174). Geneva: International Institute for Labour Studies.

Karamouzis, N., Monokroussos, P., & Anastasatos, T. (2017). From a vicious to a virtuous cycle? Turning Greece into an attractive investment destination: Opportunities and Challenges. *Economy & Markets, 11*(3), 1–38.

Karanikolos, M., Kentikelenis, A., McKee, M., Reeves, A., & Stuckler, D. (2014). Greece's health crisis: From austerity to denialism. *Lancet, 383*(9918), 748–753.

Kasimis, C., Papadopoulos, A., & Zacopoulou, E. (2003). Migrants in rural Greece. *Sociologia Ruralis, 43*(2), 167–184.

Katrougalos, G., & Lazaridis, G. (2003). *Southern European welfare states: Problems, challenges and prospects*. Houndmills, Basingstoke, UK/New York: Palgrave Macmillan.

Kelsey, D., Mueller, F., Whittle, A., & KhosraviNik, M. (2016). Financial crisis and austerity: Interdisciplinary concerns in critical discourse studies. *Critical Discourse Studies, 13*(1), 1–19.

Konstantinidis, C., & Vlachou, A. (2018). Appropriating nature in crisis-ridden Greece Part 2: Deepening neoliberal capitalism. *Capitalism Nature Socialism, 29*(2), 108–121.

Koratzanis, N., & Pierros, C. (2017).Assessing the impact of austerity in the Greek economy: A sectoral financial balances approach. *Real World Economics Review, 82*, 122–142.

Kosmidou, K. (2008).The determinants of banks' profits in Greece during the period of EU financial integration. *Managerial Finance, 34*(3), 146–159.

Kougias, K. (2017). *'Real' Flexicurity Worlds in action: Evidence from Denmark and Greece.* (GreeSe Papers No. 106). London: Hellenic Observatory, European Institute. Retrieved from www.lse.ac.uk/europeanInstitute/research/hellenicObservatory/CMS%20pdf/Publications/GreeSE/GreeSE-No.106.pdf

Ladi, S. (2012).*The Eurozone crisis and austerity politics: A trigger for administrative reform in Greece?* (GreeSe Papers No 57). London: Hellenic Observatory, European Institute. Retrieved from http://eprints.lse.ac.uk/43383/

Ladi, S. (2014). Austerity politics and administrative reform: The Eurozone crisis and its impact upon Greek public administration. *Comparative European Politics, 12*(2), 184–208.

Laeven, L., & Valencia, F. (2010).*Resolution of banking crises: The good, the bad, and the ugly.* (IMF Working Paper No. 10/146).Washington, DC: International Monetary Fund. Retrieved from www.imf.org/external/pubs/ft/wp/2010/wp10146.pdf

"'Less State' announced Ev. Venizelos" (2011, September 18). «Λιγότερο κράτος» προανήγγειλε ο Ευ. Βενιζέλος, *To Ethnos* [online newspaper]. Retrieved from www.ethnos.gr/oikonomia/arthro/ligotero_kratos_proaniggeile_o_eu_benizelos-63387060/

Linera, G. (2016). *Restauación conservadora y nuevas resistencias en Latinoamérica.* [Conservative restoration and new resistances in LatinAmerica].Paper presented at Conferencia dictada, Facultad de Ciencias Sociales, Universidad de Buenos Aires, organized by Fundación Germán Abdala. Retrieved from www.youtube.com/watch?v=-iRjp28fhco

MacEwan, A. (2005). Neoliberalism and democracy: Market power vs. Democratic power. In D. Johnston & A. Saad-Filho (Eds.), *Neoliberalism: A critical reader* (pp. 170–178). London/Ann Arbor, MI: Pluto Press.

MacGregor, S. (2005).The welfare state and neoliberalism. In D. Johnston & A. Saad-Filho (Eds.), *Neoliberalism: A critical reader* (pp. 142–148). London/Ann Arbor, MI: Pluto Press.

Martin, C. (2015). Southern welfare states: Configuration of the welfare balance between State and the family. In M. Baumeister & R. Sala (Eds.), *Southern Europe? Italy, Spain, Portugal & Greece from the 1950s until the present day.* Frankfurt: Campus.

Mavroudeas, S. (2010).*Greece and the EU: Capitalist crisis and imperialist rivalries.* Paper presented at the First International Conference of Political Economy "*Beyond the crisis.*" Rethymnon, Greece.

Milios, J. (2005).European integration as a vehicle of neoliberal hegemony. In D. Johnston & A. Saad-Filho (Eds.), *Neoliberalism: A critical reader* (pp. 208–217). London/Ann Arbor, MI: Pluto Press.

Mingione, E. (2001). The Southern European welfare model and the fight against poverty and social exclusion. In M. K. Tolba (Ed.), *Our fragile world: Challenges and opportunities for sustainable development* (Vol. 1, pp. 1041–1051). Oxford: EOLSS Publisher.

Ministry of Foreign Affairs (2014).Η π ορεία της Ελλάδας στην Ευρωπαϊκή Ένωση. [Greece's pathway to the European Union]. Retrieved from www.mfa.gr/exoteriki-politiki/i-ellada-stin-ee/i-poreia-tis-elladas-stin-europaiki-enosi.html

Munck, R. (2005). Neoliberalism and politics, and the politics of neoliberalism. In D. Johnston & A. Saad-Filho (Eds.), *Neoliberalism: A critical reader* (pp. 60–69). London/Ann Arbor, MI: Pluto Press.

Mundell, R. (1961). A theory of Optimum Currency Areas. *The American Economic Review, 51*(4), 657–665.

Mylonas, Y. (2014). Crisis, austerity and opposition in mainstream media discourses of Greece. *Critical Discourse Studies, 11*(3), 305–321.

N. D. (abbreviation for Nea Dimokratia) – Public consultation: Citizens demand less State (2016, August 8). Ν. Δ.-Δημόσια διαβούλευση: Οι πολίτες ζητούν λιγότερο κράτος, *To Vima* [online newspaper]. Retrieved from www.vimaonline.gr/20/article/25207/nd-dimosia-diavouleusi-oi-polites-zitoun-ligotero-kratos-

Neiman, G. (2011, March 13). Boom agrícola y empleo. [Agricultural boom and employment]. *Página 12* [online newspaper]. Retrieved from www.pagina12.com.ar/diario/suplementos/cash/17-5025-2011-03-13.html

Newmoney (2017, June 28). Τσακαλώτος για τις ιδιωτικοποιήσεις: «Δεν έγινε μετάλλαξη, αλλά συμβιβασμός». [Tsakalotos about privatizations: "There was no mutation but compromise"]. *Newmoney* [online newspaper]. Retrieved from www.newmoney.gr/palmos-oikonomias/ellada/326838-tsakalotos-gia-tis-idiotikopoiiseis-%C2%ABden-egine-metallaksi,-alla-simbibasmos%C2%BB

Nikolaou, N. (2008, January 12). Αφηγησεις: Η σταθεροποίηση της οικονομίας από τον Σημίτη. [Narrations: The stabilization of the economy by Simitis]. *Kathimerini* [online newspaper]. Retrieved from www.kathimerini.gr/309847/article/epikairothta/ellada/afhghseis-h-sta8eropoihsh-ths-oikonomias-apo-ton-shmith

Ong, A. (2007). Neoliberalism as a mobile technology. *Transactions of the Institute of British Geographers, 32*(1), 3–8.

Pagones, J. (2013). The European Union's response to the Sovereign Debt Crisis: Its effect on labor relations in Greece. *Fordham International Law Review, 36*(5), 1517–1554.

Pagoulatos, G. (2002). *Greece, the European Union and the 2003 Presidency*. (Research and European Issues No. 21). Paris: Notre Europe. Retrieved from www2.aueb.gr/users/pagoulatos/Notre%20Europe%20Greek%20Presidency-EN.pdf

Papadimitriou: One of the biggest worldwide programmes of privatization, 2016–2017. (2017, May 10). Παπαδημητρίου: Από τα μεγαλύτερα διεθνώς το νέο πρόγραμμα ιδιωτικοποιήσεων 2016–2017, *To Vima* [online newspaper]. Retrieved from www.tovima.gr/finance/article/?aid=878947

Papatheodorou, C., & Petmesidou, M. (2006). Poverty profiles and trends: How do southern European countries compare with each other? In C. Papatheodorou & M. Petmesidou (Eds.), *Poverty and social deprivation in the Mediterranean: Trends, policies and welfare prospects in the new millennium* (pp. 47–94). London/New York: CROP-International Studies in Poverty Research, International Social Science Council, & Zed Books.

Pappas, T. (2010). Macroeconomic policy, strategic leadership, and voter behaviour: The disparate tales of socialist reformism in Greece and Spain during the 1980s. *West European Politics, 33*(6), 1241–1260.

Patergiannaki, Z., & Pembetzoglou, M. (2017). Debt-driven water privatization: The case of Greece. *European Journal of Multidisciplinary Studies, 5*(1), 102–111.

Peck, J. (2010). *Constructions of neoliberal reason*. Oxford/New York: Oxford University Press.

Peck, J., & Tickell, A. (2002). Neoliberalizing space. *Antipode, 34*(3), 380–404.

Peet, R. (2009). *Unholy trinity: The IMF, World Bank and WTO* (2nd ed.). New York: Zed Books.

Polychroniou, C. J. (2012). *The Mediterranean conundrum: The link between the state and the macroeconomy, and the disastrous effects of the European policy of austerity*. (Public Policy Brief, No. 124). New York: Levy Economics Institute of Bard College.

Poulantzas, N. (1978). *State, power, socialism*. London/New York: NLB.

Pouliakas, K., & Theodossiou, I. (2007). *Socio-economic differences in the perceived quality of high and low-paid jobs in Greece*. (Discussion Paper 2007-05). Epicurus–Center for European Labour Market Research. Retrieved from http://econwpa.repec.org/eps/lab/papers/0506/0506002.pdf

Radice, H. (2005). Neoliberal globalization: Imperialism without empires? In D. Johnston & A. Saad-Filho (Eds.), *Neoliberalism: A critical reader* (pp. 91–98). London/Ann Arbor, MI: Pluto Press.

Reisigl, M., & Wodak, R. (2009). The Discourse-Historical Approach (DHA). In M. Meyer & R. Wodak (Eds.), *Methods of Critical Discourse Studies* (2nd ed.) (pp. 87–121). London: Sage.

Saad-Filho, A. (2005). The political economy of neoliberalism in Latin America. In D. Johnston & A. Saad-Filho (Eds.), *Neoliberalism: A critical reader* (pp. 222–229). London/Ann Arbor, MI: Pluto Press.

Schmidt, V. A. (2002). Does discourse matter in the politics of welfare state adjustment? *Comparative Political Studies*, *35*(2), 168–193.

Spanou, C. (2008). State reform in Greece: Responding to old and new challenges. *International Journal of Public Sector Management*, *21*(2), 150–173.

Theodossopoulos, D. (2014). The ambivalence of anti-austerity indignation in Greece: Resistance, hegemony and complicity. *History and Anthropology*, *25*(45), 488–506.

Toussaint, E. (2017, January 18). Ελλάδα: Οι τράπεζες προκάλεσαν την κρίση. [Greece: The banks induced the crisis]. Info-War online news. Retrieved from https://info-war.gr/ellada-i-trapezes-prokalesan-tin-krisi/

Varoufakis, Y. (2016). *And the weak suffer what they must? Europe's crisis and America's economic future*. New York: Nation Books.

Voloshinov, V. (1973). *Marxism and the philosophy of language* (L. Matejka & I. R. Titunik, Trans.). New York: SeminarPress.

Weber, M. (1904). *The Protestant ethic and the spirit of capitalism*. London: Routledge.

5 Discourses of crisis and representation of Greece in a period of austerity

Bessie Mitsikopoulou and Christina Lykou

The discursive construction of crisis in media political discourse

Following the Greek bailout in 2010 and the enforcement of strict austerity policies, different discourses of crisis and representations of Greece appeared in the European and international press which were used to (de)legitimize the politics of austerity. Based on the premise that the crisis is discursively construed and reproduced through the media, this study explores a corpus of articles from two British political magazines on debt crisis and the future of Greece. It particularly draws on the tradition of critical discourse analysis which it combines with corpus linguistics tools in order to explore the ways the Greek case was communicated in public discourses of different political orientation and to investigate changes in discourses and representations during different phases of the crisis.

Political discourse in the media has become the subject of investigation in several disciplines, especially in periods of crisis. The term may refer, according to Lauerbach and Fetzer (2007, p. 15), to the discourse *of* political agents in the media, to the discourse of journalists *with* politicians, or, as is the case in this chapter, to the discourse of journalists *about* politics and political agents in the media. Discourse *about* politics is then defined as journalistic discourse covering genres such as report, analysis, and commentary. The importance of this discourse is that it constitutes the only way through which most people in mediatized mass democracies ever come into contact with politics (Lauerbach & Fetzer, 2007, p. 3). Recently, several discourse studies *about* politics concerning the Eurozone crisis have suggested that this crisis has acted as a critical juncture for identity discourses in Europe. For instance, Bogain (2014) argues that the Eurozone crisis has actually put at stake France's self-identity, while in another study of the Southern European press, Macmillan (2014) identifies an alternative narrative with a Gothic theme (associated with fear and terror) vilifying Germany as responsible for the economic difficulties in the Eurozone periphery.

Overall, crisis research has generally developed along three broad approaches, according to De Rycker and Mohd Don (2013). The first is a political and social theorization which conceptualizes crisis in terms of social change and strategies, and places emphasis on economic, political, cultural, and religious implications. The second is a narrative approach of crisis (Hay, 1996) which conceptualizes crisis as a moment of transition and a process of transformation, constituted in and through narrative. The third, and the one adopted in this chapter, is a discourse analytic approach within the context of social constructionism which argues that crisis is socially and discursively construed, located in specific sociohistorical and cultural contexts (see, for instance, Goutsos & Hatzidaki, 2017; Kutter, 2014; Lampropoulou, 2014; Wodak & Angouri, 2014).

Considering the importance of analyzing the discursive construction of crisis and the role of the media, Stråth and Wodak (2009) argue that media discourses often reflect and reinforce crisis in the public sphere (see, for instance, Juko, 2010) and are responsible for reducing complex processes to certain images (positive or negative) masking accompanying contradictory positions, thus creating a reality which serves specific political interests and relates to normative and dogmatic concepts (Wodak, 2009). For instance, the repeated use of the same metaphors in the Spanish press has been found to lead to a problematic, one-sided interpretation of the crisis (Arrese, 2015). The importance of analyzing the discursive construction of crisis is further supported by studies which connect specific discourses with politicians' inability to offer solutions. In one of these studies, Schmidt (2014) identifies a disconnection between the discourse used by EU leaders at the EU level (what she calls *coordinative discourse*) and the *communicative discourse* that EU leaders use in their attempt to communicate their decisions to the European people and the global markets. This disconnection has, according to Schmidt, significant political effects concerning the continuation of the recent economic crisis. Consequently, the role of the media in this discursive construction, according to Mylonas (2012), is significant both for the mediation of discourses of the social elites to the general public and for the construction of social consensus.

Similarly, the role of mediated discourse regarding austerity is also crucial since it contributes to the legitimation of austerity policies. The mainstream narrative of austerity as necessary in order to deal with the public debts and to ensure a sustainable growth prevails over the less widespread narrative which views austerity as a cause of further economic recession or stagnation (Blyth, 2013) and it is widely reproduced in European media discourse, according to several recent studies. Sommer (2014), for instance, shows how the German media portray austerity as the "only logical and possible consequence both in politics and the public sphere" (p. 22) by construing the European crisis as a state debt crisis and an accumulation of national crises. In this line, the crisis-stricken countries, mainly the southern European countries, are viewed as compelled to conduct rigid austerity measures and budgetary consolidation. The same representation of austerity as the consequence of the economic crisis is developed in the British press regarding the Spanish crisis. As reported by Breeze (2014), the emergence of the North-South dichotomy construes crisis as economic and places its causes on cultural resonance. According to Caldas (2012), the European media have generally construed austerity as the only solution for the economic crisis and have greatly contributed to the emergence of austerity policies as a political priority in Europe.

Greece in the international press

During the beginning of the Eurozone crisis in 2009, Greece was not the only country struggling with the crisis, but it was the only one so negatively represented in the international media, according to Tzogopoulos (2013). This scandalization of the Greek case by the media signaled for Kutter (2014) "a symbolic-catalytic moment with profound policy impact" (p. 447) that both defined the notion of crisis within the specific sociohistorical context and, at the same time, dictated a particular approach to its management in the Eurozone: through austerity and deflation policies.

However, media representations and discourses concerning Greece have generally been found to be quite unstable. For instance, the success story discourse following the 2004 Olympic Games in Athens was replaced a few years later by a spiteful discourse about the corrupt country and its people (Sevastakis & Stavrakakis, 2012). Similarly, the abrupt change from Grexit to Grecovery discourse in 2013 indicates, according to Wodak and Angouri (2014), the dynamics of media accounts and illustrates in the most eloquent way that, far from remaining stable, discourses and representations constantly change to serve the interests of particular social elites.

While recent studies focus on analyzing crisis discourses in the Greek media (e.g., Goutsos & Hatzidaki, 2017), several other discourse and media studies explored how Greece was portrayed in the international press during the crisis. Regarding the first years of the crisis (2009–2011), Antoniades (2012) explored how crisis emerged in the public discourse of different countries and identified three dominant themes (corruption, lack of credibility, and irresponsibility) which damage the image of Greece internationally, emphasizing morality, ethics, and the notion of excess. He concluded that Greece was transformed into a negative signifier and the corrupted 'other' of rational Western society. Conducting a frame analysis of the German tabloid *Bild-Zeitung*, Mylonas (2012) showed that the newspaper systematically concealed information about the structural causes of the crisis, while at the same time vilifying Greek people as Europe's scapegoats. Similarly, Kutter (2014) analyzed editorials from the business daily *Handelsblatt* in terms of content, argumentation, and persuasion discourse strategies, and she found that, in addition to negative stereotypes, the construction of Greece contributed to the legitimation and institutionalization of a specific model of EU governance during the crisis which prioritized austerity measures, cuts in public expenditure, deflationary policies (such as wage cuts), and oversight at the EU level. She also argues that reference to the contagion potential of the Greek crisis justified the implementation of austerity measures across the Eurozone. Focusing on how Europe is represented in the British media through the case of Greece, Touri and Rogers (2014) found a tendency towards localization of the crisis as mainly a Greek problem that resulted from poor economic policies, and not as an EU problem.

Other studies focused on analysis of newspapers after 2012. For instance, Lampropoulou (2014) analyzed articles from *The Guardian* before and after the Greek national elections of 2012 and found a polarized image of the crisis which drew on conflicting representations (in or out of the Eurozone, dependent or independent social actors, collective or individualistic Europe, powerful or powerless), while Angouri and Wodak (2014) claimed that despite discussion of Grecovery in 2013, everyday discourses revealed a deeply troubled sociopolitical and dire economic context in Greece. Similarly, in their analysis of three news magazines, Bickes, Otten, and Weymann (2014) argue that the different metaphors used in different phases of the crisis highlight the dynamics of the crisis as being beyond human control.

Contributing to the body of discourse studies which investigate aspects of the Eurozone crisis and taking into account the powerful role of mediated political discourse in the construction of the crisis, in this chapter we examine discourses of crisis and representations of Greece in two British political magazines of different ideological positioning during different phases of the crisis. We argue that changes in the crisis discourses and representations construed in the public sphere are inextricably associated with changes in the sociopolitical and economic context in different phases of the crisis. We also argue that some representations and discourses of crisis have served as a means for the legitimation of austerity measures and for the construal of the politics of austerity as the only solution. In this chapter, we also show how these discourses and representations are closely related to the political perspective adopted by each magazine.

Specifically, we address the following questions: Which are the prominent discourses with regard to Greece in British political magazines? To what extent does the political orientation of a magazine affect the types of discourses used to construe the crisis? Which crisis discourses and representations of Greece serve as legitimation strategies for imposing austerity policies? What representations of Greece and Greeks permeate prominent discourses? Are there any changes of representations of Greece and Greeks in different periods of the crisis?

Methodology and data

Assuming that the economic crisis in Europe is discursively construed and that the media (re)produce dominant knowledge, ideologies, and representations (van Dijk, 2005), in this chapter we investigate prominent discourses and representations of Greece in the UK press as part of a larger project researching the discursive construction of crisis (cf. Mitsikopoulou & Lykou, 2015; Lykou & Mitsikopoulou, 2017). The concepts of 'discourses' and 'representations' constitute analytic categories which draw on critical discourse analysis and Systemic Functional Linguistics (Fairclough, 2003; Halliday & Matthiessen, 1999, 2004). Methodologically, we employ a qualitative analysis which is assisted by corpus linguistics tools in the tradition of previous discourse studies (see, for instance, Baker, 2009; Baker, Gabrielatos, KhosraviNik, Krzyzanowski, McEnery, & Wodak, 2008; Mautner, 2008, 2009).

Defined as particular ways of representing and acting in the world (physical, social or psychological), discourses relate to people's positioning in the world, and differ in terms of how social events and social actors are represented. Aiming to identify which discourses are used to represent which social events and from whose perspectives, in our investigation we conducted a thematic analysis of the texts in the corpus in order to locate salient patterns in the data through which prominent discourses are realized.

Besides the qualitative analysis of prominent discourses, we also conducted a close grammatical analysis following the Systemic Functional Linguistics (SFL) paradigm in order to investigate the types of representations developed for two main social actors: *Greece* and *Greeks*. SFL adopts a semantic orientation to language, according to which meanings are construed through language choices. These choices are socially and ideologically meaningful since different ways of using language entail different representations of reality (Halliday & Hasan, 1989). This semantic prominence of SFL allows us to identify the different representations of *Greece* and *Greeks* developed in the two political magazines.

Moreover, SFL emphasizes the interrelation between the construed meanings and the sociocultural context in which they are exchanged. Therefore, we can interpret the representations of *Greece* and *Greeks* found in the data in relation to their broader social, cultural, political, and economic context, and in relation to the context of the crisis and the policies of austerity.

In our analysis we focus on the transitivity system, which is the grammatical resource for construing our experience of the world into meanings (Halliday & Matthiessen, 2004). The system of transitivity consists of three main elements: *events* (processes, generally realized as verbs), which constitute the core of the transitivity system as they express actions and events that realize the external and internal experiences; the *interrelated entities* (participants, realized as grammatical subjects, objects or indirect objects of verbs); and the *circumstances* (realized as various types of adverbial elements). The process types and the directly involved participants (Halliday & Matthiessen, 2004, p. 206), which have been used in the analysis of this study are presented in Table 5.1.

The grammatical analysis was assisted by the concordance software Wordsmith Tools 6.0, which was used to locate all instances in the data of the two social actors, i.e., *Greece* and *Greeks*. These instances were then analyzed in terms of processes, participants, and circumstances. The use of this corpus linguistics software proved very effective for both the quantitative and the qualitative parts of our research, since it provided computing frequencies of the search words—in this case *Greeks* and *Greece*—and at the same time it identified specific extracts from a large corpus that helped us to examine qualitatively their concordance environment. By focusing on the prominent grammatical roles assigned to Greece and Greeks and their respective types of processes, we could shed light on the ways they are construed as social actors in different phases of the crisis,

Table 5.1 Process types and participants

Process types	*Category meaning*	*Participants (directly involved)*
Material	'doing'	Actor, Goal
action	'doing'	
event	'happening'	
Behavioral	'behaving'	Behaver
Mental	'sensing'	Senser, Phenomenon
perception	'seeing'	
cognition	'thinking'	
desideration	'wanting'	
emotion	'feeling'	
Verbal	'saying'	Sayer, Target
Relational	'being'	Carrier, Attribute
attribution	'attributing'	Token, Value
identification	'identifying'	
Existential	'existing'	Existent

identify which elements of events are included, excluded, or given prominence in the representation of those events, and explore the different ways the Greek economic crisis was communicated in the public European discourse. Next, we attempted to associate particular discourses with the representations construed in each phase of the crisis and ultimately with the specific sociocultural and economic context both in Greece and in Europe. It should be stated that the aim of the analysis conducted in this study is to provide qualitative evidence of the various representations concerning the two main social actors under investigation, *Greece* and *Greeks*, and not an exhaustive statistical analysis which would be based on a much larger corpus than the one presently selected (Table 5.2).

For our investigation we selected two prestigious British political magazines, *The Spectator* and *New Statesman*. While there has been a lot of research exploring discourses and representations of the crisis in the media of several European countries, such as Germany (e.g. Kutter, 2014; Macmillan, 2014; Mylonas, 2012, 2014; 2015; Sommer, 2014), Spain (e.g. Gomez-O'Cadiz, 2014), and Portugal (e.g. Caldas, 2012; Fonseca & Ferreira, 2015), fewer studies explored the crisis in the UK media (e.g., Bickes, Otten & Weymann, 2014; Touri & Rogers, 2014). Contributing to this body of research, in this chapter we focused on UK political magazines, given the special relationship that the UK held during that time, as a member of the EU but not as a member of the Economic and Monetary Union (EMU).

The Spectator and *New Statesman* were particularly selected on the basis of the following criteria: both are political weekly magazines with a long history and high circulation (they are both in the first top ten in circulation magazines), well known for their quality of political articles and commentaries, and with extensive coverage of the Eurozone crisis. They also adopt clear, although opposing,

Table 5.2 The corpus

	2010–2011	*2012–2014*	*TOTAL*
The Spectator	15,979 words 13 articles	13,948 words 16 articles	29,927 words 29 articles
New Statesman	15,464 words 14 articles	16,429 words 16 articles	31,893 words 30 articles

political ideologies. *The Spectator* has been characterized as having closer ties with the United States rather than with the European Union and as generally adopting a Eurosceptic and a moderately conservative stance, while the *New Statesman* positions itself as having a left-of-center political orientation and is known for its vigorous and satirical analysis of British and international politics (remaining "true to its heritage of radical politics," according to its 2006 editor John Kamfner, as cited in May 29, 2006 issue).

The corpus consists of 59 texts (mainly editorials, feature articles, and reports) and a total of 61,820 words published over a period of 4 years (see Table 5.2 above). The conducted analysis treated the texts in the corpus as a coherent whole belonging to a political magazine of a specific ideological stance and it did not opt for identifying differences among text types. Consequently, the aim of analysis was to shed light on the ways different magazines systematically construe specific discourses and representations of crisis and how these change in different phases of the crisis. Overall, the texts in the corpus are subdivided into two sub-corpora, one including articles published in the period 2010–2011, an early phase of the crisis, and another one with articles published between 2012–2014. Although to a certain extent arbitrary, this distinction serves analytic purposes and is permeated by the following rationale. As the crisis expanded to other European parts from the beginning of 2012, a change was noted in the international press about Greece which was followed by discussions of 'Grecovery' in 2013. It was therefore considered appropriate to study this 'moment' of representational change and to investigate the corpus for similarities and differences across both the two political magazines and the different phases of the crisis.

Prominent discourses in *The Spectator*

The Spectator employs different discourses in the two phases of our data that result in different discursive constructions of the crisis in Greece and representations of austerity. In the first period (2010–2011), *blame*, *punishment*, and *fear of disease* discourses are the most prominent ones, whereas in the second period, *blame discourse* is still prominent (although here differently realized in terms of the target of blaming), while a new discourse of *suffering* emerges.

During 2010–2011, *blame discourse* is primarily used to construe the economic crisis as a local phenomenon, as 'exclusively Greece's fault,' independent of the broader sociopolitical and economic context. Two realizations of blaming are employed throughout this period: a) Greece used false data to enter the Eurozone, and b) the economic crisis is the result of the corruption of the Greek people in general and of Greece's ineffective political and economic management. Both strategies used in this discourse serve the aim to legitimize the austerity policies imposed on the Greek people.

The first strategy is particularly realized through the use of processes such as *lied* and *cheated* (Example 1 below). Interestingly enough, the use of collectivization (van Leeuwen, 1996)[1] is activated to make a direct reference to the people of the country through the national epithet (*Greeks*), which personifies the accusation and highlights their responsibility. The deception of Greece is also manifested in the *Greek fiasco* and the *illusionary numbers*.

Example 1

> The Greeks lied and cheated their way into the Eurozone and letting them get away with it through a bailout threatens the euro with collapse...The Greek fiasco has been a decade in the making... As it turned out, however, the numbers were largely illusionary.
>
> (SP13.1.2010)[2]

An instance of the second blame strategy is illustrated in Example 2, which is targeted to a specific social group, Greek tax collectors, whose profession is directly associated with a—temporary—solution of the financial problems of the Greek state. The representation of the tax collectors as refusing to do their job and even urging Greek citizens to neglect their financial obligations to the State construes the majority of the Greek society as 'tax-dodgers.'

Example 2

> When even the tax collectors are starting to urge non-payment of tax, you can be sure everyone else feels the same way. The tax inspectors tell me they're soon to go on strike. They are even advising fellow Greeks to defy the new 'emergency taxes' on property.
>
> (SP8.10.2011)

Blame attribution in the domestic arena is a commonly used strategy for the legitimation of the imposed austerity policies in the crisis-stricken countries. By construing moralistic representations of the crisis which foreground cultural characteristics, this discourse presents austerity as the only solution.

Tightly connected to moralizing of austerity is a *punishment discourse* which is used to discursively construe the natural consequences of the crisis: since Greece has reached this difficult point because of its own fault, it deserves to be punished and to be left helpless. As Fairclough (2003) states "moral evaluation is one way of producing discursive legitimacy to particular issues (e.g., political decisions) by referring to specific value systems, their imperatives and authority" (p. 98). That is why *punishment discourse* in most cases is accompanied by *blame discourse*, as illustrated in Example 3. At the beginning of the extract, Greece is construed as a member state not worthy of the support of the EU, and immediately afterwards this decision is justified through *blame discourse* on the grounds that Greece became a member of the EMU using false data.

Example 3

> Let Greece go bust. They should let it drown. The best thing the EU can do now is let Greece go broke… After all, if every government that fiddles its books and borrows far more than it can afford gets a blank cheque from Brussels, the euro will very quickly descend into a joke currency.
>
> (SP13.1.2010)

In the case of austerity, as stated by Mylonas (2015), the values relating to the ideological premises of austerity are based on the idea of market justice, where the guilty ones should pay. Therefore, since the Greek people are construed as fully responsible for the crisis, austerity took the form of moral punishment "that would reform the corrupt Greek. The culturalist crisis-rationales moralize austerity as a primarily educative or disciplinary program" (Mylonas, 2014, p. 311).

The *fear of disease discourse* also adds to the localized character of the crisis. The economic crisis in Greece is construed as a poisonous disease, restricted only to Greece, that, if spread, would 'contaminate' the other member states (e.g., *The sovereign-debt threat is still out there and spreading: no one knows whether the containment will work, or where the poison will come ashore*, SP5.5.2010). Another instance (Example 4) builds upon a doctor-patient—unequal by default—relationship between Germans on the one hand, and Greeks and the other southern European countries on the other: the latter seem to suffer from lack of fiscal discipline, which is presented as a disease.

Example 4

> German monetary policymakers would prefer to eject the Greeks and weaker euro members. This is unthinkable for the political leadership in Berlin, who are talking about injecting some Teutonic fiscal discipline into the southern fringe.
>
> (SP16.6.2010)

Similar discursive constructions of Greece as *a sick body* (Mylonas, 2014, pp. 310–311) and *a contagious virus and a disease-driven symptom* (Bickes, Otten, & Weymann, 2014, p. 430) are described in previous studies, together with the fear of *an epidemic* (Kutter, 2014, p. 458) and *a metastasis effect* (Tzogopoulos, 2013, p. 76).

In the second period of the crisis (2012–2014), the target of blame shifts although the local character of the economic crisis remains a key representation. The focus now lies on specific social and professional groups, which are represented as indirectly responsible for the economic crisis Greece has to endure. These groups are lawyers, doctors, and engineers who avoided declaring their exact income and thus paying the due taxes, corrupt politicians and wealthy Greeks who transferred their deposits to foreign banks (*cash exodus*), owners of super-yachts, and the Greeks who invested in the real estate of foreign countries, of the UK in particular (see Example 5 below).

Example 5

> ...of Greek holders of accounts in Luxembourg and Liechtenstein, Greek owners of super-yachts registered in the Netherlands, and (this one getting longer by the day) Greek buyers of luxury properties in London...
>
> (SP26.1.2013)

Specific groups of citizens are singled out since they are not represented through the collectivized *Greeks* and are thus dissociated from the rest of the Greek society, a strategy also largely employed in the first period of the crisis. These groups of citizens were also clearly differentiated in the data from working-class people. Example 6 below is indicative of this strategy: street cleaners—hard working people—start their work at the same hour as the young people of wealthy Greek families finish their night's amusement, after having spent a large amount of money.

Example 6

> Despite the austerity, young Greeks say they will never sacrifice their nightlife and here is the proof... The respectable hour to leave is when all the carnations have been thrown and the street cleaners are starting their morning shift.
>
> (SP19.4.2014)

While not including all of Greek society, the above extract still emphasizes the cultural characteristics of the Greek people, shifting the target of blame from structural to cultural characteristics, as "the deeper layer of the crisis' truth" (Mylonas, 2014, p. 312).

In agreement with the change of focus in blame discourse, a *suffering discourse* is employed in the second period of the crisis, which highlights the severe problems and difficulties Greek people have to endure. The same strategy of differentiating working-class people from social groups of wealthy Greek citizens is employed through this discourse, in which working-class people are voiced to express the difficulties they have to face. In Example 7, for instance, a factory worker and a technician describe their problematic financial situation:

Example 7

> 'It upsets me that they believe we get high wages. Our wages are very low,' says Alexis Athanasios, a factory worker. 'We can't even afford to support our families.' Haris Manolis, a 38-year-old technician, resents Germany for wanting 'to come here and open factories with cheap labour.'
>
> (SP19.5.2012)

Moreover, dramatic descriptions of poverty due to the austerity policies and measures unfold, which picture an unbearable situation for the Greek people (e.g., *Dr Giorgos Vihas, a volunteer cardiologist at the clinic, sometimes cannot believe the problems he's treating: men and women sick from eating out of bins; five-month-old babies underweight because the parents can't afford milk*, SP19.5.2012). During 2012–2014, media representations of the 'lazy/corrupt Greeks' are replaced with representations of a society facing a humanitarian crisis and acute social problems as a result of austerity policies. This shift in the representations of Greek society is a finding reported in other studies as well (see, for instance, Kouki, 2014). "As the crisis progresses and its effects on people start becoming visible, media texts focus on individual stories of poverty, unemployment, job hunting and desperation and the tone becomes more moderate and less offending towards Greece," argue Bickes, Otten and Weymann (2014, p. 439).

Representations of Greeks and Greece in *The Spectator*

Transitivity analysis of *The Spectator* sub-corpus 2010–2011 (see Table 5.3 below) reveals a representation of *Greeks* as dynamic social actors who have the power to act autonomously. However, this is a negative representation which assigns Greek people responsibility for the crisis and the financial problems the country is facing. The most common grammatical role of *Greeks* is Actors in material processes and especially in material processes of negative semantic load (6 times—e.g., *The Greeks cheated their way into the Eurozone. After all, the Greeks pioneered default as well as democracy*), or of negative polarity (4 times—e.g., *The Greeks weren't only not fixing the roof while the sun was shining: they were selling off the slates on the assumption rain had been abolished*). The other grammatical roles highlight this representation, and *Greeks* are represented either as Actors in material intransitive processes (3 times—e.g., *who would rather riot in the streets than accept reasonable austerity measures*), as Sayers in verbal processes (3 times—e.g., *they lied*) and as Sensers in mental processes (3 times—e.g., *it feels to these tax inspectors, and to Greeks in general, like humiliation. They feel trapped in an inescapable relationship with sadistic Germany*). The dynamic image of *Greeks* as independent and autonomous social actors is associated with the *blame* discourse employed by *The Spectator* in the first period of the crisis, which puts the Greek people at the center of blaming: since they are free to act autonomously, they are rendered solely responsible for the crisis—either because of their untrustworthiness (false data, corruption) or because of their ineffectiveness in management. Besides construing a localized view of the crisis as irrespective of the European and global context, this representation legitimizes the imposition of austerity policies.

Turning to the image of *Greece* in the first period (2010–2011), we see that, through its main grammatical role as Goal in material processes (13 times), it is represented as a powerless member state subjected to the acts of other social actors, especially other EU member states, which may occasionally be implied (e.g., *Let Greece go bust*), or even non-human actors (e.g., *profligacy and corruption … led Greece to ruin*). This representation relates to both *punishment* and *blame* discourses employed by *The Spectator* in this phase of the crisis: since the main responsibility for the crisis it is facing is ascribed to *Greece*, it has to suffer the consequences of its own actions, which may result in its financial abandonment by its co-members of the EU or even its bankruptcy. In addition, as Actor in material intransitive processes (10 times), although not directly affecting other participants grammatically, Greece's actions are presented as conditions for disastrous effects on others (e.g., *if Greece falls, then so too will the euro; when Greece defaults, Ireland will go down next*). This representation is strongly related to the *fear of disease discourse* employed by this magazine during 2010–2011, through which crisis is construed as a disease threatening to 'contaminate' the other member states. Through the same grammatical role, *Greece* is also represented as a powerless social actor dependent on the acts and decisions of other participants, a representation that is associated with *punishment discourse* (e.g., *It's up to the EU as a whole to decide whether Greece sinks or swims*).

In the second period of the crisis (2012–2014), the representation of *Greeks* shifts from their role as independent actors to social actors who have feelings and beliefs but have to endure the acts and decisions of other social actors (see Table 5.3 below). This representation is realized through their main grammatical role as Sensers in mental processes (6 times—e.g., *Whereas the Greeks are outraged by the scale of the cuts in salaries and government budgets, the Germans point in indignation to the staggering increases*) and Goals in material processes (4 times—e.g., *the ruinous culture of entitlement that pervades the southern eurozone has brought the Greeks into a new form of slavery*), both of which point to the Greek people's negative feelings and anxiety concerning austerity policies, and the extremely difficult situation they are forced to face. It is also strongly related to the *suffering discourse* employed by *The Spectator* during 2012–2014, which sheds light on Greece's severe economic problems and difficulties, especially regarding working-class people. Though their role as actors is minimized in this phase, it contributes to the construction of a negative representation for wealthy Greeks, as it involves processes of negative semantic load (see Example 5 above), a representation associated with the *blame discourse* employed by the magazine, which is targeted only to the groups of wealthy Greek citizens and not to the Greek people as a whole.

Greece in this period is grammatically realized through its role as Carrier in relational processes (6 times—e.g., *Greece is in its sixth year of recession and crisis,*

Table 5.3 Representations of *Greeks* and *Greece* in *The Spectator*

2010–2011		*2012–2014*	
GREEKS			
Grammatical role	*Frequency*	*Grammatical role*	*Frequency*
Actors in material processes of negative semantic load	6	Sensers in mental processes	6
Actors in material processes of negative polarity	4	Goals in material processes	4
Actors in material intransitive processes	3	Carriers in relational attributive or possessive processes	3
Goals in material processes	3	Sayers in verbal processes	3
Sensers in mental processes	3	Actors in material processes of negative semantic load	2
Sayers in verbal processes	3	Actors in material intransitive processes	1
Actors in material processes	2		
GREECE			
Grammatical role	*Frequency*	*Grammatical role*	*Frequency*
Goal in material processes	13	Carrier in relational attributive or possessive processes	6
Actor in material intransitive processes	10	Actor in material intransitive processes	5
Carrier in relational attributive or possessive processes	7	Goal in material processes	4
Actor in material processes	3	Actor in material processes	3
Senser in mental processes	1	Senser in mental processes	2
Part of prepositional phrases or nominal groups as possessive determiner	21	Part of prepositional phrases or nominal groups as possessive determiner	28

Greece will be out of the euro rather quickly), thus highlighting the difficult situation in Greece. This representation relates to the *suffering discourse* employed by *The Spectator* in this second period of the crisis, which focuses on the severe problems the Greek society endures, especially working-class people. In addition, the weak position of Greece as a member state and its compliance to the acts and decisions of others is grammatically realized by its role as Goal in material processes (4 times—e.g., *They complain that Germany wants to reduce Greece to Bulgarian levels of poverty*) and as Actor in material intransitive processes (5 times—e.g., *Greece descends into civic collapse and violent exit from the euro*). This representation is also associated with the *suffering discourse* employed in this period by this magazine.

Prominent discourses in *New Statesman*

Unlike *The Spectator*, in *New Statesman* similar discourses are employed in the two periods of the crisis promoting a diachronically systematic representation of the political and economic crisis. Three prominent discourses include *blame* and *suffering discourse*, which have also been found in *The Spectator* corpus, as well as a new discourse, a *historical discourse*.

In the first period of the crisis (2010–2011), blame attribution emphasizes the causes of the crisis which are here viewed not in local or cultural terms but in relation to the broader politics of a global monetary system as well as the EU context. The responsibility of the global financial system is stressed in the following example, which characterizes what happened in Greece as *theft on an epic scale*. The help provided to Greece is challenged here through the use of quotation marks in *'rescue'* while the IMF is considered *a product of a grotesque financial system*.

Example 8

> This crisis that has led to Greece's 'rescue' by European banks and the International Monetary Fund is the product of a grotesque financial system that itself is in crisis... What has happened in Greece is theft on an epic, though not unfamiliar, scale.
>
> (NS21.5.2010)

In general, blame attribution in this sub-corpus systematically lies with the European Central Bank and distinguished European leaders (e.g., *...but the incompetence of the European Central Bank (ECB) along with the French President, Nicolas Sarkozy, and Germany's Chancellor, Angela Merkel, has made a further crisis ever more likely*, NS24.6.2011).

By interpreting the crisis in relation to the EU context, its systemic character is construed either by the inclusion of other European countries as co-participants with Greece (e.g., *First Greece and now Ireland have highlighted the weaknesses in the Eurozone—and have been savaged by the bond markets in the process,* NS3.12.2010), or by referring only to other European countries (except Greece), especially those of the South (e.g., *The crisis has spread to Ireland and Portugal, and the cross hairs have moved to Spain, Belgium, Italy and perhaps even beyond. Growth has been compromised and unemployment is rising in countries that have imposed austerity measures*, NS24.6.2011).

In the second period of the crisis (2012–2014), the focus of blame changes and emphasis lies on the negative consequences of the imposed austerity policies, as well as on the social actors who impose austerity measures. The main target of *blame discourse* during this period in relation to social actors is Angela Merkel. Merkel's persistence for austerity policies as a cure to the crisis is construed as catastrophic for Europe's recovery and economic growth (e.g., *Angela Merkel's mania for austerity is destroying Europe... whose solution to Europe's financial crisis—or lack thereof—has brought the continent, and perhaps the world, to the edge of a second Great Depression*, NS20.6.2012), and characterized as 'deficit fetishism' and 'obsession' that *threatens to upset more than six decades of pan-European unity and stability*. In one of the articles in the data, Helmut Kohl, one of the founders of the EU, is reported to have stated, *"Merkel is destroying my Europe"* (NS9.12.2013).

By focusing on the negative consequences of the crisis as not restricted only to Greece but as affecting all of Europe and even the whole world, as in the above examples, and by excluding direct reference to Greece, the *New Statesman* sub-corpus stresses the European and global dimensions of the economic crisis. To this end, the problem of youth unemployment caused by austerity policies is presented as a major issue for three European countries, not just for Greece (e.g., *Merkel prefers to fiddle as Athens burns—and Madrid and Rome, too. Youth unemployment in Spain and Greece is hovering around 50 per cent*, NS20.6.2012).

Construing crisis as a systemic phenomenon takes into perspective, the role of the Eurozone "to produce further contradictions in the uneven geopolitical and economic [...], as well as in the socio-culturally diverse, context of the EU" and sees the role of Greece "as that of a periphery European country tied to the interests of the EU's core countries" (Mylonas, 2015, p. 250). Furthermore, this systemic view deconstructs austerity policies as a no-alternative solution for the crisis and highlights its European and global nature, which calls for a collective solution that is not restricted to particular countries.

The delegitimation of austerity policies is also construed through *suffering discourse*. *New Statesman* highlights the unbearable situation the Greek society has been obliged to undergo. In a systematic and diachronic way, in both periods under study, the focus lies on the financial problems that ordinary people face and on the consequences of austerity policies: unemployment, reductions in salaries and pensions, general deterioration of the public sector (e.g., *And when years of extreme austerity measures stretch out before a population, pensions are slashed, public spending is squeezed*, NS5.11.2011). However, the Greek case is not singled out here either. The effects of austerity policies are presented to be the same in Greece as in America and Britain, highlighting the view of the crisis in a broader European and global context (e.g., *In Greece, as in America and Britain, the ordinary people have been told they must repay the debts of the rich and powerful who incurred them. Jobs, pensions and public services are to be slashed and burned*, NS21.5.2010).

As the crisis extends, the difficulties augmented by austerity policies become issues of survival and, according to Eurostat (2012), this recession in Greece is the most severe recession ever experienced by an established democracy. Austerity measures caused not only unemployment, but also an increase in suicides and decrease in birth rate (e.g., *One in four Greeks is unemployed; more than half of the country's youth cannot find work. Suicides are up; the birth rate is down*, NS9.12.2013). The next example stresses the catastrophic consequences of these policies and presents austerity measures as the cause of death of a young girl:

Example 9

> On 1 December, a 13-year-old girl died after inhaling carbon monoxide fumes in the Greek city of Thessaloniki. She and her unemployed mother had been trying to use a makeshift stove to heat their freezing flat, having had their electricity cut off several months earlier. In Greece, austerity continues to kill.
>
> (NS9.12.2013)

A historical discourse is also employed by *New Statesman* in a consistent way during both periods: historical accounts of specific events from European history are drawn in order to provide a coherent understanding of the present crisis. By placing the current crisis in its sociohistorical context, these texts offer an alternative perspective to the dominant narrative and serve to deconstruct the localized dimension of the crisis. For instance, one account focuses on the London Debt Agreement, 60 years ago, to remind a case of debt forgiveness in the history of Europe, thanks to which the debtor country, Germany, succeeded in improving its economy and even becoming a world economic power (e.g., *Few historians would dispute that the astounding growth of the postwar German economy and the ascent of Germany to world economic power status wouldn't have happened without the London Debt Agreement*, NS9.12.2013). What renders this historical flashback powerful are the reverse roles that the participants have, compared to the current situation, as the debtor country was Germany and one of its creditors was Greece. In this case, *New Statesman* is drawing on history to highlight the inexcusable German obsession with policies of punishment and to suggest other alternative ways of dealing with the economic crisis. Similarly, another account of a more recent event seeks to identify the roots of the recent economic crisis in the principles agreed upon in the Maastricht Treaty of 1992: neoliberalism and monetary discipline of all member states (e.g., *Maastricht wrote the principles of an economic doctrine into a political constitution. The doctrine was neoliberalism... In Europe, however, there was an added imperative for monetary discipline: countries on the periphery of the EU would boom on entry, boosting inflation*, NS21.5.2010.2). The negative role of the European Central Bank, which exerted a rigid monetarism, is also stressed (e.g., *How we got from there to a continent-wide fiscal crisis is a story of blind adherence to neoliberal and monetarist norms—at the ECB and in Berlin*, NS21.5.2010.2)

Representations of *Greeks* and *Greece* in *New Statesman*

Unlike *The Spectator*, *New Statesman* texts have a lower frequency of *Greeks* as social actors, particularly in the first period of the crisis (see Table 5.4 below). The avoidance of direct reference to the people of the country through the national epithet, which personifies the accusation as it refers to distinct people, dissociates Greeks from the negative evolvement of the economic crisis. This representation is related to *blame discourse* as employed by *New Statesman*, according to which the economic crisis is a global issue directly associated with broader socioeconomic conditions. The grammatical role of *Greeks* in the texts of this political magazine is mainly Goal in material processes (5 times—e.g., *The re-establishment of the German mark would help not only the Greeks, but also the Irish, the Spaniards and even us*) or Actors in material intransitive processes (3 times—e.g., *The Greeks could leave, he suggests, initially floating the currency at the rate of 1 drachma to €1, and return at, say, 1.3 drachmas to €1*), grammatical roles which construe the Greek people's inability to act autonomously as powerful social actors and stress their image as 'victims.'

Representations of Greece in the first period describe the situation in Greece in the context of the economic crisis. The grammatical role mostly applied to Greece is Carrier in relational attributive and possessive processes that ascribe particular characteristics to Greece (13 times—e.g., *Greece is a microcosm of a modern class war rarely reported as such; Greece now has a national unity government under an unelected economist).* The powerless position of Greece as a member state obliged to comply with the acts of others is construed through its grammatical role of Goal in material processes (7 times—e.g., *Angela Merkel's insistence on continued austerity may indeed be reducing Greece to penury*) or, less frequently, as Actor in material intransitive processes (4 times—e.g., *They may be expecting Greece to leave the euro, which is a possibility*). This representation relates to the blame attribution strategy employed by *New Statesman* in this phase of the crisis, which deconstructs the 'local' character of the crisis and views it in a global and EU context.

The systemic character of the economic crisis—a prominent feature in the *New Statesman* sub-corpus of the first period of the crisis—is grammatically construed in two ways: a) Greece as co-participant in nominal groups with other member states that have been affected by the crisis, thus rejecting the argument of the localized interpretation of the crisis and viewing it in a broader socioeconomic European and global context (e.g., *First Greece and now Ireland have highlighted the weaknesses in the Eurozone; Greece, Portugal and Spain are, as the euphemism has it, 'young democracies'*), and b) Greece as part of a group of other member states, by the use of the inclusive term *Mediterranean countries*, which creates in-group relations among Greece and the other members of the Mediterranean (e.g., *The Mediterranean countries need to increase their productivity to pursue the long-term goal of harmonizing Ireland and the Mediterranean with the industrialized countries of northern Europe*).

In the second period of the crisis (2012–2014), the emphasis on the representation of Greeks shifts from their dissociation from the origins and causes of the

Table 5.4 Representations of *Greeks* and *Greece* in *New Statesman*

2010–2011		*2012–2014*	
GREEKS			
Grammatical role	*Frequency*	*Grammatical role*	*Frequency*
Goals in material processes	5	Actors in material intransitive processes	4
Actors in material intransitive processes	3	Carriers in relational attributive or possessive processes	4
Actors in material processes	2	Sensers in mental processes	2
Part of prepositional phrases or nominal groups as possessive determiner	2	Actors in material processes	2
		Goals in material processes	1
		Part of prepositional phrases or nominal groups as possessive determiner	6
GREECE			
Grammatical role	*Frequency*	*Grammatical role*	*Frequency*
Carrier in relational attributive or possessive processes	13	Goal in material processes	13
Goal in material processes	7	Actor in material intransitive processes	10
Actor in material intransitive processes	4	Carrier in relational attributive or possessive processes	5
Actor in material processes	2	Actor in material processes	5
Part of prepositional phrases or nominal groups as possessive determiner	53	Senser in mental processes	4
		Phenomenon in mental processes	2
		Sayer in verbal processes	1
		Part of prepositional phrases or nominal groups as possessive determiner	64

economic crisis, which was mainly developed in the first period, to the effects of austerity measures and severe difficulties Greek people face, a representation which is strongly related to *suffering discourse* employed by *New Statesman*. In particular, *Greeks* are represented as Carriers in relational attributive and possessive processes (4 times—e.g., *One in four Greeks is unemployed; A harsh summer that will bring hikes in electricity bills will find Greeks once again in discomfort*), with an emphasis on the social problems Greeks are facing, such as unemployment and poverty. The same representation is construed through their role as Actors in material intransitive processes (4 times—e.g., *Greeks are protesting*), where the emphasis is put on their difficult working and living conditions.

In the second period of the crisis, the image of Greece as a social actor also changes in *New Statesman*. The focus now is not on the descriptive characteristics of Greece but rather on the actions concerning Greece, either as a social entity subjected to the acts of other participants (as Goal, 13 times), or as Actor in acts that affect only itself, in material intransitive processes (10 times). In particular, through its role as Goal, a deconstruction of the blame on Greece regarding the crisis is attempted, pointing to the responsibility of the banking system and the ineffective policies imposed on the country (e.g., *Now, the IMF admits that forcing Greece and other debt-burdened countries to reduce their deficits too quickly would be counterproductive*). This representation is associated with the blame strategy adopted by *New Statesman*. By its role as Actor in material intransitive processes, emphasis is put on the attempts of Greece to face the crisis and reduce the suffering of its people (*"Greece has turned a corner" is the general message Yannis Stournaras, the Greek Finance Minister, has been trying to spread in the past few months*), which relates to *suffering discourse*.

Discussion

Focusing on the politics of representation of the crisis in the UK press, this study has found different discursive constructions of the economic crisis and Greece in two political magazines, as the crisis unfolded. *The Spectator* adopts an inconsistent view of Greece and Greeks in the two periods of the crisis, which is illustrated in the change of discourses employed by this magazine in the two periods. In the beginning of the crisis, through *blame*, *punishment*, and *fear of disease* discourses, *The Spectator* construes the Greek people as the main agents responsible for the crisis, who should suffer the consequences of their own actions. This image of Greece is aligned with the one described by Tzogopoulos (2013) "of a country which is responsible for its own tragic fate and one which seems like a great problem for the EU, not only by cooking the books and providing false statistics but also by failing to implement reforms" (p. 103).

In the second period, especially through the emergence of *suffering discourse*, this magazine's focus lies on the consequences of the crisis and the suffering of the Greek people from austerity measures, whereas blame is now targeted to the groups of wealthy Greek citizens and politicians. This change in the discursive construction of the crisis and Greece relates to changes in the broader political and social context, domestic as well as European, as the crisis unfolds and the negative consequences of austerity policies become more obvious. The same shift in representation of the crisis has been reported in other media studies of the same period (see Bickes, Otten & Weymann, 2014). However, it should be noted that both representations point to a localized interpretation of the crisis: whether the focus lies on the responsibility of the Greek people or on the problems they have to endure, the crisis is seen as a 'local' issue, created in Greece by Greeks, and as entirely independent of the broader sociopolitical and economic context.

This localized view of the crisis, which is found in many media crisis studies in several countries, serves as a justification for the politics of austerity. Construing crisis as a local phenomenon, independent of the politics of a global monetary system and the broader EU context, defines the treatment of the crisis in local terms and thus legitimizes austerity measures implemented in the crisis-stricken European countries, as the only 'remedy' for the crisis. For instance, in a diachronic study of crisis discourses and representations in the Greek media (Lykou & Mitsikopoulou, 2017), we found that blame attribution in local terms is a strategy used in all periods of the crisis thus far. Similarly to our findings in the present study, blame was found to be attributed not only to the ineffective Greek economic policies and political choices, but also to the cultural characteristics of the Greek people and Greek society in general. The diachronic development of the self-blaming strategy construes a localized view of the crisis through which the severe austerity measures imposed on the Greek society are legitimized and people's resistance is minimized. It also encourages an uncritical adoption of the neoliberal explanations of the European elite concerning the origins and causes of the crisis, according to Pleios (2013).

This legitimation strategy of self-blaming has been widely used in media discourses of other crisis-stricken countries, such as Spain (Gomez-O'Cadiz, 2014) and Portugal (Fonseca & Ferreira, 2015). Besides blaming foreign governments and institutions, local Spanish governmental policies and corrupted politicians, Spanish crisis discourses employ self-blaming and foreground the cultural characteristics of the Spanish people, who are described as uncultured, lazy, and indifferent towards weak governmental practices. Similarly, in Portugal blame attribution was supported by a 'state of exception' rhetoric which was used to legitimize austerity policies and their negative consequences in wages, retirement pensions, and unemployment benefits. According to this rhetoric, the country faces a state of political emergency which demands the temporal suspension of the legal order, and thus legitimizes measures that were politically and socially unacceptable under 'normal times.'

Unlike *The Spectator*, *New Statesman* construes a diachronically consistent view of the crisis throughout the two periods: the crisis is interpreted in relation to a global and European socioeconomic system, as a systemic matter of neoliberal economic policies that has affected (or will eventually affect) all European member states. This particular view of the crisis permeates all three discourses in *New Statesman*—*blame*, *suffering*, and *historical discourses*—which are used consistently in both periods of the crisis described in the study. Regarding the representations of Greeks and Greece, although the emphasis in each phase may differ, focusing on either their dissociation from the causes of the crisis or the consequences of austerity measures, they are both consistent with the magazine's view of 'institutionalization' of the crisis, that is the disengagement of the country from any responsibility concerning the origins and causes of the crisis. This systemic view of the crisis deconstructs the legitimation of austerity policies as the only solution to the crisis in the crisis-stricken countries, and presents it as a systemic European crisis that calls for major reforms in the economic policies, as well as the political decisions, of the EU.

These different views of the crisis are closely related to the general ideological platform each magazine adheres to. The magazine of a conservative orientation, *The Spectator*, is found to adopt a localized view of the crisis, putting Greece and Greek people at the center of blame and thus construing austerity policies as a consequence of the country's stance and the only solution for the crisis. On the other hand, *New Statesman,* the magazine of a left-of-center political orientation, is found to foreground the negative effects and the ineffectiveness of austerity policies in a systemic crisis placed in the broader European context.

Similar conceptualizations of the crisis have been found in a study by Lykou and Mitsikopoulou (2017), which investigated two Greek newspapers from different political orientations. The newspaper of conservative orientation was found to employ diachronically a more self-reflective perspective, treating Greece and the Greek people as 'blame takers' for the crisis along with the EU. On the other hand, the newspaper of a moderate center-left orientation foregrounded the systemic nature of the crisis, placing it within the European and global context, especially at the beginning of the crisis.

Conclusion

This study has investigated how discourses of crisis and representations of Greeks and Greece developed in two political magazines are used to (de)legitimize austerity policies in the British press. It has identified two main trends associated with different political orientations. The representations of crisis in the local trend are in line with the dominant discourses of crisis construed by European elites and reproduced in the media discourse of many European countries: the crisis as decontextualized from the broader economic European and global context. An alternative discourse was developed in the second trend which adopted a systemic view of the crisis and placed its discussion in broader sociohistorical contexts. Still, however, the impact of this discourse still remains to be seen, since it is still a peripheral discourse in the European arena.

What is of particular interest in the study is the way in which *blame discourses* have been used to legitimize and delegitimize austerity policies in these trends. The legitimation of austerity policies through moralistic and technocratic representations is a form of public manipulation which promotes a neoliberal ideological position for Europe, foregrounding a "non-systemic analysis of the crisis and a non-political understanding of its solutions" while at the same time excluding alternatives and agencies of alternatives (Mylonas 2015, p. 255).

This legitimation of austerity policies along with the similar crisis discourses developed across the continent, which promoted a neoliberal approach to the crisis in European media discourses, has contributed to the citizens' alienation from the EU and the process of European integration. As Murray-Leach, Kouki, Mattes, Mollenkamp, Radice, Saltman, & Sommer (2014) point out, the construal of the crisis as an abstract entity (rather than as the result of political and economic choices), as well as the construal of crisis discourses as discourses of elites (that is, of remote bureaucratic executives and not as citizens' discourse) resulted in a de-politicization not only of the crisis but also of the European institutions.

Notes

1 See van Leuween (1996) for a sociosemiotic account of the representations of social actors.

2 The following abbreviation system has been adopted to refer to the examples used in this text. The first two letters identify the magazine (SP: *The Spectator*, NS: *New Statesman*) followed by the date of publication (day, month, year).

References

Angouri, J., & Wodak, R. (2014). 'They became big in the shadow of the crisis': The Greek success story and the rise of the far right. *Discourse & Society, 25*(4), 540–565.

Antoniades, A. (2012). *At the eye of the cyclone: The Greek crisis in global media*. Athens: ACIPE.

Baker, P. (Ed.). (2009). *Contemporary corpus linguistics*. London: Continuum.

Baker, P., Gabrielatos, C., KhosraviNik, M., Krzyzanowski, M., McEnery, T., & Wodak, R. (2008). A useful methodological synergy? Combining critical discourse analysis and corpus linguistics to examine discourses of refugees and asylum seekers in the UK press. *Discourse & Society, 19*(3), 273–306.

Bickes, H., Otten, T., & Weymann, L. C. (2014). The financial crisis in the German and English press: Metaphorical structures in the media coverage on Greece, Spain and Italy. *Discourse & Society, 25*(4), 424–445.

Blyth, M. (2013). *Austerity: The history of a dangerous idea*. New York: Oxford University Press.

Bogain, A. (2014). Demons, ants, giants and dwarves: The construction of Germany's handling of the euro crisis in French political discourse. *Journal of Contemporary European Studies, 22*(1), 7–23.

Breeze, R. (2014). Perspectives on North and South: The 2012 financial crisis in Spain seen through two major British newspapers. *Discourse & Communication, 8*(3), 241–259.

Caldas, J. C. (2012). *The consequences of austerity policies in Portugal*. Friedrich Ebert Stiftung, August, International Policy Analysis. Available at: http://library.fes.de/pdf-files/idmoe/09311.pdf

De Rycker, A., & Mohd Don, Z. (2013). Discourse in crisis, crisis in discourse. In A. De Rycker & Z. Mohd Don (Eds.), *Discourse and crisis: Critical perspectives* (pp. 3–66). Amsterdam, Netherlands: John Benjamins.

Eurostat. (2012). *Real GDP growth rate: 1990–2013*. Retrieved from: http://epp.eurostat.ec.europa.eu/tgm/table.do?tab'Otable&init'O1&plugin'O1&language'Oen&pcode'Otec00115

Fairclough, N. (2003). *Analyzing discourse: Textual analysis for social research*. London: Routledge.

Fonseca, P., & Ferreira, M. J. (2015). Through 'seas never before sailed': Portuguese government discursive legitimation strategies in a context of financial crisis. *Discourse & Society, 26*(6), 682–711.

Gomez-O'Cadiz, M. (2014). Expressing criticism, emotionality and community in the Spanish socioeconomic crisis. *The Journal for Undergraduate Ethnography, 4*(1), 40–51.

Goutsos, D., & Hatzidaki, O. (Eds.). (2017). *Crisis and conflict in contemporary Greece: Integrating critical discourse analysis and corpus linguistics*. Amsterdam, Netherlands. John Benjamins.

Halliday, M. A. K., & Hasan, R. (1989). *Language, context and text: Aspects of language in a social-semiotic perspective* (2nd ed.). Oxford: Oxford University Press.

Halliday, M. A. K., & Matthiessen, C. M. I. M. (1999). *Construing experience through meaning: A language-based approach to cognition*. London: Cassell.

Halliday, M. A. K., & Matthiessen, C. M. I. M. (2004). *An introduction to functional grammar* (3rd ed.). London: Arnold.

Hay, C. (1996). Narrating crisis: The discursive construction of the 'Winter of Discontent'. *Sociology, 30*(2), 253–277.

Juko, S. (2010). Have the media made the Greek crisis worse? *Economic Sociology, 12*(1), 28–41.

Kouki, H. (2014). European crisis discourses: The case of Greece. In T. Murray-Leach, H. Kouki, D. Mattes, D. Mollenkamp, H. Radice, E. M., Saltman, & M. Sommer (Eds.), *Crisis discourses in Europe: Media EU-phemisms and alternative narratives* (pp. 16–20). London: London School of Economics and Political Science.

Kutter, A. (2014). A catalytic moment: The Greek crisis in the German financial press. *Discourse & Society, 25*(4), 446–466.

Lampropoulou, S. (2014). 'Greece will decide the future of Europe': The recontextualisation of the Greek national elections in a British broadsheet newspaper. *Discourse & Society, 25*(4), 467–482.

Lauerbach, G. E., & Fetzer, A. (2007). Political discourse in the media: Cross-cultural perspectives. In G. E. Lauerbach & A. Fetzer (Eds.), *Political discourse in the media* (pp. 3–28). Amsterdam, Netherlands: John Benjamins.

Lykou, C., & Mitsikopoulou, B. (2017). The chronicle of an ongoing crisis: Diachronic media representations of Greece and Europe in the Greek press. In D. Goutsos & O. Hatzidaki (Eds.), *Crisis and conflict in contemporary Greece: Integrating critical discourse analysis and corpus linguistics* (pp. 111–147). Amsterdam, Netherlands: John Benjamins.

Macmillan, C. (2014). The return of the Reich? A gothic tale of Germany and the Eurozone crisis. *Journal of Contemporary European Studies, 22*(1), 24–38.

Mautner, G. (2008). Analyzing newspapers, magazines and other print media. In R. Wodak & M. Krzyzanowski (Eds.), *Qualitative discourse analysis in the social sciences* (pp. 30–53). Houndmills, Basingstoke, UK: Palgrave Macmillan.

Mautner, G. (2009). Checks and balances. How corpus linguistics can contribute to CDA. In R. Wodak & M. Meyer (Eds.), *Methods of critical discourse analysis* (2nd ed.) (pp. 122–143). London: Sage.

Mitsikopoulou, B., & Lykou, C. (2015). The discursive construction of the recent European economic crisis in two political magazines. *On The Horizon, 23*(3), 190–201.

Murray-Leach, T., Kouki, H., Mattes, D., Mollenkamp, D., Radice, H., Saltman, E. M., & Sommer, M. (Eds.) (2014). *Crisis discourses in Europe. Media EU-phemisms and alternative narratives*. London: London School of Economics and Political Science.

Mylonas, Y. (2012). Media and the economic crisis of the EU: The 'culturalization' of a systemic crisis and Bild-Zeitung's framing of Greece. *TripleC, 10*(2), 646–671.

Mylonas, Y. (2014). Crisis, austerity and opposition in mainstream media discourses of Greece. *Critical Discourse Studies, 11*(3), 305–321.

Mylonas, Y. (2015). Austerity discoursed in "Der Spiegel" journal, 2009–2014. *TripleC, 13*(2), 248–269.

Pleios, G. (2013). The media against the crisis. In G. Pleios (Ed.), *The crisis and the media* (pp. 87–134). Athens: Papazisis.

Schmidt, V. A. (2014). Speaking to the markets or to the people? A discursive institutionalist analysis of the EU's sovereign debt crisis. *The British Journal of Politics and International Relations, 16*, 188–209.

Sevastakis, N., & Stavrakakis, Y. (2012). *Populism, antipopulism and the crisis*. Athens: Nefeli Publications.

Sommer, M. (2014). European crisis discourses: The case of Germany. In T. Murray-Leach, H. Kouki, D. Mattes, D. Mollenkamp, H. Radice, E. M., Saltman, & M. Sommer (Eds.), *Crisis discourses in Europe. Media EU-phemisms and alternative narratives* (pp. 11–15). London: London School of Economics and Political Science.

Stråth, B., & Wodak, R., (2009). Europe—discourse—politics—media—history: Constructing 'crises'? In A. Triandafyllidou, R. Wodak, & M. Krzyzanowski (Eds.), *The European public sphere and the media: Europe in crisis* (pp. 15–33). Houndmills, Basingstoke, UK: Palgrave Macmillan.

Touri, M., & Rogers, S. L. (2014). Europe's communication deficit and the UK Press: Framing the Greek financial crisis. *Journal of Contemporary European Studies, 21*(2), 175–189.

Tzogopoulos, G. (2013). *The Greek crisis in the media: Stereotyping in the international press*. Farnham, UK: Ashgate.

Van Dijk, T. (2005). *Discourse and racism in Spain and Latin America*. Amsterdam, Netherlands: John Benjamins.

Van Leeuwen, T. (1996). The representation of social actors. In C. Caldas-Coulthard & M. Coulthard (Eds.), *Texts and practices: Readings n Critical Discourse Analysis* (pp. 32–70). London: Routledge.

Wodak, R. (2009). *The discourse of politics in action: Politics as usual*. Houndmills, Basingstoke, UK: Palgrave Macmillan.

Wodak, R., & Angouri, J. (2014). From Grexit to Grecovery: Euro/crisis discourses. *Discourse & Society, 25*(4), 417–423.

Part III

The notion of 'crisis'

Rahm Emanuel, the current Mayor of Chicago and formerly President Barack Obama's chief of staff, famously once said: "You never want a serious crisis to go to waste. [...] This crisis provides the opportunity for us to do things that you could not before." The chapters in this part address how a sense of crisis has been discursively constructed, used, and indeed fostered, in the early twenty-first century to promote very specific goals—not all of which appear to have targeted the 'crisis' in question.

Working within the parameters of critical realism, Eduardo Strachman and Inês Signorini (Chapter 6) evaluate both the theoretical assumptions and the public rhetoric that supported a dramatic U-turn in Brazilian economic policy, towards austerity measures. They explain that economic theory is itself discursive and not merely an area of technical expertise wholly separate from the public debate; and they analyze various discourses on the Brazilian 'crisis' between 2014 and 2017, noting the significance of metaphor as a strategic form of argumentation. This analysis forms part of Strachman and Signorini's review of the Brazilian government's policy reversal, which reflects a common feature of the post-crisis environment and will be useful to analysts examining the situation in numerous countries.

Naoise McDonagh (Chapter 7) analyzes austerity in terms of the distribution of wealth between different social classes, focusing on the situation in Ireland where a failure of the banking system has been presented as a moral crisis of the State. Solutions to this 'crisis' were proposed which appeared to make sense when viewed through this lens, but in fact more directly served the preservation of existing wealth distribution patterns that favored elites. In this sense, the critiques of austerity made by Keynesian economists—based on its economic inefficacy—missed their mark: in terms of its real goals, as explained by McDonagh, austerity policies have actually been highly successful.

Yannis Stavrakakis and Antonis Galanopoulos (Chapter 8) reach similar conclusions in relation to the Greek situation. Their chapter describes how the fiscal crisis in Greece was presented as both a moral and a cultural crisis, within an overarching framework of 'abnormality' in which various metaphors (including illness, immaturity, and monstrosity) portrayed Greek society as 'abnormal.' This sense of the 'abnormal,' in turn, was used to create a perceived need for normalization and the imposition of a new order, with austerity measures framed as an essential normalizing instrument.

The first of these chapters exemplifies the kind of close collaboration between economists and linguists that we hope to promote in this volume, and all three chapters adopt analytical approaches that we believe can facilitate such collaboration.

Informed by modern rhetorical studies, which both resemble and differ from classical rhetoric in their focus on the "discovery of the available means of persuasion" (Aristotle, *Rhetoric*), Strachman and Signorini consider the various appeals used to justify austerity policies in Brazil—including economic theory, mini-narratives or scenarios, and both verbal and visual metaphors.

McDonagh draws on the pioneering work of Bob Jessop (and colleagues) from the emerging field of Cultural Political Economy (CPE), which relates closely to Critical Discourse Analysis as practiced by Norman Fairclough. CPE combines critical semiotics with Marxian political economy in order to explain how it is that particular economic imaginaries 'win the day' in specific historical and sociopolitical contexts. More specifically, this approach points to the selection, retention, and reinforcement of (privileged) discourses—along with efforts towards their material reproduction—as key contributors to the construction and construal of economic and social relations.

Finally, the chapter by Stavrakakis and Galanopoulos reflects the post-structuralist approach developed by the Essex School of Discourse Analysis. Following Georges Canguilhem and Michel Foucault, these authors trace the discursive genealogy of repertoires of 'normality' and 'abnormality'; and, in doing so, they draw on and extend both Ernesto Laclau's insights about the place of empty signifiers within political discourse and Jacques Derrida's observations about the fundamental interchangeability of the designations 'normal' and 'abnormal.'

Economists wishing to explore the discursive dimensions of all manner of economic issues could equally gain from and contribute to any of these approaches.

6 The recent economic crisis in Brazil and beyond

Some discussions on the weight of empirical issues, methodology and rhetoric

Eduardo Strachman and Inês Signorini

The crisis of 2007–2008 unleashed discussions over the role and weight of empirical issues, methodology and rhetoric as its causes. In this chapter, we unfold an argument that begins with a brief presentation of some important methodological and rhetorical points, which we consider relevant to understanding the crisis of 2007–2008, with its epicenter in the US. Afterwards, we unveil the effects of that international crisis on the Brazilian economy and its economic policies, detailing the steep change of course that the Brazilian Federal Government chose, after its re-election, at the end of 2014. To this end, the article presents four items, in addition to this introduction and some brief concluding remarks. First, we provide a more detailed discussion of methodological issues (Dow, 2008; Lawson, 2009; Grune-Yanoff, 2009). Second, we discuss the essential role of rhetoric in mainstream economics and its use in different proposals to explain persuasively the reasons and consequences of the financial crisis and to prepare—of course, painfully, in general, since the majority of people (even economists, policy-makers, and businessmen/women) seem to believe that 'more pain, more gain'—for another 'normal' epoch in the economy and economics (Blyth, 2013). Third, we present the recent case of the Brazilian economy, in which its Federal Government initially (2008–2009) reacted to the crisis through a creative and non-mainstream stance—profusely using public credit through its huge public banks (two commercial and one investment bank), albeit quite schizophrenically, together with a very conservative Central Bank (Guttman, 2009)—but later surrendered to austerity policies, triggering one of the worst economic crises in Brazil since the Great Depression of 1929 (and also bringing about an impeachment, less than 16 months after the re-election of Dilma Rousseff as President of Brazil). Fourth, we describe and analyze some metaphorical mappings and scenarios in authoritative discourses on crisis and austerity, with illustrative examples from the recent Brazilian case, underscoring both the crisis and the rhetoric linked to it (2014–2017).

Austerity from a methodological point of view

It is not easy to deal with austerity as a methodological issue, first because fiscal austerity is not always an event, but rather a perennial proposed direction for economic policies. However, austerity policies are anchored in an economic theory which can be analyzed methodologically, be it transitory or perennial.

The theory that supports austerity proposals is the supposed expansionary effect of a fiscal consolidation/reform. According to this theory—and in total opposition to the theoretical (and also empirical) proposals of many Keynesians, even if not all or even the majority of them—it is not fiscal spending, but mainly a fierce control over state disbursements that promotes economic growth (Blyth, 2013; Alesina, Barbiero, Favero, Giavazzi, & Paradisi, 2017); and this is held to be true, even with the imposition of an absolute ceiling, as in the USA, in 2011, or in the recently approved Constitutional Amendment by the Brazilian Congress, in December 2016. The causal link between the public expenditure cut and economic growth is understood to be given by the 'confidence recovery' of the private investor, who, once secure of the recovery of government fiscal prudence, is expected to resume her/his productive investments.

The diagnosis that supports this austerity proposal is generally that there had been an excess of irresponsible expenditures in the recent past, so that—in this conservative *weltanschauung*, quite similar to a stern family or school—there must be some kind of suffering to balance the spending spree. This implies that the sour medicine of austerity is the only way to regain the health of the economy, to make this catharsis possible (Blyth, 2013).

However, determining whether or not there had been a public expenditure excess in Brazil after 2003 is an empirical rather than a theoretical matter, amenable to empirical and chiefly objective analysis rather than a priori theorizing. A related issue worth interrogating is whether or not Brazilian public spending had been irresponsible.[1] But our main focus in this chapter concerns the validity, or otherwise, of the theory supporting austerity (which is a methodological issue) and why austerity has been seen as the "only way to restore the economy" (which is both a methodological and a rhetorical issue).

Critical realism (Lawson, 1997, 2003) proposes a meta-methodology in economics, that is, a way to appraise the methods of which economists avail themselves when they propose or use theories. For critical realism, 'ontology comes first': so, first we pose questions about the nature of the object investigated, requiring for this both previous knowledge about the object, its structure, its functioning mechanisms and its capacity to bring about certain effects, and a discussion of the effects that can appear as a result of its operation.

Taking critical realism as the main base from which we should appraise austerity policies, our initial question should concern the capacity of austerity to work. There are three mainstream theoretical underpinnings for such an assertion, each of which can be readily countered. There are also three related propositions, diametrically opposed to the mainstream theory, which raise fundamental objections to the notion of expansionary fiscal consolidation. We will now discuss each of these in turn.

The first mainstream argument is that agents in the economy (including when submitted to austerity policies) are completely rational and believe in the chief mainstream models—for their fear that public debt could result in a tax or inflation hike is a corollary of Ricardian equivalence and thus of traditional models and notions of intertemporal utility maximization. However, one might ask: why should plainly rational agents lend to irresponsible governments? After all, such agents should know objectively beforehand the chances of default or of changes in economic growth (and hence in government receipts), etc., in spite of any government decisions concerning taxation and disbursements—since, according to this mainstream understanding, rational agents can commit errors only if the government surprises them. A related but opposite proposition is that human rationality is limited (Simon, 1976), even in the best (and non-existent) condition of being without fundamental uncertainty (Dequech, 2011). After all, human calculations, at large, and the entrepreneurial one, more strictly, cannot generally produce any effective (ex-post) best solution, only a best forecast (ex-ante), to which one can compare the effective data after events occur. Consequently, it is impossible to know ex-ante if, and for how much, the maximization calculus (prognosis) will differ from the actual results.

According to the second mainstream argument, the economy should rest on a 'pure' financial system, in which banks are mere intermediaries between private savings and investing enterprises. Yet, the real financial system is not that simple and opportunities abound to apply financial resources in the financial market without bringing about any real entrepreneurial investment. Indeed, an opposite proposition can be made, that financial systems are complex.

Third, and also as a corollary of the first argument above, mainstream theory posits that the economy ought to be ergodic and, consequently, investments and other decisions should not be prone to surprises (Davidson, 2015); that is, any such surprises are likely to be ignored as absurd or, at most, would occur only in a mild fashion, making easier any entrepreneurial calculation and decision. However, the generation of innovations and surprises is central to an entrepreneurial economy (Dequech, 2011). In fact, the final oppositional proposition we will mention here is that entrepreneurial actions are both creative and disruptive.

In sum, the three mainstream propositions just mentioned violate basic characteristics even of commonsensical knowledge of the economy; after all, what are the meanings of (i) absolute rationality, (ii) a simple financial system, and (iii) an uneventful and business-as-usual entrepreneurial activity? That is why important non-mainstream economists (such as Schumpeter, Keynes, Simon, Minsky, etc.) pointed towards the problems these propositions implicated, and consequently made huge advances for the development and acceptance of an alternative framework.

Moreover, one has to come to grips with the conundrum that a fiscal consolidation, with its curtailment of public expenditures, could be expected to bring about a rise in private spending that would surpass the depressing effects of that cut in government disbursements. There is not even a sign that such a trade-off was ever achieved, despite some exercises trying to prove that many events in this same direction are the historical rule (Reinhart & Rogoff, 2009; Nersisyan & Wray, 2011; Chick & Pettifor, 2010; Alesina et al., 2017).

All of these considerations support the assertion that austerity proposals, based in the theory of expansionary fiscal consolidation, do not and cannot work. Furthermore, we can stress that, once applied, fiscal austerity generates or even deepens the very outcome that it purports to counter: the growth of the public deficit and debt (Chick & Pettifor, 2010).

We could use the 'paradox of thrift' as exposed by Keynes in the 1930s, to explain that outcome: if a) the State wants to 'save' more (spend less), another agent—b) the private or c) the external sector—must save less (spend more), knowing that the sum of those three savings must be zero (Godley & Zezza, 2006). However, that sum of savings—once more, necessarily equal to zero—in a depressed economy, in which almost every agent tries to cut her/his spending, will be attained with a smaller national product/yield: the product will go down, the debt will go up (public receipts from taxation on yield, value added, etc., will fall, and some expenditures will increase, e.g., in unemployment relief, etc.), and the relation debt/product will worsen steeply. If this is so, the recovery of entrepreneurial confidence clearly depends on an expenditure increase, not on a cut, in all of the economy and also by the State. As indicated before, which economic agent would invest or expand her/his production if her/his sales are falling, raising uncertainty in the future prospects of the economy?

However, one can stress that, in the absence of national sources of demand, an economy can try to make recourse to exports. But, if austerity measures are applied in many countries, as nowadays, those external markets will also shrink. Apparently, this outcome is what the current revival of nationalism and protectionism will beget: a reduction in the growth of the world trade or even in its absolute numbers (Blyth, 2013). The parsimony paradox thus states an impossibility: we cannot all be austere at the same time, be that in the individual, national, or international levels.

For instance, in the Brazilian case, as we will see in more detail below, there was no public expenditure excess and, hence, these disbursements did not bring about any inflation increase nor any rise of *default* of the public debt, which remained extremely low. Certainly, there was a bunch of badly chosen fiscal incentives, which, thus, unfortunately contributed to Brazil's slow economic growth generating a rise in public deficits, after 2013. Nevertheless, inflation dynamics, in Brazil, are nowadays mainly a result of the behavior of prices in the non-tradeable and administered sectors (Strachman, 2013; de Paula & Saraiva, 2015), with no demand-pull inflation, or even any risk of it. We can question the quality and direction of public spending and of misused public incentives,[2] but there was no 'excess' or fiscal 'irresponsibility' in this case. The debt/GDP relation which amounted to 57.2% in 2014 (the same average level of the ten years before), increased to 66.2% in 2015, and shall attain 76.0% by the end of 2018 (Pupo, 2018). This is not a huge level, in international terms, however, despite the recent growth rate, which is explained chiefly by the fiscal incentives and the fall in economic expansion.

This brings us to our last remark about methodology. If fiscal austerity does not work—if, once applied, it breeds effects opposed to those expected—and if the 'fiscal crisis' is commonly overblown, why are these policies persistently announced as 'the only game in town,' the unique solution for the recovery of economies?

Austerity from a rhetorical point of view

The so-called "rhetoric of economics" (McCloskey, 1983, 1994, 1997) can help us to explain this puzzle. As pointed out by Hanan and Chaput (2015), "through a focus on the narratives, metaphors, and other symbolic figures of speech" used by economists, the rhetoric of economics "showed that, far from being neutral and objective, the discipline of economics required persuasion for the adoption of its views and value systems" (p. 16). According to this perspective, theoretical and practical reason in economics is embedded in language and culture, i.e., in a "web of social, cultural, and political influences" (p. 19). Therefore, this point of view "complicate[s] the positivist foundations of modern economics" (p. 16) as it calls into question the idea that specific theories are true or false, compared to what the world 'really is.' Instead, theories are considered largely in terms of their productivity-instrumentality in accomplishing certain purposes, thus in producing, explaining, and acting upon reality. Indeed, all ontological, epistemological, and empirical arguments can be perceived as strategic discursive devices which shall face the sieve of the proponent and of the audience. If accepted, they will be considered valid; if not, they will be discarded.[3] Thus, a theory that comes to be accepted is one that successfully persuades the target audience, e.g., the academic community and/or the general public.

Expert discourse on economic crisis and austerity, for example, encodes culturally and historically constructed conceptualizations that could explain its great persuasive power for the general population. In this sense, it has several persuasive attributes: it sounds simple ("if we spent, we must pay"), intuitive ("the government should take care of its finances as a housewife takes care of hers"—although we should not forget the aforementioned, well-known paradox of thrift), and it has a moral appeal ("in difficult moments, we all should fasten our belts").

But equally important is the fact that these persuasive attributes, as explained by Blyth (2013), serve both ideological commitments (e.g., an attack on the welfare state and a defence of a tiny State) and material interests: austerity sacrifices have important impacts, for instance, on distribution, because of the consequences of public austerity on **public services**; meanwhile, upper deciles of income can count on the private provision of those same services. Moreover, many **public goods**, which can beget several positive externalities that are particularly important for the bottom deciles, can also suffer an interruption in their production and use—lots of them, though of course not all, having been produced by the public sector. And all of this mostly, if not only, in order that public debt owners can continue receiving high interest for assets free from risks; meanwhile the very value of liquidity is increased, because of the resultant recession/depression.[4] Thus, the logic of austerity policies can be summed up as a distributive conflict being forced into society through authoritative discourses of austerity that justify and legitimize the social cost—moreover unequal among social and economic groups—of restrictive policies during economic crisis.

In the context of the Brazilian crisis, as described in the following sections, authoritative discourses of austerity have a crucial role in the public political arena, in which restrictive measures under the liberal/conservative policies adopted by Dilma's and Temer's administration were explained and justified. Drawing on Lakoff's (1993) conceptual metaphor theory and on Musolff's (2006) concept of metaphor scenario or mini-narrative, we show how metaphorical mappings and scenarios are used to explain, persuade, reason, question, and argue for new interpretations of reality in this specific context.

The amazing case of the Brazilian reaction to the crisis: A tale in three acts

Act I (2008–2009)

Almost immediately after the onset of the crisis in Brazil—with the traditional private banking retrenchment that accompanied it, which included the trend towards important capital outflows—the leftist Lula[5] government adopted a huge series of countercyclical policies ("Veja as medidas contra a crise," 2008). Among them, the government decided to avoid a great devaluation of the Brazilian currency (Real), just four days after the crash of September 15, 2008—a policy that would be complemented at other moments, as needed. On October 8, 2008, for example, the Brazilian Central Bank sold US dollars in the spot market.

In addition, the Lula government reduced the compulsory reserves of commercial banks, in order to stir up lending to firms and families, and allowed major banks to buy the whole or shares of the credit portfolio of smaller banks facing difficulties, despite the fact that there was no parallel between these portfolios and those of the American banking system.[6] The government also diminished some taxes on durable goods, and on credits for these goods (autos, motorcycles, refrigerators, furniture, etc., as noted by Barbosa & Souza, 2010). This action stimulated banks located in the country to increase lending directed to this kind of acquisition and also to small and medium enterprises ("Veja as medidas contra a crise," 2008). Moreover, in 2009, the government induced two major commercial banks, of which it is the main owner—that is, Banco do Brasil and Caixa Econômica Federal, corresponding to approximately 30% of the total assets and 39% of the total credits of all banks in Brazil (de Paula, Oreiro, & Basilio, 2013)—to increase their lending and cut both spreads and interest rates. This was achieved in 2009 (as compared to 2007 and 2008), bringing about a reduction in delinquencies.[7] As a matter of fact, the private commercial banks had to follow this lead of the public commercial banks, in order to stop losing market share: the public banks increased their loan share from 31% in 2007 to 42% in 2009; meanwhile the private banks' share declined from 42% to 33% in the same period (Soihet & Cabral, 2012, pp. 8–11; Almeida, 2011, p. 332).[8] As a consequence of these measures, in the second semester of 2009, credit to firms again increased (Almeida, 2011, p. 332).

This policy was complemented by those of another government bank, the National Bank for Economic and Social Development (BNDES), which is the only Brazilian investment bank and augmented its loans to the private sector, in order to keep stable the country's aggregated product and demand. BNDES increased its loans by 140%, in real terms, from December 2008 to December 2009 (Soihet & Cabral, 2012, pp. 11–12). This activism from BNDES, trying to increase the investment/product rate—even if one can dispute the priorities (related to sectors, firms, etc.) given by the bank and the government—would be maintained wisely until the end of the second presidential term of Dilma Rousseff.[9]

These policies attained the stabilization of the Brazilian Gross Domestic Product, in 2009, with only a minor decrease of 0.13% in relation to 2008 and with a strong performance in the following two years (2010–2011), as shown in Figure 6.1. However, this performance could have been better if Brazil's monetary and fiscal policies had been more aggressive (Kaltenbrunner, 2010)—as they were in India and China during the same period—since the

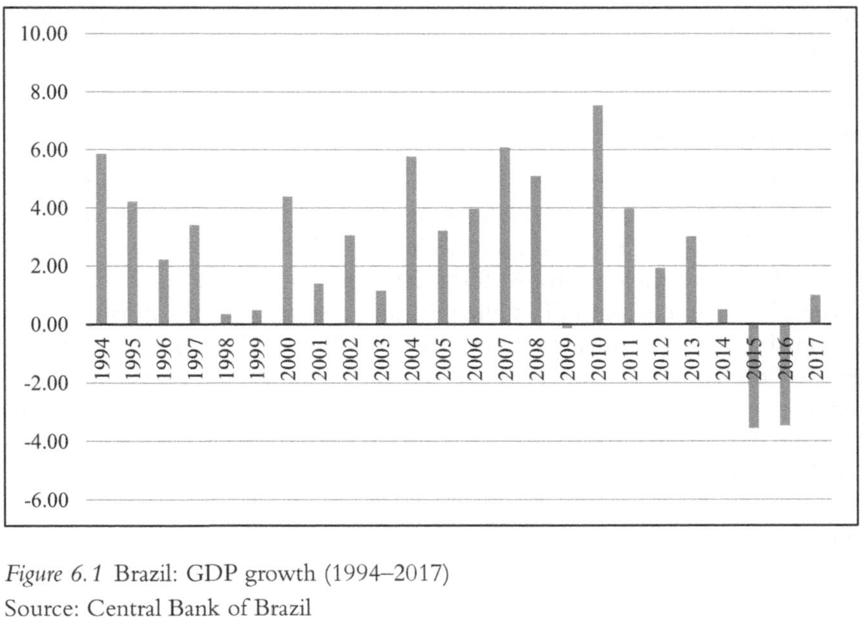

Figure 6.1 Brazil: GDP growth (1994–2017)
Source: Central Bank of Brazil

countercyclical policies described above quite schizophrenically were adopted together with a very conservative stance by the Brazilian Central Bank, almost always maintaining very high nominal and real interest rates (Guttman, 2009): on the other hand, the reduction of the interest happened too late. Only in January 2009 there was the first reduction of the basic rate… [it] would fall from 13.75% to 8.75% annually, between January and July 2009 (Almeida, 2011, p. 330).

Summing up, the main measures adopted by the Brazilian government intended to foster economic growth, after the beginning of the crisis, were (Almeida, 2011; Barbosa & Souza, 2010): (i) monetary measures which, however, were adopted quite late and less aggressively than in other countries (Guttman, 2009); (ii) fiscal measures, also taken up more timidly than in other nations; (iii) the liquidity supply by the Central Bank, protecting the banking system against the risk of a systemic crisis; and (iv) the increase of credit by the public banks, which was the more active of the policies adopted.

In addition to these policies, however, we should underscore the maintenance or deepening of some measures which were already then in course: huge investments by Petrobras, the largest firm of the country, owned mainly by the Federal Government;[10] an important public housing project (called "My house, my life"), which would have a stronger impact after 2010; the Program of Investment Support, chiefly aimed to sustain the acquisition of less expensive capital goods, through a reduction to 4.5% per year of the nominal interest rates by the BNDES, making them zero or even negative in real terms; and augmented money transfers to poorer families and the raise of the minimum wage. All of these measures granted a less steep decrease in formal employment between October 2008 and March 2009 (692,000 workers, preeminently in the primary and industrial sectors); they also generated some minor gains in employment in services, and later increases across all sectors.

Act II (2010–2014)

In 2010 and 2011, a series of more restrictive policies were adopted in Brazil. In April 2010, the basic rate (Selic) started to rise from 8.75% per annum in March to 12.5% in July 2011, but declined to 7.25% in October 2012—the lowest level in decades (Silva & Terra, 2012, p. 10)—where it remained until March 2013. As a matter of fact, the institutions supporting the inflation target regime in Brazil (de Paula & Saraiva, 2015; Strachman, 2013) induce the interest rates—"the basic instrument" of this regime—almost always upward, in their intention to bring about a deflationary trend through a reduction of economic activity. But this kind of policy is also based on the impact of an appreciation of the national currency over some costs and prices (Kaltenbrunner, 2010), in a mix of very short run horizons—with harsh consequences for investment, economic growth, etc. over the long run (Carvalho, 2008)—*and* political pressures stirring them up (Drummond, 2016; Sayad, 2014). This can explain the strong fluctuation in the basic interest rates, stressed above, which most of the time are running against the other policies (fiscal, investment, development, social, etc.).

Nevertheless, this time, fiscal policies were leaning in the opposite direction of the former period—that is, reducing tax breaks, increasing tax rates, etc.—in order to achieve a huge fiscal surplus, which materialized effectively at the end of the year: 2.3% of the GDP, excluding interest payments for the public debt (Silva & Terra, 2012). All this performance was accompanied by some measures, such as taxes on short run transactions, intended both to dampen speculation with the Real and to increase the stabilization of the exchange rate.

In May 2012, the Government made recourse to tax breaks on the consumption of durables, as they had done in 2008–2009, but with only minor repercussions for demand, despite significant costs to the public budget.[11] These tax breaks were maintained until the end of 2014, coinciding with the end of Dilma's first presidential term. They also represented—together with their minor repercussion over the domestic product and a really silly attempt to cajole the financial sector and the Brazilian political and economic right—the main reason she would later opt for an incredible U-turn, from the inception of her second term (Serrano & Melin, 2015), although doing so would ultimately destroy her government, causing her to lose political support from some important social groups.

Act III (2015–2017)

However, the liberal U-turn had actually begun more mildly, during the second period (Act II, discussed above). After her victory in the October 2014 election, Dilma decided to embrace liberal/conservative policies, with at least implicit support from Lula. In doing so, she proceeded in opposition to her election program, her constituency, and the economics she had been taught at least twice while a post-graduate student at the quite heterodox State University of Campinas—albeit without completing the course, since she never presented a MSc or PhD dissertation.

In particular, Dilma opted for a Minister of Finance, Joaquim Levy—nicknamed by some Joaquim "Scissorhands" because he is proud to cut public expenditures—whose former job had been on the Executive Board of one of Brazil's two largest banks. With international reserves at their peak of US$374 billion, a mild deterioration of the public debt in relation to GDP, and a controlled inflation of 6.41% per annum (inside the target, as it had been without interruption since 2004), the new Minister decided to cut public expenditures, increase interest rates abruptly (both basic rates and those of the public banks), curtail credit, and abruptly correct utility prices. This decision created a perfect economic storm (Serrano & Melin, 2015, p. 3), plunging the economy into a GDP decline of –3.55% in 2015 and –3.46% in 2016, with only minimal recovery of +0.99 in 2017. Thus, in just two years, the economy shrank by 6.88%, and by 5.97% over three years (2015–2017). In addition, 7.9 million formal jobs were lost by the end of September 2017, increasing the unemployment rate to 12.4%, from 6.8% at the end of 2014. By the end of 2017, 12.96 million people were unemployed in Brazil, and formal employment fell from 41.2 million at the end of 2014, to 33.3 million at the end of 2017: a stunning decline of 19.2%, in less than three years ("Brasil tem 12,961 milhões," 2017). Nevertheless, in 2015, Scissorhands curtailed access to unemployment insurance and took other measures to reduce social protection and pensions.

Furthermore, Petrobras investments declined from the US$44 billion originally planned to US$31 billion in 2015, with further cuts planned for 2015–2019, from US$221 billion to US$130 billion (Serrano & Melin, 2015, p. 10). This economic policy disaster was complemented by an inflation of 10.67% in 2015, the first year since 2004 that did not reach the government's target, and the first year of two-digit inflation since 2002. Hence, the total real wage bill fell only 10.4% in 2015 (Serrano & Melin, 2015, p. 11). The real fiscal adjustment achieved an increase of the gross public debt to a declining GDP (since tax revenues fell dramatically after the onset of the recession), from 56.2% in December 2014 to 75.3% in March 2018 (data from the Brazilian Central Bank). This result was also thanks to the sharp rise in interest rates of 3.25% in nine months, after Dilma's election in October 2014, to 14.25% per year, where it remained from July 2015 to October 2016, before falling to 7.0% in December 2017.

In short, this new policy direction begot (or at least augmented) the worst economic crisis in modern Brazilian history (Rossi & Mello, 2017)—worse even than the 1930s and beginning of the 1980s (the age of the Latin American external debt crises)—as well as a political crisis that would in less than 16 months imply the impeachment of this very government.

Metaphorical mappings and scenarios in authoritative discourses on crisis and austerity (2014–2017)

As pointed out in the literature (McCloskey, 1994, 1997), metaphors are a pervasive component of economic rhetoric. But the term 'rhetoric' needs clarification due to the expansion of the range of modern rhetorical studies into different domains and disciplines. Hence, in this section, we will use the following working definition of 'rhetoric' proposed by Killingsworth (2005), namely: "a concern for audience manifested in the situation and form of a communication" (p. x, emphasis original).

As explained by Killingsworth, "a concern for audience" can involve a range of desires or intentions, from persuading through formal argumentation, to communicating and sense-making in everyday life. "Situation and form" are related both to social, historical, and local or immediate contextual features, and to genre and mode of communication. Thus, when viewed from this perspective, rhetorical phenomena are an integral part of meaning-making within social communication and involve the mobilization of socio-semiotic tools—like language, images, or sounds—as well as historical and sociocultural knowledge, including implicit knowledge that group members take for granted in their everyday social practices.

In order to show the relevance of rhetoric in modern contexts, Killingsworth recontextualizes the classical notions of *ethos*, *pathos*, and *logos* to situate appeals to character, emotion, and logic or reasoning within a model of appeals that includes "at least four elements—three positions and [one] medium of exchange" (p. 1): the position of the author or "agent of production" (p. 1), the position of the audience, and the position of authority or value "to which the author refers (p. 1)," all of which are mediated through a text.[12] For Killingsworth (2005), interpretation always involves the rhetorical action of appealing, and "[s]uccessful appeals move the audience, the result of which is the alignment of the three positions" (p. 1).

As fundamental resources for making, enacting and managing meanings, tropes and imageries, particularly metaphors, play a relevant role in the rhetorical action of appealing. In fact, as metaphor studies has been arguing since the 1980s (e.g., Lakoff & Johnson, 1980; Lakoff, 1993; Gibbs & Steen, 1999; Kövecses, 2002), metaphors provide a way of structuring attention and reasoning from an angle or perspective from which the object, concept, argument, or event will be viewed by interlocutors, suppressing other aspects which are inconsistent with the value referred: "Each angle, each shift of perspective, will create a different kind of appeal" (Killingsworth, 2005, p. 10). Thus, metaphor may enhance efficacy and persuasive power, particularly in strategic discourse. Therefore, it is a powerful influencing tool in the sociopolitical arena.

Going back to economics, however, the rhetorical approach sheds light on the transactional character of knowledge production in the field, as well as on the epistemological and heuristic role of metaphorical representations and expressions in economic expert discourses. As described in the literature (e.g., Cameron & Low, 1999), metaphorical framing not only facilitates understanding of the subject, but also invites the audience to accept a certain politico-economic view, i.e., it contributes to the 'alignment' process described by the Killingsworth model. This alignment occurs because metaphors "appear to instantiate frame-consistent knowledge structures," including common sense and stereotype, and they also "invite structurally consistent inferences" (Thibodeau & Boroditsky, 2011, p. 1).

Similarly to other contexts described by the literature on economic crisis (e.g., Arrese, 2015; Cardini, 2014; Charteris-Black, 2000), metaphorical framing in the conceptualization of the Brazilian crisis mobilizes a structured cluster of conceptual metaphors articulated through mini-narratives or scenarios (Musolff, 2006, 2016) which predominantly depict it as something negative. Some examples—to cite just the most frequent metaphorical expressions used during the period in focus—include:

- a disease: *Dilma points to herself before prescribing 'bitter medicine' against crisis* ("Dilma aponta para si antes de prescrever 'remédio amargo' contra a crise", 2017),

- a natural/man-made disaster: *Public accounts were allowed to slip out of control* (Oliveira & Coronato, 2016),
- a living harmful organism: *The economic crisis began to hit the country last year* (Betim, 2015), and
- a technical/mechanical failure: *This economic train is back on track. The machine needs to be fixed to get it moving* (Nogueira, 2017).

And, as also noticed by Cardini (2014) in relation to conceptualizations of the English crisis of 2008, "viewing a state of economic/financial crisis as a damaged or destroyed object appears to be the most widely adopted metaphor" (p. 54).

As a matter of fact, as we have seen above, metaphorical framings displayed in official and expert discourses since the inception of the Brazilian financial crisis unfold the following three main conceptual schemes: (i) economy/finance is like a living organism/a human being; (ii) economy/finance is like a natural force/a natural flaw; and (iii) economy/finance is like a movement.

As these conceptual schemes are reverberated and amplified by the press and social media,[13] they play a fundamental role in shaping information, perception, and, thus, 'knowledge' of the crisis, highlighting its profoundly negative and harmful (*catastrophic*) effects on the one hand and, on the other, its circumstantial (*flows of instability*) and technical (*lack of financial control*) character, i.e., a phenomenon not necessarily related to sociopolitical issues.

A relevant aspect to be noticed about these conceptual schemes is that they embed values, beliefs, and attitudes, i.e., ideological positionings among and/or within competing interpretations of financial and economic phenomena. As emphasized by O'Mara-Shimek, Guillén-Parra, and Ortega-Larrea (2015), "[w]hile metaphor in itself is not ideological, its use can serve functions of ideology," particularly through entailments or "associated secondary concepts that accompany metaphors" (pp. 104–105).

Aiming to illustrate how metaphorical concepts and expressions contributed to the process of 'alignment' described by Killingsworth's model in the Brazilian public arena, we examine below three examples of strategic argumentative talk and reasoning based on metaphorical frameworks of crisis and austerity, addressed by: (i) an expert in economics; (ii) official government speeches; and (iii) both supportive and critical interlocutors in the public arena.

Appealing to the 'victims of crisis'

The shallow blog post "Metaphors to calm down the victims of crisis" (Constantino, 2015) is an exemplary representative of the published materials produced by Brazilian 'experts' in economics in order both (i) to explain in a didactic way the financial, economic, and political crisis described in earlier sections of this chapter; and (ii) to persuade non-experts that austerity measures are rational, logical, and therefore unavoidable. In his blog, Constantino supported Dilma's impeachment campaign in order to *get rid of the PT party* [that is, Dilma's Partido dos Trabalhadores or "Workers' Party"] *once and for all*. His appeals to the reader are framed by an association with one of the most frequent conceptual frameworks through which economics is understood and categorized by experts and non-experts alike in Brazilian media, namely: the view of the economy as a living organism, and, thus, of financial/economic crisis as an illness, and austerity as **the** (i.e., the only) treatment.

In order to provide supportive evidence and avoid rebuttals or refutations that the reader might apply in that highly opaque context of controversial issues (for example, in his explanation on context of *the victims of crisis*), Constantino instantiates this framework quite unimaginatively (Blyth, 2013) through a scenario or mini-narrative (Musolff, 2016) in which the shared embodied experience of illness and treatment is activated and associated with shared social knowledge of Judeo-Christian doctrine about sin and redemption. Therefore, the success of Constantino's argumentative reasoning—that is, the success of his appeal towards the audience (Killingsworth, 2005, pp. 2–3)—in favor of austerity depends upon closing the distance between the appeal to Health and Paradise as indisputable and desired values on the one hand, and his endorsement of austerity policies as not only inevitable but rather the desired solution to *the victims of crisis*, on the other hand.

Three scenarios are described in Constantino's blog post, as summarized below:

> **(i) From alcoholic intoxication to liver cirrhosis: The fatal disease, its causes and its painful treatment**
>
> You, dear reader, have had too much to drink at least once in your life, I assume. You know the feeling of euphoria caused by alcohol. The subject feels immortal, brave; thinks that everyone looks at him with admiration and respect; feels funnier, excited; glimpses a future with no restrictions.
>
> Then comes that damn hangover. [...] But we know there is no alternative. Actually, there is: continue drinking to prolong the artificial euphoria. But this path leads to an even greater hangover, perhaps cirrhosis of the liver. It is better to accept the torment with the resignation of those who understand that it is a necessary process to rid the body of the excesses, the poison.
>
> The diagnosis of the exams comes and the individual is struck dumb: it is indeed cancer, and it is malignant! The body's cells are being destroyed by the 'invader.' The doctor goes straight to the point: a radical treatment now, or death. [...]
>
> (Constantino, 2015)

> **(ii) From Hell to Paradise: the sin, its causes and the painful path to purification**
>
> The Catholic myth makes it very clear: between Hell and the Kingdom of Heaven lies Purgatory. It is a process of purification, a temporary punishment for the sinner. [...] Yes, he turned away from God, he made very bad choices, driven by greed, seduced by the Devil. He abandoned morals and

> ethics. He embraced the Golden Calf. But if he really repents, then he can be forgiven and cross Purgatory onto paradise.
>
> (Constantino, 2015)

(iii) And then, from the depression-suffering to the treatment, after Purgatory: after the current Brazilian crisis, explained its causes and after the painful path, the nation can be sent back to normality

> Inflation above 9%, unemployment rising, the dollar at R$ 3.40, the country being downgraded by risk agencies, economy expected to suffer from a 2% decrease in 2015: we have arrived at Purgatory, we are paying for our sins, it is the hangover from the 2010 euphoria, produced by government artificial liquidity. The sensation is of malaise, depression discomfort. We are taking the medicine to attack this cancer. The body reacts, the suffering is evident. (…) If the body of Brazil overcomes this phase, it will come out stronger further ahead, free of the cancer that bothers us, ready to embark on a journey to 'paradise', or at least away from Bolivarian hell.
>
> (Constantino, 2015)

In these examples, economic crisis and austerity are explained by a double analogy or metaphorical mapping (Gentner, 1988, 1989) from one domain (the base) into the other (the target), as follows: shared, ordinary information about fatal illness (cancer) and about the sinner's condition is the basis for the interpretation of financial crisis; shared, ordinary information about the painful treatment of cancer and suffering in Purgatory is the basis for the interpretation of the audience's growing discomfort as 'victims' of austerity policies. Thus, the attributes of the highlighted ordinary 'objects' and the common relational structure of this ordinary, shared information are articulated as the basis for the interpretation of austerity policies as the 'the only game in town,' the unique solution for recovery of normality.

One must nevertheless notice that the intended problem to be solved is a political problem, rather than a financial or economic problem, namely getting rid of a left-wing 'populist' group, i.e., the PT party as a major problem (or major source of problems) to the neoliberal agenda. According to Constantino (2015):

> We will have more solid Republican institutions and people more averse to populism. If this moment of crisis is the price necessary to pay for Brazil to get rid of PT once and for all, then let's go citizens! The alternative is much worse!

Appealing to the electorate

Since the liberal U-turn described in prior sections, President Rousseff's official statements, for instance, on a large-scale project to build 10,000 kilometers of new railroads across the country—"Putting Brazil on the Rails"—have been replaced by references to the railroad as a metaphor for the economy. Although her former Economic Minister Joaquim Levy had emphasized the need to establish a new economic structure, i.e., a new track to put the economy on (Silva, 2015), the conceptualization of the economic recovery was structured also by this metaphorical representation of a derailed train put 'back on track.' In fact, "putting Brazil on track" has simply become the most overused political slogan later on.

In the midst of the political crisis caused by Dilma's impeachment, she used this metaphorical expression to justify her appointment of Lula as her Chief of Staff: "My government will have better conditions to put Brazil back on track with Lula next to me" ("Governo terá condições de recolocar Brasil," 2016, March 17). In his first speech as President, Michel Temer took up the same metaphor to describe his commitment to government on a national television network: "My commitment is to rescue the strength of our economy and put Brazil back on track."[14]

Particularly in Temer's official statements about economic governance, fiscal and economic issues are figured as the missing or broken rail tracks that caused a catastrophic derailment, but which can be extensively and expertly repaired through fiscal austerity and reformist policies aimed to "rescue the strength" of the Brazilian economy. Thus, while drawing on the conceptual metaphor "finance/economy is movement," his commitment to make essential repairs to the damaged rail line entails the figure of a vehicle that cannot move under its own power, i.e., the figure of a derailed train corresponding to the weak economy which needs to be 'rescued' from 'chaos.' Therefore, although putting the vehicle back on track is the first step towards motion, it is not enough, as Joaquim "Scissorhands" Levy explained before Dilma's impeachment:

> It will be a slow recovery. When things are structured, we expect to see the economy stop going down and then start going up, slowly.
>
> (Silva, 2015)

In fact, as postulated by Lakoff (1990) and Lakoff and Johnson (1983), conceptual schemes related to motion highlight the upward movement—'start going up'—as a metaphorical mapping of progress through purposeful and efficient action. Hence, several sets of conceptual correspondences related to motion—forward/backward movement, acceleration/slowness, lack of movement, lack of direction—have been associated with the conventional image of the train and other vehicles for speaking and reasoning about the Brazilian sociopolitical and economic issues since 2014. In addition, these conceptual schemes played an essential role in the rhetorical action of appealing to public opinion, as in Temer's and his subordinates' interventions, as well as in both supportive and critical accounts of government policy.

In Temer's and his subordinates' statements on crisis and austerity, the recurrence of the metaphorical expression *putting Brazil back on track* ("'Brasil começa a entrar nos trilhos', diz Temer em reunião de cúpula do Brics," 2016) presupposes that the tensions among different viewpoints, values, and positionings within the social and political arena may be resolved or attenuated through the formulation of a unifying and consensual appeal to voters and politicians concerned about economic stagnation. Thus, in Killingsworth's (2005) terms, this metaphorical leitmotiv plays a pivotal role in the rhetorical process of audience 'alignment' with the government agenda: through metaphorical framing, the audience is invited to recognize and reason about common relational structures across different sets of elements, as in the following three interrelated scenarios:

(i) From chaos to 'order and progress': a path/direction to put Brazil back on track

Our motto—which is not from today—, our motto is order and progress.
(Portal Planalto, 2016, May 12)

Gentlemen, my administration has a direction! (…) I say for sure: Brazil will not get off track. I will continue to lead the government.
(Portal Planalto, 2017, May 20)

(ii) From socioeconomic delay to the twenty-first century economy: a new track/location to put Brazil on/into

Brazil is moving more and more towards modernity.
(UOL Economia, 2017, July 11)

[O]ur main goal is to put the government into the 21st century, put Brazil into the 21st century.
(Portal Planalto, 2017, November 22)

(iii) From stagnation to economic growth and industrial development: the market-based track to put Brazil back on

The results show that the strategy proposed and executed by the government is right. We left the crisis behind and resumed the path of development.
(Temer, 2017, November 8)

Now, Brazil will advance more.
(Temer, 2017, November 8)

One must, nonetheless, notice that rhetorical processes involving a fragmented audience are always uncertain, even risky, as interpretation is not an automatic result and also depends upon the ability of the performer to affect and sustain collective attention.

Supporting and challenging through metaphorical mappings

Among the government policy evaluations published in mass and social media during the period in focus, those produced by experts in economics very often reinforced and expanded positively the figures and mappings used by official representatives. A director of the Brazilian Central Bank, for example, expressed his opinion during an interview in the following terms:

> I had a very negative understanding of what was going on in the previous administration. I thought Brazil was headed for chaos. I really did. This path has now been reversed. [...] Today, Brazil remains vulnerable, but that feeling that it was a runaway train, from which we were going to the precipice, passed. The mission that they are facing is not easy, because they were given a piece of scorched earth, to pick up the pieces, and have been able to move forward, despite everything that is happening in the political arena and in the judiciary.
>
> (Fucs, 2017)

In the excerpt above, the director instantiates already existing scenarios and representations in order to provide a simplified binary account of Dilma's (negative account) and Temer's (positive account) economic models and policies. In so doing, he mobilizes the image of the same vehicle, but this time it is in motion and it turns 'fortunately' to Temer's safer track, despite the difficulties encountered in reversing the direction of Dilma's erratic path towards 'abyss,' 'chaos,' or 'scorched landscape.' Thus, the author's rhetorical strategy for convincingly describing his own values as isomorphic with those of one of the two opposite governments is based on a dramatization of existing metaphorical scenarios, representing them as contradictory and therefore as excluding one another—and, moreover, arguing that one of them was irrational and irresponsible. As in the example discussed above, the argument here is that there is only one option with which the audience can align.

Among negative evaluations of government policies, the same cluster of metaphorical mappings and scenarios related to the figure of the train (whether derailed or in motion) are instantiated, but displaying inverted roles (a dangerous device), positions and directions (running over people) as a way of defining and communicating doubts and alternative interpretations. Take for example the warning from a financial expert concerned about corruption scandals: "we must persevere in the reforms without which we will have a new chicken flight in the economy, and the light at the end of the tunnel will be a train that comes to knead us" (Bandeira, 2017, October 3).

Nonetheless, further layers of inferential processes involved in the reading of metaphorical expressions and scenarios were better explored by cartoons and memes published in the social media. It represented a popular responsive critical understanding/reframing of what was happening in the country, frequently based on a literal translation of the metaphorical expression "putting Brazil on track."

A good example is a cartoon published in *Humor Político* (Oliveira, 2017), where a terrified Brazil is stuck on the rail at risk of being hit by the PMDB (the governing party) train controlled by President Temer, who says: "by 2018 I will have put this country on track!" The representation of a risk situation is alluding to the socioeconomic conditions of the poorest and most disadvantaged population groups, significantly deteriorated at that time, in contrast with the richer groups that support the reformist agenda.

The same argument is alluded to in another cartoon published in *Humor Político* (Dantas, 2017), which depicts an imminent disaster involving wagons racing to an abyss. The representation of Brazil as a train full of people—that is, not a generic train, as in the first cartoon and in the textual figures discussed above—alludes to the non-abstract or technical character of economic issues. The concrete components involved are brought together: citizens and their rights; the nation and its resources; all going down to the abyss. Temer claims: "I have put the country on track!" A sign of approval from Uncle Sam, also depicted in this cartoon, points to the 'development' model pursued by the Brazilian government, as well as to other meanings related to the economic and political power of the United States, which has been historically relevant to the Brazilian political economy.

In fact, as illustrated by the examples discussed in this section, scenarios carry evaluative and attitudinal biases, display particular political reasons and framed imagery of the national discourse communities. In this sense, scenarios are relevant argumentative and rhetorical resources (Musolff, 2016), particularly relevant in the Brazilian context, which was trapped in an escalating partisan-ideological polarization within social media since the 'war' against institutional corruption. It is almost at the level of scenarios that the ongoing complex cultural and ideological dispute between competing and clashing interests and values takes place.

Concluding remarks

In this chapter, we started with a discussion of some of the methodological and rhetorical issues underpinning austerity policies, in order to better understand them, and their causes and consequences—that is, the scourge they represent for societies and economies. This was followed by a brief review of the economic policies adopted in Brazil after the 2007–2008 crisis, with special attention to the quite schizophrenic choice in 2015 of a U-turn in those policies, just after Dilma was re-elected in October 2014 (representing the fourth federal government election win in a row for the Workers' Party).

We also explored a core component of theoretical and practical reasoning in economics, which articulates disciplinary and sociocultural knowledge in verbal discourses on crisis and austerity, that is language framing. As a selection of "some aspects of a perceived reality" in order to "make them more salient in a communicating text" (Entman, 1993, p. 52), linguistic and discursive frames "define problems," "diagnose causes," "make moral judgments," and "suggest remedies" (Entman, 1993, p. 52). Focusing on some metaphorical mappings and scenarios in the discourses on crisis and austerity from Brazilian experts and political authorities, we showed how linguistic and discursive frames operate in (re)defining and recontextualizing common-sensical perceptions of the Brazilian case, just before, and after, that 2015 U-turn in economic policy.

As a result, more emphasis should be given to Alejo González's (2011, p. 76) and Schiller's (2017, pp. 48–50) appeals, among others, that there is room for collaborative research on the articulation between disciplinary and sociocultural knowledge through linguistic and discursive framing, which may in turn contribute to better insights into the pervasive presence of metaphors and narrative in economics.

Notes

1 These empirical issues are not under scrutiny in this particular section, but we do deal with them in Section 3. In this direction, we must stress that the credit transfers from the Brazilian Treasury to public banks, responsible for many of the finance operations concerning social policies in the last three presidential mandates—and foundational to the impeachment process of President Rousseff—may be discussed for the sake of a rather objective appraisal of the administration (was it bad or not?), but not of any expenditure 'excess.'

2 Orair, Siqueira, & Gobetti (2016) analyzed in a disaggregated manner the multipliers of the Brazilian public expenditure. They noticed that direct spending by the government (e.g., in infrastructure) brings about more effects over economic activity than indirect incentives to private spending (as with fiscal incentives). The reason for this is quite simple: In the first case, there is a direct and unambiguous injection of **demand**, besides that of **purchase power**, in the economy, while in the case of the incentives there is a direct increase only in purchase power, but without any guarantee that this power will be effectively spent and converted in demand.

3 Thus, rhetoric is considered more distant from critical realism, in the methodological spectrum, and nearer to instrumentalism and constructivism.

4 In the Brazilian case, the interest rate bearing on government bonds is never discussed, also because it is viewed as part of the monetary (inflation target) policy in the New Consensus Macroeconomics and, therefore, untouchable.

5 President of Brazil between 2003 and 2011, Luiz Inácio Lula da Silva is known widely as "Lula."

6 There was a zero contamination of the country's financial institutions with the infamous 'toxic' assets of the international financial *boom* (Almeida, 2011, p. 330).

7 Barbosa & Souza (2010) assert that in 2008 approximately 20% of the funding of Brazilian credits was obtained offshore. This funding simply disappeared in the aftermath of the crisis, reducing the supply of credit in Brazil. At the same time, there was a liquid capital outflow of US$27 billion from the country, in the last four months of 2008.

8 Singer (2015) postulates that this aggressive stance in using the public commercial banks—by Lula, at this moment, and by the first Dilma Rousseff Government (2011–2014)—was one major fact responsible for Dilma Rousseff's impeachment at the beginning of her second presidential term, in April 2016 (cf. also Drummond, 2016).

9 Like Lula before her, former President of Brazil (2011–2016), Dilma Rousseff is generally known simply as "Dilma."

10 Barbosa & Souza (2010) calculated that, in 2009, the share of the Federal Government and Petrobras together corresponded to 16% of the total investment in Brazil.

11 "After growing at an average annual rate of 8.0 percent between 2004 and 2010, peaking at 18 percent in 2010, the real growth rate of gross fixed capital formation fell to 6.7 percent in 2011 and actually shrank –0.6 percent in 2012. Investment recovered in 2013, growing 6.0 percent, but soon contracted again in 2014, with investment collapsing –4.3 percent. The average annual growth rate over 2011–2014 was 1.8 percent, lower than the growth rate of private consumption and substantially lower than investment growth over the previous period" (Serrano & Summa, 2015, p. 23). Many critics stressed that these funds should have been expended in direct investments by the government or, as a second best policy, in tax breaks directed to investments by the private sector.

12 Temer's finance minister, Francisco Meirelles, seemed to be aware of this when he justified his visit to the evangelical churches in the following terms: because they invited me and expressed their agreement with the values of society. It is, in part, the message of the churches: to spend only what is earned, not to borrow money for running expenses (Tereza, Rodrigues Alvares, & Fernandes, 2017).

13 In the period focused on in this article, texts and images explaining the crisis were profusely found in the national print media, as well as in television and social media, through visual and multimodal materials, like videos, cartoons, and memes.

14 In this five-minute address, Temer also introduced the most common metaphorical commonplace to explain and justify the new government's austerity program: A government is like your family. If you are in debt, you need to reduce expenses to pay off the debt. (…) Our motto is to spend only the money we collect. (as cited in Chagas, 2016).

References

Alejo González, R. (2011). The container schema in economics and its discourse. *International Journal of Innovation and Leadership in the Teaching of Humanities, 1*(1), 64–79.

Alesina, A., Barbiero, O., Favero, C., Giavazzi, F., & Paradisi, M. (2017). *The effects of fiscal consolidations: Theory and evidence.* (Working Paper No. 23385). Washington, DC: NBER. Retrieved from www.nber.org/papers/w23385

Almeida, J. S. G. (2011). Como o Brasil superou a crise. *Revista de Economia Política, 31*(2), 330–332.

Arrese, A. (2015). Euro crisis metaphors in the Spanish press. *Communication & Society, 28*(2), 19–23.

Bandeira, A. (2017, October 3). Economia: Luz no fim do túnel pode ser um trem que vai nos amassar. Retrieved from https://dinheirama.com/blog/2017/10/03/economia-luz-trem-amassar/

Barbosa, N., & Souza, J. A. P. (2010). A inflexão do Governo Lula: Política econômica, crescimento e distribuição de renda. In E. Sader & M. A. Garcia (Eds.), *Brasil: Entre o passado e o futuro* (pp. 1–42). São Paulo: Boitempo.

Betim, F. (2015, November 4). OCDE descreve o atual momento econômico do Brasil como 'crítico.' *El País*. Retrieved from https://brasil.elpais.com/brasil/2015/11/04/economia/1446663237_818015.html

Blyth, M. (2013). *Austerity: The history of a dangerous idea.* New York: Oxford University Press.

"'Brasil começa a entrar nos trilhos' diz Temer em reunião de cúpula do Brics." (2016, October 16). *Agência Brasil.* Retrieved from http://agenciabrasil.ebc.com.br/politica/noticia/2016-10/brasil-comeca-entrar-nos-trilhos-diz-teme-cupula-do-brics

"Brasil tem 12,961 milhões de desempregados, diz IBGE." (2017, October 31). Retrieved from http://epocanegocios.globo.com/Economia/noticia/2017/10/epoca-negocios-brasil-tem-desemprego-de-124-no-trimestre-ate-setembro-diz-ibge.html

Cameron, L., & Low, G. (Eds.). (1999). *Researching and applying metaphor*. Cambridge, UK: Cambridge University Press.

Cardini, F. E. (2014). Analysing English metaphors of the economic crisis. *Lingue Linguaggi*, *11*, 59–76.

Carvalho, F. J. C. (2008). Financial liberalization in Brazil and Argentina. In P. Arestis & L. F. De Paula (Eds.), *Financial liberalization and economic performance in emerging countries* (pp. 121–141). Houndmills, Basingstoke, UK: Palgrave Macmillan.

Chagas, P. (2016, August 31). Na TV, Temer cita reformas e que vai "recolocar o Brasil nos trilhos." *Agência Brasil*. Retrieved from http://agenciabrasil.ebc.com.br/politica/noticia/2016-08/na-tv-temer-cita-reformas-e-que-vai-recolocar-o-brasil-nos-trilhos

Charteris-Black, J. (2000). Metaphor and vocabulary teaching in ESP economics. *English for Specific Purposes*, *19*, 149–165.

Chick, V., & Pettifor, A. (2010). *The economic consequences of Mr. Osborne–Fiscal Consolidation: Lessons from a century of UK macroeconomic statistics*. Retrieved from www.annpettifor.com/wp-content/uploads/2010/06/Fiscal-Consolidation1.pdf

Constantino, R. (2015, July 28). Metáforas para acalmar as vítimas da crise [Blog post]. Retrieved from www.gazetadopovo.com.br/rodrigo-constantino/artigos/metaforas-para-acalmar-as-vitimas-da-crise/

Dantas, B. (2017). Colocando o Brasil nos trilhos … *Humor Político*. Retrieved from www.humorpolitico.com.br/bira/colocando-o-brasil-nos-trilhos/

"Dilma aponta para si antes de prescrever 'remédio amargo' contra a crise." (2017, September 7). *O Globo*. [Video]. Retrieved from https://oglobo.globo.com/brasil/dilma-aponta-para-si-antes-de-prescrever-remedio-amargo-contra-crise-17432479

Davidson, P. (2015). What was the primary factor encouraging mainstream economists to marginalize post Keynesian theory? *Journal of Post Keynesian Economics*, *37*(3), 369–383.

de Paula, L. F., Oreiro, J. L., & Basilio, F. A. C. (2013). Estrutura do setor bancário e o ciclo recente de expansão do crédito: O papel dos bancos públicos federais. *Nova Economia*, *23*(3), 473–520.

de Paula, L. F., & Saraiva, P. J. (2015). Novo consenso macroeconômico e regime de metas de inflação: algumas implicações para o Brasil. *Revista Paranaense de Desenvolvimento*, *36*(128), 19–32.

Dequech, D. (2011). Uncertainty: A typology and refinements of existing concepts. *Journal of Economic Issues*, *45*(3), 621–640.

Dow, S. C. (2008). Mainstream methodology, financial markets and global political economy. *Contributions to Political Economy*, *27*, 13–29.

Drummond, C. (2016, September 21). As elites agem politicamente para manter os juros altos? *Carta Capital* [online news portal]. Retrieved from www.cartacapital.com.br/revista/918/os-colecionadores-de-moedas

Entman, R. (1993) Framing: toward clarification of a fractured paradigm. *Journal of Communication*, *43*(4), 51–58.

Fucs, J. (2017, February 6). 'A sensação de trem desgovernado passou', diz Arminio Fraga. *O Estado de S. Paulo*. Retrieved from http://economia.estadao.com.br/noticias/geral,sensacao-de-trem-desgovernado-passou,70001654271

Gentner, D. (1988). Metaphor as structure mapping: The relational shift. *Child Development*, *59*, 47–59.

Gentner, D. (1989). The mechanisms of analogical reasoning. In S. Vosniadou & A. Ortony (Eds.). *Similarity and analogical reasoning*. Cambridge, UK: Cambridge University Press.

Gibbs, R.W., Jr., & Steen, G.J. (Eds.). (1999). *Metaphor in Cognitive Linguistics*. Amsterdam, Netherlands: John Benjamins.

Godley, W., & Zezza, G. (2006). *Debt and lending: A cri de coeur*. (Policy Note, 2006/4). New York: Levy Economics Institute of Bard College.

"Governo terá condições de recolocar Brasil nos trilhos com Lula," diz Dilma (2016, March 17). *Correio do Povo*. Retrieved from www.correiodopovo.com.br/Noticias/Politica/2016/3/582165/Governo-tera-condicoes-de-recolocar-Brasil-nos-trilhos-com-Lula,-diz-Dilma.

Grune-Yanoff, T. (Ed.). (2009). Economic models as credible worlds or as isolating tools [Special issue]. *Erkenntnis, 70*(1).

Guttman, R. (2009). Financial globalization and post-crisis perspectives. *The Perspective of the World Review, 1*(1), 53–68.

Hanan, J. S., & Chaput, C. (2015). A rhetoric of economics beyond civic humanism: Exploring the political economy of rhetoric in the context of late neo-liberalism. *Journal of Cultural Economy, 8*, (1), 16–24.

Kaltenbrunner, A. (2010). International financialization and depreciation: The Brazilian Real in the international financial crisis. *Competition and Change, 14*(3–4), 296–323.

Killingsworth, M. J. (2005). *Appeals in modern rhetoric: An ordinary language approach*. Carbondale, IL: Southern Illinois U.P.

Kövecses, Z. (2002). *Metaphor. A practical introduction*. New York/Oxford: Oxford University Press.

Lakoff, G. (1993). Contemporary theory of metaphor. In A. Ortony (Ed.). *Metaphor and thought* (2nd ed.) (pp. 201–251). Cambridge, UK: Cambridge University Press.

Lakoff, G., & Johnson, M. (1980). *Metaphors we live by*. Chicago, IL: University of Chicago Press.

Lawson, T. (1997). *Economics and reality*. London: Routledge.

Lawson, T. (2003). *Reorienting economics*. London: Routledge.

Lawson, T. (2009). The current economic crisis: Its nature and the course of academic economics. *Cambridge Journal of Economics, 33*(4), 759–777.

McCloskey, D. (1983). The rhetoric of economics. *Journal of Economic Literature, 21*(2), 481–517.

McCloskey, D. (1994). *Knowledge and persuasion in economics*. Cambridge, UK: Cambridge University Press.

McCloskey, D. (1997). *The rhetoric of economics* (2nd ed.). Madison: University of Wisconsin Press.

Musolff, A. (2006). Metaphor scenarios in public discourse. *Metaphor and Symbol, 21*(1), 23–38.

Musolff, A. (2016). *Political metaphor analysis: Discourse and scenarios*. London: Bloomsbury Academic.

Nersisyan, Y., & Wray, L. R. (2011). Review of the book *This time is different: Eight centuries of financial folly*, by Carmen Reinhart and Kenneth Rogoff. *Challenge, 54*(1), 113–120.

Nogueira, L. A. (2017). O trem econômico já voltou aos trilhos. Falta colocá-lo em movimento. *Istoé Dinheiro*. Retrieved from www.istoedinheiro.com.br/o-trem-economico-ja-voltou-aos-trilhos-falta-coloca-lo-em-movimento/

Oliveira, A. de (2017, June 1). Temer vai botar o país nos trilhos... *Humor Político*. Retrieved from www.humorpolitico.com.br/michel-temer/temer-vai-botar-o-pais-nos-trilhos/

Oliveira, G., & Coronato, M. (2016, April 4). Como o Brasil entrou sozinho na pior crise da história. *Época*. Retrieved from https://epoca.globo.com/ideias/noticia/2016/04/como-o-brasil-entrou-sozinho-na-pior-crise-da-historia.html

O'Mara-Shimek, M., Guillén-Parra, M., & Ortega-Larrea, A. (2015). Stop the bleeding or weather the storm? Crisis solution marketing and the ideological use of metaphor in online financial reporting of the stock market crash of 2008 at the New York Stock Exchange. *Discourse & Communication*, *9*(1), 103–123.

Orair, R. O., Siqueira, F. F., & Gobetti S. W. (2016). *Política fiscal e ciclo econômico: Uma análise baseada em multiplicadores do gasto público*. Brasília: Tesouro Nacional.

Portal Planalto. (2016, May 12). Discurso do Presidente da República, Michel Temer, durante cerimônia de posse dos novos ministros de Estado. Retrieved from www2.planalto.gov.br/acompanhe-planalto/discursos/discursos-do-presidente-da-republica/discurso-do-presidente-da-republica-michel-temer-durante-cerimonia-de-posse-dos-novos-ministros-de-estado-palacio-do-planalto

Portal Planalto. (2017, May 20). Declaração à Imprensa do Presidente da República, Michel Temer—Brasília/DF. Retrieved from www2.planalto.gov.br/acompanhe-planalto/discursos/discursos-do-presidente-da-republica/discurso-do-presidente-da-republica-michel-temer-durante-cerimonia-de-posse-dos-novos-ministros-de-estado-palacio-do-planalto

Portal Planalto. (2017, November 22). Discurso do Presidente da República, Michel Temer, durante cerimônia de anúncio da Política de Governança Pública. Retrieved from www2.planalto.gov.br/acompanhe-planalto/discursos/discursos-do-presidente-da-republica/discurso-do-presidente-da-republica-michel-temer-durante-cerimonia-de-anuncio-da-politica-de-governanca-publica

Pupo, F. (2018, January 11). Economistas preveem déficit primário menor em 2018, aponta Prisma. *Valor Econômico*. [online news portal]. Retrieved from www.valor.com.br/brasil/5253929/economistas-preveem-deficit-primario-menor-em-2018-aponta-prisma

Reinhart, C., & Rogoff, K. (2009). *This time is different: Eight centuries of financial folly*. Princeton, NJ: Princeton University Press.

Rossi, P., & Mello, G. (2017, April). Choque recessivo e a maior crise da história: A economia brasileira em marcha à ré. Centro de Estudos de Conjuntura e Política Econômica–IE/UNICAMP. Nota do Cecon, No. 1. Retrieved from www.eco.unicamp.br/images/arquivos/NotaCecon1_Choque_recessivo_2.pdf

Sayad, J. (2014, August 31). Pé ante pé: O preço da salada e outros mitos da moeda. *Folha de São Paulo*. Retrieved from www1.folha.uol.com.br/fsp/ilustrissima/183380-pe-ante-pe.shtml

Schiller, R. J. (2017, January 7) Narrative economics. Presidential address delivered at the 129th annual meeting of the American Economic Association. Retrieved from cowles.yale.edu/sites/default/files/files/pub/d20/d2069.pdf

Serrano, F., & Melin, L.E. (2015, December). *Political aspects of unemployment: Brazil's neo-liberal U-turn*. Retrieved from www.excedente.org/wp-content/uploads/2015/12/Serrano-Melin-U-Turn.pdf

Serrano, F., & Summa, R. (2015, August). *Aggregate demand and the slowdown of Brazilian economic growth from 2011–2014*. Center for Economic and Policy Research (CEPR).

Retrieved from http://cepr.net/publications/reports/aggregate-demand-and-the-slowdown-of-brazilian-economic-growth-from-2011–2014

Silva, A., Jr. (2015, June 1). Recuperação da economia precisa ser construída 'tijolo a tijolo', diz Levy. *Estadão*. Retrieved from http://economia.estadao.com.br/noticias/geral,recuperacao-da-economia-precisa-ser-construida-tijolo-a-tijolo--diz-levy,1698432

Silva, C. G., & Terra, F. H. B. (2012). O desempenho econômico brasileiro em 2011 e perspectivas para 2012: Uma análise rápida em um período complexo. *Economia & Tecnologia*, *8*(1), 7–18.

Simon, H. A. (1976). From substantive to procedural rationality. In S. J. Latsis (Ed.), *Method and appraisal in economics* (pp. 129–148). Cambridge, UK: Cambridge University Press.

Singer, A. (2015). Cutucando onças com varas curtas: O ensaio desenvolvimentista no primeiro mandato de Dilma Rousseff (2011–2014). *Novos Estudos CEBRAP*, *102*, 43–71.

Soihet, E., & Cabral, C. M. N. (2012). *Crise de 2008 e o papel determinante dos bancos públicos na recuperação da economia Brasileira*. Paper presented at the Fifth Conference of the Brazilian Keynesian Association (AKB), São Paulo.

Strachman, E. (2013). Metas de inflação no Brasil (1999–2012): Uma análise institucional. *Ensaios Econômicos FEE*, *34*(2), 407–438.

Temer, M. (2017, November 8). O Brasil voltou aos trilhos. *Diário de Notícias*. Retrieved from www.dn.pt/opiniao/opiniao-dn/convidados/interior/o-brasil-voltou-aos-trilhos-8901702.html

Tereza, I., Rodrigues A., M., & Fernandes, A. (2017, October 8). Em cultos, ministro Henrique Meirelles prega austeridade. *Estadão : Economia & Negócios*. Retrieved from http://economia.estadao.com.br/noticias/geral,em-cultos-ministro-henrique-meirelles-prega-austeridade,70002032568

Thibodeau, P. H., & Boroditsky, L. (2011). Metaphors we think with: The role of metaphor in reasoning. *PLoSOne*. *6*, e16782. doi: 10.1371/journal.pone.0016782 PMID: 21373643

UOL Economia. (2017, July 11). Após reforma passar, Temer diz que governo está "conectado com o século 21." Retrieved from https://economia.uol.com.br/noticias/redacao/2017/07/11/apos-reforma-passar-temer-diz-que-governo-esta-conectado-com-o-seculo-21.htm?cmpid=copiaecola

"Veja as medidas contra a crise já tomadas pelo governo no Brasil." (2008, December 28). Retrieved from http://economia.uol.com.br/ultnot/2008/12/11/ult4294u2001.jhtm

7 Tales of austerity, and a crisis of wealth distribution

Naoise McDonagh

> *I accept that there were failures in the political system. I accept that I have to take responsibility as a member of the governing party during that period for what happened. But let's be fair about it. We all partied.*
>
> — Brian Lenihan, Irish Finance Minister (2010)

Austerity, referring to drastic cuts in public spending, dominated the Irish state's policy response to the financial crisis that erupted in 2008. The political framing of austerity proceeded in two distinct ways. The first strategy involved discursively constructing the crisis "as a moral spectacle" (Kelsey, Mueller, Whittle, & KhosraviNik, 2016, p. 3), with the above statement from Ireland's Finance Minister made during a nationally broadcast 'Prime Time' interview an exemplar of this approach. Lenihan argued that austerity was penance for national hedonism in the form of profligate state spending, thereby universalizing guilt amongst all Irish citizens for national debt levels that exploded post-2008. However, Ireland's public debt explosion post-2008, like elsewhere in Europe, occurred not as a result of overly-generous public spending, but as a result of public funding for bank bailouts.

Consequently, moral storytelling should be seen as a discursive strategy, a 'blame game' which shifted responsibility for the economic crisis away from private finance capital and onto the State (Morgan, Froud, Quack, & Schneiberg, 2011). A second discursive strategy pursued by Ireland's governing class supported the first, whereby economic experts argued that austerity was the most effective technical solution to resolve a fiscal crisis. Here the "quintessential 'austerian' is the technocrat" who is presented as an advocate of "unpleasant but necessary measures" (Schui, 2014, p. 4). While prominent neo-Keynesian economists have challenged the technical arguments supporting austerity (Krugman, 2012; Stiglitz, 2012), such arguments miss the deeper structural issues motivating arguments for austerity.

I argue in this chapter that austerity is not primarily designed to solve an economic crisis, but rather to solve a crisis of wealth distribution. This fact has been hidden by political framing strategies. In reformulating a capitalist economic crisis as primarily a sociopolitical distributional crisis, I seek to sharpen into view the fundamental issue at stake. Austerity is a neoliberal strategy to preserve an institutional pattern of wealth distribution, one that favors owners of capital under conditions of a shrinking economic surplus. Consequently, when seen through a lens of social stratification, austerity works extremely well. Discursively framing austerity in moral and technical terms is strategic. It follows from the fact that in order to dictate the sociopolitical response to a crisis of distribution a group must be able to provide the dominant framing of the nature of the crisis and its logical solution (Sum & Jessop, 2013).

Drawing theoretically upon concepts from 'cultural political economy' (Sum & Jessop, 2013) and the theory of social stratification (Harris, 1959; Angle, 1986), this chapter challenges public framings of austerity that appeared during January 2009 in the *Irish Times*, a nationally disseminated medium considered Ireland's newspaper of record (McDonagh, 2016a). At this key period in Ireland's emerging financial crisis, politicians and elite economic actors utilized privileged media access to frame austerity for political ends. The chapter will proceed in six sections. Section 1 assesses literature on the discursive production of austerity as moral penance during Europe's financial crisis. Section 2 draws upon social stratification theory to argue that austerity is primarily a policy solution to a crisis of wealth distribution. Section 3 discusses the role of neoliberal policy in Ireland's political economy in the run-up to the 2008 financial crisis. Section 4 discusses data collection and methodology. Section 5 provides an analysis of data. Section 6 provides a discussion of key findings and summarizes the argument.

1. Greek myths and austerity as penance

In cultural political economy, 'semiosis' refers to the sense- and meaning-making required for actors to 'get on' in the world, with discourse being a key resource through which this occurs (Sum & Jessop, 2013). Meaning-making is an activity that typically occurs in relation to material events, which can then be discursively understood in various and contingent ways. Ontologically, cultural political economy is concerned with the ways in which social actors reduce otherwise endless and overwhelming social complexity into manageable subsets, through practices such as discourse construction. Complexity reduction is further provided through the historical fixing of institutional and ideological limits on possible forms of social relations at any given point in time-space (Sum & Jessop, 2013, p. 6). Such historical fixing produces patterns of social structuration that reduce the scope for some social practices while increasing the scope for others. For example, a neoliberal state is more likely to seek fiscal consolidation through wage suppression and spending cuts than through wealth taxation, and will have pre-given institutional and ideological resources that make such an approach both feasible and logical-sounding. By contrast, a socialist government would be more likely to take the latter option, and have the requisite resources that make that option appear most plausible.

Irrespective of the historically fixed context, a crisis can be said to objectively occur when a set of social relations can no longer go on. To elaborate, we can say that crises "disrupt accepted views of the world and how to 'go on' within it and also call established theoretical and policy paradigms into question" (Sum & Jessop, 2013, p. 395). For this reason a crisis is usually disorientating, and opens space for alternative ideas previously ignored. A contest to instill dominant interpretive narratives is likely to emerge between actors with different interests and prerogatives. The 2008 global financial crisis was just such a profoundly disorientating crisis, and for that reason initially resulted in an equally disorientating potpourri of narratives as to what happened, why it had happened, and what should be done in response (see Galbraith, 2014, pp. 4–17).

Two accounts of the crisis became dominant within the Eurozone after the initial shock subsided. One account focused on the story of individual, immoral behavior while the other focused on the sovereign debt crisis engulfing states such as Portugal, Ireland, Italy, Greece and Spain, grouped under the 'PIIGS' acronym. Both narratives became intertwined and self-reinforcing in many instances, both in Ireland and elsewhere, producing both a moral and a technical veil covering deeper structural motivations driving the story of the crisis and its solution. Some examples of this veiling process will now be highlighted.

The financial crisis as moral spectacle in the mass media was one way in which complexity was considerably reduced in public discourse. While "moral storytelling can enhance or enlighten our understanding of an issue, it can also be used as a tool for manipulating an audience or suppressing other knowledge" (Kelsey et al., 2016, p. 4). For this reason such stories ought to be carefully scrutinized, both for what they may hide from view, as much as for what they explicitly tell us. A number of studies have focused on how individuals such as corporate bankers utilized moral reconstructions in order to shift responsibility for the crisis. One method was to present themselves as penitent learners who were willing to improve (Tourish & Hargie, 2012); another was the use of public apologies to attribute blame and responsibility (Hargie, Stapleton, & Tourish, 2010). Moral stories were also used to blame governments and national populations for a sovereign debt crisis caused by finance capital. Here, the myth of the 'lazy Greek' (Kitromilides, 2013; Mylonas, 2014; Pentaraki, 2013) stands out in particular.

The myth goes as follows: Greek society is responsible for its sovereign debt crisis post-2008. A corrupted and inept state mismanaged national affairs; tax evasion was endemic; the public sector was overblown and inefficient, while powerful labor unions and protected professions blocked entrepreneurial activity. This critique was reinforced by a disturbing caricature of Greek society as "inherently lazy, profligate and irresponsible," given as reasons for why the State was living beyond its financial means (Kitromilides, 2013, p. 626). The clear moral of the story was that Greek austerity was both necessary and deserving as penance for immoral behavior. Pentaraki (2013), however, highlights the spurious quality of these myths, noting that the public sector was not overblown, but proportionally one of the smallest in the Eurozone; and that Greece's welfare system before austerity was less generous than the EU average. Likewise, OECD data on average hours worked per worker in 2008 gives the truth to the lazy Greek myth, showing that Greeks worked on average 2,120 hours a year, a full 690 hours more than the average German (OECD, 2017).

Greek ethnicity suffered most as the target of direct and sustained ethnic abuse in the politics of European austerity. However, other states captured by the derogatory 'PIIGS' acronym were all subject through association to share national characteristics homologous with the lazy Greek caricature. Less vitriolic discourse, using the technical language of 'inefficiency,' was more often used to code the public sectors of these states as deserving the penance of austerity. For PIIGS states, becoming efficient meant engaging in 'much-needed' market-orientated reforms according to Germany's finance minister Wolfgang Schäuble (2011). Reforms here included making labor markets more flexible, raising the retirement age, suppressing wages and cutting pension benefits, with the public sector the main target. For Schäuble, this is no more than moral penance for the "undisputable fact that excessive state spending has led to unsustainable levels of debt and deficits" (Schäuble, 2011).

What Schäuble fails to acknowledge is, first, that it was the cost of bank bailouts post-2008 that had led to enormous fiscal deficits in the PIIGS, and second, that much of this bailout money went directly to German and French banks, which had exposure to PIIGS economies estimated at $1 trillion in 2010 (Blyth, 2013, p. 86). In light of such facts, I suggest that moral storytelling in European political discourse post-2008 had been mobilized not to enlighten, but rather to veil deeper political-economic motivations.

Before discussing these motivations, I will briefly highlight a number of recent studies assessing the role of the Irish media in framing the financial crisis to the public (McDonagh, 2016a, 2016b; Mercille, 2014). Previously, I have analysed corporate mass media over a two-year period (2009–2010), assessing how organizational bias determined who received media access in order to project narratives about Ireland's economic crisis (McDonagh, 2016a). That study argues that the *Irish Times* provided privileged access to business leaders and orthodox economists during Ireland's financial crisis, helping to 'capture' debate on recovery within the logic of capital. Elsewhere (McDonagh, 2016b), I have analysed framing strategy used to legitimate bank bailout policy, focusing on how the frame "Too big to fail" was deployed within Ireland's two leading daily newspaper media during 2008–2009. Mercille's (2014) study provides a quantitative overview of 431 articles appearing in three leading Irish newspapers, assessing each medium's editorial position on fiscal consolidation (austerity) between 2008 and 2012.

Mercille's study is relevant to the concerns of this chapter with austerity discourse. Regarding the *Irish Times*, the media investigated here, Mercille finds that over the time period in question 57% of articles support fiscal consolidation, 16% are against it, and 27% are neutral (2014: 296). In addition, Mercille's study highlights article titles in the *Irish Times* that are highly suggestive of the moral and technical veiling of austerity discussed in this chapter, titles such as "Commitment and Stamina are Required for Fiscal Consolidation" (*Irish Times*, 6 September 2008), "Austerity Vital to Maintain our Economic Sovereignty"

(*Irish Times*, 11 October 2010), "Bill is Tough but Necessary" (*Irish Times*, 22 January 2011), and "Tough Budget Needed to Stave Off Grimmer Future" (*Irish Times*, 4 November 2009). However, while Mercille's study comprehensively categorizes the *Irish Times* stance towards austerity in relation to a large number of articles, it also elides the rich qualitative data on narrative construction. This chapter will provide such an analysis of austerity narratives in Irish public discourse, theorized in a framework that uniquely illuminates the crisis of distribution on which austerity politics turn.

2. A Surplus of wealth and a deficit of distribution

A second discursive veiling of the political character of austerity post-2008 has occurred through public discourse that treats fiscal spending cuts as a neutral technical issue. Under this 'technical veil' proponents of austerity argue that state spending has gotten out of control, and that fiscal consolidation is a painful but necessary policy to restore growth. On the other hand, detractors of austerity reproduce this technical framing by also arguing in technical terms about the validity of the policy. Members of this latter group, typically economists within the Keynesian tradition, argue that austerity is a wrong-headed policy solution resulting from a misdiagnosis of economic factors (Calcagno, 2012; Krugman, 2012; Reich, 2010; Stiglitz, 2012). Misdiagnosis is argued to be a result of mistaking the symptom of the crisis, fiscal indebtedness, as the cause of the crisis. However, in presenting austerity as a policy failure, Keynesians eschew analysis of underlying capitalist class relations as the source of structural motivations for particular policy positions (Hossein-zadeh, 2014). Consequently, Keynesian economists have a significant blind spot in their analysis of austerity.

As far as it goes, it is correct that austerity is a poor choice to resolve an economic crisis, since the weight of evidence shows that it leads to downturns that are "longer and deeper than necessary" (Schui, 2014, p. 5). However, when the 2008 financial crisis is viewed primarily as a class-based crisis of distribution and as an economic crisis second, austerity takes on a different hue. To elaborate, austerity is a form of fiscal consolidation that seeks to boost 'business confidence' by cutting public expenditure, suppressing wages, and replacing government service provision with private service provision (Blyth, 2013, p. 2). These are all central aspects of neoliberal economic restructuring (Fraser, Murphy, & Kelly, 2013; Larner, 2000), a project Harvey (2005) argues is itself a reactionary movement designed to restore capitalist class power weakened by the rising influence of labor unions and Keynesian welfare policy post-1945. In highlighting the congruence between austerity and neoliberalism, the former can be placed as a policy within the neoliberal paradigm, one designed to maintain favorable wealth distribution patterns for owners of capital under conditions of economic recession. To develop this argument further, the surplus theory of social stratification will provide a more detailed context in which to understand the political economy of austerity.

The "surplus theory of social stratification" (Harris, 1959) regards the development of agricultural technology as pivotal in ushering in the era of fixed human settlements through supply of a consistent and growing economic surplus. This surplus allowed for the emergence of a population of specialized non-food producers, including "craftsmen, merchants, priests, officials and clerks" (Childe, 1942, p. 18), and with this differentiation of roles a concomitant dramatic revolution in social organization. Of particular concern here is the impact of economic surplus on patterns of distribution, which shift from being largely egalitarian in pre-surplus societies to increasingly unequal in surplus economies (Fried, 1967; Mann, 2012). For example, archaeological excavations have consistently found that evidence of substantial inequality of wealth appears in the same strata as evidence of early agriculture and plentiful food (Angle, 1986). Consequently, it appears that at the point in history when the necessities for material reproduction of life become increasingly plentiful we also see increasing evidence of political contests over the distribution of that surplus. This marks the transformation of 'economy'—meaning the struggle against nature for material survival—into political economy, a distributional struggle between various social classes for a share of the surplus produced by society.

In reformulating a capitalist economic crisis as a sociopolitical distributional crisis, I seek to sharpen into view the fundamental issue at hand in austerity politics, with which this chapter, and indeed the whole book, is concerned. At stake is our ability to distinguish between necessary outcomes resulting from a given event, for example rationing of goods during a famine because of absolute shortages, and socially determined outcomes in reaction to a given event, for example austerity that impacts the lowest socioeconomic group to ensure privileged distributional patterns are maintained for others. Consequently, it has been suggested that the study of social stratification could be renamed the study of 'distributive process,' since what is at stake is the question of "[w]ho gets what and why?" (Lenski, 1966, p. 1).

Consistent and growing inequality under capitalism (Piketty, 2014), therefore, follows the historical trend identified with the emergence of an economic surplus, namely the startlingly universal fact that "…the equal distribution of wealth in societies with surpluses is so rare as to be almost non-existent" (Herskovits, 1940, p. 371). The issue at hand is that once a surplus has been established, a contraction in economic output at a given moment is less likely to produce a general economic crisis threatening all strata, and increasingly likely to become a social crisis of distribution. Depending on institutional arrangements and cultural norms, a distribution crisis may result in a competitive scramble whereby each economic class aims to maintain their pre-crisis share of a now shrinking economic surplus. Only the losers in this distributional crisis will experience an actual economic crisis.

Under contemporary capitalism, two key institutions that decide distribution of surplus are wage-labor (Marx, 1990) and the welfare state (Gough, 1979). Capitalist wage-labor ensures a greater share of the produced economic surplus goes to owners of capital relative to labor. The welfare state collects through taxation a share of the total surplus produced and then redistributes this share through public expenditure that benefits both capital (providing costly public goods such as railways, highways, police forces, judiciary, etc., that are necessary for a functioning economy) and labor (providing transfer payments such as unemployment support, healthcare, and state pensions). At any given moment both the exact level of wages paid to labor and the distribution policies of the welfare state are open to contestation. Structurally, therefore, the central fault lines in capitalist distributional politics are the contest between labor and capital over a share of the economic surplus generated during production (Silver, 2003), and the role of the State in redistributing a portion of the surplus collected through taxes. Austerity operates simultaneously on both of these sites of contestation and in ways that favor capital over labor.

3. Ireland's political economy

Kirby (2010) and Kirby and Murphy (2011) have comprehensively detailed why Ireland's economic development during its 'Celtic Tiger' era of high growth during the 1990s and 2000s is best conceptualized as a form of neoliberal 'competition state' economy. The competition state is an analytical construct used to assess the ways in which industrially developed states began to restructure themselves during the 1990s in response to the opportunities and constraints resulting from the ongoing global liberalization of capital (Kirby & Murphy, 2011, p. 23). Factors of economic globalization including highly mobile capital, international competitiveness for mobile capital, and growing international trade forced economic restructuring away from the Keynesian welfare orthodoxy of the post-war era and towards a neoliberal policy paradigm.

The Irish state's policy response to globalization involved neoliberal measures including privatization of public services, minimal regulation of key economic sectors, and supply-side incentives such as favorable tax structures and investment grants to attract foreign direct investment. Policies such as these led some to view Ireland as an "exemplar of the [neoliberal] competition state, where social policy is subordinated to the needs of the economy" (Boyle, 2005, p. 16; Kirby & Murphy, 2011). This was especially the case in the financial sector, where institutional patterns of economic regulation and surplus distribution followed the Anglo-Saxon model of economic liberalization, with disastrous results.

Ireland's banking crisis was the direct result of its competition state model of development championing neoliberal deregulation of the State's financial sector, in a policy termed 'light-touch' regulation (Chari & Bernhagen, 2011). The light touch approach to regulation was based upon prevailing approaches in Anglo-Saxon financial policy circles since the Thatcher and Reagan era reforms (Donovan & Murphy, 2013). The supporting economic philosophy for these reforms was based on the Efficient Market Hypothesis (Fama, 1970), which argued that markets are most efficient at allocating resources when left to self-regulate. Implementation of light-touch regulation in Ireland during the 1990s and 2000s set in place the conditions for the financial crisis of 2008, as bank lending became increasingly speculative in the drive for more profit. The fallacy of self-regulation rests in ignoring the fact that the inevitable pressure between banks to compete for market share tends to reduce incentives to act prudently, while increasing incentives to act speculatively. For example, as competition increased between Irish banks to fund a growing construction boom across the State, lending criteria became ever more lax. This allowed property speculation to increase, driving more lending in a self-expanding cycle.

The result of massive credit expansion was predictable. Between 1991 and 2007 house prices in Ireland quadrupled on average, while during the same period building costs and wages only doubled. By 2007 the average house price represented a multiple of 11.9 times the average industrial wage (Kitchin, O'Callaghan, Boyle, Gleeson, & Keaveney, 2012). A standard prudential measure of a sustainable multiple between median income and house prices is considered to be between three and five, highlighting the degree of speculation in Ireland's property market. The freezing of interbank credit as a result of the US subprime crisis beginning in 2007 was simply the proximate cause triggering deflation of Ireland's extreme property bubble. Without further credit to fuel speculation there was a precipitous drop in prices over the subsequent years, so that by 2010 house prices in the capital Dublin were 52% lower than at their highest level in early 2007, with the rest of the country averaging a drop of 42% (Kitchin et al., 2012).

The share of banks' assets in property-related lending had by 2006 grown to over 60% (Honohan, 2010). As a result, the significant drop in property valuations would have been disastrous absent intervention for the Irish banking system, as loan-to-value ratios turned negative and increasing numbers of loans became non-performing. Financial collapse threatened the whole scheme of financial wealth built on property speculation during the latter years of Ireland's boom. Thus began Ireland's social crisis of distribution as a result of the financial sector's economic crisis. To protect financial claims on wealth, Ireland's government followed two strategies that became commonplace in many states impacted by the financial crisis.

First, the State implemented bank bailouts to socialize private debts, initially spending €5.5 billion in September 2008 to take controlling stakes in the State's three main banks—Allied Irish Bank (AIB), Bank of Ireland (BoI), and Anglo Irish Bank—with tens of billions added to this over the next two years. It was these bailout costs rather than spending on public services or wages that led to an explosion in Irish state debt in 2009. Second, starting in 2009, the State implemented a multi-year austerity plan to fund the costs of the bank bailouts. The social costs of austerity ensure it is politically unpopular. When austerity is required to protect private financial wealth invested for private gain on the market, it becomes a potentially explosive political issue. Consequently, in 2009 Irish elites began a concerted effort to publicly frame austerity in technical and moral terms in order to distract from its political-economic function of making the general public pay the costs for a party to which they were never invited.

4. Data collection and methodology

This study draws upon data from a larger corpus collected from the *Irish Times* during the period of January 2009 to December 2010. The *Irish Times* is the second highest circulation daily during this period and is considered Ireland's newspaper of record. The corpus was collected using the following search commands in the *LexisNexis* news database:

> Ireland AND HLEAD (financial crisis OR banking crisis) AND (comment OR opinion OR editorial OR analysis)
> INDEXING 'Economic Conditions'

The search returns 204 articles. The search utilizes the 'HLEAD' command to target specific terms in the headline of an article in order to return comment, opinion, editorial, and analysis articles that have either 'financial crisis' or 'banking crisis' in their frame of reference These categories of article are indicative of the *Irish Times* overall editorial stance, since access to present an article is dependent upon editorial gatekeepers. Further, these articles are intended to present a strong argumentative position regarding solutions to Ireland's financial crisis, highlighting the priorities of elite actors. Once unrelated articles, which included 'Letters to the Editor' on various other topics, are removed 140 articles remain.

In a previous study, I have analyzed the entire corpus relative to organizational bias in the production of public media discourse on economic recovery (McDonagh, 2016a). For the purposes of this study, I will restrict analysis to articles returned in January 2009, which number six in total. January 2009 is the start of a year in which a new fiscal reality of multi-year state spending cuts becomes the dominant political issue in Ireland, and initial arguments for 'austerity' are presented to the public at this time. It is a time of profound disorientation for Irish citizens, and a prime moment in which to instill a dominant narrative so as to be able to dictate policy response. Articles have been read iteratively in order to identify themes specifically relating to moral and technical framings of austerity. In addition, by taking a small-*n* approach to data collection, this study aims to provide rich details of narrative construction that are missing in studies on austerity discourse in Irish media. The qualitative 'small-*n*' approach taken here accepts the view that "in a complex social world, cases are at some level unique" (Bennett & Elman, 2006, p. 258). Nevertheless, while every case is unique to a degree, it is also true that cases typically share characteristics, since social action is reproduced in reoccurring stable patterns across time, by way of institutions and ubiquitous cultural values (Campbell, 2004). As a result, individual cases may, as I argue here, present an 'instance of type' that provide insight into wider phenomena (Hammersley & Gomm, 2009, p. 4).

5. Analysis

January 2009 represents a period in Ireland when a crisis of wealth distribution has emerged. I will now assess how this played out within discourse in the *Irish Times*. Table 7.1 below provides an overview of the data, providing information on the author, article type, title, and date of publication. All articles are argumentative opinion pieces written by the named authors, except for one article which is an interview article with Brian Cowen, Ireland's Prime Minister of the period. Table 7.1 highlights common moral and technical themes across the six articles, showing which themes appeared in which articles. Three moral veils, and two technical ones, are prominent within the corpus. Each of these will now be highlighted through quotes and then discussed.

Austerity as morality

The politics of redistribution that underlie austerity were suppressed through moralizing discourse that manifested in at least three ways within the corpus investigated here. First, the myth of the 'lazy Greek' finds in Ireland its

Table 7.1 Moral and technical veiling in the *Irish Times*

Article information and thematic overview	*Moral Veiling*	*Technical Veiling*
B. Cowen, Prime Minister, interview, "Cowen wants public to get behind him" (January 3)	"'Lazy Greek' homology" "National duty to pitch in"	No
Editorial, opinion, "No time for whingers" (January 3)	"'Lazy Greek' homology" "National duty to pitch in"	No
A. Ahearne, Economist, opinion, "Income taxes will need to rise" (January 27)	"'Lazy Greek' homology" "National duty to pitch in" "Public and private sector must suffer equally"	"Cost competitiveness"
J. Fitzgerald, economist, opinion, "Government must detail real plan to take us out of crisis" (January 12)	"National duty to pitch in"	"Cost competitiveness"
G. Fitzgerald, former politician, opinion, "Loss of competitiveness remains most serious issue"' (January 31)	"National duty to pitch in" "Public and private sector must suffer equally"	"Cost competitiveness"
P. O'Mahony, Irish Times journalist, opinion, "'Bad bank" strategy luring regulators internationally" (January 21)	No	"Nationalize non-performing private debts"

homology in the myth of the 'inefficient' or 'archaic' public sector; second, the idea of a moral equivalence between public sector and private sector employees regarding the costs of austerity is constructed; third, a moral duty calling on individual sacrifice for the national good emerges. All three veils relate primarily to arguments seeking wage repression, reductions in public service provision, and reductions to transfer payments. I will provide examples of each in turn.

The lazy Greek myth is a powerful moral story that seeks to make austerity for specific groups a form of moral penance. In that sense it provides a compelling and relatively simple explanation that effectively reduces complexity by allowing citizens to understand a technical issue in terms of everyday moral reasoning. In effect, the lazy Greek narrative is a means to legitimate distribution of costs on moral grounds. In Ireland it has typically been the public sector cast in the role of the lazy Greek. The myth of the 'lazy public sector' is vividly constructed in the *Irish Times* across three articles. An interview article with Ireland's Prime Minister of the time, Brian Cowen (January 3), uncritically presents arguments that subtly prepare the ground for public sector cutbacks. Cowen argues that "short-term measures would have to be taken this year in the health service and other areas of the public service to get better value for money." Or again, Cowen argues that the nation must "satisfy ourselves that we are doing it [public spending] in the most efficient and best possible way."

These two quotes subtly position the public sector as slothful, but in ways that avoid politically risky outright attacks by Cowen on his own civil servants. For example, inefficiency or poor value for money may simply be bad practice. On the other hand, it may also be read as inferring a poor work ethic, in which case wage cuts would be fair penance. Consequently, the wider discursive environment is important here, since it nudges interpretation of more ambiguous statements in certain directions.

The article by economist Alan Ahearne (January 27) is less ambiguous in coding the public sector as lazy and anti-progressive, arguing: "Parts of the public sector are wedded to archaic structures and systems that act as barriers to improvements in efficiency." This is followed up by the claim that "During the boom, surging tax revenues from the property sector allowed the Government to meet the increased demand for public services without major improvements in productivity." Like in the Cowen article, no evidence is forthcoming; however, this narrative fits with the generic neoliberal narrative that juxtaposes a wasteful and lazy public sector against an entrepreneurial private sector (Mazzucato, 2013). I will provide evidence that calls this narrative into question below in discussing the technical framing of austerity as a necessity of regaining cost competitiveness.

A third article, this time an editorial (January 3), is most reminiscent of the direct abusive coding of Greek culture that has marred political discussion in Europe. The editorial engages in a scathing attack on low-wage public sector workers, referring to them as 'whingers' for protesting against coming wage-cuts even as billions of public money are made available to absorb private financial losses. The editorial compares current worker resistance with historical cronyism and greed embedded in Irish culture generally, arguing:

> greed has been endemic in Irish life for a very long time, sometimes wrapped in the cloak of politics, whether it was the land hunger of past generations shrouded in the green flag of nationalism or, occasionally, the selfishness of workers in powerful positions.

This moralistic historical revisionism strays far from the current causes of Ireland's crisis, speculative finance capital, and is suggestive of the moral story that seeks to hide more than reveal the issues at stake.

Two articles argue that there is a moral imperative that wage suppression, which is occurring at a faster rate in the private sector, must be matched in the public sphere. Ahearne (January 27) argues that

> because of the competitiveness crisis facing many private sector firms, some employees and employers are already agreeing deals to cut nominal wage rates to save jobs. If such a pattern occurs across the private sector it will be vital that this is also reflected in a similar (or even a greater) fall in the public sector.

Similarly, Garrett Fitzgerald (January 31), a former Irish Prime Minister, argues that "A significant divergence between current pay trends in the public service and the private sector would be impossible to defend." Just why there should be a moral coupling of wages between these fundamentally different sectors is not articulated in any substantive manner. It is simply assumed that it is morally appropriate that wage suppression should be across the board. The potential strategic value of this type of moral equivalence is that it drives a wedge between private and public sector workers at a time when solidarity would serve both groups better in defending their overall share of the economic surplus.

A third moralizing veil calls for national sacrifice and a renewed work ethic during a time of crisis. Cowen (January 3) talks of "all of us putting our shoulders to the wheel," or that "We have to roll up our sleeves and just try and be as competitive as others in other markets." In calling for a renewed work ethic, Cowen simultaneously imputes the opposite, a lack of work ethic, without having to directly state it, since renewal is only required when decay has first occurred. Ahearne argues that "The public will presumably not be willing to put their shoulders to the wheel unless the burden-sharing associated with the fiscal consolidation is perceived as equitable" (January 27), also drawing on notions of national sacrifice, and in ways that reinforce a moral equivalency for public workers to accepts cuts similar to private workers. Economist John Fitzgerald (January 12) takes a similar position as Ahearne, arguing "Before a recovery can begin, the effects of this fall in output have to be shared out more evenly across the economy." Considering the focus on national sacrifice and equitable distribution of costs, one might find it strange that the given solutions all focus on wage suppression and public service spending. Such austerity policies prevent equitable cost distribution by primarily affecting those on the lowest incomes in society (Blyth, 2013).

Austerity as technicality

As noted in the introduction, a major factor driving austerity in Ireland was increased public debt due to the State assuming responsibility for bad banking debts. One article weighs up the technical merits of this approach, pointing to Sweden's experience during the 1990s. O'Mahony (January 21) notes that the Swedish government spent around 4% of GDP buying toxic bank assets, which were then restructured and sold on at a loss of 50%. He concludes that this "investment" is "a small price to pay in the circumstances, most agree." Invoking common sense is one way to passively nudge a reader to accept an argument, as well as normalize what is a drastic solution. Two per cent of any state's GDP is a significant number. Furthermore, what O'Mahony does not discuss is where the funds would come from to pay for an Irish bank bailout. Is it coincidence that simultaneous to a growing realization that the government would bail out the Irish banking sector, various elites began calling for public spending cuts?

Technical arguments for general wage suppression in January 2009 focus exclusively on the concept of cost competiveness between national economies. It is claimed that there has been "a disastrous decline in our national competitiveness" (G. Fitzgerald, January 31); that "in the short term [we] have to address competitiveness issues" (Cowen, January 3); that the "crucial feature of the current crisis is the very serious loss of competitiveness in recent years" (J. Fitzgerald, January 12), or again that "[t]wo conditions are necessary for a revival in exports: a rebound in economic activity abroad and a substantial improvement in cost competitiveness at home" (Ahearne, January 27).

While these commentators are sure that cost competitiveness is the problem, they are less sure as to how this has occurred. Ahearne notes prices in Ireland have risen 25% relative to Ireland's trading partners, continuing

> [s]ome of the faster pace of increase in prices and wages can probably be justified by improvements in productivity, but there can be little doubt that wages in both the private and public sectors overshot their sustainable levels during the bubble years.

However, no evidence is shown as to why we should have no doubt on the causes of price inflation.

This is not surprising since the economic literature on the concept of international competitiveness suggests that the concept is largely ill-defined and open to "a wide variety of notions and extreme difficulties of measurement and application" (Buckley, Pass, & Prescott, 1988, p. 175; Siggel, 2006). That said, international business ratings have long been considered a key resource for assessing national competitiveness (Buckley et al., 1988). An assessment of Ireland's public service according to the World Bank's 'Doing Business' global index is one way of assessing the robustness of competitiveness claims. Multiple measures within this index refer to public sector efficiency in facilitating business activity, including getting construction permits, registering property, paying taxes, enforcing contracts, and resolving insolvency. In 2006, Ireland ranked 11 out of 190 countries; the same assessment in 2009 ranked Ireland four places higher at number seven globally (World Bank, 2006, 2009). The myth of the 'uncompetitive public sector' seems as dubious and objectionable as the myth of the 'lazy Greek'.

Nevertheless, there was no shortage of solutions to this unproven claim, namely to reduce the costs. Ahearne argues that "[r]educing public sector pay is a necessary part of the effort to improve Ireland's cost competitiveness," along with cuts in current spending and transfer payments. For J. Fitzgerald a sharp "5 per cent fall in nominal wages in 2009" does the trick, while G. Fitzgerald argues the State must "tackle effectively the excess of our pay levels above those of our EU competitors." What is noteworthy here is that while no real evidence is put forth to exhibit Ireland's lost competitiveness, the above commentators come to a decisive agreement that austerity for both workers (through wage suppression) and the poorest in Irish society (through cuts to public services and transfer payments) is the solution.

6. Discussion and conclusion

Ireland did not experience a general economic crisis in 2009, as an array of social elites connected to economic governance across public and private realms claimed. The country did experience a crisis of distribution, the outcome of which resulted in marginalized social groups experiencing an economic crisis. I have argued that austerity ought to be seen primarily as a form of neoliberal retrenchment designed primarily to solve the dilemma posed to incumbent wealth distribution patterns during an economic recession. The policy is not, therefore, primarily designed to solve an economic recession, as typically claimed by proponents, nor is it morally legitimate penance for state hedonism or a slothful cultural work ethic. I will now discuss further the implications of this argument for unsettling the narrative of austerity.

Beginning with technical arguments, it is not the case that fiscal austerity is entirely incidental to economic recovery, even if the policy primarily addresses distributional concerns. What I mean here is that in capitalist economies private sector growth "is not just a function of strong demand but also of low costs, which often means low employment and low wages" (Hossein-zadeh, 2014, p. 28). However, it is precisely because the private sector will automatically adjust wages and employment levels during a recession that Keynes's (1936) great insight was that public sector spending must be counter-cyclical to the business cycle. Spending on public services, transfer payments and capital projects during a recession would all work to increase demand, shortening the duration and reducing the intensity of a given economic downturn. Of course, the immediate objection to this proposal is that a growing deficit leads to higher borrowing costs and is therefore unsustainable. But this objection presupposes that the only way to raise funds is through borrowing, when other reasonable options exist, to which I now turn.

Philo (2010) has challenged the claimed necessity of austerity in the United Kingdom by providing a fully costed proposal for clearing national debt through a one-off graduated wealth tax. Since much wealth is tied up in property and other non-liquid assets, the proposal allowed for payment after death, with interest on what is owed paid in the meantime. Philo also conducted a YouGov poll which showed that 74% of the British public supported this proposal. As Philo noted, aside from being technically feasible, the moral argument is entirely on the side of a wealth tax rather than austerity, which is in effect a new tax on the already impoverished (Blyth, 2013, p. 8). However, this type of proposal never entered serious public debate in either the United Kingdom, Ireland or to the best knowledge of this study any other state that enacted austerity post-2008. Why not? Philo's wealth tax involves a redistribution of wealth that is anathema to neoliberal ideology and its institutional forms of wealth distribution.

In Ireland, a state economy generally structured along neoliberal lines in recent times, an absence of solutions such as a wealth tax in crisis narratives presented by political and economic elites are therefore not surprising. Likewise, the implementation of austerity in Ireland has had severe and predictable costs for the lowest socioeconomic groups, for example by increasing persistent poverty rates from 4.2% in 2008 to 6.9% in 2011 (Fraser, Murphy, & Kelly, 2013, p. 48). Consequently, the costs of financial speculation that led to Ireland's crisis were foisted onto citizens who had the least responsibility for the State's economic crisis. This fact is typical of austerity policy in general, therefore the paradox lies in the fact that moral arguments for austerity are made precisely to hide the fact that the policy's preferred distribution of costs is grossly immoral. It is for this reason that narrative-fixing is a vital means to influence public sentiment and government policy, particularly when democratic consent is required.

To conclude, let me reiterate once more that austerity works. It works, if and when, the goal is to protect financially those who least require such protection. Austerity ensures an asymmetrical distribution of costs where the wealthiest contribute the least proportional to their ability to pay, and the poorest contribute the most. Austerity, therefore, is a highly successful distributional strategy for owners of wealth—one that comes with high social costs. It is for this latter reason that it is imperative to construct a new narrative about austerity, a narrative that rejects moralizing myths and technical solutions devoid of evidence. Austerity is neither technically necessary nor a deserved moral penance. It is a politics of wealth distribution through and through. Given these facts, austerity can and ought to be resisted.

References

Angle, J. (1986). The surplus theory of social stratification and the size distribution of personal wealth. *Social Forces, 65*(2), 293–326.

Bennett, A., & Elman, C. (2006). Qualitative research: Recent developments in case study methods. *Annual Review of Political Science, 9*(1), 455–476.

Blyth, M. (2013). *Austerity: The history of a dangerous idea*. Oxford: Oxford University Press.

Boyle, N. (2005). *FAS and Active Labour Market Policy 1985–2004. Studies in Public Policy, 17*. Dublin: Trinity College Dublin.

Buckley, P. J., Pass, C. L., & Prescott, K. (1988). Measures of international competitiveness: A critical survey*. *Journal of Marketing Management, 4*(2), 175–200.

Calcagno, A. (2012). Can austerity work? *Review of Keynesian Economics, 1*, 24–36.

Campbell, J. L. (2004). *Institutional change and globalization*. Princeton, NJ: Princeton University Press.

Chari, R., & Bernhagen, P. (2011). Financial and economic crisis: Explaining the sunset over the Celtic Tiger. *Irish Political Studies, 26*(4), 473–488.

Childe, V. G. (1942). *What happened in history*. Harmondsworth, UK: Penguin books.

Donovan, D., & Murphy, A. E. (2013). *The fall of the Celtic Tiger: Ireland and the Euro debt crisis* (1st ed.). Oxford: Oxford University Press.

Fama, E. F. (1970). Efficient capital markets: A review of theory and empirical work. *The Journal of Finance, 25*(2), 383–417.

Fraser, A., Murphy, E., & Kelly, S. (2013). Deepening neoliberalism via austerity and 'reform': The case of Ireland. *Human Geography, 6*, 38–53.

Fried, M. H. (1967). *The evolution of political society: An essay in political anthropology* (Vol. 7). New York: Random House.

Galbraith, J. K. (2014). *The end of normal: The great crisis and the future of growth*. New York: Simon and Schuster.

Gough, I. (1979). *The political economy of the welfare state*. London: Palgrave Macmillan.

Hammersley, M., & Gomm, R. (2009). Introduction. In R. Gomm, M. Hammersley, & P. Foster (Eds.), *Case study method: Key issues, key texts*. London: Sage.

Hargie, O., Stapleton, K., & Tourish, D. (2010). Interpretations of CEO public apologies for the banking crisis: Attributions of blame and avoidance of responsibility. *Organization, 17*(6), 721–742.

Harris, M. (1959). The economy has no surplus? *American Anthropologist, 61*(2), 185–199.

Harvey, D. (2005). *A brief history of neoliberalism*. Oxford/New York: Oxford University Press.

Herskovits, M. J. (1940). *Economic life of primitive peoples*. New York: Knopf.

Honohan, P. (2010). *The Irish banking crisis: Regulatory and financial stability policy 2003–2008*. Retrieved from https://inquiries.oireachtas.ie/banking/evidence/the-irish-banking-crisis-regulatory-financial-stability-policy-2003–2008/

Hossein-Zadeh, I. (2014). *Beyond mainstream explanations of the financial crisis: Parasitic finance capital*. New York: Routledge.

Kelsey, D., Mueller, F., Whittle, A., & KhosraviNik, M. (2016). Financial crisis and austerity: Interdisciplinary concerns in critical discourse studies. *Critical Discourse Studies, 13*(1), 1–19.

Kirby, P. (2010). *Celtic tiger in collapse: Explaining the weaknesses of the Irish model* (2nd ed.). Houndmills, Basingstoke, UK/New York: Palgrave Macmillan.

Kirby, P., & Murphy, M. (2011). Globalisation and models of state: Debates and evidence from Ireland. *New Political Economy, 16*(1), 19–39.

Kitchin, R., O'Callaghan, C., Boyle, M., Gleeson, J., & Keaveney, K. (2012). Placing neoliberalism: The rise and fall of Ireland's Celtic Tiger. *Environment and Planning A, 44*(6), 1302–1326.

Kitromilides, Y. (2013). Stories, fables, parables, and myths: Greece and the Euro Crisis, toward a new narrative. *Journal of Economic Issues, 47*(3), 623–638.

Krugman, P. (2012). *End this depression now!* New York: W.W. Norton & Company, Inc.

Larner, W. (2000). Neo-liberalism: Policy, ideology, governmentality. *Studies in Political Economy, 63*, 5–25.

Lenski, G. E. (1966). *Power and privilege: A theory of social stratification*. New York: McGraw Hill.

Mann, M. (2012). *The sources of social power: A history of power from the beginning to AD 1760* (New Edition ed.Vol. 1). New York: Cambridge University Press.

Marx, K. (1990). *Capital: A critique of political economy* (B. Fowkes, Trans.Vol. 1). London: Penguin Classics.

Mazzucato, M. (2013). *The entrepreneurial state: Debunking public vs. private sector myths*. London: Anthem Press.

McDonagh, N. (2016a). One-dimensional times: A dialectical response to the *Irish Times*' coverage of the global financial crisis. *Culture and Organization*, 1–20.

McDonagh, N. (2016b). How to frame a bank bailout: Lessons from Ireland during the Global Financial Crisis. *Przestrzeń Społeczna/SocialSpace, 12*(2), 84–112.

Morgan, G., Froud, J., Quack, S., & Schneiberg, M. (2011). Capitalism in crisis: Organizational perspectives. *Organization, 18*(2), 147–152.

Mylonas, Y. (2014). Crisis, austerity and opposition in mainstream media discourses of Greece. *Critical Discourse Studies, 11*(3), 305–321.

OECD. (2017). Average hours actually worked per worker. Retrieved from http://stats.oecd.org/Index.aspx?DataSetCode=ANHRS

Pentaraki, M. (2013). 'If we do not cut social spending, we will end up like Greece': Challenging consent to austerity through social work action. *Critical Social Policy, 33*(4), 700–711.

Philo, G. (2010). The Daily Politics. *BBC*. Retrieved from www.youtube.com/watch?v=Pmmf-cLnuq0

Piketty, T. (2014). *Capital in the twenty-first century*. (A. Goldhammer, Trans.). Cambridge, MA: The Belknap Press.

Reich, R. (2010). *Aftershock: The next economy and America's future*. New York: Alfred A. Knopf.

Schäuble, W. (2011, September 5). Why austerity is only cure for Eurozone. *The Financial Times*.

Schui, F. (2014). *Austerity: The great failure*. New Haven, CT: Yale University Press.

Siggel, E. (2006). International competitiveness and comparative advantage: A survey and a proposal for measurement. *Journal of Industry, Competition and Trade, 6*(2), 137–159.

Silver, B. (2003). *Forces of labour: Worker's movements and globalization since 1870*. New York: Cambridge University Press.

Stiglitz, J. (2012). Austerity – Europe's man-made disaster. *Social Europe Journal*. Retrieved from www.socialeurope.eu/austerity-europes-man-made-disaster

Sum, N.-L., & Jessop, B. (2013). *Towards a cultural political economy: Putting culture in its place in political economy*. Northampton, MA: Edward Elgar Publishing.

Tourish, D., & Hargie, O. (2012). Metaphors of failure and the failures of metaphor: A critical study of root metaphors used by bankers in explaining the banking crisis. *Organization Studies, 33*(8), 1045–1069.

World Bank. (2006). Doing Business, 2006. Retrieved from www.doingbusiness.org/~/media/WBG/DoingBusiness/Documents/Annual-Reports/English/DB06-FullReport.pdf

World Bank. (2009). Doing Business, 2009. Retrieved from www.doingbusiness.org/~/media/WBG/DoingBusiness/Documents/Annual-Reports/English/DB09-FullReport.pdf

8 Discursive uses of 'abnormality' in the Greek crisis

Yannis Stavrakakis and Antonis Galanopoulos

In crisis-ridden Greece, a strict austerity program has been applied, from 2010 onwards—when the global and mainly European economic crisis hit the shores of the Aegean—under the supervision of the European Commission, the European Central Bank, and the International Monetary Fund (the so-called *troika*). In order to provide an adequate framing and legitimization to this program, the crisis was discursively constructed not only as an economic one but also as a *moral* and a *cultural* crisis. Within this framework, the implementation of the austerity program became increasingly associated with discourses about 'normality.'

In this chapter, we will follow and attempt to analyze the emergence and the forms this normalizing discourse has acquired between the eruption of the crisis and the elections of January 2015, paying particular attention to the construction of *abnormality* and/or *monstrosity* it involves and on which it seems to rely, which usually takes the form of 'populism.' More specifically, we survey two types of this discourse: the political and the journalistic. Utilizing a variety of theoretical resources (from discourse theory to Canguilhem, Foucault. and Derrida), this chapter deconstructs the narrative claims involved, provides a genealogy of the discursive repertoires on which they draw, accounts for their distinct ideological articulations, and highlights their often camouflaged political implications.

Historical background: The (Greek) crisis and its politico-discursive management

Our story begins with George Papandreou, then Prime Minister of Greece, announcing his decision to appeal to the EU support mechanism (April 23, 2010), with the implementation of the program starting on May 3. The financial situation that made the country appeal to a bailout included a deficit that—for 2009—had risen to 15.4% of GDP and a total public debt that had reached 126.7% of GDP. Several years of draconian austerity and severe recession followed, in which the remedy seems to have exacerbated the illness diagnosed: Greece's GDP declined cumulatively—between 2010 and 2014—by

24.5%, legitimizing comparisons with the Great Depression of 1929 (World Bank, n.d).

Salaries, pensions, allowances, public health, employment in the public and private sector, all received major blows. For example, in 2014, unemployment reached 26.5% for the general population and 52.4% for young people under 25 years old, the highest rates of unemployment in Europe (Eurostat, August 2016). At the same time, Greek public debt was recorded at 180.1% of GDP in 2014 and at 176.9% of GDP in 2015, while according to the May 2016 IMF report it was projected to reach 183.7% of GDP in 2016. According to the projections of the IMF, Greek debt is supposed to fall below 150% of GDP in 2028 (IMF, May 2016) (Table 8.1). In this sense, the very program of economic measures implemented to address the debt problem seems to have made the problem worse, failing to combat one of the supposed root causes of the Greek malaise.

In the face of massive social dislocation, a violent downward shift in social mobility, mounting political crisis and protests, the consecutive fiscal adjustment programs agreed between the troika and the Greek governments—the so-called *memoranda*—have struggled to win popular acceptance. Overall, this attempt has been pivotally connected with a call to make Greece 'a normal country,' 'a normal state' closer to European standards, a call that relied on the rejection of the Greek 'way of life' before the crisis as 'abnormal.' Moralistic and disciplinary arguments gained a privileged position in this dominant discourse. According to the medical, therapeutic repertoire they often utilized, crisis was presented as a serious illness, the result of a virulent social pathology, calling for the administration of a bitter medicine, a painful treatment. On the other hand, according to a parallel pedagogical repertoire used, the cause of the crisis was attributed to the immaturity of the Greek people. Therefore, the country needed guidance, discipline and punishment in order to put its house in order and be rehabilitated into the family of 'normal' 'healthy' and 'responsible' states (Stavrakakis, 2013, 2014b).

The criticism could be detected both within the country and also abroad with highly derogatory articles in the international press mocking the lazy and corrupt Greeks. It was also crucially supported and illustrated by zoomorphic metaphors like that of the so-called 'PIIGS' (comprising the

Table 8.1 Greece, 2009–2015: Comparison of basic economic indicators

Indicator	*2009*	*2015*
GDP (billions)	231.7	176
Debt (billions)	298	311.5
Debt/GDP	126.8%	176.9%
Unemployment	9.6%	24.9%

Source: Hellenic Statistical Authority, Eurostat

delinquent countries with debt problems, putting more or less in question their humanity and dignity). Indeed, politicians, technocrats and the mainstream media worldwide presented Greece as a truant child or a delinquent member of the European family (Mylonas, 2014, p. 310). Within the country as well, Greece was portrayed as an exception to the norm and excessive debt was the evidence of this peculiarity within the European setting; it was thus stigmatized as the dysfunctional party deviating from a European standard of normality. As it has been paradigmatically articulated by the parliamentary spokesman of PASOK,[1] the junior partner in the coalition government between 2012–2015, "if something has brought us to the crisis it is our deviation from normality" (Koukoulopoulos, 2014). The presentation of the country and its people in this way made it possible to apply exceptional and punitive policies, and to demonize 'the people' in order to preempt popular resistance (Mylonas, 2014, p. 307; also see Stavrakakis, 2014a). Those who have sinned must suffer without protesting and/or resisting. Thus a 'negative; mechanism of producing guilt and terror through the dual tactics of stigmatization and shock was accompanied by a 'positive' mechanism projecting the vision of a 'normal country' at the end of the process. Austerity policies and 'creative destruction' were simply presented as the necessary steps in this process leading from purgatory to salvation.

Nevertheless, the management of the crisis along these lines by the established political class, provocatively described by Saskia Sassen as an "economic version of ethnic cleansing" (Sassen, 2014, p. 36), resulted in a wider intensification of social dislocations that deepened the indignation and discontent for both the dominant regime of democratic representation (two party system) and the EU, stimulating massive protest movements (including demonstrations, strikes, and square occupations). This process eventually led to the emergence of the Greek Indignados (*Aganaktismenoi*) and the gradual channeling of its political potential into the radical left party of SYRIZA,[2] which was slowly transformed from fringe party to the main party of the opposition expressing resistance to austerity and the memoranda (Spourdalakis, 2014; Stavrakakis & Katsambekis, 2014). Now, if mainstream pro-memoranda discourse relied on a series of normalizing dichotomies between good and evil utilizing therapeutic, zoomorphic and pedagogical metaphors (health vs. illness, responsibility vs. irresponsibility, maturity vs. immaturity, humanity vs. animality, normality vs. abnormality), the opposition articulated a very different crisis narrative defending 'the people; against the policies implemented and their agents.

SYRIZA also divided the social space into two opposing camps: '*them*' (the 'establishment') and '*us*' ('the people'), power and the underdog, the elite (domestic and European) and the non-privileged, those 'up' and the others 'down.' Within this dichotomous framework, blame for the crisis was attributed towards the 'external troika' (institutions like the IMF, the ECB and the European Commission) and its local 'collaborators,' the so-called 'internal troika' (see, on this aspect, the relevant research of Stavrakakis & Katsambekis, 2014, p. 131). This narrative has been successful in articulating a variety of heterogeneous reactions and emotions against austerity into a new—retroactively and radically constructed—political subject ("the people in the leading role"), thus ascribing to SYRIZA's confrontational discourse a hegemonic appeal. Since 'populism' is currently the 'convenient name' hiding "the exacerbated contradiction between popular legitimacy and savant legitimacy, the difficulty of the government of science to accommodate the manifestation of democracy and even the mixed form of its representative system" (Rancière, 2006, p. 80), SYRIZA was quickly and summarily denounced as 'populist.' Within the ensuing politico-discursive choreography, populism emerged thus as the condensation of all the pathologies accounting for the abnormal profile of the Greek society and economy, as a nodal synecdoche of abnormality, and thus as the main cause for the crisis and the punishment that followed.

Discourses of normalization: political and journalistic

The first coherent appearance of the idea of the 'normal country' can be traced back to a questionnaire sent by PASOK to its members in view of its forthcoming ninth conference (March, 1–3, 2013): "The central aim of our conference is to create a party that can guarantee the transformation of Greece into a normal country." To the question "Whom should it address and whom does PASOK represent?" one of the options offered was the following: "All those people who believe in the need for Greece to become a normal state." To the question "What strategy, concerning the country, should PASOK consider fundamental?" there was as an option to answer "The need for Greece to become a normal state, a normal economy, a normal society" ("PASOK opens the debate on its future," 2013). Since then, the idea of the (ab)normal country evolved into a central frame, a nodal point, in the discourse of the Greek government. We have traced this expression in PASOK's website in 50 different cases during 2014. The elevation of the phrase "normal country" into such a prominent role was also indicated by the president of PASOK and Deputy Prime Minister in a speech in April 2014 where he argued: "The country's new brand is a Greece that surpasses the crisis, is a Greece coming back to normality, is a Greece that once again becomes self-reliant within the EU, the Eurozone and the international markets" (Venizelos, 2014b).

Emerging in the discourse of PASOK, this reference to 'normality' soon colonized the discourse of both the main governing parties (New Democracy[3] and PASOK), exhibiting remarkable fluidity. Normality here is identified with a posited *European* normality, alluding to the participation of Greece in the EU as an equal partner. But it also acquires an economic meaning indicating, for example, an exit to the markets in search of sustainable loans. It is also connected to political normality, i.e., the completion of the four-year term of a government and the avoidance of early elections. It is worth referring in some detail to a few indicative examples. The parliamentary spokesman of PASOK has provided a cogent example of the rhetoric of normality in the first sense:

> So if the desired thing, as we believe, is the search of a European—let's say—normality—because Greece is not a normal country—we should face with honesty some things. [...] This is the way to become step by step a normal country.
>
> (Koukoulopoulos, 2014)

Moving to an economic connotation of normality, in one of his speeches, the Deputy Prime Minister characteristically stated about the country's exit to the markets: "Greece is returning. It is returning to the markets, to positive growth rates, to normality." In another speech, he reiterated: "The return to the markets symbolizes the gradual return to normality" (Venizelos, 2014a). The former Prime Minister Antonis Samaras had earlier stated that, "In 2014 Greece will return to the markets, will start becoming a normal country, like the others" (Samaras, 2013).

Passing now to the political connotation mentioned earlier, as Antonis Samaras had stated in a meeting with members of his party: "We must become a normal country and have elections every four years as the Constitution specifies" (Samaras, 2014a). All in all, normality had been firmly established as the only—and indisputable—aim of the policies implemented under European economic and political guidance: "We are negotiating closely with our lenders the next day after the end of the program, a prudent exit to normality" (Samaras, 2014d), stated then Prime Minister Antonis Samaras in Brussels shortly after the end of the Eurozone summit of October 2014.

Several times in this discourse one encounters the phrase 'return to normality' which gives the impression that what is meant is that the country was normal in the past and needs to return to a prior state. However, speaking at the Conference of the Greek Union of Entrepreneurs in October 2014, Venizelos stressed that "the return to normality is not a return to the past, but a return to the future" (Venizelos, 2014c). Thus references to normality should be understood as indicating the establishment of a *new* normal resulting from the implementation of the austerity measures. Indeed, when the speakers are called to describe in more detail what this normality involves, the link between this normality and an overall restructuring of Greek state and society along entrepreneurial (neoliberal) lines is clearly revealed. In December 2013, for example, the Deputy Prime Minister once more stated:

> The first condition is to have a normal state, a state whose administration is friendly towards investments and is associated with a society friendly to investments. [...] A state that can provide legal certainty and mainly a secure, stable and simple tax regime.
>
> (Venizelos, 2013)

To move to two other relevant examples, the then Minister of Labor, Social Security and Welfare similarly argued that

> The Prime Minister Antonis Samaras kept the country on its feet, and at the same time proceeded with a number of critical structural reforms across the entire range of economic, social and political life gradually transforming Greece into a normal European country.
>
> (Vroutsis, 2014)

And the Minister of Development and Competitiveness concluded that "Thanks to the sacrifices of the Greeks and the efforts of the government, the country is becoming a normal country" (Hatzidakis, 2014).

If, during the period under examination, 'normality' thus emerges as the predominant goal in dominant political discourse, the media have also played an important role in spreading the idea of normality and in highlighting its salient meanings. By accepting 'normality' as the only legitimate ideal for the crisis-ridden country, they elevated it into a benchmark to be used when judging the practices and policies of the various political parties. For example, several articles on this theme were published in the newspaper *Imerisia*. In one of them the author asks: "Will we create a normal country or will we shut it down?" Then he goes on:

> It is inconceivable for a country that is supposed to be European, with a rich past, which came close to collapse, to need a 'troika' in order to act in an acceptable way, to become a normal state, with a beginning, a middle and an end.
>
> (Papadis, 2014)

In another article in the same newspaper, one reads:

> Can the country celebrate because it appears that it is coming out of the tunnel? Isn't there much more to be done in order for Greece to become a 'normal' country? […] All that implies two major changes. The first concerns the citizens themselves, who should understand that the normality of a state requires sacrifices by themselves too.
>
> (Kanellis, 2014)

In this sense, this idea of normality, and of the normal country, is being constructed as an objective that all citizens should adopt, and do whatever it takes in order to achieve.[4] Here governmental discourse and mainstream journalistic discourse seem to be in line, fueling each other and providing mutual support as they multiply the effects of their common message.

Now, gradually, the aforementioned idea of normality and of the 'normal country' was elevated into a controversial matter in the public sphere triggering ideological confrontation. Thus, from an oppositional point of view, SYRIZA MP and current economy minister, Euclid Tsakalotos, addressed this issue directly during a speech in Parliament in December 2014, through a *resignification* of the empty signifier 'normality,' one that can arguably involve many different significations, one that is revealed as a signifier without a (fixed) signified: "If you dare, you should go to your voters and tell them, we will reduce the number of schools and hospitals, we will make you a normal Third World country" (Tsakalotos, 2014). Similarly, the then Secretary of SYRIZA Dimitris Vitsas argued in an interview that

> the normality of Mr. Samaras involves 1.5 million unemployed. The normality of Mr. Samaras involves privatizations. The normality of Mr. Samaras involves the sellout of airports and ports. This is not normality. This is a normal continuous surveillance and degradation of the life of Greek people.
> (Vitsas, 2014)

Challenges to the attempted 'normalization' were also advanced by a part of the press, with the most characteristic example probably being *Efimerida ton Syntakton*, an anti-memorandum co-operative newspaper. In September 2014, the newspaper published an article entitled "Poverty Contradicts the 'Normal' Country of the Prime Minister," in which figures of a Budget Office report were used to disprove a statement of the then Prime Minister according to which "month after month Greece is becoming a normal country." A few days later in the same newspaper the article of an editor was published, which concluded with the following words: "Sorry, Prime Minister, but that is not the image of a serious and normal country, like the one that you are telling us we are becoming. It is the image of a devastated country" (Pappas, 2014).

Crucially, in order to acquire political effectivity in the face of oppositional discourses, the new normal seems to have relied on the production and demonization of its Other. In other words, in the Greek case, normality presupposed the localization of abnormality. This is far from surprising. Not only because, as we know already from de Saussure, identity necessarily relies on difference (de Saussure, 1959, p. 120), but also because hegemony relies on establishing particular sequences and distributions between positive and negative. 'Populism' seems to be directly implicated in this function as it has surfaced in crisis-ridden Greece. Populism indeed emerges as the condensation or synecdoche of everything pathological and evil: irresponsibility, demagogy, immorality, corruption, destruction, irrationalism. It operates as a *negative* empty signifier that, by its mere existence, proves the value of the *positive* empty signifier of 'normality,' providing cohesion to the discourses of normalization. Not only is it to blame for the crisis itself, but it is also what obstructs the implementation of the required rational solutions (austerity).

According to Ernesto Laclau, hegemonic struggles typically involve such a differential dialectic between negativity and positivity, lack and fullness. Even if a utopian social "fullness and universality [...] is unachievable," yet "its need does not disappear"; the need for fullness "will always show itself through the presence of its absence" (Laclau, 1996, p. 53). In political antagonism, both absence and presence are represented by signifiers that, in order to acquire wider appeal, are tendentially 'empty' and thus operate at a relatively formal level:

> In a situation of radical disorder, 'order' is present as that which is absent; it becomes an empty signifier, as the signifier of this absence. In this sense, various political forces can compete in their efforts to present their particular objectives as those which carry out the filling of that lack. To hegemonize something is exactly to carry out this filling function.
>
> (Laclau, 1996, p. 44)

Laclau suggests, moreover, that signifiers other than 'order'—signifiers like 'unity,' 'revolution,' 'justice,' 'change,' 'happiness,' etc.—can function in a similar way: "Any term which, in a certain political context becomes the signifier of the lack, plays the same role. Politics is possible because the constitutive impossibility of society can only represent itself through the production of empty signifiers" (Laclau, 1996, p. 44). Indeed, what this argument ultimately suggests—although this is not fully developed by Laclau himself—is that political discourses with hegemonic pretensions need to win consent both (i) in the diagnosis of a malaise, and thus have to localize negativity through the production of a *negative empty signifier* (disorder, disunity, injustice, etc.), and (ii) in putting forward a solution to this *malaise*, and thus also have to positivize the localized negativity they have highlighted through the production of a *positive empty signifier* (order, unity, justice, etc.). Our analysis of the way 'normality' and 'populism' have been articulated in the Greek case can provide a revealing illustration of this discursive choreography.

Once more, and exactly like articulations of the 'normal country,' this reference to populism traverses both governmental and mainstream media discourse. For example, apart from being a prominent agent of normalization, Antonis Samaras repeatedly presented himself as a fierce opponent of populism. In September 2014, in one more statement indicating that Greece was returning to normality, the former Prime Minister argued that

> The enemies of reforms are preparing their last attack, they do what they can with false promises, but the more they try to convince that they have a credible alternative, the more they are exposed. What we have accomplished cannot be sacrificed on the altar of populism and extremism.
>
> (Samaras, 2014b)

Speaking in a celebration for the 40 years since the establishment of his New Democracy party, Samaras added:

> Populism gave the ultimate rearguard battle to take Greece out of the euro and to destroy its participation in European integration. It failed! Populism gave the ultimate battle to prevent the unraveling of statism. It fails in that too. This is the new political changeover that has already begun! (Samaras, 2014c)

Such references continue into 2015 and well into 2016. Hence, in November 2015 Samaras castigates populism as a 'disease' (Samaras, 2015); no wonder that, in 2016, upon congratulating the new leader of his party, the only thing he does stress is, once more, the need for New Democracy to unite in order "to embrace all Greeks and win conclusively the battle against populism" (Samaras, 2016). In fact, this was something that the new leader, Kyriakos Mitsotakis, had already highlighted in his acceptance speech: "We have one goal. New Democracy must express all the forces in this land confronting the populism of an incompetent government" (Mitsotakis, 2016). Needless to say, this discursive repertoire pitting the normality of structural reforms against the abnormality of populism, is not restricted to New Democracy, but also encompasses parties and personalities with social-democratic sensibilities. In a typical interview with the newspaper *Kathimerini* under the title "Populism Cuts Across the Parties," after criticizing populism and depicting it as the greatest evil, Alekos Papadopoulos, a former PASOK Minister, concludes:

> Only one road exists. The establishment of an anti-populist, anti-peronist democratic front of the leading social forces of realism and rationality present in the our territory. Only in that way will Greece get rid of the idols of populist delusion which have reigned for decades in the current political system and all the so-called leading classes of the country, which are deeply selfish, atrophic and dangerous in their majority. This is the only way for Greece to become a normal, modern European social state, with a hierarchical value-society.
>
> (Papadopoulos, 2014)

What is striking about such discursive articulations is that this denouncement of the abnormality of populism can perform its political role only if invested with an extra-political, anthropological value. Hence, we often see populism being opposed to 'rationality' and 'common sense,' characteristics that are commonly recognized as universal features of the human species (presumably including 'populists'). Thus, in February 2012, Andreas Loverdos (PASOK MP and then Minister of Health and Social Solidarity) applied to Greek MPs a distinction between 'populists' and 'rationalists,' while two months later an editorial in the *Athens Review of Books*, preaching against the "intolerable Actually Existing Populism," concluded that "Greece needs today more than ever the forces of reason, which are surely at war with populism, and its European course and perspective" (Athens Review of Books, 2012). At the extreme end of such depoliticized arguments we meet the downgrading of 'populists' to sub-humans: 'cave men,' 'Neanderthals' and 'troglodytes' (Michas, 2011; for a detailed analysis see Stavrakakis, 2014a).

Last but not least, metaphors of *monstrosity* are enlisted to strike the final blow—as in the case of ex-Minister of Education, Lifelong Learning and Religious Affairs, Anna Diamantopoulou:

> populism has always been more than a threat—it has been an executioner of democracy, societal development, and of peace [...] the monster of

> populism must be crushed for good. Currently, it continues to feed on the mistakes of the past, the failures of the reform program and the desperation of people at the prolonged austerity. As long as populism remains powerful it will continue to appeal and attract more followers to its path, eventually poisoning healthy prospects terminally.
>
> (Diamantopoulou, 2016)

In this discursive frame then, 'populism' is indeed presented as pure negativity, a pure negativity that is to be contrasted with the pure positivity with which the aforementioned return to normality is credited. Therefore two chains of equivalence seem to emerge: on the one hand, that of *normality* which comprises rationality, responsibility, reforms and modernization, and, on the other hand, that of a *monstrous* abnormality which includes populism and its many negative connotations: irresponsibility, irrationalism, and so on.

Turning now to the media, in his discursive analysis of editorials of the *Kathimerini* daily—a respectable center-right newspaper emblematic of the pro-memorandum, anti-populist camp—Yiannis Mylonas concludes that its editors also create a chain of equivalence representing the desired identity that encompasses the rational, realistic and pro-European segments of Greek society. The opposite equivalential chain comprises 'populism' and 'extremism.' This chain includes all those who are opposed to austerity and are characterized as lazy, anti-Europeans, etc. (Mylonas, 2014, p. 315). Indeed, extreme anti-populist rhetoric is not restricted within partisan political antagonism. It also marks the field of the media. Using both qualitative and lexicometric methods, a relevant analysis of newspaper articles published in the Greek printed press between June 1, 2014 and May 31, 2015 has registered, once more, a clear division between ostensibly 'anti-populist' and 'pro-populist' media. What emerges as well is, on the one hand, the polarization implicit in pro-populist discourse, but also the demonization of 'populism' (and the political forces denounced as populist, mainly SYRIZA) marking the anti-populist press. Indeed, common adjectives accompanying references to populism in this camp comprise the following: extreme, vulgar, dangerous, cheap, fanatical, clientelist, catastrophic, unbearable, lumpen, irresponsible, savage, total, unscrupulous, etc. In a similar vein, a lot of metaphors utilized in forming sentences about populism emanate from medical discourse and associate it with some sort of illness, either of the body (contamination, plague, gangrene, cancer, etc.) or of the soul (madness, schizophrenia, irrationality, etc.). Another salient category of metaphors employed originate from the natural sciences, especially meteorology (tsunami, storm, etc.) and zoology, either real (parasite, wolf, etc.) or imaginary (beast, monster, etc.) (Nikisianis, Siomos, Stavrakakis, & Dimitroulia, 2016).

This discourse is far from restricted to fringe journalists and media; it constitutes a prominent feature of mainstream media and celebrity journalists. The case of Alexis Papachelas, singled out by the news portal *Politico* as one of "the twenty eight people from twenty eight countries who are shaping, shaking and stirring Europe" is indicative (Politico, 2015). As editor-in-chief and leading columnist of *Kathimerini*, Papachelas has published, throughout the last few years, numerous articles on populism invariably utilizing the metaphor of the 'beast.' Already from 2010 he refers to the "beast of populism," to which in 2014 he will attribute all that has gone wrong in post-authoritarian Greece: "All that angers us has an explanation and is not a momentary product, for it took several decades for the hungry beast of populism to rear its ugly head" (Papachelas, 2014). The repertoire of monstrosity will continue to feed this anti-populist discourse well into 2015, when many articles will be published utilizing this graphic metaphor.

Normality, abnormality and monstrosity

We have seen how, by disrupting economic spaces and relations, by destabilizing social identities and severing politico-ideological affiliations, the Greek crisis has created a lack of meaning that two main camps sought to cover over. As a moment of dislocation, it opened a field of possibilities within which various warring sides attempted to impose a new order, putting forward antithetical hegemonic interventions that promised to stabilize again the social field. Extreme polarization ensued, in which blame attribution took the form of constructing normal/abnormal distributions and chains of equivalence. Normality here was mainly understood as the name for the imposition of a new order. This was exactly the attempt of the previous governments. 'Normality' operated as the point of reference of this hovering hegemonic project. This attempt, however, has relied heavily on the construction and demonization of a *constitutive outside,* of something crucial for the legitimation of 'normalization' processes precisely because it is presented as incarnating the radical negation of normality. The hegemonic intervention of a *positive* empty signifier presupposed the localization of a *negative* empty signifier. Thus dominant discourses of normalization have singled out 'populism' as the emblematic incarnation of abnormality, illustrating it with the use of a very graphic grammar of deviation and monstrosity. What is, however, the exact operation of such articulations? How can one further reflect on their political input? Do they constitute a Greek peculiarity? Arguably the Greek conjuncture is far from unique; indeed repertoires of abnormality and monstrosity have been operative throughout modernity, if not before. A theorization of the political function of such mechanisms as well as a brief genealogy of their manifestations could be useful in situating the language games developed within the Greek crisis and in drawing some broader conclusions.

It is clearly with Canguilhem and Foucault that such a theorization has to start. They both highlight the political function of the idea of the 'norm' and 'normality.' It is a thoroughly polemical concept in Canguilhem's case, a clearly political concept for Foucault. In his celebrated study, *The Normal and the Pathological*, Canguilhem concludes that "the normal is not a static or peaceful, but a dynamic and polemical concept" (Canguilhem, 1991, p. 239). It legitimizes a decision (Canguilhem, 1991, p. 245) and, most importantly, it does so on the basis of an inverted causality that, crucially, relies on the production of 'abnormality':

> The abnormal, as ab-normal, comes after the definition of the normal, it is its logical negation. However, it is the historical anteriority of the future abnormal which gives rise to a normative intention. The normal is the effect obtained by the execution of the normative project, [...] Consequently it is not paradoxical to say that the abnormal, while logically second, is existentially first.
>
> (Canguilhem, 1991, p. 243)

For Foucault, likewise, the norm is involved in a (retro-)*active* exercise of power. It is simultaneously

> a principle of qualification and a principle of correction. [...] The negative formulation of the 'normal' through the knowledge of what it is not—rather than what it is—is paralleled by the power exercised in order to protect that normalcy.
>
> (Elden, 2001, p. 103)

Indeed, during his lectures at the *Collège de France* during the academic year 1974–1975, Foucault attempted to chart a genealogy of abnormality in the West. He identified three main types: the human monster, the individual to be corrected, the masturbating child/the onanist. What is at stake here is not merely the description, specification or identification of a normality but rather its construction through the productive power of normalizing processes that work through differential identification, through the juxtaposition of the normal to the abnormal:

> The norm consequently lays claim to power. The norm is not simply and not even a principle of intelligibility; it is an element on the basis of which a certain exercise of power is founded and legitimized. [...] it is always linked to a positive technique of intervention and transformation, to a sort of normative project.
>
> (Foucault, 2003, p. 50)

What Foucault singles out as the *dispositif* of 'normalization' provides thus privileged access to his understanding of the power/knowledge nexus: "This is how society is defended: both an exclusion established through knowledge and an inclusion policed through power" (Elden, 2001, p. 103).

Deconstructing the normative authority of the normal/abnormal distribution and revealing the hierarchical functions of its inverted causality, Canguilhem and Foucault unveil normalizing processes as discursive technologies of domination. They thus offer new angles in understanding the mechanisms through which the choreography between positive and negative empty signifiers with hegemonic pretensions has marked throughout the discursive struggles triggered by the Greek crisis.

For his part, Jacques Derrida will offer, well before the current crisis, an example of the contemporary political uses of such differential distributions through his discussion of the idea of the 'rogue' and especially of the deployment of the designation of the so-called 'rogue states' in international politics. What is at stake here is, once more, a normalizing exercise of legitimation and delegitimation. Derrida cogently details the way certain states are "denounced, confronted, and repressed by the police of supposedly legitimate states, those that respect an international law that they have the power to control" (Derrida, 2005, p. 68). With an almost prophetic insight, he includes the IMF in the international formations regulating such distributions, something that would prove particularly crucial in the Greek case. Model cases comprise Noriega's Panama and Sadam's Iraq. Of course, the point of Derrida is not to defend such barbarous, dictatorial regimes; it is merely to show that their fall from grace in the eyes of the euro-atlantic gaze had nothing to do with a truly ethical decision, but was the result of pragmatic policy reversals that required such processes of normalization as a means of discursive legitimization.

This is demonstrated when one takes into account two crucial dimensions. First of all, the fact that such states are stigmatized as 'rogue' after many years of being supported by the great powers despite their diachronic neglect for international law and human rights; have we really forgotten that, before being stigmatized as the "beast of Baghdad," Sadam had been, "like Noriega, a long-standing ally and valuable economic partner" of the West? (Derrida, 2005, p. 97). Second, the ultimate interchangeability of the assumed exceptional abnormality or even monstrosity between the 'rogue' and the supposedly legitimate 'sovereign':

> those states that are able or are in a state to denounce or accuse some 'rogue state' of violating the law, of failing to live up to the law, of being guilty of some perversion or deviation, those states that claim to uphold international law and that take the initiative of war, of police or peacekeeping operations because they have the force to do so, these states, [...] are themselves, as sovereign, the first rogue states.
>
> (Derrida, 2005, p. 102)

No wonder that, immediately before being ridiculed as perhaps the filthiest of the 'PIIGS,' just before it was denounced as the *bette noire* of Europe, Greece had staged the 2004 Athens Olympics, had entered the Eurozone, and was widely celebrated as the preferential partner of Europe in the Balkans.

This latter claim takes us to Derrida's (2009) analysis of what he calls the "great zoopolitics" (p. 4) that binds into a paradoxical choreography the beast and the sovereign:

> there is between sovereign, criminal, and beast a sort of obscure and fascinating complicity, or even a worrying mutual attraction, a worrying similarity, an unheimlich, uncanny, reciprocal haunting. Both of them, all three of them, the animal, the criminal, and the sovereign, are outside the law, at a distance from or above the laws: criminal, beast, and sovereign strangely resemble each other while seeming to be situated at the antipodes, at each other's antipodes.
>
> (p. 17)

Thus, the metaphor of the animal or the beast forms a discursive repertoire that is utilized to represent both the sovereign—the king as wolf in La Fontaine and the fable of the Fox man in Machiavelli are two good cases in point (p. 211)—and the leaders of rogue states, "who are often, in the political rhetoric of the most powerful states, compared to 'beasts'" (p. xiv).

A brief discursive genealogy indeed reveals that the repertoire of monstrosity is far from novel in its deployment within normalizing language games. We know that already before the English Civil War, new idioms of monstrosity "were to become crucial rhetorical figures through which struggles over political power were played out, only to be reworked and reanimated as means of interpreting the conflicts of the French Revolution, nearly a century and a half later" (McNally, 2011, p. 46). Now, interestingly enough, these idioms were mainly used to demonize popular participation and popular demands and movements. Thus two main rubrics dominated the representation of the *monstrous* crowd during the English Civil War of the 1640s:

> First, the multitude is portrayed as a 'headless' beast (one that has lost its mind, as represented by the monarch) or, what is meant as the same thing, as 'many headed', a reference to its democratic proclivity for rule by the many. In addition, the mob is said, secondly, to consist of a monstrous 'confusion' of parts, detached bits lacking order and form.
>
> (McNally, 2011, p. 71)

The multiple strands of the early-modern discourse of monstrosity found no more sensitive a registrar than Shakespeare (McNally, 2011, pp. 62–63). For example, all of the abusive representations of "the many headed multitude" (Shakespeare, 1976, p. 180) materialize in his *Coriolanus* mainly through the aristocratic hero's gaze. Portraying both sides, the patricians and the plebs, with great eloquence, Shakespeare illustrates cogently "the *us* and the *they* as emerging political identities in struggle," something that "was to mark literature and history ever since" (Politi, 2012, p. 87, emphasis original).

Metaphors of monstrosity acquire a central status in processes of normalization precisely because the monster is defined as both

> a violation of the laws of society but also a violation of the laws of nature. Its very existence is a breach of the law at both levels. [...] The monster is

> the limit, both the point at which law is overturned and the exception that is found only in extreme cases. The monster combines the impossible and the forbidden.
>
> (Foucault, 2003, pp. 55–56).

This unprecedented plasticity accounts for the potency and political effectivity as well as for the trans-historical insistence of this metaphor, of which our account of the Greek case has provided ample evidence. It is also what allows its many antithetical formulations. Foucault recounts, for example, how, around the time of the French Revolution two antagonistic representations of monstrosity clashed: the "monster from below" and the "monster from above":

> the cannibalistic monster represented above all by the figure of the people in revolt, and the incestuous monster represented above all by the figure of the king are important because in the nineteenth century we find them at the very heart of the juridico-medical theme of the monster. In their very twinship, these two figures will haunt the problematic of abnormal individuality.
>
> (Foucault, 2003, p. 101)

Conclusion

In austerity-struck Greece, a draconian program of structural adjustments has been applied, from 2010 onwards, under the supervision of the so-called *troika* (comprising the European Commission, the European Central Bank, and the International Monetary Fund). In an attempt to secure legitimation and compliance, mainstream public discourse has attempted to link the implementation of this program with a particular understanding of the crisis as a radical moral and cultural failure, if not a subjective failure affecting each and every Greek citizen. Within this context, the implementation of the austerity program—as a remedy to such failures—became increasingly associated with discourses about 'normality.' In this chapter we have followed the emergence and mapped the forms this normalizing discourse takes, focusing on the construction of *abnormality* and/or *monstrosity* it seems to have also required, which usually takes the form of 'populism.'

More specifically, we have identified and explored two types of this discourse: the political and the journalistic. According to the coalition government of New Democracy and PASOK, during 2012–2014, for example, austerity measures and structural reforms should have been accepted and actively supported because they would transform Greece into a 'normal' European country. In a similar vein, many journalists from mainstream media also presented 'normality' as the ultimate target that Greece had to achieve at any cost. This was juxtaposed to a supposedly 'abnormal' state of affairs usually associated with populist actors, which were typically depicted in terms of 'monstrosity' (references to the 'populist beast' abound). Drawing on a variety of theoretical resources (from Canguillhem, Foucault and Derrida to Ernesto Laclau), this chapter attempted to interpret the narrative claims involved, provide a genealogy of the discursive repertoires on which they have drawn, and account for their distinct political implications. Far from being a Greek peculiarity, repertoires of abnormality and monstrosity have been operative throughout modernity and seem to betray a diachronically relevant discursive technology of domination. Its prominent position in the language games developed within the Greek crisis alerts us to the continuing importance of tracing and critically deconstructing it. By tackling other types of discourse, like academic discourse, future research on the Greek case can further enrich this research orientation, extending its scope and interpretative implications.

Notes

1 PASOK (Panhellenic Socialist Movement) was founded by Andreas Papandreou in 1974. Emerging as a radical left political force in the 1970s, it would adopt a more pragmatic and moderate profile when in office in the 1980s, before gradually joining the trajectory of third-way European social democracy.
2 SYRIZA (Coalition of Radical Left) was initially founded as an electoral coalition of radical left political parties and extra-parliamentarian organizations in 2004. Its main constituent, Synaspismos (founded in 1992), originates in the Greek Eurocommunist tradition.
3 Founded in 1974 by Konstantinos Karamanlis, ND (New Democracy) is a center-right party and had functioned as one of the main pillars—together with PASOK—of the Greek two-party system (1974–2012).
4 For a psychoanalytic take on the unmistakably superegoic mechanism at work here (one operating through guilt and sadistic discipline) see Stavrakakis (2013).

References

Athens Review of Books. (2012, April 28). Στη χώρα της κατουρημένης ποδιάς. [Editorial] Retrieved from athensreviewofbooks.com/?m=201204
Canguilhem, G. (1991). *The normal and the pathological.* New York: Zone Books.
Derrida, J. (2005). *Rogues.* Stanford: Stanford University Press.
Derrida, J. (2009–2011). *The beast and the sovereign* (Vols. 1–2). Chicago, IL: The University of Chicago Press.
de Saussure, F. (1959). *Course in general linguistics.* New York: Philosophical Library.
Diamantopoulou, A. (2016, September 1). *Populism and social democracy's distress.* Social Europe. Retrieved from www.socialeurope.eu/2016/09/populism-social-democracys-distress/
Elden, S. (2001). The constitution of the normal: Monsters and masturbation at the College de France. *Boundary 2, 28*(1), 91–105.
Foucault, M. (2003). *Abnormal: Lectures at the Collège de France, 1974–1975.* New York: Picador.
Hatzidakis, K. (2014, April 10). Χατζηδάκης: Χάρη στις θυσίες των Ελλήνων η χώρα γίνεται κανονική χώρα. [Hatzidakis: Thanks to the Sacrifices of the Greeks,

the Country Becomes a Normal Country]. *Alpha TV*. [online news magazine]. Retrieved from http://omega.alphatv.gr/news/politics/hatzidakis-hari-stis-thysies-ton-ellinon-i-hora-ginetai-kanoniki-hora

Hellenic Statistical Authority. (2016a). *Labor force (Monthly data)*. Retrieved from www.statistics.gr/en/statistics/-/publication/SJO02/-

Hellenic Statistical Authority. (2016b). *Fiscal data (Annual)*. Retrieved from www.statistics.gr/en/statistics/-/publication/SEL03/-

Hellenic Statistical Authority. (2016c). *Gross domestic product*. Retrieved from www.statistics.gr/en/statistics/-/publication/SEL15/-

International Monetary Fund. (2016). *Greece: Preliminary debt sustainability analysis: Updated estimates and further considerations*. (IMF Country Report No. 16/30). Retrieved from www.imf.org/external/pubs/ft/scr/2016/cr16130.pdf

Kanellis, V. (2014). Καλά τα νούμερα, αλλά πότε θα γίνουμε κανονική χώρα. [The numbers are good, but when will we become a normal country?]. *Imerisia*. [online newspaper]. Retrieved from www.imerisia.gr/article.asp?catid=26533&subid=2&pubid=113362560

Koukoulopoulos, P. (2014, February 28). Ομιλία στην ολομέλεια της Βουλής. [Speech in the Greek Parliament]. Retrieved from koukoulopoulos.gr/index.php/-video/1264-28-02-2014-omilia-stinolomeleia-tis-voulis

Laclau, E. (1996). *Emancipation(s)*. London: Verso.

McNally, D. (2011). *Monsters of the market: Zombies, vampires and global capitalism*. Leiden/Boston: Brill.

Michas, T. (2011, January 11). Ο λαϊκισμός που σκοτώνει [The populism that kills]. *Protagon*. [online news magazine]. Retrieved from www.protagon.gr/?i= protagon.el.article&id=4767

Mitsotakis, K. (2016, January 11). Εκτακτο συνέδριο στην ατζέντα των 100 ημερών του Κυριάκου Μητσοτάκη. [Extraordinary Congress on the Agenda of Kyriakos Mitsotakis]. *Ta Nea*. [online newspaper]. Retrieved from www.tanea.gr/news/politics/article/5325118/allagh-selidas-sth-nea-dhmokratia-me-kyriako-mhtsotakh/

Mylonas, Y. (2014). Crisis, austerity and opposition in mainstream media discourses of Greece. *Critical Discourse Studies, 11*(3), 305–321.

Nikisianis, N., Siomos, Th., Stavrakakis, Y., & Dimitroulia, T. (2016). Λαϊκισμός εναντίον αντιλαϊκισμού στον ελληνικό τύπο. [Populism vs. anti-populism in the Greek press]. *Synchrona Themata, 132*(3), 52–70.

Papachelas, A. (2014, June 11). Βορά στα θηρία του λαϊκισμού. [Prey to the beasts of populism]. *Kathimerini*. [online newspaper]. Retrieved from www.kathimerini.gr/771165/opinion/epikairothta/politikh/vora-sta-8hria-toy-laikismoy

Papadis, T. (2014). Θα δημιουργήσουμε μια κανονική χώρα ή θα την κλείσουμε;. [Will we create a normal country or will we shut it down?]. *Imerisia*. [online newspaper]. Retrieved from www.imerisia.gr/article.asp?catid=26533&subid=2&pubid=113354466

Papadopoulos, A. (2014, June 22). Ο λαϊκισμός διατρέχει οριζόντια τα κόμματα. [Populism cuts across the parties]. *Kathimerini*. [online newspaper]. Retrieved from www.kathimerini.gr/772908/article/proswpa/synentey3eis/o-laikismosdiatrexei-orizontia-ta-kommata

Pappas, T. (2014, September 25). Ετσι είναι οι κανονικές χώρες, κύριε πρωθυπουργέ. [Is this how normal countries look, Mr. Prime Minister?]. *Efimerida ton Syntakton*. [online newspaper]. Retrieved from http://archive.efsyn.gr/?p=237726

PASOK opens the debate on its future. (2013, February 4). Το ΠΑΣΟΚ ανοίγει το διάλογο για το μέλλον του. *Kathimerini*. [online newspaper]. Retrieved from www.kathimerini.gr/27514/article/epikairothta/politikh/to-pasok-anoigei-to-dialogo-gia-to-mellon-toy

Politi, J. (2012). "A swinish multitude" versus "a crowd of golden daffodils." In R. Parkin-Gounelas (Ed.), *The psychology and politics of the collective: Groups, crowds and mass identifications* (pp. 86–102). London: Routledge.

Politico. (2015). The 28 people from 28 countries who are shaping, shaking and stirring Europe. Retrieved from www.politico.eu/list/politico-28/

Poverty contradicts the 'normal country' of the Prime Minister. (2014, September 26). Η φτώχεια διαψεύδει την «κανονική χώρα» του πρωθυπουργού. *Efimerida ton Syntakton*. [online newspaper]. Retrieved from http://archive.efsyn.gr/?p=237985

Rancière, J. (2006). *Hatred of democracy* (S. Corcoran, Trans.). London, New York: Verso.

Samaras, A. (2013, December 31). Μήνυμα του Πρωθυπουργού, Αντώνη Σαμαρά, για τη Νέα Χρονιά. [Message of the Prime Minister, Antonis Samaras, for the New Year]. Retrieved from https://primeminister.gr/2013/12/31/12518

Samaras, A. (2014a, January 18). Ο λαός θέλει εκλογές το 2016. [The people want elections in 2016]. *Ethnos*, p. 9.

Samaras, A. (2014b, September 16). Η Ελλάδα επέστρεψε, η προσπάθεια συνεχίζεται. [Greece returned, the effort continues]. *Naftemporiki*. [online newspaper]. Retrieved from www.naftemporiki.gr/video/856946/ant-samaras-i-ellada-epestrepse-i-prospatheia-sunexizetai

Samaras, A. (2014c, October 4). Σαμαράς: «Πρέπει να ξεριζωθεί από τη χώρα ο λαϊκισμός, να γίνουμε Ευρώπη». [Samaras: "Populism must be eradicated from the country, we have to become Europeans"]. *Ta Nea*. [online newspaper]. Retrieved from www.tanea.gr/news/politics/article/5166144/ta-40-ths-xronia-giortazei-h-nd/

Samaras, A. (2014d, October 23). Samaras: A prudent exit from bailouts. *The TOC*. [online newspaper]. Retrieved from www.thetoc.gr/eng/news/article/samaras-a-prudent-exit-from-bailouts

Samaras, A. (2015, November 11). Σαμαράς: Εγώ είμαι ακόμα εδώ – Οι Ευρωπαίοι διευκόλ υναν τους λαϊκιστές. [Samaras: "I am still present—Europeans facilitated the populists]. *Proto Thema*. [online news magazine]. Retrieved from www.protothema.gr/politics/article/ 523387/samaras-ego-eimai-akoma-edo-oi-europaioi-dieukolunan-tous-laikistes/

Samaras, A. (2016, January 11). Σαμαράς: Η ΝΔ ενωμένη να κερδίσει τη μάχη κατά του λαϊκισμού. [Samaras: "A united New Democracy can win the battle against populism"]. *Kathimerini*. [online newspaper]. Retrieved from www.kathimerini.gr/845238/article/epikairothta/politikh/samaras-h-nd-enwmenh-na-kerdisei-th-maxh-kata-toy-laikismoy

Sassen, S. (2014). *Expulsions*. Cambridge, MA: Harvard University Press.

Shakespeare, W. (1976). *Coriolanus*. P. Brockbank (Ed.). London: Methuen.

Spourdalakis, M. (2014). The miraculous rise of the 'Phenomenon SYRIZA'. *International Critical Thought, 4*(3), 354–366. doi:10.1080/21598282.2014.931022

Stavrakakis, Y. (2013). Dispatches from the Greek lab: Metaphors, strategies and debt in the European crisis. *Psychoanalysis, Culture & Society, 18*(3), 313–324.

Stavrakakis, Y. (2014a). The return of 'the People': Populism and anti-populism in the shadow of the European crisis. *Constellations, 21*(4), 505–517.

Stavrakakis, Y. (2014b). Debt society: Psychosocial aspects of the (Greek) crisis. In K. Kenny & M. Fotaki (Eds.), *The psychosocial and organization studies: Affect at work* (pp. 33–59). London: Palgrave Macmillan.

Stavrakakis, Y., & Katsambekis, G. (2014). Left-wing populism in the European periphery: The case of SYRIZA. *Journal of Political Ideologies*, *19*(2), 119–142.

Tsakalotos, E. (2014, December 8). Κρυφή ατζέντα της Ν.Δ. να γίνουμε μια κανονική τριτοκοσμική χώρα. [The hidden agenda of New Democracy is to transform Greece into a normal third world country]. *Avgi*. [online newspaper]. Retrieved from www.avgi.gr/article/5114969/eukl-tsakalotos-krufi-atzenta-tis-n-d-na-ginoumemia-kanoniki-tritokosmiki-xora-me-38-tou-aep-gia-kratikes-dapanes-video-

Venizelos, E. (2013, December 2). Ομιλία Αντιπροέδρου της Κυβέρνησης και Υπουργού Εξωτερικών Ευ. Βενιζέλου στο 24ο Ετήσιο Συνέδριο του Ελληνοαμερικανικού Επιμελητηρίου. [Speech of the Deputy Prime Minister and Minister of Foreign Affairs Ev.Venizelos at the 24th Annual Meeting of the American-Hellenic Chamber of Commerce]. Retrieved from www.evenizelos.gr/speeches/conferences-events/186-conferencespeech2013/4260-24.html

Venizelos, E. (2014a, April 4). Εθνικό αγαθό η σταθερότητα. [Stability is a national good]. *Mega TV*. [online news magazine]. Retrieved from www.megatv.com/megagegonota/article.asp?catid=27371&subid=2&pubid=33365524

Venizelos, E. (2014b, April 29). Ομιλία Αντιπροέδρου της Κυβέρνησης και Υπουργού Εξωτερικών Ευ. Βενιζέλου σε 1η ετήσια συνάντηση διαπιστευμένων Πρέσβεων στην Αθήνα «The Ambassadors Circle». [Speech by Deputy Prime Minister and Minister of Foreign Affairs Venizelos at the First Annual Meeting of Accredited Ambassadors in Athens, "The Ambassadors Circle"]. Retrieved from www.evenizelos.gr/speeches/conferences-events/384-conferencespeech2014/5312-1-the-ambassadors-circle.html

Venizelos, E. (2014c, October 7). Ομιλία του Αντιπροέδρου της Κυβέρνησης και Υπουργού Εξωτερικών, Ευ. Βενιζέλου, στο συνέδριο της Ελληνικής Ένωσης Επιχειρηματιών. [Speech of the Deputy Prime Minister and Minister of Foreign Affairs Ev.Venizelos at the Conference of the Greek Union of Entrepreneurs]. Retrieved from www.evenizelos.gr/speeches/conferences-events/384-conferencespeech2014/4633-2009.html

Vitsas, D. (2014, October 24). Η κανονικότητα του κ. Σαμαρά είναι συνεχής επιτήρηση και υποβάθμιση της ζωής του ελληνικού λαού. [The normality of Mr. Samaras is equal to continuous supervision and deterioration of life standards of the Greek people]. *Left*. [online news magazine]. Retrieved from https://left.gr/news/d-vitsas-i-kanonikotita-toy-k-samara-einai-synehis-epitirisi-kai-ypovathmisi-tis-zois-toy

Vroutsis, I. (2014, November 9). Συνέντευξη του υπουργού Εργασίας Γιάννη Βρούτση στην Καθημερινή της Κυριακής και στη δημοσιογράφο Ρούλα Σαλούρου. [Interview of the Minister of Labour, Ioannis Vroutsis]. *Kykladiki*. [online news magazine]. Retrieved from www.kykladiki.gr/?p=2510

World Bank (n.d.). GDP Growth (annual %). Retrieved from data.worldbank.org/indicator/NY.GDP.MKTP.KD.ZG?locations=GR

Part IV
Metaphors

In this short part, we investigate the prevalence and character of metaphorical language in austerity discourses. It is now well established, thanks to the work of a generation of scholars in linguistics and cognitive science, that metaphor plays a vital role in shaping abstract concepts. Metaphor is an essential element, for example, in building frames, defending positions, and shaping opinions. Consequently, perhaps, metaphors are also the aspect of economic discourse that has been most thoroughly explored to date; and the chapters in this part bring two important questions to that growing body of work.

First, Catherine Resche (Chapter 9) explores the extent to which the metaphors underlying institutional and academic discourses on austerity are reliable predictors of the stances adopted. Analyzing the use of metaphors by various key policymakers—representing the Fed, the Bank of England, the European Central Bank, the International Monetary Fund, and the European Commission—as well as several well-known academics between 2008 and 2015. Resche locates the metaphorical networks within which pro- and anti-austerity discourses are located. In doing so, she establishes that advocates of and opponents to austerity often recruit different properties of the same 'problem' and 'solution' metaphors, thus evidencing the elasticity and expansive argumentative power of metaphor.

Second, Antonella Luporini (Chapter 10) posits that early metaphorical framing of the 2008 financial crisis by the international media may have contributed to legitimizing austerity policies, but that such framing was not limited to word choice alone. Focusing on representations in the British (*The Financial Times*) and Italian (*Il Sole 24 Ore*) financial press, Luporini demonstrates that metaphorical frames can also be generated by grammatical structures, rendering their detection and contestation more difficult.

As in the earlier parts of this book, these chapters make creative use of well-established linguistic theories and methods, in particular—although to differing degrees—Conceptual Metaphor Theory (CMT), and corpus-assisted analysis.

Also known as Cognitive Metaphor Theory, CMT has been foundational to numerous analyses of economic metaphors; indeed, since its origin in the work of George Lakoff and Mark Johnson over 40 years ago, CMT has arguably become the leading interdisciplinary approach to studying metaphor. Both

Resche and Luporini accept its basic claim that abstract domains are made comprehensible via associations with bodily or concrete experience, which in turn are forged through metaphor. For Resche, this foundation prompts both a search for the 'mega-metaphors' underpinning austerity policies, and a comparison of the contexts in which different metaphors are deployed. Luporini's study, by contrast, involves a more fine-grained linguistic analysis drawing on Systemic Functional Linguistics (SFL), which we first met in Chapter 5. In this part, however, SFL lends the insight that metaphors can be created by altering the grammatical elements conventionally used to depict certain meanings: by using a noun, in lieu of a verb, for example.

In both chapters, the nature and distribution of metaphorical associations are explored using tools borrowed from corpus linguistics. First, Resche and Luporini built their own multi-sectioned corpora to serve as strategic samples, designed selectively to represent each author's object of inquiry. Next, they followed a stepwise approach, using corpus analytic software to run automated inquiries, which they supplemented with manual analysis. Both quantitative and qualitative findings are possible in corpus linguistic studies, which we believe makes it a potentially very interesting and fruitful analytical approach for economic inquiries.

9 Are the metaphors underlying institutional and academic discourse on austerity reliable predictors of the stances adopted?

Catherine Resche

Metaphors in specialized and disciplinary domains have been studied extensively from various angles in the past decades, and their iconic (Hiraga, 2005), heuristic (Klamer & Leonard, 1994), and pedagogical functions (Hesse, 1980) have been underlined. Apart from their useful role for research and teaching, metaphors can also be used to build frames, defend specific viewpoints, justify decisions, and influence others (McCloskey, 1998). Kövecses (2002) mentions "the experiential bases or motivation of conceptual metaphors" (p. 75), pointing at their easily-exploitable argumentative power.

Austerity metaphors have already been studied by a number of researchers (Negrea-Busuioc, 2013; Soares da Silva, 2016) who focused their analyses on the press coverage of the latest crisis, whether they dealt with cartoons referring to the Greek crisis or the Portuguese press. So far, however, institutional and academic discourse on austerity does not seem to have been studied with a view to determining whether the underlying metaphors can be reliable predictors of the stances adopted by their authors.

Precisely, the goal of the present chapter is to analyze the choice and use of metaphors in the discourse of various policymakers and academics over the 2008–2015 period. Metaphors may highlight diverging opinions, and thus help identify whether their author is an 'austerian'—a term coined in 2010 by economist Rob Parenteau, i.e., a deficit hawk exhorting governments to reduce their debt levels—, an opponent of austerity, or a supporter of a less drastic, more gradual or milder form of austerity. However, the likelihood that the same metaphorical frame will be used by opposite camps should not be set aside. If this hypothesis is verified, it will be necessary to determine the extent to which the properties selected by each camp for a given metaphor converge or diverge, and whether any change in the metaphorical discourse within the same institution can also point to a change in attitudes and policies.

The chapter is organized as follows: Section 1 describes the methodological perspective; Section 2 offers an overview of the main metaphors retrieved from the corpus (pl: corpora) analysis; Section 3 analyses the findings, putting them in perspective, and discusses the extent to which metaphors are reliable predictors of their authors' stances in the debate for or against austerity. The concluding remarks underline the most salient features of the chapter and offer suggestions on how to supplement and enrich the analysis.

1. Methodology

In the context of crisis management and austerity measures, where the aim is to address real-world problems, studying metaphors requires exploring them in terms of the social and discursive context in which they are used (Low, Todd, Deignan, & Cameron, 2010). Accordingly, the present research borrows from cognitive metaphor theory (Lakoff & Johnson, 1980; Gibbs & Steen, 1999), relying on the existence of a widely-shared set of concepts drawing from individuals' everyday experience, combined with a corpus linguistic approach (Charteris-Black, 2004).

The corpora that served as a basis for the analysis are of two kinds (as illustrated in Table 9.1 below); one set gathers the transcripts[1] of official speeches by the heads of central banks—the Fed, the Bank of England (BoE) and the European Central Bank (ECB)—in addition to speeches by the Presidents of the International Monetary Fund (IMF) and the European Commission (EC); the other set is a collection of texts by a number of well-known academics.[2]

The analysis also keeps in mind research on theory-constitutive metaphors (Boyd, 1993; Resche, 2012) and more precisely on the two main metaphorical veins that flow through economic theory, namely the mechanistic and organic/body metaphors stemming from the historical influence of physical mechanics and hydraulic physics[3] as well as that of biology[4] on economic thought (Resche, 2013). Unsurprisingly, the mega-metaphors (Partington, 2003) THE ECONOMY IS A MACHINE and THE ECONOMY IS A (SICK) BODY/A PATIENT are present in the corpora, alongside other metaphors that are used to frame and contextualize them.

An important point to bear in mind is that the underlying metaphorical frames are not necessarily expressed through metaphorical lexical units or phrases, which makes their identification all the more challenging. If corpus-based methods have been successfully applied to linguistics research dealing with grammar, lexis and various aspects of language use, they have proved less helpful when it comes to extracting metaphors or detecting conceptual mappings (Stefanowitsch, 2006). As a rule, authors rarely draw attention to their own metaphors, though a few examples in the corpora gathered for this research can be quoted:

> It is one thing to have information which, *like blood*, flows through the *veins* of the system; it is another to ensure that everything beats at the same rhythm and all *organs of the body* get all they need from the same single flow.
> (Draghi, 2014, Oct ober 15, emphasis added)[5]

Table 9.1 The corpora

Corpus A: Institutions / heads (number of words)	*Number of words per institution*
The IMF	128,562
- Dominique Strauss-Kahn (50,275)	
- Christine Lagarde (78,287)	
The European Commission (EC)	223,735
- Manuel Barroso (191,186)	
- Jean-Claude Juncker (32,549)	
The Federal Reserve (Fed)	138,459
- Ben Bernanke (78,099)	
- Janet Yellen (60,360)	
The Bank of England (BoE)	125,656
- Mervyn King (71,425)	
- Mark Carney (54,231)	
The European Central Bank (ECB)	153,832
- Jean-Claude Trichet (35,775)	
- Mario Draghi (118,057)	

Corpus B: Academics	*Number of words per academic*
de Grauwe Paul (London School of Economics)	4,946
Krugman Paul (Princeton University; 2008 'Nobel' Laureate)	43,153
Picketty Thomas (EHESS, Paris School of Social Studies)	4,894
Roubini Nouriel (New York University, Stern School of Business)	7,440
Sachs Jeffrey (Earth Institute, Columbia University, New York)	4,924
Sen Amartya (Harvard University; 1998 'Nobel' Laureate)	5,445
Shiller Robert (Yale University; 2013 'Nobel' Laureate)	2,834
Stiglitz Joseph (Graduate School of Business, Columbia University; 2001 'Nobel' Laureate, with George Akerlof and Michael Spence)	26,599
Tirole Jean (School of economics, Toulouse, France; 2014 'Nobel' Laureate)	1,375
Varoufakis Yanis (University of Athens)	15,531
Wren-Lewis Simon (Merton College, Oxford)	16,390

> An analogy can help to make the point clearer: it is as if a person had asked for an antibiotic for his fever, and been given a mixed tablet with antibiotic and rat poison. You cannot have the antibiotic without also having the rat poison.
>
> (Sen, 2015, June 4, emphasis added)[6]

Even though similes and explicit analogies should not be overlooked as they may signal corresponding metaphors, they cannot serve as an exclusive basis

Table 9.2 Preliminary list of key lexical items and associated notions

cuts (budget / job / spending / wages)	abuse / assistance
debt; debt-to-GDP ratio	belt-tightening
deficit	contagion
default	damage, discipline
excess	efforts
fiscal cliff	(ir)responsibility, (in)stability
fiscal consolidation	misconduct, mistakes
reduction, restriction	overspending
sequester	pain, profligacy
sovereign debt crisis	reform, remedies, repair, rescue
tax increases	rigor, risk-taking
	sacrifice, sanctions
	suffering, sustainability

for identifying metaphors, so that other strategies have to be put in place by researchers in the field. Accordingly, in the present chapter, both bottom-up and top-down approaches have been chosen: close reading was essential to help identify the main metaphorical source or target domains.[7] Then, the corpora were fed into the AntConc concordancer[8] and lexical items relevant to source or/and target domain were sought. Two preliminary steps were taken to gain more insight into the austerity issue.

On the one hand, dictionary definitions of 'austerity,' as well as the range of possible austerity measures, were checked,[9] and a first list based on the key terms was drawn; in addition, associated notions deserving attention were added (see Table 9.2).

As shown in the first column, austerity measures are called for when a country risks defaulting because its debt-to-GDP level is excessively high. They consist in stringent cuts in government spending—which can reduce the quality of government services—and/or tax increases in order to increase government revenue. Whatever the measures, they will affect citizens' living standards and impose restrictions. Depending on the arguments used by pro- or anti-austerity camps, austerity measures may be put forward as either recessionary (paralyzing growth) or expansionary (stimulating growth), though it is important to distinguish between the short-term and the longer-term horizons. As evidenced in the second column of Table 9.2, a number of associated notions were added on the basis of the metaphors identified during the close reading phase of this analysis, so that queries based on the initial findings could be submitted to the concordancer and dealt with more systematically.

On the other hand, using the concordancer to retrieve all of the collocates[10] of 'austerity' yielded insightful information: the word 'austerity' is absent from the Fed and ECB corpora, limited to one occurrence in the BoE corpus, and used sparingly in the EC and IMF corpora (respectively 10 and 7 hits). By contrast, it is frequently used in academic discourse (except for Jean Tirole). Its greatest users are anti-austerity campaigners like Paul Krugman and Joseph

Table 9.3 'Austerity' and its collocates[1]

***austerity* (in left position) + noun forms**	advocates; agenda; alternatives; camp; backlash; crowd; *cult*; *death* spiral; debacle; delusion; doctrine; drive; dynamics; economics; economy; efforts; experiment; *fatigue*; *fever*; gang; line; madness; measures; *medicine*; mistake; movement; orthodoxy; plans; policies; pro-business; process; program(me)s; push; regime; rhetoric; scheme; sentiment; *sermons*; strategy; trap; zombie.
***austerity* (in right position) + nouns**	budget austerity; Ponzi austerity; public-sector austerity.
***austerity* (measures/ programmes) + adjectives or compound forms**	acute; *belt-tightening*; conservative; contractionary; counterproductive; creditor-imposed; deficit-obsessed; destructive; draconian; dramatic; excessive; expansionary; fiscal; Greek-style; harmful; harsh; imposed; indiscriminate; intense; irrational; mild; *painful*; panic-driven / induced; recessionary; *savage*; self-defeating; self-inflicted; severe; sharp; sudden; tough; uncalled-for; unsustainable.
***austerity* + verbs**	brings economic decline; causes recession; *cripples* long-term growth; deepens economic problems; depresses growth; destroys jobs; *harms* the economy; *hurts* growth; inflicts damage; is a gamble / a huge mistake / a *suicide* pact; *kills* jobs; makes recession worse; reduces tax receipts; ruins lives; shrinks the economy; threatens/undermines/weakens economic recovery/growth; worsens the crisis.
verbs + *austerity*	*preach* austerity; sell austerity; *tighten the screws* of austerity.
Others	anti-austerity sentiment; austerity-hit countries; austerity-induced depression / recession/ slump; *austerity's bitter medicine*
	European leaders wedded to austerity; governments' devotion to austerity
	the champions of austerity; the costs of austerity; the *cult* of austerity; the failure of austerity; the *medicine* of austerity; the *merchants* of austerity; the *prophets* of austerity

1 Italics signal potentially metaphorical fields.

Stiglitz (respectively 360 and 95 hits), and most of its collocates have negative connotations (see Table 9.3).

In order to have a more representative network of clues as to how different camps convey their message and what mega-metaphors they rely on to support their arguments, other queries were deemed necessary: a number of lexical units like 'rigor'/'rigorous,' 'severe,' 'harsh,' 'stringent,' 'strict,' 'restrictive'/'restriction' were also focused on. They yielded additional information as to how both camps may use them to prove different points (see Table 9.4 below): for example, 'harsh austerity' or 'strict conditions' can be either recommended or denounced, and 'severe cuts' in public expenditure can be presented either as a solution or as a problem.

Table 9.4 Collocates of lexical items pertaining to the field of austerity

harsh	austerity; conditions; effects; lessons; reality; spending cuts; terms
restriction / restrictive	criteria / fiscal policies; regulation
rigor / rigorous	budgetary –; fiscal– / adjustments (policy); clean-up of the banking system; conditions; consolidation; fiscal orthodoxy; governance; policies; processes; procedures
severe	adjustment programs; adverse economic effects; austerity; cuts; collateral damage; cuts; distortions; due diligence; income disparity; job losses; limitations; medicine; monitoring; pressure; squeeze; (fiscal) tightening; toll
strict	bonuses for bankers; conditionality; conditions; constraints; enforcement; implementation; objectives; laws; respect; regulation; solutions; supervision (of banks)
stringent	application; borrowing conditions; conditionality; regulations (capital and liquidity); requirements (reporting); risk control; standards; stress tests; supervision

2. Findings

As underlined by Charteris-Black (2004), metaphor is "concerned with framing a coherent view of reality" (p. 28) and, accordingly, the results will be presented with a view to understanding and highlighting the rationale behind the metaphorical frames chosen by policymakers and academics to convey their ideas. But before the main austerity metaphors are introduced, attention must be drawn to the background metaphors feeding them.

Setting the scene for austerity metaphors

Austerity discourse does seem to be rooted in a preliminary metaphorical network appealing to any citizen's experience, which helps prepare the public to understand the need for exceptional measures, given the great shocks and extraordinary character of the events referred to.

In both the institutional and the academic corpora analyzed here, the crises are first presented in terms of natural catastrophes or fast spreading contagious diseases. The ship "Economy" is caught in extraordinary storms and winds at sea; the economic structure, like that of a building, is threatened by devastating earthquakes or fire, and economies must be protected from a deadly epidemic. King highlights "the economic winds buffeting [the] economy" and the need to "reach the calmer waters of low inflation," while Carney (2014, November 17) mentions "the first tremors of the earthquake." Bernanke (2012, April 9) warns against "the propagation of shocks" and Varoufakis (2013, October 23) also refers to "the shockwaves of the 2008 global earthquake." Barroso underlines the "unprecedented economic shocks and seismic shifts in global geopolitics" (2014, October 20), while Krugman (2012, April 18) refers to Greece as "the epicenter of the crisis." Strauss-Kahn (2010, March 19), for his part, states that "we have all been burnt by the crisis," insisting on the need for "fire brigades to intervene when things get out of hand," and Bernanke (2013, November 8) raises "the question of how to better fireproof the system." Wren-Lewis (2011, September) notes that the crisis is "spreading around the world, leaving no country unscathed" and Krugman (2012, July 2) points out that the euro's crisis has "metastasized."

The severity and magnitude of these phenomena pave the way for a second series of metaphors highlighting the difficult task ahead and the skills required of policymakers to face the turmoil and turbulence (White, 2004), and guide the economy on a long and risky journey. Faced with such challenges, policymakers are called upon to play a number of roles as described in Table 9.5 below. Whether these roles are seen to be performed well, or even acknowledged, is a matter which will be investigated with the aid of the entire corpus.

Many of the roles mentioned in Table 9.4 are related to the machine or patient metaphors. In times of crisis, these metaphors can be modified as THE ECONOMIC MACHINE NEEDS REPAIR, or THE ECONOMIC STRUCTURE RISKS CRUMBLING, and THE ECONOMIC PATIENT IS IN POOR HEALTH. Machine and patient metaphors can also be mixed in the same speech:

> In the beginning, central banks focused their attention on easing liquidity, *to lubricate* financial markets and *get the machinery working again*. [...] Central banks then began to move into new territory, deploying unconventional measures *to resuscitate* markets.
>
> (Strauss-Kahn, 2009, May 15, emphasis added)[11]

The metaphorical frames for analyzing problems

Now turning to the austerity metaphors proper, it is important to bear in mind that metaphorical frames are not necessarily built on explicit metaphors and that the logic behind them is therefore to be derived from key notions expressed in ordinary, non-metaphorical words. In both the institutional and the academic corpora, a number of serious mistakes, flaws and excesses are pointed out as the root causes of economic problems. It therefore seemed relevant to focus on the collocates of the words 'excess'/'excessive' (Table 9.6) and on lexical items starting with the 'over' or 'mis' prefixes (Table 9.7) in order to gain more insight into the way problems were assessed.

Authors in both corpora denounce excessive greed, which pushed financial institutions to "place undue emphasis on returns over risks" (Trichet, 2008, December 8), a lack of self-discipline, of rigor, and ethics, in addition to lies by some countries, like Greece, which provided "misleading statistics" (King, 2011, June 25), "ran large and unsustainable budget deficits," and "forged its books"

Table 9.5 The various roles of policymakers

Roles	*Institutional discourse*	*Academic discourse*
drivers	Countries need to *keep a steady hand on the wheel* (7 May 2012, Lagarde)	
captains	We have to *pass through turbulent waters, but we have set the right course.* (15 June 2011, King)	The major emerging-market countries, which *steered* successfully *through the storms* of 2008 and 2009, may not cope as well with the problems *looming on the horizon* (Stiglitz, 13 Jan. 2012).
architects / housebuilders	A system *built precariously on sand* will *stand more firmly on rock*. [...] By fixing the *fault lines* that caused the last crisis we have created *strong foundations* for a truly global financial system. (17 Nov. 2014, Carney, BoE)	The euro crisis [...] was due to the *faulty architecture* of the particular form of monetary Union we chose (Văroufákis, 23 Oct. 2013).
firefighters	In the middle of a *storm* we had to be *fire-brigade* and *architects* at the same time. (5 Nov. 2013, Barroso, EC)	
doctors	I promised the president I would do my very best, working with my Fed colleagues, to help *restore the health of the economy* (5 March 2014, Yellen, Fed)	The economy's *doctors* say that the *patient* must stay the course. [...] The reality, though, is that the *cure is not working*, and there is no hope that it will – that is, without *being worse than the disease* (Stiglitz, 6 March 2013).
mechanics	Encouraging demand is the first step, to get *the economic engine* to run faster and *stop it stalling out*. But we need to make sure that *the spark* to demand will *fuel* sustained growth. (7 May 2012, Lagarde, IMF)	The Tories stopped *tightening the screws* [...] and sure enough the nation started feeling better (de Grauwe, 21 Feb. 2014).
defense officers	Policymakers immediately *deployed the monetary arsenal* as the first *line of defense* against the crisis. (15 May 2009, Strauss-Kahn, IMF)	
guides / mountaineers	[The crisis] *shook* the financial system. It opened *crevices*, raised *mountains*, and *diverted streams* in the central banking and monetary policy landscape. On this new *terrain*, central bankers are quickly learning to be *mountaineers* and have been busily developing new ideas and new *tools* for this more *challenging terrain*. (Lagarde, 2014, July 2)	

Table 9.6 Collocates of 'excess' / 'excessive'

excess	... and abuse; demand; leverage; liquidity; payments; reserves; savings
excessive	austerity; bonuses; debt (accumulation/ratios); deficit; dependence on unstable short-term funding; exuberance; faith in the virtues of markets; indebtedness; leverage; macroeconomic imbalances; money creation; penalties; price pressures; public borrowing; reliance on consumption; risk-taking; speculation; spending.

Table 9.7 Items starting with *over-* or *mis-*

over- + co-occurrences	*mis- (adjectives or noun forms) + co-occurrences*
overblown (construction sector; optimism)	misaligned (incentives) / misalignment (price –)
overburdened (households)	misallocated (capital) / misallocation (of scarce capital) /
overcapacity	misbehavior
overconfidence	misconduct (in FX markets / and rigging of markets)
over-extension (of balance sheets)/ overextended (financial sector)	misdiagnosis (Maturity – in shadow banking / between assets and liabilities)
over-indebtedness	misguided (policies)
over-leveraged (mortgage debtors/ positions)	misleading (practices / statistics)
overheating / overheated (housing market; economies)	mismanagement (of public finances)
overreliance (on models / on short-term funding)	mismatches
oversized (banking system)	misreporting (statistical –)
over-spending	mistrust
overstated (capital)	misuse of confidential information
overvalued / overvaluation	

(Roubini, 2013, April 16). The authorities are blamed for failing to control the system properly, or to analyze the situation adequately; and for being partly responsible for the fragility of the financial system and/or of the European Union. Reckless behavior and excessive indebtedness cannot be tolerated and scandals in the banking sector must end, as Carney (2014, November 17) insists metaphorically: "It is simply untenable now to argue that the problem is one of a few bad apples. The issue is with the barrels in which they are stored."

All of these flaws give rise to value judgments that contribute to shaping metaphorical frames likely to influence people's views and understanding (Fillmore, 1985): the authors appeal to the public's moral sense. In Corpus A (institutions), discipline and efforts are praised as virtues. Barroso (2013, January 10), for example, expresses his admiration and respect for the Irish who are "suffering the hardships to fix the problems now so that we can build a better future together" and he congratulates Ireland for "fighting its way through an economic crisis with remarkable resilience and resolution," and for showing "an unwavering commitment to implementing the economic adjustment programme." Ireland seems to be a good pupil, a metaphor anyone can understand: it made efforts, was disciplined, and heeded the recommendations, so that it deserves praise, and can therefore be quoted as an example for the others. Conversely, when countries are guilty of non-compliance with the rules, or when they "are not making sufficient progress towards medium-term budgetary objectives" (Trichet, 2010, June 21), sanctions should be applied. Another underlying metaphor is that based on an analogy between a country and a family, that failed to "save money for a rainy day" (Strauss-Kahn, 2008, February 13). Such an analogy with elementary housekeeping rules is easily acceptable because it is based on common sense[12]: everyone will be familiar with the idea that an over-indebted family will have to spend less in order to rebalance its budget, which means accepting such sacrifices as dining out less often, and saving on what is considered superfluous. Irresponsible behavior such as greed or any other form of excess is presented as a sign of weakness of character, namely the inability to resist temptation. Under such circumstances, belt-tightening is called for. Lagarde (2012, May 7) highlights the need "to shed excess weight to become fit and healthy," and King warns that people must prepare to behave more soberly:

> The next decade is likely to be *a sober decade*, a decade of *savings*, *orderly budgets*, and *equitable rebalancing*. [...] *A sober decade* may not be fun, but it is *necessary* for our economic *health*.
>
> (King, 2010, October 19)[13]

The moral considerations of having to pay for one's mistakes are given religious and biblical overtones. It all becomes a matter of crime and punishment, sin and expiation, hubris and nemesis:

> Failure to tackle the imbalances during *the seven years of plenty* before 2007 threatens *seven lean years* thereafter for at least part of the world economy.
>
> (King, 2011, June 15, emphasis added)[14]

In Corpus B (academic), where parallel metaphors are used, the institutional diagnosis is often questioned. For example, the very metaphor of countries living beyond their means is denounced as a "simplistic diagnosis" (Stiglitz, 2013, March 6) and its flawed premise is underlined:

> [W]hile that approach to debt works well for a single household in trouble, it does not work well for an entire economy, for the spending cuts only worsen the problem. This is the paradox of thrift: belt-tightening causes people to lose their jobs, because other people are not buying what they produce, so their debt burden rises rather than fall.
>
> (Shiller, 2012, January 19)

The value judgments differ, though the same metaphorical fields of discipline, efforts, mistakes, sacrifices, and religion are resorted to. The divergence lies in their exploitation. Krugman, for example, wonders whether it is worth being a good pupil: "Even Austerity's star pupils, countries that, like Portugal and Ireland, have done everything that was demanded of them, still face sky-high borrowing costs" (2012, February 19). Stiglitz presents the pain/sacrifice/expiation metaphor by insisting on the 'innocent victims' that are made to 'pay the price' of others' sins: "If there is pain to be borne, the brunt of it should be felt by those responsible for the crisis, and those who benefited most from the bubble that preceded it" (2011, January 3). As for "the moral appeal of austerity," it is resisted by Sen (2012, July 3) as being "deceptively high ('if it hurts, it must be doing some good') [...], and also self-defeating in reducing public deficits, because austerity tends to depress growth." The echoes of the religious frame are meant to warn against "the cult of austerity, a morality play, a tale of countries that lived high and now face the inevitable reckoning. Sin and its consequences is their story and they are sticking to it" (Krugman, 2012, September 28).

In assessing the situation, authors in both corpora add to the list of roles already mentioned in Section 1. Institutional actors seek to picture themselves as people whose duty is to right wrongs, guarantee discipline and avoid abuses. They are sometimes led to become chaperones:

> The role of a central banker is to *take the punch bowl away just as the party is getting going*. [...] If banks feel they must keep on dancing while the music is playing and that at the end the central bank will make sure everyone gets home safely, then over time the parties will become wilder and wilder.
>
> (Mervyn King, 2008, June 10, emphasis added)[15]

Corpus B offers an echo to the punch bowl metaphor, only to point out that it is a double-edged sword since the chaperones may fail in their mission:

> So, yes, the economy is showing some signs of healing itself. But that healing process won't go very far if policy makers stomp on it, in particular by raising interest rates. That's not an idle worry: A Fed chairman famously declared that his job was to take away the punch bowl just as the party was really warming up; unfortunately, history offers many examples of central bankers pulling away the punch bowl even before the party even starts.
>
> (Krugman, 2013, July 7)

Corpus B authors exploit the religious metaphor somewhat differently, denouncing the moralizing posture and the sermon-like speeches of 'austerians,' referred to as 'prophets' or 'apostles' of the austerity religion, "preaching the virtues of pain and suffering" (Stiglitz, 2011, January 3), and even as 'merchants' selling austerity, through an underlying analogy with the Merchants in the Temple:

> Under [Jean-Claude Trichet's] leadership the bank began preaching austerity as a universal economic elixir that should be imposed immediately everywhere.
>
> (Krugman, 2011, May 22)

Once the diagnosis has been made either by mechanics, engineers, architects, or doctors, the appropriate instruments and tools must be selected to repair the damage, and solutions and remedies offered.

The metaphors dealing with the recommended solutions

In institutional austerity discourse, the first preoccupation is to restore the public's confidence by introducing the toolkit metaphor. Policymakers insist that they "have considerably widened their set of tools" (Bernanke, 2011, October 18), including less conventional ones, and that they will make full use of "the array of instruments [they] have at hand" (Draghi, 2014, April 24) to control the situation, fine-tune the economic engine, strengthen the architecture, and cure the patient. Controls, rules, restrictions, and discipline are key notions.

The medical register is abundantly relied on, both by the advocates of and opponents to austerity. While the former recommend a slimming diet that will rid the financial world of its excesses and the countries of their debts, the latter point to the risks of excessive weight loss that could lead to anorexia and eventually death:

> [I]t can be concluded that the sharp austerity measures that were imposed by market and policymakers' panic not only produced deep recessions in the countries that were *exposed to the medicine*, but also that up to now *this medicine did not work.*
>
> (de Grauwe, 2013, February 21, emphasis added)

The remedies are sometimes questioned in a very sarcastic manner:

> To say that *the medicine is working* because the unemployment rate has decreased by a couple of percentage points, or because one can see a glimmer of meager growth, is akin to *a medieval barber saying that a bloodletting is working because the patient has not died yet*.
>
> (Stiglitz, 2014, October 1, emphasis added)

> Our finance ministers resemble *doctors who misdiagnose* a cancer patient in severe pain as afflicted with a pain-crisis.
>
> (Varoufakis, 2013, October 23, emphasis added)

The 'economic doctors,' for their part, insist that full recovery will take time, all the more so as the injuries were serious, a metaphor easy to understand by anyone familiar with health problems:

> Since late 2008, the Fed has taken *extraordinary* steps to *revive* the economy. [...] But the *scars* from the Great Recession remain, and reaching our goals *will take time.*
>
> (Yellen, 2014, March 31, emphasis added)

Once emergency remedies, described as "a shot in the arm" (Lagarde, 2015, April 9), have been administered, it is important to reconsider the situation for, "as with many *medicines*, there are *side-effects* from [...] *prolonged use*" (King, 2013, January 22, emphasis added). So shock therapy or initial life support need to be followed by longer-term measures, in order for the patient to recover and be more resilient:

> Government and central banks put a massive sticking *plaster on the wounds* in the form of an *extraordinary* degree of monetary and fiscal stimulus. But there is *a long period of healing* ahead.
>
> (King, 2010, January 19, emphasis added)[16]

> [A]ll of us who have a leadership role, facing this unprecedented set of circumstances, will be judged by history, not just on how we try to *anesthetise short term pain*, but on whether we *take a holistic view of the whole body*, and whether we put forward measures to *strengthen it* in order to *prevent injury* in the face of future falls or stumbles.
>
> (Barroso, 2011, May 18, emphasis added)

Although not all academics in the corpus are opponents of austerity, the more vocal ones are those who wish to share with their audience the idea that austerity is counterproductive: in order to do so, they use metaphors with a view to countering the metaphors used in institutional discourse. While institutional discourse highlights the need for efforts, strict controls and reforms, academics question the need for self-inflicted pain, which they analyze through the lens of the baseball bat metaphor:

> Suppose that for some reason you decided to start hitting yourself in the head, repeatedly, with a baseball bat. You'd feel pretty bad. Correspondingly, you'd probably feel a lot better if and when you finally stopped. [...] Your head wasn't hurting because you were sick; it was hurting because you kept hitting it with that baseball bat. [...] Britain's government has declared its intention to pick up the baseball bat again—to engage in further austerity.
>
> (Krugman, 2014, December 28)

And in order to point at what they consider flawed arguments used by austerity advocates to convince the public to accept sacrifices, the anti-austerity campaigners created a new metaphor, that of the 'confidence fairy':

> Advocates of austerity believe that mystically, as the deficits come down, confidence in the economy will be restored and investment will boom.[...] The *confidence fairy* that the austerity advocates claim will appear never does, partly perhaps because the downturns mean that the deficit reductions are always smaller than was hoped.
>
> (Stiglitz, 2010, October 19, emphasis added)

3. Analysis

It is now time to analyze the results further and see the extent to which they can provide answers to the questions raised at the beginning of this chapter.

The main answer lies in the fact that, apart from 'the confidence fairy' and 'the baseball bat' metaphors, both corpora use the same metaphorical fields, relying on the widely-shared everyday experience of human beings: excesses and necessary restraints, mistakes and sanctions, misconduct and moral considerations, pain and relief. The differences lie in the way the metaphorical fields are exploited to express opposite outcomes.

If a 'battle of metaphors' can be considered as a relevant notion here, it should not be understood in terms of competing metaphorical fields, but rather in terms of competing semantic traits and metaphorical extensions within the same metaphorical source fields (Prandi, 2012). In both camps, the metaphors are presented along diverging logical lines, but are likely to find an echo in the public's shared experience.

Table 9.8 offers an overview of the way metaphors stemming from the same metaphorical vein lead to different interpretations and conclusions, depending on the camp that uses them.

Another initial question raised in the introduction to this chapter dealt with the likelihood of changing metaphors to accommodate changing attitudes towards austerity; in other words, could a change in metaphors help identify a turning point in their authors' stances?

In a 2010 paper, Alesina and Ardagna made a case for expansionary austerity, comforting the advocates of austerity as to the merits of such policies. Yet, in 2011, another paper by Guajardo, Leigh, and Pescatori came to the opposite conclusion: austerity could be contractionary. Two subsequent IMF papers (Blanchard & Leigh, 2012, 2013) pointed out that the initial projections about the fiscal multiplier had been underestimated, and that the IMF had underestimated the damage that spending cuts inflict on a weak economy. The question raised by the last three papers mentioned was whether such cuts were likely to trigger a turning point in the IMF's approach to austerity, a change that might be mirrored in the IMF's metaphors. Analysis of Christine Lagarde's discourse in Corpus A shows that, although the metaphors remain the same (navigation, belt-tightening, morality, bookkeeping), they are exploited with a view to mitigating the institution's positions:

> Fiscal policy must *navigate* between *the twin perils* of losing credibility and undercutting recovery. [...] *It does not necessarily mean drastic upfront*

Table 9.8 Various interpretations of the same metaphorical fields

Metaphorical fields	*Pro-austerity camp*	*Anti-austerity camp*
misconduct	A country that cheats about its deficit is guilty of misconduct; so are people who take advantage of the situation, endangering others.	Those who take advantage of the weak (borrowers) or punish innocent victims (through austerity measures) are guilty of misconduct.
sin / moral considerations	Reckless lending and borrowing, overspending, cheating are sins that must be paid for.	Excessive austerity is a sin in itself; innocent victims should not be expected to foot the bill.
religion	Rigour and abstemiousness are virtues; sacrifices and efforts will be rewarded.	Are the prophets of the austerity religion entitled to impose suffering on others?
excess	The economic patient must go on a diet.	Excessive dieting may lead to anorexia and death.
medicine	An ailing economy needs skillful doctors able to administer the right remedies: shock therapy and longer-term prescriptions.	An ailing economy is at the mercy of doctors choosing the wrong remedies that may do more harm than good.
pain	Pain is a necessary ill but it is worth it.	Is pain worth it? It may lead to depression and even suicide.
housekeeping	Economies, like families, need to manage their budget in a sensible manner.	Economies have nothing in common with households.
machine	The economic engine risks stalling if the proper measures (austerity) are not taken to reboot the machine; skillful engineers are called for.	Over-tightening the screws of the economic engine may damage the mechanisms and delay recovery.

> *belt-tightening* if countries address long-term fiscal risks like rising pension costs or healthcare spending, they will have more space in the short run to support growth and jobs.
>
> (Lagarde, 2011, August 27, emphasis added)

> This brings me to another *worrisome tendency* in many quarters – to view fiscal policy as *a morality play between profligacy and responsibility*.
>
> (Lagarde, 2012, January 23, emphasis added)

> A measured and steady pace will generally strike *the right balance* between *putting the books in order* and *supporting the recovery*.
>
> (Lagarde, 2013, March 3, emphasis added)

In a parallel way, Manuel Barroso echoes the IMF's qualified position, alluding to the potentially counterproductive effect of all-out harsh austerity:

> Some say that Europe just needs more *discipline*, more *rigour*, more *sanctions*. Others say that more *solidarity* and *flexibility* are what is needed. Both sides are wrong. We need both approaches. We need to shoulder *responsibility* and to show *solidarity*.
>
> (Barroso, 2013, January 7, emphasis added)

From 2013 onwards, the more frequent mentions of the ordinary citizens' difficult living conditions in central bank discourse also points to the policymakers' greater consideration for the pain inflicted on 'innocent victims.' The EC also evolved in its approach to austerity: as Vivien Schmidt (2015) put it, the EC abandoned the idea of a one-size-fits-all rule of budgetary austerity, which had caused it to be considered as "ayatollah of austerity," to become more accommodative as a "minister of moderation."

Again, changes in attitudes cannot be said to coincide with the introduction of new metaphors: they are only visible in the way metaphorical source fields are used to support slightly different approaches which do not call into question the principle of austerity but only reconsider its degree and timing. In the pro-austerity camp discourse, both dimensions draw from the medical and religious conceptual frames: if shock therapy (i.e., monetary injections or fiscal stimulus) can be used at first to save the patient in a situation of emergency, and if austerity measures can be delayed for a while, a stricter, longer cure requiring efforts and sacrifices will be inevitable in the longer term, as Dominique Strauss-Kahn underlined as early as 2009: "with fiscal policy, *there is a time to sow and a time to reap*, and loose policies today must go hand in hand with tight policies tomorrow" (emphasis added).

Concluding remarks

The need to embrace the broader metaphorical landscape behind discourse, rather than focusing on isolated metaphors, has been evidenced: such an approach yields a better idea of the metaphorical frames underpinning and supporting each camp's message.

Analysis of the corpora has provided answers to the questions raised. It has established that, whatever the position of the authors, the same metaphorical fields are borrowed from: only they are deployed differently, depending on the semantic properties deemed relevant in order to convey the desired message. Thus, the persuasive and manipulative force of metaphors is revealed: through the specific metaphors used in the implementation and justification of harsh austerity policies—namely the metaphors of obesity/diet, an indebted family, good pupils, and sacrifice—austerity is conceptualized as self-discipline, necessary punishment, and the moral imperative not to "live beyond one's means." These moral metaphors serve the ideological agenda of austerity, and foster the beliefs that budget deficits are always a problem, or that the principles of household management can be applied to a country's economy. The message is that austerity can help economies resume their long-term growth path. However, metaphors can also be used to highlight the reverse—the mischievous and immoral features of austerity measures—in the context of a widespread perception that austerity and sacrifices were not worth it. From this perspective, austerity is not seen as a real economic solution, but rather as a cruel, misguided, and counterproductive policy of crime and punishment, or sin that should necessarily be paid for. The diachronic perspective has also made it possible to verify that even when standpoints evolve as a result of new research, i.e., when policies are somewhat softened, the metaphorical frame remains the same, but is used slightly differently.

The present chapter has shown that there is much to be gained from considering metaphorical fields, and approaching them as dynamic networks (Prandi, 2012), looking out for any evolution in the metaphorical landscape that may signal changing positions. Keeping in mind the argumentative potential of metaphors, it is easier to understand their underpinning logic, and to beware of their persuasive and manipulative power. Comparing the metaphors used by institutions and academics with the metaphors used by politicians over the same period would most certainly provide interesting insights as to the extent to which the metaphorical frames used by the latter converge or diverge depending on their positions towards austerity.

Notes

1 The transcripts are available on the official websites of the various institutions: www.imf.org; ec.europa.eu; www.federalreserve.gov; www.bankofengland.co.uk; www.ecb.europa.eu

2 The texts are available on their authors' blogs, web pages, or can easily be retrieved by entering the academics' names alongside 'austerity' on Google.

3 Irving Fisher's price machine and A.W.H. Phillips's machine, with their tanks, pipes, sluices, valves, pulleys and levers both provide illustrations of the economy-as-a-machine metaphor, while they also account for the importance of the liquid metaphor in economics, borrowed from fluid dynamics (see Resche, 2013, pp. 146–148).

4 The liquid metaphor also permeates economics as a result of François Quesnay's use of the analogy between the circulation of blood in the human body and the circulation of riches in the economy, as represented in his 1758 "*tableau économique.*" Obviously, his training as a physician inspired the analogy.

5 www.ecb.europa.eu/press/key/date/2014/html/sp141015.en.html

6 www.newstatesman.com/politics/2015/06/amartya-sen-economic-consequences-austerity

7 In the metaphor 'The economy is a mechanism,' the source domain is the mechanical field, while the target domain is the economy.

8 AntConc is a freeware corpus analysis toolkit for concordancing and text analysis developed by Laurence Anthony at Tokyo's Waseda University. The version used here is AntConc 3.5.0 (2015). It is available from www.laurenceanthony.net/

9 Financial Times lexicon: lexicon.ft.com/Term?term=austerity-measure; Investopedia: www.investopedia.com/terms/a/austerity.asp

10 Here collocates are words occurring in conjunction with the word 'austerity.'

11 www.imf.org/en/News/Articles/2015/09/28/04/53/sp051509

12 The lay person may not be aware of how central to economics the household metaphor is, since in ancient Greek 'οἰκονομία' literally meant 'household management.' However, the analogy is used in the corpus as an argument that anyone can easily grasp.
13 www.bis.org/review/r101021a.pdf
14 www.bankofengland.co.uk/-/media/boe/files/speech/2011/speech-by-mervyn-king-at-the-lord-mayors-banquet-at-mansion-house.pdf
15 www.bankofengland.co.uk/-/media/boe/files/speech/2008/banking-and-the-bank-of-england.pdf
16 www.bankofengland.co.uk/-/media/boe/files/speech/2010/mervyn-king-speech-at-the-university-of-exeter.pdf

References

Alesina, A., & Ardagna, S. (2010). Large changes in fiscal policy: Taxes versus spending. In J.R. Brown (Ed.). *Tax policy and the economy* (Vol. 24, pp. 35–68). Chicago, IL: University of Chicago Press.

Boyd, R. (1993). Metaphor and theory change: What is 'metaphor' a metaphor for? In A. Ortony (Ed.). *Metaphor and thought* (2nd ed.) (pp. 481–532). Cambridge, UK: Cambridge University Press.

Blanchard, O., & Leigh, D. (2012). *World economic outlook: Coping with high debt and sluggish growth.* Washington, DC: International Monetary Fund.

Blanchard, O., & Leigh, D. (2013). *Growth forecast errors and fiscal multipliers.* (Working Paper No. 13/1). Washington, DC: International Monetary Fund.

Charteris-Black, J. (2004). *Corpus approaches to critical metaphor analysis.* Houndmills, Basingstoke, UK: Palgrave MacMillan.

Fillmore, C. J. (1985). Frames and the semantics of understanding. *Quaderni di Semantica, 6*, 222–254.

Gibbs, R. W., & Steen, G. J. (1999). *Metaphor in cognitive linguistics.* Amsterdam, Netherlands/New York: John Benjamins.

Guajardo, J., Leigh, D., & Pescatori, A. (2011). *Expansionary austerity: New international evidence.* (Working Paper No. 11/158). Washington, DC: International Monetary Fund.

Hesse, M. (1980). *Revolutions and reconstructions in the Philosophy of Science.* Brighton, UK: Harvester.

Hiraga, M. J. (2005) *Metaphor and iconicity.* New York: Palgrave Macmillan.

Klamer, A., & Leonard, T. C. (1994). "So what's an economic metaphor?" In P. Mirowski (Ed.) *Natural images in economic thought: Markets read in tooth and claw* (pp. 20–51). Cambridge, UK: Cambridge University Press.

Kövecses, Z. (2002). *Metaphor: A practical introduction.* Oxford/New York: Oxford University Press.

Lakoff, G., & Johnson, M. (1980). *Metaphors we live by.* Chicago, IL: University of Chicago Press.

Low, G., Todd, Z., Deignan, A., & Cameron, L. (Eds.). (2010). *Researching and applying metaphors in the real world.* Amsterdam, Netherlands: John Benjamins.

McCloskey, D. (1998). *The rhetoric of economics* (2nd ed.). Madison, WI: The University of Wisconsin Press.

Negrea-Busuioc, E. (2013). What does austerity 'look' like? An analysis of visual metaphors in three newspaper cartoons depicting the Eurozone crisis. In P. Gill, J. Barnden, M. Lee, R. Moon, A. Wattington, & C. Shank (Eds.). *Corpus-based approaches to figurative language: Metaphor and austerity* (pp. 4–7). Birmingham: The University of Birmingham.

Partington, A. (2003). *The Linguistics of political argument*. London/New York: Routledge.

Prandi, M. (2012). A plea for living metaphors: Conflictual metaphors and metaphorical swarms. *Metaphor and Symbol, 27*(2), 148–170.

Resche, C. (2012). Towards a better understanding of metaphorical networks in the language of economics: The importance of theory-constitutive metaphors. In H. Herrero & M. White (Eds.). *Metaphor and mills: Figurative language in business and economics* (pp. 77–102). Berlin: De Gruyter Mouton.

Resche, C. (2013). *Economic terms and beyond: Capitalising on the wealth of notions*. Bern: Peter Lang.

Schmidt, V. A. (2015). *The Eurozone's crisis of democratic legitimacy: Can the EU rebuild public trust and support for European economic integration*? (European Economy Discussion paper No. 015). Luxembourg: Publications Office of the European Union. Retrieved from https://ec.europa.eu/info/sites/info/files/file_import/dp015_en_2.pdf

Soares da Silva, A. (2016). The persuasive (and manipulative) power of metaphor in 'austerity' discourse. In M. Romano & M. D. Porto (Eds.). *Exploring discourse strategies in social and cognitive interaction*. Amsterdam, Netherlands: John Benjamins.

Stefanowitsch, A., & Gries, S. T. (2006). *Corpus-based approaches to metaphor and metonymy*. Berlin/New York: de Gruyter Mouton.

White, M. (2004). 'Turbulence' and 'turmoil' in the market or the language of a financial crisis. *Ibérica,* 7, 71–86.

10 Metaphors in times of crisis

Legitimizing austerity?

Antonella Luporini

This chapter focuses on the metaphorical framing of the global crisis in the British and the Italian financial presses in 2008—the year when the global outlook on the slowdown following the financial tensions in the US changed for the worse—discussing results of research into crisis-related conceptual and grammatical metaphors (nominalizations) in a corpus of articles from *The Financial Times* and the Italian business newspaper *Il Sole 24 Ore*.[1]

Theoretical background

Metaphor in language and thought

Our view on metaphor, and on the implications of metaphorical language, has radically changed over the past decades. One of the main reasons for this change was the publication of Lakoff and Johnson's *Metaphors We Live By* (1980), and the subsequent inception of Conceptual Metaphor Theory (henceforth CMT). This novel approach, originating within cognitive linguistics, put an end to the long-standing supremacy of the 'ornamental' view, which conceived of metaphor as a rhetorical device, having a purely stylistic function.[2]

Indeed, one of the main tenets of CMT is that metaphor is ubiquitous, not only in language, but also—crucially—in thought: linguistic (*lexical*) metaphors are seen as the pervasive, visible output of *conceptual* metaphorical links which play a key role in comprehension, meaning construction and social action (see, e.g., Lakoff & Johnson, 1980; Lakoff, 1993).[3] In the words of Lakoff and Johnson: "Our ordinary conceptual system, in terms of which we both *think* and *act*, is fundamentally *metaphorical* in nature" (1980, p. 3, emphasis added). From this perspective, metaphor becomes a powerful cognitive and linguistic tool, which "helps constrain the way we *think* and *speak* of our ordinary lives" (Gibbs, 1994, p. 7, emphasis added).

A second major assumption is the bodily basis of metaphorical reasoning. We tend to comprehend the non-physical (less readily accessible) through metaphorical mappings with the physical, which is observable and more directly experienced (cf. Kövecses, 2015, pp. 21–22).[4] This phenomenon is clearly illustrated by an expression like the following (from Soares da Silva, 2016, p. 94):

(1) This quick and painful *cure* demanded by the Troika [...] is the only solution

The example shows that the physically-grounded domain HEALTH (the *source* domain, in CMT terminology) is mapped onto the abstract *target* concept AUSTERITY, yielding the conceptual metaphor (CM): AUSTERITY IS MEDICAL TREATMENT (but also entailing THE CRISIS IS A MEDICAL CONDITION).[5] It is worth noting that excerpt (1) forms part of a coherent set of similar linguistic resources (in English and in other languages), which, however, may not be ordinarily perceived as being metaphorical at all.

This leads to a further consideration, directly relevant to this study, concerning how metaphors can 'organise our view' of reality (as Black noted, back in 1955, p. 288). First, metaphorical mappings are *selective*: while some areas of the target concept are foregrounded in and by the overlap with the source, other areas are inevitably backgrounded (cf. Lakoff & Johnson, 1980, Chapter 3). For instance, in excerpt (1) above, the risks to which the State's economy is exposed are implicitly emphasized; however, since only some parts of the source concept come into play in structuring the metaphor, other possibilities (e.g., a wrong diagnosis? too-aggressive treatment?) are obscured. Second, since conceptual metaphors (CMs) are systematic and inherent in our conceptual system, their linguistic manifestations—which we resort to continuously, if inadvertently—are for the most part *conventionalized*: they are natural ways of talking about certain domains of experience.The two aspects together make metaphor a powerful tool for construing reality, as the metaphorical framing of an event (especially in general interest areas such as political and media discourse) inevitably impacts on its reception and conceptualization, while often going unnoticed.

Substantial research has been carried out in this area, at the intersection between CMT and critical discourse analysis (for which see, e.g., Fairclough, 1995 [2010]). Space permits but a few examples (but see also Goatly, 2007; Underhill, 2011). In their seminal work, Lakoff and Johnson discuss the WAR metaphor used by US President Carter with reference to the 1970s energy crisis, arguing that "metaphors can be self-fulfilling prophecies" (1980, p. 156). Lakoff has continued to pay attention to the presence and effects of metaphor in political communication, e.g., analysing the metaphorical apparatus used by the US administration to justify the Gulf Wars (1991, 2003), the 'metaphors of terror' involved in the September 11 attacks (2001), and the different models underlying the liberal and the conservative views of morality (1996 [2016]). More recently, Bednarek (2005) has focused on CMs, newspaper language and *event-construal*, defined as "the way in which a particular event in the 'real world' is construed via textualization when it is reported in a newspaper" (p. 9), probing the strategic importance of CMs in establishing event-construals.

In the language of economics, which is our focus here, the role played by metaphor is widely acknowledged. Numerous corpus-assisted studies have addressed the metaphors used to frame economic/financial issues in the press, as well as their impact on the readers' reception (e.g., Charteris-Black, 2004,

Chapter 7; Rojo López & Orts Llopis, 2010). The pervasiveness of metaphor in the language of financial actors is also the topic of an article that was published in August 2016 in *The Wall Street Journal* (Sindreu & Gold, 2016). The authors quote, among others, economist Kallum Pickering, who, interestingly, makes reference to the potential for construing biased representations of reality inherent in metaphor: "Here's the problem I have with metaphors: *sometimes you don't give a true picture of what's happening*" (emphasis added).

Austerity-related metaphors have also attracted scholarly attention of late, especially during the recent financial crisis, when, as Kitson, Martin, & Tyler (2011, pp. 289–291) put it, a NICE economy (characterized by "non-inflationary consistent expansion") was replaced by a VILE economy ("volatile inflation, little expansion"), calling for austerity measures to be implemented in the US and the Eurozone.[6]

The 2013 *Workshop on Corpus-Based Approaches to Figurative Language* was specifically dedicated to exploring the connections between metaphor and austerity; the contributions (Philip, Barnden, Lee, Moon, Wallington, & Shank, 2013) addressed the metaphors used to structure the discourse of austerity, and related issues, in different languages, particularly within CMT (e.g., ECONOMY IS HOUSEHOLD BUDGET; see also Krugman, 2012a; on the ideological and persuasive power of austerity metaphors, see Soares da Silva, 2016). Lakoff himself (2012) has written on the implications of the misleading *fiscal cliff* metaphor, after Krugman's (2012b) appeal to replace it with the more fitting *austerity bomb*, noting that "if the economy is a vehicle moving forward without control toward the cliff, there is great and immediate danger, and so the 'fiscal cliff' metaphor engenders fear," but also warning that "metaphors cannot be proposed at will and be expected to work, even if they are intended to fit reality better than existing metaphors."

Following up on this, the study presented here focuses on the metaphors used in the British and the Italian presses to construe the global crisis at its onset, in the conviction that the resulting pessimistic outlook—to be discussed—may have contributed to justifying the adoption of urgent and exceptional measures, thus paving the way for the narrative of austerity that predominated in the following years. As noted at the beginning, my analysis goes beyond CMT to include the framework of grammatical metaphor, to which I now turn.

Grammatical metaphor and nominalization

I began this chapter by saying that our view on metaphor has dramatically changed over the past decades, and dedicating the previous section to a discussion of the main tenets of CMT. There is, however, another approach to metaphor, nascent in the same years, which has made a fundamental contribution to our understanding of the pervasiveness and significance of metaphorical mechanisms: the framework of grammatical metaphor (henceforth GM) developed within Systemic Functional Linguistics (SFL).

SFL assumes that metaphorical variation often goes beyond word choice (the focus of interest in CMT), affecting grammatical structures: "there is also such a thing as grammatical metaphor, where the variation is essentially in the grammatical forms, although often entailing some lexical variation as well" (Halliday, 1985, p. 320). The underlying principle is the same: Meaning is *transferred* from the linguistic element that is most naturally associated with it to a different one. In fact, in the same way as *lexical units* (see Note 3) have *literal* meanings, so *grammatical structures* in SFL are said to have *congruent* (i.e., default) functions within the system of a language. Thus, both GM and lexical metaphor imply a semantic shift, and can be seen as second-order linguistic phenomena: "a linguistic expression can only be labelled 'metaphorical' by virtue of there being a comparable non-metaphorical expression" (Taverniers, 2006, p. 326).

This framework embraces distinct types of GM (ideational, interpersonal and, according to some scholars, also textual), which correspond to the three metafunctions played by language in context identified by SFL (ideational, interpersonal, and textual: see Halliday 1985 and subsequent editions). The rest of this section is dedicated to the type dealt with in this study, nominalization, which falls within the category of ideational metaphors (comprehensive accounts of the GM framework and the theory behind it can be found in, e.g., Halliday & Matthiessen, 1999, Chapter 6; Thompson, 1996 [2014], Chapter 9).

Whereas the interpersonal metafunction has to do with language as a means of enacting personal and social relationships, and the textual metafunction focuses on how speakers and writers choose to organise the message, the ideational metafunction accounts for the fact that speakers use language "to make sense of their experience of what goes on around them and inside them" (Halliday, 1985, p. 101). The lexico-grammatical system enabling speakers to represent experience in language is that of TRANSITIVITY,[7] which includes options to construe the factual content of the message through configurations of: a) activities or states (*processes*); b) entities involved (*participants*); and c) circumstantial information. Processes are congruently encoded in language as verbs; they may also involve the qualities being ascribed to entities or facts, which are congruently encoded as adjectival or adverbial forms. Participant roles are congruently realized by nouns. Nominalization is the most productive and studied form of GM in this realm: it consists in the (non-congruent/metaphorical) use of a nominal form to express a 'process' or 'quality' meaning, as in the following examples (from Devrim, 2015, p. 11):[8]

(2) [Congruent] The taxpayers are anxious, because the government passed a new bill.

(3) [Metaphorical] The *passing* of a new bill caused *anxiety* among taxpayers.

As a comparison between (2) and (3) shows, nominalization has a knock-on effect on ideational semantics in the whole clause. First, meanings and wordings are compressed: (2) features two clauses (one for each verb congruently instantiating a process), hypotactically linked (i.e., one clause is subordinated to another) through the conjunction *because*, while (3) is a simple clause, with two nominalizations. Second, nominalized processes and qualities are *reified*, i.e., metaphorically portrayed as things: therefore, they become atemporal (pass*ed* → *the passing*; *are* anxious → *anxiety*) and tend to be de-personalized through agency deletion (in (3), for example, the 'Doer' of the material action of *passing* disappears, and *anxiety* is portrayed as an entity spreading among taxpayers, as if of its own accord). As a consequence, clauses containing nominalizations are less open to inter-speaker negotiation (Thompson, 1996 [2014], p. 245).

So then, nominalization, like CM, has effects on the ways reality is construed in discourse. Indeed, GM has started to complement CMT in the critical analysis of texts (see, e.g., Koller & Davidson, 2008; Ritchie & Zhu, 2015; Luporini, 2017).

Corpus construction and methodology of analysis

The preliminary stage of my research involved the construction of an ad hoc corpus, collecting articles from all of the 2008 issues of *The Financial Times* (London edition) and *Il Sole 24 Ore*. This year was chosen for the significance of its financial events, among which the federal takeover of Fannie Mae and Freddie Mac (announced September 6), and the Lehman Brothers crash (September 15), after which concerns about the global aftermath of the US economic downturn spread worldwide.[9] The newspapers were selected for their authoritativeness and wide circulation, with a view to carrying out a comparative analysis of the metaphorical representation of the crisis in the two languages and countries.

For each issue, the main first page article and the leader were stored in electronic format. First page articles reflect the editorial board's perception of the main events of the day and, thanks to their visibility, are likely to reach a wider audience (including non-specialists). Leaders, on the other hand, are "the voice of the newspaper," one of their primary functions being "that of persuading the newspaper's readers of its point of view" (Morley, 2004, p. 239). In both cases, the role played by CMs and nominalizations in terms of event-construal (cf. Bednarek, 2005) was potentially significant.

At the end of the data collection stage, the corpus [plural: corpora] amounted to 863,277 words and included four sub-corpora: *FT_First_page* (*Financial Times* first page articles) + *FT_Leaders* (*Financial Times* lead articles) (154,408 + 152,773 words respectively) and *S24O_First_page* (*Il Sole 24 Ore* first page articles) + *S24O_Leaders* (*Il Sole 24 Ore* lead articles) (311,640 + 244,456 words respectively). The corpus was uploaded to the online Corpus Query System *Sketch Engine* (Kilgarriff, Rychlý, Smrz, & Tugwell, 2004). To ensure a smoother running of automated queries, it was part-of-speech tagged (so that formally identical words belonging to different classes would be clearly distinguishable: e.g., *use* noun vs. *use* verb) and lemmatized (so that different forms of a lemma [i.e., the standard citation form of a word] would be retrieved and counted together, e.g. *used*, *using* and *uses* as different instantiations of the same basic form *use*).

Analysis focused on the lemma *crisis* and its Italian equivalent *crisi* (including both their singular and plural instantiations in the corpus), and involved the following steps:

i) Sentence-length keyword-in-context concordances (i.e., a display of all instances of the search term in context, showing the entire sentence in which they each occur) were retrieved for all instances of the two lemmas.
ii) Irrelevant occurrences, not referring to economic/financial issues (e.g., mentions of the 2008 Georgian crisis) were discarded.
iii) The final set of concordances resulting from step (ii) (1,356) was preliminarily scanned for instantiations of CMs and nominalizations, through a combination of automated techniques (collocate lists and word sketches, cf. Kilgarriff et al., 2004) and manual analysis. Two subsets of *metaphorical* concordances (concordances, i.e., including at least one instance of CM or nominalization linked to *crisis/crisi*) were thus identified. The exact number of metaphorical concordances, in terms of CM and nominalization respectively, is given in Tables 10.1 and 10.2 below.
iv) Finally, all of the lexical metaphors in the metaphorical concordances were classified according to the CM they realized in context, taking into account the distinction between ontological, orientational and structural metaphors (Lakoff & Johnson, 1980). For instance, expressions like *to be in crisis* and *emerge from the crisis* (It. *essere in crisi, uscire dalla crisi*) were treated as instantiations of the ontological CM THE CRISIS IS A CONTAINER; *the crisis arose*, or *escalating crisis* (It. *la crisi che monta*) were linked to the orientational CM MORE IS UP; finally, different occurrences of the expression *immune to the crisis* (It. *immune alla crisi*) were classified as instantiations of the structural CM THE CRISIS IS A HEALTH PROBLEM. Nominalizations were also marked off for subsequent qualitative scrutiny. For instance, the noun *loss* and its Italian counterpart *perdita* were treated as nominalized forms of the material process *losing* (*perdere*), whose congruent realization would be a verb. A functional analysis of the nominalized element, including its effects on the semantics of the clause (cf. examples (2) and (3) above), was then carried out. Co-occurrence of CMs and nominalizations was also considered.

Findings rundown and discussion

Table 10.1 shows a statistically significant total percentage (54.7%) of concordances with evidence of CMs involving the crisis (log-likelihood = 12.10, df = 1, $p < 0.01$). The total percentage of metaphorical concordances in Table 10.2

Table 10.1 Number and percentage of metaphorical concordances (CM)

Sub-corpus	*Analyzed concordances*	*Metaphorical concordances (CM)*	*% of metaphorical concordances*
FT_First_page	180	95	52.8%
FT_Leaders	177	102	57.6%
S24O_First_page	514	282	54.9%
S24O_Leaders	485	263	54.2%
Total	**1356**	**742**	**54.7%**

Table 10.2 Number and percentage of metaphorical concordances (GM: nominalization)

Sub-corpus	*Analyzed concordances*	*Metaphorical concordances (nominalization)*	*% of metaphorical concordances*
FT_First_page	180	94	52.2%
FT_Leaders	177	88	49.7%
S24O_First_page	514	204	39.7%
S24O_Leaders	485	201	41.4%
Total	**1356**	**587**	**43.3%**

(nominalization) is lower (43.3%), but still significant (log-likelihood = 10.64, df = 1, $p < 0.01$).

Tables 10.3 and 10.4 focus on CMs, providing an in-depth look at the main source concepts mapped onto the target concept CRISIS in the four sub-corpora, as emerging from analysis in step (iv) above (the full list of metaphorical lexical units, with their classification in terms of CMs, is provided in Luporini, 2013a, pp. 129–148).

As can be seen, the CMs involved in the representation of the crisis are substantially uniform across the data, with only slight differences in their relative frequencies: a small set of conceptual domains (PHYSICAL ENTITY, CONTAINER, HEALTH, WAR and NATURAL FORCE/DISASTER) accounts for the majority of lexical metaphors in all the sub-corpora. We will now take a closer look at each of these metaphorical classes; the discussion will focus on both the lexical metaphors instantiating the CM and, when present, the nominalization(s) involved (the case for the synergies between the two types of metaphor, and their tendency to co-occur, has been made elsewhere: see Luporini, 2017).

The crisis is a physical entity

PHYSICAL ENTITY is the main source of metaphorical expressions in all the sub-corpora (with, co-incidentally, exactly the same number of occurrences in *FT_First_page* and *FT_Leaders*). This is also the least defined category, since the linguistic metaphors realizing it may actually highlight different areas of the

Table 10.3 Main categories of CM for CRISIS in FT

	FT	
	FT_First_page *Total no. of lexical metaphors* = **118**	**FT_Leaders** *Total no. of lexical metaphors* = **118**
1.	PHYSICAL ENTITY [33 occurrences, **28%**]	PHYSICAL ENTITY [33 occurrences, **28%**]
2.	WAR [28 occurrences, **23.7%**]	CONTAINER [25 occurrences, **21.2%**]
3.	CONTAINER [18 occurrences, **15.3%**]	HEALTH [20 occurrences, **17%**]
4.	NATURAL FORCE/DISASTER [13 occurrences, **11%**]	–
	Others = below 10% each	*Others = below 10% each*

Table 10.4 Main categories of CM for CRISIS in S24O

	S24O	
	S24O_First_page *Total no. of lexical metaphors* = **330**	**S24O_Leaders** *Total no. of lexical metaphors* = **314**
1.	PHYSICAL ENTITY [96 occurrences, 29.1%]	PHYSICAL ENTITY [93 occurrences, 29.6%]
2.	CONTAINER [50 occurrences, 15.2%]	CONTAINER [54 occurrences, 17.2%]
3.	WAR [48 occurrences, 14.6%]	HEALTH [44 occurrences, 14%]
4.	HEALTH [47 occurrences, 14.2%]	WAR [42, 13.4%]
5.	NATURAL fORCE/DISASTER [46 occurrences, 13.9%]	–
	Others = below 10% each	*Others = below 10% each*

physical domain, as we shall see below. Overall, PHYSICAL ENTITY metaphors tend to portray the crisis (marked in bold below) as a tangible presence within human society, and to foreground its repercussions on human beings and economic activities, as in:

(4) *Si proietterà* [...] sul prossimo anno [...] *la durezza* dell'attuale **crisi** ["*The hardness* of the current crisis [...] will *project itself* onto the next year"; *S24O_First_page*, December 17]

The lexical unit activating the CM is the verb *proiettarsi* ("to project oneself onto something") which in its literal sense refers to a physical action performed by a corporeal entity; indeed, it is classified in the SFL TRANSITIVITY SYSTEM as a material process (i.e., involving 'doing,' as opposed to a mental process involving 'sensing' or a relational process involving 'being' or 'having,' for example). The lexical metaphor combines with the nominalization *la durezza* ('the hardness'), which metaphorically represents the quality of being 'hard' as a thing, through a nominal group, and takes on the function of 'Doer' (or 'Actor,' in SFL terminology) of the material process. The two types of metaphor together have important effects on the way information is organized and conveyed in and by the text. On the one hand, they both bring about "a move in the direction of objectifying" (Halliday & Matthiessen, 1999, p. 233), in the sense of construing the crisis as an almost 'perceptible' object. On the other hand, the nominalization condenses the related proposition ('the crisis is hard'), making it less contestable; it also activates a contextually meaningful component of SEVERITY and, possibly, even HARM (construing the crisis as a stiff object, which can have serious consequences if and when it impacts on something else), thus making the statement more vivid.

One of the sub-areas of the physical domain most frequently activated by the lexical units in the corpus (especially in the English section) is MOTION, with a total of 23 occurrences in *FT_First_page* + *FT_Leaders* (34.8%) and 35 occurrences in *S24O_First_page* + *S24O_Leaders* (18.5%). From this perspective, the crisis is conceptualized as a MOVING OBJECT/SUBSTANCE, having its own energy, and capable of spreading through the economy. An example follows:

(5) The [...] **crisis** *emerged* as house prices fell and mortgage defaults rose [*FT_Leaders*, October 8]

The CM in (5) is triggered by the lexical metaphor *emerged*, another material process.[10] The lexical choice here is particularly interesting, since it implies that the crisis was already 'out there,; and that it came out of a place where it was 'hidden' (underground? underwater?) thanks to a set of favorable conditions. Thus, besides implying the usual shift towards concreteness, this CM tends to efface human involvement: a further inference may be that finding a solution—in a metaphorical world where financial events act of their own accord, so to speak—becomes even more urgent.

Another sub-area involved in the conceptualization of the crisis as 'physical' is that of EXPLOSIVE SUBSTANCES. Interestingly, this sub-type of PHYSICAL ENTITY metaphor is specific to the Italian sub-corpora, where it occurs 23 times in total (12.2%). Let us briefly consider the following instance:

(6) La **crisi** *innescata* dai mutui subprime
["Crisis *set off* by subprime loans"; *S24O_Leaders*, April 13][11]

By construing the crisis as a bomb, these metaphorical expressions underline not only its harmful potential, but also its instability and unpredictability. The related wordings, once again, tend to conceal human agency: this is evident in

(6), where the crisis is said to be triggered by *subprime loans* (personified, while 'real' human agency is excluded).

The crisis is a container

CONTAINER metaphors are a specific type of PHYSICAL ENTITY metaphors, in which the crisis is portrayed as a container having an entrance (usually easy to find) and an exit (hidden or difficult to reach). The linguistic instantiations generally involve the metaphorical use of the prepositions *in/out of/from* and their Italian equivalents *in/da* (which, when used literally, refer to a 'truly' physical location); these, however, frequently combine with other lexical units, such as motion verbs, or adjectives expressing qualities of the container (particularly *deep/profondo*):

(7) credito e immobiliare [...] ci hanno fatto *piombare nella* più difficile **crisi** economica
["the credit and housing markets [...] made us *fall into* the worst economic crisis"; *S24O_Leaders*, January 29]

(8) we are *in the depths of* the [...] **crisis** [*FT_First_page*, April 19]

In (7) above, the verb *piombare* (meaning "to fall down with a sudden and rapid movement," according to the *Treccani* Italian dictionary) focuses on motion towards the container *crisis*, highlighting the feature HIGH SPEED; the lexicogrammatical structure of the sentence once again involves a non-human Subject ("the credit and housing markets"), construed as responsible for the event through a causative verbal group complex ("made (us) fall"). Example (8) above is another instance of conflation between lexical metaphor (the preposition *in*) and nominalization (*depths*), through which the underlying CM is reinforced. The nominalization, as in (4) above, involves a shift from (congruent) quality to (non-congruent) thing (*deep* → *depth*); this not only works consistently with the scenario set up by the CM, adding to the sense of 'perceptibility' of the crisis as a container, but also contributes to the emergence of an additional property, i.e., its INESCAPABILITY, assuming that the deeper the container, the harder it is (e.g., because more energy or abilities are needed) to escape. Clearly, even highly conventional metaphorical expressions like this can have noteworthy effects in terms of event-construal.

The crisis is war/a health problem

These two metaphorical classes are discussed in the same section because they share an important aspect, namely that the crisis is conceptualized as something that can cause physical injury or, in the worst cases, even kill. Interestingly, the English sub-corpora show a noticeable difference in the relative frequency of these two source concepts (Table 10.3): WAR metaphors account for 23.7% of the total CMs in *FT_First_page*, where they rank second, but fall below 10% in *FT_Leaders*, which, by contrast, shows a preference for HEALTH metaphors (17%). Such difference may be motivated by a tendency towards 'eye-catching' wordings in first page articles in English; the difference in the Italian data is too small to draw similar conclusions with impunity.

As far as WAR metaphors are concerned, the lexical metaphors activating them, in both English and Italian, represent the crisis as an enemy attacking us—through, e.g., the verbs *face/threaten* and their Italian equivalents, *fronteggiare/minacciare*. On several occasions, the physical struggle between the 'enemy' and the institutions and authorities involved (e.g., the IMF, banks, financial markets, policymakers, regulators) is explicitly signalled through verbs instantiating material processes like *combat* (It. *combattere*), *hit* (It. *colpire*) or *strangle*, which can be nominalized, as when the IMF is said to have launched an appeal to the banks to collect fresh capital in order to better:

(9) sopportare *i colpi* della **crisi**
["withstand *the blows* of the crisis"; *S24O_First_page*, July 29]

Another example from the English section follows:

(10) a pledge [...] to implement an *aggressive* [...] *plan to combat* the financial **crisis** [*FT_First_page*, October 11/12]

The most notable difference between (9) and (10) lies in the role played by the crisis in terms of the underlying ideational semantics (for which see the introductory section on GM and nominalization above). Indeed, in (9), the nominalization *colpi* condenses the proposition "the crisis is hitting (something/someone)," in which the crisis has an agentive role ('Actor' of the material process *colpire*, 'to hit'); in (10), by contrast, the crisis is the element that undergoes the material process *combat* (or the 'Goal,' in SFL terminology). There is, however, another (subtler) distinction to be considered. Example (9) shows an instance of lexical metaphor/nominalization conflation in the word *colpi* ('blows'). This brings about a metaphorical shift from 'verb' (which would be the standard, congruent realization of the material process of *hitting*) to 'thing': the action itself is reified, being represented through its agnate (i.e., semantically similar, though grammatically different) nominal form *blow*; the nominalization makes it appear more tangible, even more 'real.' In (10), by contrast, the possibility of fighting the crisis is located on a theoretical, non-factual level by the lexical unit *plan*, even if this is explicitly qualified as *aggressive*.

Turning to HEALTH metaphors, their instantiations in the data frame the crisis as either a generic cause of death, or (more frequently) as a medical condition, while the role of patient/victim can be taken by: a) people working at financial institutions; b) metonymically, the institutions themselves; c) abstractions such as *economy*. One example must suffice:

(11) *la fine* della **crisi** [...] non si vede, mentre *si allarga il contagio*
["the end of the crisis [...] is *nowhere in sight*, while *the contamination is spreading*"; *S24O_First_page*, July 29]

Here, the crisis is simultaneously conceptualized as a PHYSICAL ENTITY (its end being nowhere *to be seen*) and as a DISEASE, whose 'contamination' (with a nominalization) is spreading through finance and economy like an epidemic—once again foregrounding its concrete presence.

Overall, the main effect of WAR metaphors seems to be that of highlighting the crisis's violence and resilience, especially when the lexical instantiations combine with nominalizations that foreground the physical aspects of the struggle. This class of CMs, however, brings with it another relevant corollary, namely that urgent and *exceptional* measures are not only justified, but also required, as noted by Lakoff with reference to different contexts (1991, 2001, 2003). HEALTH metaphors also foreground the crisis's severity, and tend to portray it as something that is largely inevitable (just like a serious disease), or that might have been averted only by taking all reasonable precautions.

The crisis is a natural force/disaster

This category accounts for more than 10% of the total occurrences only in the sub-corpora collecting first page articles (again, this may be linked to the search for 'effectiveness' characterizing this section of the newspaper). This particular type of usually 'catastrophic' metaphors is realized by lexical units like *storm*, *upheaval*, or—in the Italian data—*cataclisma* ('cataclysm'), *ciclone* ('tornado'). In the following example, the lexical metaphor *epicentro* ('epicenter') evokes the specific CM THE CRISIS IS AN EARTHQUAKE:

(12) le grandi banche [...], *epicentro* della **crisi**
["the big investment banks [...], the *epicenter* of the crisis"; *S24O_First_page*, June 29]

The English data, however, show evidence of a particular sub-class of NATURAL DISASTER metaphors which is absent from the Italian section, namely: THE CRISIS IS A NUCLEAR DISASTER. This is instantiated by the lexical units *fallout* and *meltdown* (in which, again, the lexical metaphor is conflated with a nominalization). There is space for but one example:

(13) After escaping being [...] hit by the *fallout* from the US subprime mortgage **crisis** [...] eurozone economies have been slowed down [*FT_First_page*, August 15]

Fallout is a 'dead' nominalization from the verb *fall out* in its literal sense, as a look at the online etymological dictionary *www.etymonline.com* confirms: it refers to radioactive dust spreading in the air after a nuclear explosion. Here too, lexical metaphor and nominalization work cohesively: the 'thingified' process *fallout* ('Actor') may concretely *hit* (another material process) economies; these are, in turn, objectified and represented as (slowly) moving objects (compatibly with the basic orientational metaphors LESS/LOSING CONTROL IS DOWN: see Note 10), thus creating a multiple-layered metaphorical scenario. Luporini (2013b) provides further discussion of this category.

In closing this section, I will only note that the different instantiations of the CM THE CRISIS IS A NATURAL FORCE/DISASTER have as their main effect that of conceptualizing economic and financial processes as natural phenomena, following their own rules, and ultimately beyond human control.

Conclusions

This chapter has addressed the metaphorical framing of the global financial crisis as it emerges from analysis of a corpus of articles from *The Financial Times* and *Il Sole 24 Ore*.

Quantitative analysis unveiled a significant presence of CMs and nominalizations in crisis-related discourse in both newspapers: both types of metaphor, already in 2008, were frequently used to construe the crisis and related events in the specialized press; as we have seen, this is in line with findings on the language of economics in general.

Qualitative analysis for CMs revealed that the main metaphorical patterns instantiated in the corpus represent the crisis as:

- i) capable of 'concretely' impacting on human society, through mappings with the source concept PHYSICAL ENTITY, sometimes also highlighting its destructive potential (as is the case with the CM, specific to the Italian sub-corpora, THE CRISIS IS AN EXPLOSIVE SUBSTANCE);
- ii) a physical and almost inescapable CONTAINER;
- iii) an enemy threatening us or engaging us in physical conflict, through WAR metaphors, or a disease/cause of death, through metaphors based on the HEALTH domain; and
- iv) something that may occasionally be forecasted, but not averted, often having catastrophic consequences, through NATURAL FORCE/DISASTER metaphors.

Thus, overall, the metaphorical conceptualization of the crisis, foregrounding its 'tangible' aspects, seems to construe the necessity for urgent and exceptional a posteriori action (as is the case with, e.g., a military invasion or a tornado).

Qualitative analysis for nominalizations (often working synergistically with CMs, within the same concordances: see Luporini, 2017) revealed the crucial role played by this type of GM in reifying the crisis and its effects, construing them as less readily negotiable, and thus also justifying the need for an immediate solution.

Against this background, my answer to the question posed by the title is a qualified 'yes.' Although further research into the metaphorical framing of the crisis, at different times (e.g., pre- and post-austerity) and in different text-types, would be needed to corroborate this assertion, the data discussed above suggest that, already in 2008, the economic situation was being presented in highly negative terms in the two countries. Such a pessimistic representation may arguably have contributed to justifying their upcoming drive for austerity. As Lakoff and Johnson (1980) put it, "[i]n most cases, what is at issue is not the truth or falsity of a metaphor but the perceptions and inferences that follow from it and the actions that are sanctioned by it" (p. 158). It is perhaps no coincidence that the package of austerity measures put forward by the Monti government in December 2011 came with a resonant name: the "*Save* Italy" decree.

Notes

1 The study is a development of a PhD research project. The complete analysis can be found in Luporini (2013a).

2 For an overview of other contributions that questioned the ornamental view before CMT, see Johnson (1981).

3 By linguistic metaphors, scholars working within CMT generally mean *lexical* metaphors, i.e., non-literal uses of lexical units: words or multi-word expressions which may belong to various classes: nouns, verbs, adjectives, adverbs, and also prepositions (cf. Lindstromberg, 1998, [2010]). There is already a long tradition of corpus-assisted research into lexical metaphors as surface realizations of conceptual metaphors in naturally occurring language (see, e.g., Deignan, 2009 [2012]).

4 On the notion of *embodiment* in CMT, see, e.g., Johnson (1987), Gibbs, Lima & Francozo (2004); on the 'embodiment turn' in cognitive science, see in particular Shapiro (2011).

5 Throughout the chapter, concepts involved in CMs are conventionally indicated in small capitals; related linguistic metaphors are in italics.

6 In the EU, though with local specificities, austerity emerged as a common response to the crisis, overseen by the Troika (cf. example (1) above). In the UK, it took the form of "the biggest cuts in state spending since World War II" (Kitson, Martin, & Tyler, 2011, p. 294). In Italy, the austerity turn was signalled by the appointment by the President of the Republic of the cabinet led by Mario Monti in November 2011.

7 In Systemic Functional Linguistics, systems are conventionally indicated in small capitals.

8 Nominalizations are indicated in italics.

9 The impact of the 2008 financial tensions, especially of Lehman Brothers 'death,' on our collective imagination is testified by the body of fiction on the topic that appeared in the following years (see Shaw, 2015). Also in 2015, a movie directed by Adam McKay (*The Big Short*, based on the book by Michael Lewis) drew attention to the connections between the US housing bubble (and the unscrupulous practices behind it) and the subsequent crisis.

10 It should be noted, however, that the whole sentence is highly metaphorical, and shows evidence of what Lakoff and Johnson (1980, Chapter 4) call *orientational* metaphors (metaphors, i.e., based on basic spatial concepts) in *house prices fell* (LESS IS DOWN) and *mortgage defaults rose* (MORE IS UP). The expression *the crisis emerged* itself makes use of the basic orientational metaphors MORE/HAVING CONTROL IS UP.

11 In Italian, the verb *innescare* in its literal sense is specifically used in relation to bombs and explosives in general.

References

Bednarek, M. (2005). Construing the world: Conceptual metaphors and event-construal in news stories. *Metaphorik.de*. 9/2005, 6–32. Retrieved from www.metaphorik.de/en/journal/09/construing-world-conceptual-metaphors-and-event-construal-news-stories.html

Black, M. (1955). Metaphor. *Proceedings of the Aristotelian Society*, 55 (1954/1955), 273–294.

Charteris-Black, J. (2004). *Corpus approaches to Critical Metaphor Analysis*. Houndmills, Basingstoke, UK: Palgrave Macmillan.

Deignan, A. (2009 [2012]). Searching for metaphorical patterns in corpora. In P. Baker (Ed.), *Contemporary Corpus Linguistics* (pp. 9–31). London/New York: Continuum.

Devrim, D.Y. (2015). Grammatical metaphor: What do we mean? What exactly are we researching? *Functional Linguistics*, *2*(3). Retrieved from http://functionallinguistics.springeropen.com/articles/10.1186/s40554-015-0016-7.

Fairclough, N. (1995 [2010]). *Critical Discourse Analysis: The critical study of language* (2nd ed.). London/New York: Routledge.

Gibbs, R.W., Jr. (1994). *The poetics of mind: Figurative thought, language, and understanding*. Cambridge, UK: Cambridge University Press.

Gibbs, R. W., Jr., Lima, P., & Francozo, E. (2004). Metaphor is grounded in embodied experience. *Journal of Pragmatics*, *36*(7), 1189–1210.

Goatly, A. (2007). *Washing the brain: Metaphor and hidden ideology*. Amsterdam, Netherlands/Philadelphia: John Benjamins.

Halliday, M. A .K. (1985). *An introduction to Functional Grammar*. London: Arnold.

Halliday, M. A. K., & Matthiessen, C. M. I. M. (1999). *Construing experience through meaning: A language-based approach to cognition*. London: Cassell.

Johnson, M. (Ed.). (1981). *Philosophical perspectives on metaphor*. Minneapolis: Minnesota University Press.

Johnson, M. (1987). *The body in the mind: The bodily basis of meaning, imagination, and reason*. Chicago, IL: University of Chicago Press.

Kilgarriff, A., Rychlý, P., Smrz, P., & Tugwell, D. (2004). The sketch engine. In G. Williams & S. Vessier (Eds.), *Proceedings of the Eleventh EURALEX International Congress* (pp. 105–115). Lorient: Université de Bretagne Sud. Retrieved from www.euralex.org/elx_proceedings/Euralex2004/.

Kitson, M., Martin, R., & Tyler, P. (2011). The geographies of austerity. *Cambridge Journal of Regions, Economy and Society*, *4*(3), 289–302.

Koller, V., & Davidson, P. (2008). Social exclusion as conceptual and grammatical metaphor: A cross-genre study of British policy-making. *Discourse & Society*, *19*(3), 307–331.

Kövecses, Z. (2015). *Where metaphors come from: Reconsidering context in metaphor*. Oxford: Oxford University Press.

Krugman, P. (2012a, May 31). The austerity agenda. *The New York Times*. Retrieved from www.nytimes.com/2012/06/01/opinion/krugman-the-austerity-agenda.html

Krugman, P. (2012b, August 12). The austerity bomb. *The New York Times*. Retrieved from https://krugman.blogs.nytimes.com/2012/11/14/the-austerity-bomb August 2017

Lakoff, G. (1991). Metaphor and war: The metaphor system used to justify war in the Gulf. *Peace Research, 23*(2/3), 25–32.

Lakoff, G. (1993). The contemporary theory of metaphor. In A. Ortony (Ed.), *Metaphor and thought* (2nd ed., pp. 202–251). Cambridge, UK: Cambridge University Press.

Lakoff, G. 1996 [2016]). *Moral politics: How Liberals and Conservatives think* (3rd ed.). Chicago, IL: University of Chicago Press.

Lakoff, G. (2001). Metaphors of terror. Retrieved from www.press.uchicago.edu/sites/daysafter/911lakoff.html

Lakoff, G. (2003). Metaphor and war, again. Retrieved from www.alternet.org/story/15414/metaphor_and_war,_again

Lakoff, G. (2012, March 12). Why it's hard to replace the 'Fiscal Cliff' metaphor. *The Huffington Post*. Retrieved from www.huffingtonpost.com/george-lakoff/why-its-hard-to-replace-t_b_2230577.html

Lakoff, G., & Johnson, M. (1980). *Metaphors we live by*. Chicago, IL: University of Chicago Press.

Lindstromberg, S. (1998 [2010]). *English prepositions explained* (2nd ed.). Amsterdam, Netherlands/Philadelphia: John Benjamins.

Luporini, A. (2013a). *Metaphor in times of crisis: Metaphorical representations of the global crisis in* The Financial Times *and* Il Sole 24 Ore *2008*. Unpublished PhD dissertation. Pisa: University of Pisa. Retrieved from: http://etd.adm.unipi.it/t/etd-05132013-001020/.

Luporini, A. (2013b). Metaphor and culture in the business press: A corpus-assisted study of *The Financial Times* and *Il Sole 24 Ore*. *Rassegna Italiana di Linguistica Applicata. 45*(1), 163–177.

Luporini, A. (2017). 'In the depths of the world's credit crisis': Compelling synergies between conceptual and grammatical metaphor in a corpus-assisted study of the British and Italian financial press'. *Textus, 30*(1), 169–184.

Morley, J. (2004). The sting in the tail: Persuasion in English editorial discourse. In A. Partington, J. Morley, & L. Haarman (Eds.). *Corpora and discourse* (pp. 239–255). Bern: Peter Lang.

Philip, G., Barnden, J., Lee, M., Moon, R., Wallington, A., & Shank, C. (Eds.) (2013). *Corpus-based approaches to figurative language: Metaphor and austerity*. Birmingham, UK: University of Birmingham.

Ritchie, L. D., & Zhu, M. (2015). "Nixon Stonewalled the Investigation": Potential contributions of grammatical metaphor to Conceptual Metaphor Theory and analysis. *Metaphor and Symbol, 30*(2), 118–136.

Rojo López, A. M., & Orts Llopis, M. A. (2010). Metaphorical pattern analysis in financial texts: Framing the crisis in positive or negative metaphorical terms. *Journal of Pragmatics, 42*(12), 3300–3313.

Shapiro, L. (2011). *Embodied cognition*. Abingdon, UK: Routledge.

Shaw, K. (2015). *Crunch lit*. London: Bloomsbury.

Sindreu, J., & Gold, R. (2016, August 29). Bazookas! Sinks! Aggressive doves! Nobody loves silly metaphors more than central bankers. *The Wall Street Journal*. Retrieved from www.wsj.com/articles/bazookas-sinks-aggressive-doves-nobody-loves-silly-metaphors-more-than-central-bankers-1472481317?tesla=y

Soares da Silva, A. (2016). The persuasive (and manipulative) power of metaphor in 'austerity' discourse: A corpus-based analysis of embodied and moral metaphors of austerity in the Portuguese press. In M. Romano & M. D. Porto (Eds.). *Exploring discourse strategies in social and cognitive interaction* (pp. 79–108). Amsterdam, Netherlands/ Philadelphia: John Benjamins.

Taverniers, M. (2006). Grammatical metaphor and lexical metaphor: Different perspectives on semantic variation. *Neophilologus*, *90*(2), 321–332.

Thompson, G. (1996 [2014]). *Introducing Functional Grammar* (3rd ed.). Abingdon, UK: Routledge.

Underhill, J.W. (2011). *Creating worldviews: Metaphor, ideology and language*. Edinburgh: Edinburgh University Press.

Part V
Argumentation

As the contributors to earlier parts in this book have demonstrated, the strategic recruitment of both economic theory and linguistic features (including, but not limited to, metaphor) has been central to the legitimation of twenty-first century austerity policies. In this part, we turn to the mechanics of arguments made for and against austerity, again considering both economics and linguistics, as well as their interrelationship. In doing so, we are mindful of Blaise Pascal's well-known aphorism, that "People almost invariably arrive at their beliefs not on the basis of proof but on the basis of what they find attractive" [*On the Art of Persuasion*, 1658]—and so we ask of austerity policies not only "what proof(s)?" but also "attractive to whom?"

In his analysis of the European Fiscal Compact (FC) and, particularly, its implementation and media representation in Austria, Stephan Pühringer (Chapter 11) explains the increasing role of economic experts as purveyors of political discourse, and economic proofs (including market exigencies) as the foundation of European policy-making. He notes that, unlike in France and Germany, in Austria the FC was chiefly supported by Social Democrats via moral, financial and political (pro-European) arguments, but opposed by the Greens and right-wing parties with financial, political (nationalist, pro-democratic), and legal arguments. He concludes that both the content of the European Union's Fiscal Compact and the process by which it was implemented in Austria represent a post-democratic development.

Giuseppe Mastromatteo and Sergio Rossi (Chapter 12) masterfully summarize the economic theory supporting both sides of the austerity debate. Focusing on the main arguments for austerity, they expose the underlying ideological principles of these arguments, most prominently belief in the ineffectiveness of the State as an economic actor and faith in market mechanisms. They also present a solution to some of the policy dilemmas of contemporary public finance, noting that its implementation has been impeded by powerful vested interests in debtor and creditor countries alike. In doing so, Mastromatteo and Rossi lay down a challenge that aligns perfectly with the interests of critical discourse analysis, namely to examine power relations within the austerity debate, including who wins and who loses.

Emanuele Brambilla (Chapter 13) analyzes the arguments not of theoreticians but, rather, of political leaders anxious to sell austerity to their respective electorates in the UK, USA and France. Most notably, we see here the recurring metaphorical depiction of the State as a household, in the shape of the well-known admonition by Charles Dickens's fictional character, Mr. Micawber, to spend no more than one earns. Yet, there is more than meets the eye in the way this seemingly simple argument is employed by political leaders in different countries and contexts: while the central topic of austerity measures remains constant, it is strategically combined with diverse sub-topics and rhetorical devices, building varied argumentation schemes that are tailored to and reflect contextual differences, and serve varied political agendas.

All of these chapters point to the fact that a detailed knowledge of how argumentation works in practice—including the ability to identify (often unspoken) premises, distinguish between topics and sub-topics, and attend to linguistic detail—is part and parcel of understanding not only how particular propositions come to 'win the day,' but also who stands to gain (and lose) therefrom. Mastromatteo and Rossi focus on the *content* of arguments in favor of austerity, while Pühringer and Brambilla focus on the *language* with which those arguments are constructed. Yet each of these authors makes clear that, although some arguments appear consistently across different genres and time periods, they remain highly-situated and call for close consideration of not only content but also genre, context, and language use.

To this end, both Pühringer and Brambilla draw on aspects of corpus linguistics (which we first encountered in Chapter 3) and Critical Discourse Analysis (major variants of which also appear Chapters 1, 4 and 7). In addition, Pühringer borrows from Cognitive Metaphor Theory (also used in Chapter 9), while Brambilla makes use of Pragma-dialectics. Initiated by Frans van Eemeren and Rob Grootendorst in the 1970s, Pragma-dialectics has since been both widely adopted and developed, and is now arguably the leading international approach to argumentation theory. It is both descriptive and normative, integrating *dialectics* (or the study of reasoned argument) and *pragmatics* (that is, the study of language in use); and, as such, its scope ranges from the philosophical and theoretical to the empirical, analytical and practical—and more recently has also included rhetorical considerations under the notion of 'strategic maneuvering.'

Readers will find interdisciplinary orientations here that may be fruitfully taken up in relation to other topics, and in other fields.

11 The 'eternal character' of austerity measures in European crisis policies: Evidence from the Fiscal Compact discourse in Austria

Stephan Pühringer

There was a strong tendency to interpret the financial and economic crisis in its aftermath mainly as a sovereign debt crisis without any reference to the preceding crises. Although the financial crisis initially could have offered a possibility for a fundamental paradigm shift in economic thought and economic policies, yet a few years after the bankruptcy of Lehman Brothers there are hardly any signs of such a shift (Heise, 2017; Green & Hay, 2015; Pühringer, 2015a). In contrast, the core 'economic imaginary' (Jessop, 2013 [BOB-008]3; Sum & Jessop, 2013) of a 'functioning (financial) market,' which had a formative impact on economic and particularly financial market policies still seems to be dominant in European crisis policies. A striking example of the subordination of political discourse to 'the market' is given by the German Chancellor Angela Merkel: "Of course we live in a democracy and it is a parliamentary democracy [...] so we shall find ways to shape parliamentary co-determination so that it nonetheless conforms to the markets" (Merkel, 2011).

Merkel's concept of a "democracy in line with the market" (*marktkonforme Demokratie*) can be rooted in German ordoliberalism[1] which was and is still the core narrative in European crisis policies after 2009 (Pühringer, 2018). Due to the strong economic and political position of Germany in the EU and the Eurozone (Bulmer & Paterson, 2013; Schoeller, 2016), many scholars stressed a return or a revival of ordoliberalism during the financial crisis (Young, 2014; Biebricher, 2014) or even an 'ordoliberalization' of Europe (Blyth, 2013). Streeck (2015), referring to EU monetary policy and the central role of the Bundesbank, argued that "European money (...) is Austrian, ordoliberal and neoliberal money" (p. 365). In a similar vein, Rommerskirchen (2015) speaks of "EMU's[2] disciplinary neoliberalism" (p. 756). In the field of fiscal policy, the strong influence of Germany is echoed in the European Fiscal Compact which builds on the concept of a 'debt brake,' already introduced in Germany in 2009 (Fabbrini, 2013).

The European Fiscal Compact (FC) entered into force on January 1, 2013 in 25 EU Member States.[3] With ratification, the signatory countries commit significant parts of their budget to the European Commission and the European Court of Justice, which indicates a shift of power from legislative to executive authorities and the judiciary. Following Colin Crouch's (2004, 2011) conception of 'post-democracy,' the process of the implementation of the European FC thus can be interpreted as an example of a post-democratic phenomenon: while on the surface all democratic institutions and rules are working properly, an increasing number of core political decisions is made 'behind closed doors,' justified mainly with recourse to inherent economic necessities. Moreover, economic experts in multiple roles continuously increase their impact on political discourse, and economic rationality is becoming the main guideline for policy-making (Lebaron, 2006; Maesse, 2015). The shift of power from political representatives, particularly members of national parliaments and the European Parliament to seemingly independent experts of the European Commission also manifests itself in EU crisis policy in the aftermath of the economic crisis. Oberndorfer (2012) describes the process of a shift of power as 'authoritarian constitutionalism' which led to a huge loss of democracy.

The implementation of the European Fiscal Compact in Austria offers a good opportunity to analyze the austerity discourse in the EU because, as the social democrats also ratified the Treaty, a variety of arguments in favor of the FC can be analyzed. It can be shown that the public discourse about economic policies—in a period when economics is going through a crisis (a potential 'crisis of economics')—is still dominated by 'economic imaginaries' (implicitly) preferring austerity measures to active fiscal policies. The main purpose of this chapter thus is twofold. First, I will argue that the process of the implementation as well as the content of the Fiscal Compact can be interpreted as an example of a post-democratic development, which potentially hollows out and in the long term even endangers democracy in the EU. Second, based on the example of the Austrian Fiscal Compact discourse, it will be shown that the support for austerity policies particularly in public discourses often rests on moral arguments. Simultaneously, expansive fiscal policies are framed as an immoral and irresponsible behavior.

The remainder of this chapter is structured as follows. The first section outlines the historical context and the main features of the FC and discusses the specific case of Austria. Section 2 presents the methodological framework of the chapter. Section 3 provides the results of discourse analysis of the debate on the FC in leading Austrian newspapers. A short summary and discussion of the core arguments of this chapter and some concluding remarks are given in Section 4.

1. The Fiscal Compact as a means to make austerity measures legally binding

Historically, the FC can be seen in the tradition of the European Economic and Monetary Union (EMU) laid down in the Maastricht Treaty adopted in 1992 and the Growth and Stability Pact (GSP) adopted at the Council of Amsterdam in 1997. This EMU framework comprised economic convergence criteria (budget deficit below 3% and sovereign debt ratio below 60% of GDP) in order to achieve a better coordination of national fiscal policies and thus was the first step towards a common currency (Euro). The core of the EMU are the 'four freedoms' (i.e., free movement of capital, goods, services, and people) which paved the way for liberalization and privatization and restrictive fiscal policies in many sectors of the economy (Rommerskirchen, 2015; for privatization policies in Austria, see Mesch, 2015). In this context, the economic austerity policy in the European Union in the aftermath of the financial and economic crisis beginning in 2008 is just a consistent continuation of neoliberal policies already introduced in 1992, or an example of the "strange non-death of neoliberalism" (Crouch, 2011) after the crisis.

As a reaction to the economic and euro crisis in 2009–2010, treaties such as the European Semester, the program for Economic Governance (Six Pack), and the European Stability Mechanism (ESM) can be interpreted as signposts on the way towards the FC and led to a 'new constitutional architecture' (Fabbrini, 2016, p. 11) of European economic governance. The European Semester for instance permits European Commission supervision of national budgets for the subsequent year. The then EU Commissioner for Economic and Monetary Affairs, Olli Rehn (2010) argues that this "will help us to correct imbalances and prevent deviations in due time, when Member States prepare their national budgets and national reform programs." Moreover, Rehn also anticipates automatic sanctions similar to the FC: "Sanctions should be the normal, almost automatic, consequence to be expected by countries in breach of their commitments." The ESM as part of the Euro rescue package was designed to support countries in financial difficulties under the provision that they fulfill strict requirements. Hence, the ESM allows the European Commission to put (economic) pressure on potential debt-countries to run a balanced budget. Finally, the six components of Economic Governance ('six-pack') can be seen as the last step towards the FC. Hence, some of the core measures of the FC—such as balanced budgets (max. 0.5% structural budget) and the maximum sovereign debt of 60%, as well as punitive payments in case of non-compliance with recommendations of the European Commission (0.1% of the GDP), and in case of forged statistics (0.2% of the GDP)—have already been formulated. In a comment on EU Economic Governance, Rehn (2011) pointed out that these agreements are the only possible way out of the severe crisis in the EU and thus urged for strict control: "I will not hesitate to fully apply the new rules with rigor from the first day these tools enter into force." Rehn concluded, about the causes of the crisis: "Countries living beyond their means, the lack of economic reforms in the context of open markets, the building up of financial bubbles... The price we have paid is high, too high, and it should prevent us from falling again into the same traps" (Rehn, 2011).

Following the main thesis of this chapter, the FC has to be seen as the logical consequence of a reinforced neoliberal policy in the aftermath of the financial and economic crises in the EU. Hence, several 'heavily-indebted countries' (Schulden-Staaten) have to be blamed for 'living beyond their means,' where at the same time there is hardly any discussion about the fact that sovereign debts in most European countries are a direct consequence of the massive bank rescue programs and stimulus packages of 2008 and 2009 (Lane, 2012).

The economic consequences of the FC are discussed controversially in academic economic debates. Heinemann, Mössinger, and Osterloh (2011) argue that a treaty on fiscal discipline similar to the German debt brake improves the credibility of the whole Eurozone on financial markets. Strict budgetary limitations would therefore be an important prerequisite to solve the European economic crisis. Truger and Will (2012) in contrast criticize such an argument as 'fundamentally flawed' (p. 1). Truger and Will, as well as Truger (2013), argue first, that unstable fiscal policy was not the main cause for the euro crisis, second, that there are still overlooked foreign trade imbalances, and third, that such an argument still rests on the flawed assumption that financial markets behave rationally. Apart from the debate on the long-term consequences of strict fiscal discipline employed simultaneously in the whole European Union (see Keynes's paradox of thrift[4]), other criticisms of the economic consequences of the FC and new European economic governance in general have been made.

De Grauwe and Ji (2013), as well as Sapir, Wolff, de Sousa, and Terzi (2014), have shown that the Troika (IMF, ECB, and European Commission) used their economic power and the financial dependence of peripheral countries like Greece, Portugal. and Ireland to force them to consider heavy cuts in government spending and wages. Greer (2014) even compares these measures to the Structural Adjustment Programs imposed on African and South East Asian countries in the 1980s and 1990s. The consequences were a strong decrease in demand, a heavy increase in (especially youth) unemployment and thus, particularly in Greece, a severe crisis of the social insurance and health system (Kentikelenis, Karanikolos, Reeves, & McKee, 2014). Hence, even the OECD warns about the long-term consequences of austerity policies in countries heavily hit by the crisis: "It is still too early to quantify the longer-term effects on people's health, but unemployment and economic difficulties are known to contribute to a range of health problems, including mental illness" (OECD, 2014, p. 11).

Particularly the calculation methodology for the structural deficit and the Potential Output (PO) model of the European Commission, respectively, have been criticized. Schulmeister (2014) argues that, because of the huge number of variables used to define the structural deficit, experts of the European Union are given the potential power to determine European economic policy in a specific neoliberal sense. Heimberger and Kapeller (2016) particularly blame the PO model used by the European Commission for vindicating pro-cyclical fiscal policies (i.e., a 'downward loop' after the crisis) and hence strengthening the effects of the crisis in the Euro periphery. They conclude that the PO model "serves as a restrictive and opaque 'experts' cage'" (Heimberger & Kapeller, 2016, p. 22). In a similar vein, Mathieu and Sterdyniak (2010) showed that the estimations of ECOFIN experts concerning the potential output in the EU substantially deviate from estimations of OECD experts based on different expectations. As these estimations after the inception of the FC are legally binding and in case of non-compliance result in automatic sanctions against EU countries, this process indicates a shift of power from politicians to bureaucrats who are allegedly neutral economic experts. Mathieu and Sterdyniak (2010) describe this shift of power as a process where "a technical issue (...) becomes a political one..." (p. 15).

On the political level, the consequences of the FC are still difficult to assess. Nevertheless, the content as well as the genesis of the FC allow some insights into the general trend of the respective European crisis policy.

First, the FC should be implemented at the constitutional level (of 'binding force'), which indicates that changing political majorities should not have the ability to change the treaty in the future. On the one hand, debt brakes should 'calm' the financial markets, while on the other hand this ambition can be interpreted as an effort to establish neoliberal austerity policy in the framework of a new European economic governance (Fabbrini, 2013).

Second, the implementation process of the FC shows a continuing shift of power away from national parliaments and the European Parliament, to the European Council and the European Commission, i.e., institutions with much lower or even no democratic legitimacy. The European Parliament was hardly involved in the debate during the implementation of the FC and members of the European Parliament only had observer status in the working group formulating the content of the FC in the first rounds of negotiation. Thus, the treaty can be seen as a transfer of power from the legislative assembly to the executive authority (Oberndorfer, 2012) and to the judiciary, respectively. Whereas the former transfer of power supports the post-democracy thesis of Crouch (2004, 2011), the latter transfer of power particularly manifests itself in the provisions for the automatic correction mechanism (Fabbrini, 2013). The European Commission now has the possibility to bring an action against a particular EU Member state before the European Court of Justice in case of non-compliance with the budgetary obligations of the FC. In contrast to the provisions of the Maastricht Treaty, the FC operates with a reverse qualified majority voting. Hence, an action against a Member state can only be prevented by a qualified majority.

Third, the FC contains no legal procedure for a signatory state's withdrawal from the treaty. As the FC is not part of EU law, by virtue of the provisions of the Vienna Convention on the Law of Treaties, all signatory states would have to agree on a modification of the FC. This complicated procedure paves the way for Angela Merkel to promote the 'eternal character' of the FC.

2. Methodological framework

The basic analytical approach employed in this chapter is based on the theoretical and methodological framework of critical discourse analysis (CDA) (Fairclough & Wodak, 1997; Wodak & Meyer, 2009). CDA is a sociolinguistic approach, focusing on the use of language in combination with social and cultural hegemonic processes. This means that CDA deconstructs the formation of social power in discourses and analyses the interactions between discourses and the social world. Hence, discourses are understood as a complex of statements and discursive practices which generate hierarchical systems of knowledge and form social reality (Wodak, 2013). In particular, I used a corpus-based CDA approach as suggested by Baker (2006) and Mulderrig (2011). The analysis of metaphorical content of basic patterns of arguments in the public discourse on the FC furthermore builds on the conceptual metaphor theory (CMT) developed by Lakoff and Johnson (1980, 1999; for a critical overview of CMT, see also Kövecses, 2008). According to CMT, metaphors reflect the way people think and speak. Hence, CMT does not interpret language as a rhetorical element but rather stresses the impact of a specific use of language and metaphors in the process of how realities are constructed.

The analysis of the public media discourse on the FC as an example of the new architecture of European economic governance offers a possibility to examine the predominant patterns of argument brought forward in defence of and in opposition to the FC, respectively. I focus on the discourse in opinion-leading Austrian media because media discourses reflect the political struggle for discursive power in the debate on crisis policies (Pilkington & Sinapi, 2014; Heinrich & Jessop, 2014).

The analysis in this chapter is based on a corpus of newspaper articles of the three main Austrian supranational quality newspapers. The 800 articles—about 1,200 pages of text—were retrieved from the media archives on the basis that they contained the catch-phrase 'Fiskalpakt' (the German equivalent to 'Fiscal Compact').

The text corpus was then reduced to discourse fragments comprising statements or indirect quotes about the causes or the consequences of the FC in order to focus the analysis on the process of problem construction and solution. The result is a list of discourse fragments which were used to illustrate the trajectory of the debate on the FC in Austrian media. The discourse fragments were assigned to a thematic classification system of patterns of argument in favor of, as well as against, the FC, and served as the basis for a detailed analysis of language and metaphors used in the debate, in order to highlight both how relevant actors think about the FC and the main implications of the FC.

3. The Austrian media discourse on the Fiscal Compact

The chronological starting point of the debate on the FC was December 9, 2011 at the Summit of Heads of State and/or Governments of the EU Member States (except the United Kingdom) in Brussels. After three negotiation rounds, the final version of the treaty was presented at an informal Summit of Heads of State and/or Governments on January 30, 2012. On March 2, the FC was signed by 25 EU Member states. Only the UK and the Czech Republic refused their approval. The FC entered into force after at least 12 out of 17 Eurozone states ratified the treaty by January 1, 2013. The ambitious goal of the treaty was that the implementation should have provisions of "binding force and permanent character, preferably constitutional" (FC, Article 3, 2). The critical discourse analysis in this chapter focuses on the time span between December 2011 and

July 2012 in order to cover the beginning of the debate on the FC at European level and the ratification of the treaty in the Austrian parliament, respectively. In contrast to Germany, where the FC was ratified with a constitutional majority (two-thirds), in Austria only a simple majority of parliamentarians voted for the FC. Nevertheless, again in contrast to Germany and France, the Austrian Social Democrats (then in a grand coalition with the Austrian Conservative Party) mainly supported the FC, whereas the Greens and the two right-wing parties BZÖ and FPÖ were against the FC.

Quantitative and qualitative analysis of public discourse about the Fiscal Compact in leading Austrian newspapers

First, a simple quantitative analysis of the discourse on the FC (see Figure 11.1 below) gives a first overview of both the intensity and the course of the debate, and is therefore an indicator for the structure of the discourse on the implementation of the FC in the Austrian context.

The first peaks of the debate were prior to the Summit of the European Council in January 31, 2012 and then in March 2012 after the signature of the Treaty on March 2, 2012. The highest number of hits for the term 'Fiscal Compact' was in May, 2012. This can be explained mainly by the French election campaign where François Hollande, the socialist challenger of President Sarkozy, urged for a re-negotiation of the FC which in turn also had a strong impact on the debates of social democratic parties in Austria and Germany. Additionally, there was a debate about the Irish referendum about the FC on June 1, 2012.

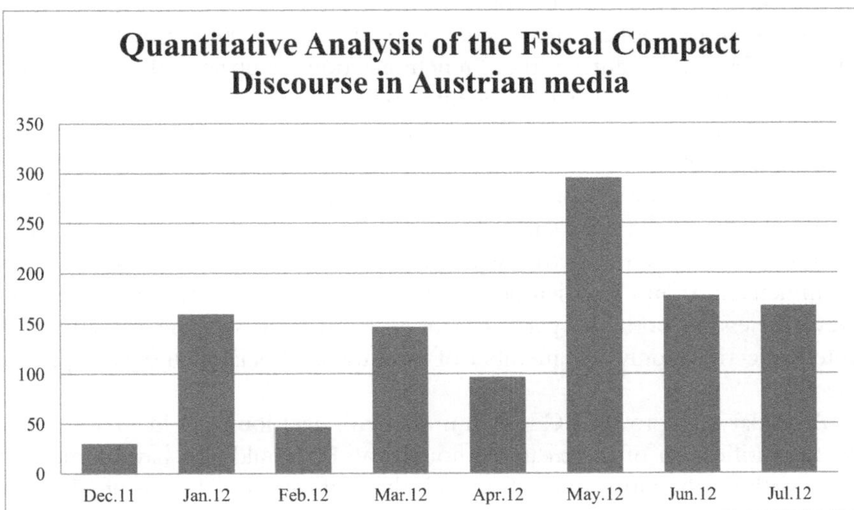

Figure 11.1 Hits for 'Fiscal Compact' in the Austrian newspapers *Salzburger Nachrichten*, *Presse* and *Standard* (from December 9, 2011 to July 31, 2012)

In June and July, the main reference points for the Austrian FC debate were the ratification process in the Austrian and German parliaments in July, and the debate on the constitutional conformity of the FC culminating in complaints of unconstitutionality in Austria and Germany.

Second, I analyzed the dominant lines of discourse and dominant discursive patterns in the media in order to highlight the different perceptions of the FC and its consequences. Table 11.1 below combines the dominant discourses and arguments with the implementation process of the FC on a political level.

The analysis of the FC debates in Austrian media from December 2011 to February 2012 reveals two dominant countervailing patterns of discourse. First, the FC is interpreted as a step towards a 'necessary' European harmonization. This goal rests on an ambivalent concept of 'European solidarity.' Particularly the German Minister of Finance, Wolfgang Schäuble, stresses that "solidarity goes hand in hand with solidity" (Salzburger Nachrichten (SN), December 20, 2011). Hence, and as an immediate reaction to the 'debt crisis' in the EU periphery, it is argued that EU member states have to "submit their budgetary policy to stricter rules" (SN, January 31, 2012). Second, there is an ongoing claim for harsh sanctions and punishments to calm the financial markets: "The markets want to see action" (Schäuble, as cited in SN, December 20, 2011). According to such a logic, where political decision-making is often subordinated to the requirements of the financial markets, it is straightforward to interpret incompatibilities of the FC with national constitutions as 'difficulties,' one has 'to handle' (Austrian Chancellor Faymann in Presse, January 27, 2012).[5] Summing up, in the initial (and politically decisive) phase of the debate on the FC, there is hardly any public criticism about the FC.

The Summit of the EU Council in late January 2012 initiated a political debate on a potential shift of power to the EU and the threat of a centralization of economic policy. At the same time, the announcement by the socialist François Hollande, during the French election campaign, that he would renegotiate the FC as French President also fed into the Austrian discourse. The Austrian Minister of Finance, Maria Fekter, warned that any re-negotiations could send fatal signals to the financial markets and thus would intensify the European economic crisis. Moreover, the French election campaign had a strong impact on the Austrian and also the German discourse on the FC, forcing the Social Democrats to discuss the disadvantages of the treaty and a few prominent Austrian social democrats criticized the FC heavily, at least in public. Nevertheless, in both the party executive committee and the parliamentary vote, respectively, only one member of the Austrian Social Democrats opposed the FC.[6]

A similar threat to the FC is seen in the Irish decision to hold a referendum on the ratification of the treaty. Although the FC could also have come into force without the ratification of Ireland (the ratification of 12 out of 17 Euro-member states is enough), the rejection of the FC in a public vote would have had an enormous impact on the political debate in the European Union. The debate around the Irish referendum thus often reflected the logic of economic

Table 11.1 Course of the discourse about the implementation of the Fiscal Compact

Year-month	*Political events connected to the Fiscal Compact*	*Dominant patterns of discourse*
2011–12	• EU Summit decision	• Stability of the economy due to 'budgetary rules of the game' • Solidarity and European harmonization
2012–01	• Negotiation rounds and Summit of the ministers of finance • UK refuses to sign the Fiscal Compact (FC)	• FC as immediate reaction to the 'debt crisis' • Calming of the financial markets ('predictable politics') • Harsh sanctions and debt brakes • Threat to the budgetary authority of the parliament
2012–02	• Czech Republic refuses to sign the FC	• Fear of French elections • Transfer of power to the EU Commission • Sanctions are much too weak
2012–03	• No constitutional majority for the FC in Austrian parliament • Signing of FC on March 2	• FC as an 'important signal' and milestone for financial markets • Constitutional conformity of the FC?
2012–04	• Irish referendum on the FC to be held on June 1 • Open letter of ATTAC against 'Loss of democracy and falling social standards.' • Leading Austrian Social Democrats against FC.	• FC as step into 'political union' • Referendums and elections as elements of uncertainty • FC is 'not politically negotiable' but additional growth initiatives • Criticism on central power of EU and Germany
2012–05	• Hollande wins French presidential election • Merkel-Hollande: Agreement on an additionally 'growth pact' • Special EU-Council Summit for growth	• Social democrats want to postpone Austria decision • TINA: no money from the ESM without FC • Resistance of the Social Democrats and Greens in Germany against the FC
2012–06	• Irish vote for FC • German opposition claims financial market tax as a counter-move to a ratification of the FC	• 'time of running up debts is over' • Threats of complaints of unconstitutionality in Austria/ Germany • Opposition to the FC is a minority position in Austrian SD • Criticism of the exclusion of the European Parliament
2012–07	• Ratification of the FC and complaints of unconstitutionality in Austria and Germany	• Economic criticism (structural deficit) • Solid and predictable policy • Harsh punishment for 'budgetary sinners' • German 'Saving dictate"'

practical constraints. On the one hand, the European Commission put strong economic pressure on Ireland, because potential subsidies from the ESM were linked to the ratification of the FC and, on the other hand, the Irish were warned that their "international reputation would fall to a Greek level" (Presse, May 31, 2012) in case the FC should be rejected.

From June 2012 on, the FC debate was almost completely reduced to the question of whether growth strategies should be included in the FC or be just a supplement to the FC. Hollande and Merkel, the two key actors in this debate at the European level, agreed to leave the FC unchanged, but additionally introduced a common strategy for growth, particularly to fight youth unemployment. The core disparity between the implementation of the FC and the agreement on growth is, however, that the former should have a binding character and be included in national constitutions, whereas the latter remained a declaration of intent without any binding character.

Dominant patterns of argument and discourse profiles

The analysis of dominant patterns of discourse in this section is now divided into arguments in favor of and against the FC, in order to analyze the two countervailing discourses on the FC in more detail.

Arguments in favor of the FC are often moral ones and therefore special emphasis is put on 'strict discipline,' 'harsh sanctions' and a moral responsibility to have balanced budgets. This 'moral tale' (Fourcade, 2013, p. 621) can be found in the whole discourse on austerity programs in the European crisis policy and culminates in the phrase "We have lived beyond our means." The rejection of the FC, in contrast, is then framed as immoral or irresponsible behavior, often with reference to metaphors supporting a dichotomy between 'good' and 'bad' economic policies. In this context, the President of the Austrian economic research institute IHS, Keuschnigg (SN, April 28, 2012) declares that only "fiscal discipline" avoids the fate that "the burden of excessive sovereign debt is rolled on future generations" and "debt states" are denoted as "budgetary sinners." In a similar vein, Matthijs (2016, p. 376) analyzed the role of Germany in European crisis policies and also found a strong narrative of "Northern Saints" and "Southern Sinners" based on moral arguments.

The first important pattern of discourse of supporters is that the FC should serve as a safeguard against "recurring errors of debt making" or the "antiquated recipes of the past" (Fekter, Standard, May 22, 2012). This position, which had the strongest impact on the FC discourse, can be interpreted as a fundamental rejection of Keynesian demand-oriented economic policy, which had a short revival during the crisis policy in the form of stimulus packages in 2008 and 2009.[7]

The second line of argument in favor of the FC, mainly in the initial phase of the discourse, is on a prospective European political union and therefore claims the need for European solidarity. Hence, the FC is framed as one central milestone in the process of closer European integration and partly even as an expression of European solidarity. Nevertheless, this is always a solidarity with reservations, because "solidarity goes hand in hand with solidity" as Schäuble stressed (Standard, December 19, 2011).

Third, the FC is framed as an immediate reaction to the sovereign debt crisis. This pattern of discourse is based on the neoliberal argument that political decision has to follow economic necessities, which was prominently stressed in Merkel's idea of a 'market-conform democracy' (Pühringer, 2015b). As a consequence, it is argued that "there is no alternative"—a phrase coined by Margaret Thatcher—to the implementation of the FC. This subordination of political decision-making to seemingly economic necessities can be shown in the Irish debate on the referendum, but also more generally in the threat to prospectively heavily-indebted states. In this context, the Austrian Minister of Finance, Fekter, warns that "the freedom to determine one's own budget will be reserved to those who play by the rules of the game" (*Standard*, June 19, 2012).

Fourth, and building on the third pattern of discourse, the supporters of the FC stress its importance to calm the financial markets. This argument similarly serves as a threat towards particular 'debt states' but also against re-negotiations of the treaty in general. Veit Sorger, then president of the influential Federation of Austrian Industrialists (IV), in this context speaks of 'fatal signals' for the markets (SN, May 22, 2012) and a member of the ECB directory and close confidant of Merkel, Jörg Asmussen, urgently warns against a 'substantial weakening' of the treaty (Standard, Jan. 13, 2012). The delegation of responsibility for political decision-making to a seemingly neutral category as 'The Market' thus reflects a perception of the market as a superior moral authority (Ötsch, 2014), and/or as having a 'disciplinary function' (Rommerskirchen, 2015).

Whereas it can be shown that the debate on the FC in Austrian media was dominated by a discourse supporting the FC and austerity policies based on the treaty, there has also been a countervailing discourse of criticism against the FC, which is presented in the following part of this section.

First and foremost, and particularly after the successful election campaign of Hollande, several actors ranging from trade unions and NGOs to members of the Green party and parts of the Social Democratic party stressed the need for a 'growth package' to overcome the threat of economic recession. Nevertheless, economic criticism remains rather superficial and is mainly driven by the debate between Hollande and Merkel on growth initiatives. Detailed criticism of the fundamental shift of power to the European Commission as a result of the provision for the structural deficit, in contrast, is hardly present in this discourse or is limited to comments by the Keynesian economist Stephan Schulmeister and in an open letter of the globalization-critical NGO ATTAC.

Second, discourse on the transfer of power to the EU is shaped by nationalist prejudices against the EU in general and thus mainly put forward by members of the two right-wing populist or national-conservative parties in Austria (FPÖ and BZÖ). The special role of Germany in the debate about the FC leads to a discursive equation of austerity policies and 'German dominance.' Hence, Merkel is labeled "Europe's mother of saving" (Presse, May 3, 2012).

The third core argument against the FC involves the potential unconstitutionality of the FC, which is present in the debate on the ratification of the FC in the Austrian parliament in June and July 2012. This critique is focused on the limitation of the budgetary sovereignty of the Austrian parliament as a result of the ratification of the FC. Despite their great ideological differences, all three opposition parties agreed on a complaint of unconstitutionality of the FC, which however was rejected by the Austrian Constitutional Court.

The fourth pattern of discourse which was present in Austrian media was the framing of the FC as a loss of democracy, especially due to the automatic sanction mechanism and the threat that the political debate is continuously replaced by bureaucratic and legal procedures. This discourse was indeed mainly brought forward by NGOs like ATTAC and had no severe impact on the course of public debate on the FC.

4. Conclusion

To sum up, the analysis of public debate on the FC in leading Austrian newspapers showed that many of the potential consequences of the treaty were not discussed and criticism therefore remained on a rather superficial level. Particularly, the policy implications and legal consequences hardly entered into the debate either from the supporters or from the critics of the FC. The French election campaign played an important role, particularly for the social democratic parties in Germany and Austria. Claims for growth strategies and re-negotiations of the FC initiated a debate about the prospective economic consequences of one-sided austerity measures. Nevertheless, the analysis also showed that the FC was often justified as an immediate reaction to the debt crisis in order to calm the financial markets and hence austerity was often framed as positive, or at least as the only possibility to prevent 'economically irresponsible behavior' in periphery countries. The claim for a predictable policy with reference to apparent economic necessities was hardly opposed by fundamental critique. This discursive imbalance induced a moral and in many cases derogatory discourse on 'budgetary sinners' and 'debt states.' In such a moral framing, austerity policies were discussed as necessary measures to punish and sanction the immoral behavior of 'heavily-indebted states.' The moralization of debt however also reflects the influential narrative of the 'crisis countries' having 'lived beyond their means.'

The dominant discourse on the FC focused on the necessity of 'harsh sanctions' and punishment in case of non-compliance with the 'strict rules' of the FC. The superficiality of the debate about the FC and the blatant ignorance of central political practitioners in the discourse indicate that the implementation of the FC can be interpreted as a perfect example of a post-democratic process, where the political power has moved away from legitimate democratic representatives to expert groups or the bureaucracy. In fact, the whole initial debate on debt brakes and automatic sanction mechanisms was held behind closed doors (Oberndorfer, 2012). The course of the debate on the FC, as well as its core claim for austerity, supports the idea that the FC can be understood as the provisional culmination point of neoliberal European policies. Although the FC in many parts is still the consequence of a process initiated with the Maastricht Treaty, due to its reversed majority voting and its constitutional status, the FC goes even one step further.

The FC today provides a very strong legal and political framework for austerity measures which can be used for direct attacks against European welfare states. In this context, it is quite enlightening that German Chancellor Angela Merkel, still in the initial phase of the implementation of the FC, pointed out its intended 'eternal character': "The debt brakes will be binding and valid forever (…) Never will you be able to change them through a parliamentary majority" (Merkel, as cited by Traynor, 2012). For sure there have also been some political countermovements against austerity policies in Europe (e.g. the recent Yellow vests movement in France) and furthermore events such as the Brexit-debate challenge the EU legal and political framework. Nevertheless, after the successful implementation of the FC, this 'eternal character' hinders opposition to neoliberal austerity policies in Europe to a great extent.

Notes

1 According to Mirowski (2013), ordoliberalism (beside Hayekian Austrian legal theory and Chicago School neoclassical economics) has been one of the main strands in the initial era of the neoliberal thought collective. Starbatty (2001), one of the leading ordoliberal German economists denoted ordoliberalism as "the German variety of neoliberalism" (p. 252).
2 European Economic and Monetary Union
3 In fact only the United Kingdom and the Czech Republic refused to sign the Treaty.
4 Keynes argued that when many countries or individuals try to reduce their expenditures or increase their savings during an economic recession, this leads to a fall in aggregate demand and could even result in an overall increase of debts and thus in an economically harmful situation for everybody.
5 Quotations of media text fragments were translated and can be provided by the author; they are also available at the electronic archives of the respective media.
6 In contrast to Germany, the Austrian Social Democrats were in coalition with the Christian Democrats and part of the government during that time.
7 Krugman (2008) called this the short "Keynesian Moment" of global economic policy.

References

Baker, P. (2006). *Using corpora in discourse analysis.* London: Continuum.

Biebricher, T. (2014). The return of ordoliberalism in Europe: Notes on a research agenda. *i-lex*, *21*, 1–24.

Blyth, M. (2013). *Austerity: The history of a dangerous idea.* Oxford: Oxford University Press.

Bulmer, S., & Paterson, W. (2013). Germany as the EU's reluctant hegemon? Of the economic strength and political constraints. *Journal of European Public Policies 20*(19), 1387–1405.

Crouch, C. (2004). *Post-democracy: Themes for the 21st century*. Cambridge, UK: Polity Press.

Crouch, C. (2011). *The strange non-death of neo-liberalism*. Cambridge. UK: Polity Press.

de Grauwe, P., & Ji, Y. (2013). From panic-driven austerity to symmetric macroeconomic policies in the Eurozone. *Journal of Common Market Studies*, *51*(S1), 31–41.

Fabbrini, F. (2013). The fiscal compact, the 'Golden Rule,' and the paradox of European federalism. *Boston College International and Comparative Law Review*, *36*(1), 1–38.

Fabbrini, F. (2016). *Economic governance in Europe: Comparative paradoxes and constitutional challenges*. Oxford: Oxford University Press.

Fairclough, N., & Wodak, R. (1997). Critical discourse analysis. In T.A. van Dijk (Ed.). Discourse studies: A multidisciplinary introduction (pp. 258–284). London: Sage.

Fourcade, M. (2013). The economy as morality play, and implications for the Eurozone crisis. *Socio-economic Review*, *11*(3), 620–627.

Green, J., & Hay, C. (2015). Towards a new political economy of the crisis: Getting what went wrong right. *New Political Economy*, *20*(3), 331–341.

Greer, S. (2014). Structural adjustment comes to Europe: Lessons for the Eurozone from the conditionality debates. *Global Social Policy*, *14*(1), 51–71.

Heimberger, P., & Kapeller, J. (2016), The performativity of potential output: Pro-cyclicality and path dependency in coordinating European fiscal policies. (ICAE Working Paper No. 50). Linz: Johannes Kepler University Linz. Retrieved from www.econstor.eu/bitstream/10419/171425/1/icae-wp50.pdf

Heinemann, F., Mössinger, M.-D., & Osterloh, S. (2011). *Nationale Fiskalregeln—Ein Instrument zur Vorbeugung von Vertrauenskrisen: Summary of a research study by the Centre for Economic Research Mannheim*. [Monthly Report of the Germany Ministry of Finance (BMF), August], pp. 58–66.

Heinrich, M., & Jessop, B. (2014). Interpretations of the EU crisis and their policy implementation. In B. Jessop, B. Young, & C. Scherrer (Eds.), *Cultures of finance and crisis dynamics* (pp. 278–283). London: Routledge.

Heise, A. (2017). Die Ökonomik als wissenschaftliches Macht- und Schlachtfeld. In J. Maesse, H. Pahl, & J. Sparsam (Eds.), *Die Innenwelt der Ökonomie* (pp. 55–81). Wiesbaden: Springer VS.

Jessop, B. (2013). Recovered imaginaries, imagined recoveries: A cultural political economy of crisis construals and crisis-management in the North Atlantic financial crisis. In M. Benner (Ed.), *Before and beyond the global economic crisis: Economics, politics, settlement* (pp. 234–254). Cheltenham, UK: Edward Elgar.

Kentikelenis, A., Karanikolos, M., Reeves, A., McKee, M., & Stuckler, D. (2014). Greece's health crisis: From austerity to denialism. *The Lancet*, *383*(9918), 748–753.

Kövecses, Z. (2008). Conceptual metaphor theory. Some criticisms and alternative proposals. *Annual Review of Cognitive Linguistics*, *6*, 168–184.

Krugman, P. (2008, November 29). The Keynesian moment. *New York Times*. Retrieved from https://krugman.blogs.nytimes.com/2008/11/29/the-keynesian-moment/

Lakoff, G., & Johnson, M. (1980). *Metaphors we live by*. Chicago, IL: University of Chicago Press.

Lakoff, G., & Johnson, M. (1999). *Philosophy in the flesh: The embodied mind and its challenge to Western thought*. New York: Basic Books.

Lane, P. (2012). The European sovereign debt crisis. *Journal of Economic Perspectives*, 26(3), 49–67.

Lebaron, F. (2006). 'Nobel' economists as public intellectuals: The circulation of symbolic capital. *International Journal of Contemporary Sociology*, *43*(1), 88–101.

Maesse, J. (2015). Economic experts. A discursive political economy of economics. *Journal of Multicultural Discourses*, *10*(3), 279–305.

Mathieu, C., & Sterdyniak, H. (2010). European Debt Crisis and Fiscal Exit Strategies. (OFCE Working Paper, No. 2010–11). Paris: OFCE—Centre de recherché in économie de Sciences Po.

Matthijs, M. (2016). Powerful rules governing the Euro: The perverse logic of German ideas. *Journal of European Public Policy*, *23*(3), 375–91.

Merkel, A. (2011). Press Statement of German Chancellor Angela Merkel, September 1, 2011. Retrieved from www.bundesregierung.de/ContentArchiv/DE/Archiv17/Mitschrift/Pressekonferenzen/2011/09/2011-09-01-merkel-coelho.html (translation provided by the author)

Mesch, M. (2015). Nationale arbeitsbeziehungen und lohnpolitik in der EU. In M. Mesch, M. Marterbauer, & S. Zuckerstätter (Eds.). *Nationale Arbeitsbeziehungen und Lohnpolitik in der EU 2004–2014* (pp. 9–67). Vienna: ÖGB Verlag.

Mirowski, P. (2013). *Never let a serious crisis go to waste: How neoliberalism survived the financial meltdown*. London/New York: Verso.

Mulderrig, J. (2011). Manufacturing consent: A corpus-based critical discourse analysis of New Labour's educational governance. *Educational Philosophy and Theory*, *43*(6), 562–578.

Oberndorfer, L. (2012). "Vom neuen zum autoritären Konstitutionalismus". *Kurswechsel*, 2012/2, 62–67.

OECD (2014). The crisis and its aftermath: A stress test for societies and for social policies. *Society at a Glance 2014. OECD Social Indicators* (pp. 15–75). Paris: OECD Publishing. Retrieved from www.oecd-ilibrary.org/docserver/download/8113171ec005.pdf?expires=1519009879&id=id&accname=guest&checksum=A3A1668E6A276303B458BC29A2CEE83E

Ötsch, W.O. (2014). The deep meaning of 'market': Understanding neoliberal-market-radical reasoning. *Human Geography*, *6*(2), 11–25.

Pilkington, M., & Sinapi, C. (2014). Crisis perception in financial media discourse: A concrete application using the Minskian/mainstream opposition. *On the Horizon*, *22*(4), 280–296.

Pühringer, S. (2015a), *The strange non-crisis of economics. Economic crisis and crisis policies in economic and political discourses*. (Unpublished PhD thesis), Johannes Kepler University, Linz.

Pühringer, S. (2015b). Markets as 'ultimate judges' of economic policies: Angela Merkel's discourse profile during the economic crisis and the European crisis policies. *On the Horizon*, *23*(3), 246–259.

Pühringer, S. (2018). The success story of ordoliberalism as guiding principle of German economic policy. In J. Hien & C. Joerges (Eds.). *Ordoliberalism: Law and the rule of economics* (pp. 134–158). Oxford: Hart Publishing.

Rehn, O. (2010, September 7). Statement by Commissioner for Economic and Monetary Affairs Olli REHN on the endorsement of the 'European Semester' by the EU Council. [Press release]. Retrieved from http://europa.eu/rapid/press-release_MEMO-10-394_en.htm?locale=en

Rehn, O. (2011, October 5). Commissioner Rehn comments on the new rules for EU economic governance [Press release]. Retrieved from http://europa.eu/rapid/press-release_MEMO-11-664_en.htm

Rommerskirchen, C. (2015). Debt and punishment: Market discipline in the Eurozone. *New Political Economy*, *20*(5), 752–782.

Sapir, A., Wolff, G., de Sousa, C., & Terzi, A. (2014). The Troika and financial assistance in the euro area: Successes and failures. [European Parliament Committee study on the request of the Economic and Monetary Affairs Committee, February 2014]. Retrieved from http://bruegel.org/wp-content/uploads/imported/publications/20140219ATT79633EN_01.pdf

Schoeller, M.G. (2016). Providing political leadership? Three case studies on Germany's ambiguous role in the Eurozone crisis. *Journal of European Public Policy*, *24*(1), 1–20.

Schulmeister, S. (2014). EU-Fiskalpakt: Hauptkomponente einer Systemkrise. (WIFO Working Paper, No. 480). Vienna: Austrian Institute of Economic Research (WIFO). Retrieved from www.wifo.ac.at/jart/prj3/wifo/resources/person_dokument/person_dokument.jart?publikationsid=47515&mime_type=application/pdf

Starbatty, J. (2001). Ordoliberalismus. In O. Issing (Ed.), *Geschichte der Nationalökonomie* (pp. 251–269). Munich: Vahlen.

Streeck, W. (2015). Heller, Schmitt and the Euro. *European Law Journal*, *21*(3), 361–370.

Sum, N.-L., & Jessop, B. (2013). *Towards a cultural political economy: Putting culture in its place in political economy*. Cheltenham, UK: Edward Elgar.

Traynor, I. (2012, January 31). Germany to set the terms for saving the euro. *The Guardian*. Retrieved from www.theguardian.com/business/2012/jan/30/eu-summit-eurozone-treaty-deal

Truger, A. (2013). Austerity in the Euro area: The sad state of economic policy in Germany and the EU. *European Journal of Economic and Economic Policies: Intervention*, *10*(2), 158–174.

Truger, A., & Will, H. (2012). *The German 'debt brake': A shining example for European fiscal policy?* (Working paper No. 15/2012). Berlin: Institute for International Political Economy. Retrieved from www.ipe-berlin.org/fileadmin/downloads/working_paper/ipe_working_paper_15.pdf

Wodak, R. (Ed.) (2013), *Critical discourse analysis* (Vol. 1). London: Sage.

Wodak, R., & Meyer, M. (Eds.). (2009). *Methods for critical discourse analysis: Introducing qualitative methods*. London: Sage.

Young, B. (2014). German ordoliberalism as agenda setter for the Euro crisis: Myth Trumps reality. *Journal of Contemporary European Studies*, *22*(3), 276–287.

12 The mirage of expansionary fiscal consolidation to resolve the euro-area crisis

Giuseppe Mastromatteo and Sergio Rossi

The euro-area crisis is not a 'sovereign debt' crisis, as the conventional view depicts it. As a number of non-mainstream economists have been explaining since the euro-area crisis broke out (at the end of 2009), this crisis is the result of unsustainable macro-economic imbalances across the private sector of the euro-area, which have built up and remained largely unaddressed in the first ten years of the European Monetary Union (EMU). Some of these economists—for instance Cesaratto and Stirati (2011)—argue that the EMU has been experiencing a balance-of-payments crisis, to wit, a crisis that results from huge current account imbalances across the euro-area, but particularly between 'core' countries like Germany (recording current account surpluses above 6% of GDP) and the 'PIIGS' (named apparently with a view to indicate that this crisis originates in excessive public debt across the member countries of the euro-area, particularly in its 'periphery'—the PIIGS are: Portugal, Ireland, Italy, Greece, and Spain). This elicited an external-debt-sustainability crisis (Bagnai, 2013). Other economists within the heterodox camp explain by contrast that the euro-area crisis originates, in fact, in a monetary-structural flaw encapsulated in the euro-area-wide payment system, namely TARGET2 (see Rossi, 2013). Be that as it may, all these unconventional views are far away from the orthodox account of the origins of the euro-area crisis. As a result, it does not come as a surprise that heterodox economists are, in general, against the policy stance taken by euro-area governments to address this major crisis along the conventional view based on fiscal consolidation (that is to say, a series of austerity measures intended to rebalance the public sector's budget by different spending cuts aimed at kick-starting economic growth).

This chapter offers a survey of the mainstream conceptual frameworks in economic analysis of public finances; the aim is to point out the ways in which the arguments in favor of austerity have been validated on 'scientific' grounds (in public debates as well as in those media supporting fiscal consolidation as the solution to the euro-area crisis). We will then expose the core hypotheses underlying this policy stance, explaining why they are wrong on both theoretical and empirical grounds, with a view to pointing out which categories of economic agents actually benefit from this stance (in both the financial and non-financial sectors of the economy). The last section will show that the theoretical benefits of fiscal consolidation do not materialize in practice, as the structural reforms on the labor market, coupled with the public sector's austerity, give rise to deflationary pressures that aggravate the socio-economic situation across the euro-area as a whole rather than contributing to solve the euro-area crisis for good. This chapter therefore ends with a pessimistic conclusion, but also points out how such a bad scenario can be averted before too long.

The arguments in favor of fiscal consolidation

Fiscal consolidation is the politically-correct expression to indicate, in fact, a series of austerity policies consisting in reducing public spending drastically. Moved by the clear ideological stance that "government is not the solution to our problem; government is the problem" (Reagan, 1981),[1] these cuts in government expenditure are meant to increase economic agents' trust in the future. This would increase their private spending, notably as a result of a significant reduction in interest rates over the long run, since the public sector's budget is rebalanced and thus less demanding in terms of private savings. As a result of the lower demand coming from the public sector for loanable funds, the market rate of interest is lower, as its level is determined in this framework by the market forces of supply and demand, that is, the supply of savings and the demand for loanable funds.[2] This framework may give rise to higher unemployment as a result of the reduction in public expenditure (on the labor as well as on the goods markets). However, this problem on the labor market is considered to be a transitory phenomenon necessary to reduce the wage level, in order to increase firms' competitiveness and thereby their profits so that, in the end, they will hire more workers and gradually increase their compensation. This is then expected to support aggregate demand and eventually economic growth, rebalancing also the public sector's budget with higher tax receipts as well as lower expenditure for the welfare system, particularly unemployment benefits (see, among others, Giavazzi & Pagano, 1990, 1996; Alesina & Perotti, 1995, 1997; Alesina & Ardagna, 1998, 2010). In this theoretical framework, some economists refer to the so-called "Ricardian equivalence theorem" to claim that consumers increase their expenditures when they consider that they will have to pay lower taxes as a result of the fiscal consolidation occurring in the public sector (see, for instance, Barro, 1974, 1989; Buchanan, 1976; Seater, 1993).

The mainstream support for austerity policies goes beyond the public sector's budget and considers indeed the whole economic system of a country, as fiscal consolidation also impacts on the country's balance of payments: the reduction of public expenditure and a subsequent similar impact on private spending, notably by households, reduces imports—all the more so if the exchange rate of the national currency depreciates, as a result of the different forms of behavior induced by an austerity policy stance. Whilst the impact of this policy stance might affect economic growth negatively over the short run, orthodox economists consider that its "medium to long-term effects are favourable and more than compensate any short-term shortfall" (European Central Bank,

2012, p. 85). This should occur, according to Cottarelli and Jaramillo (2012), as "[r]eforms in goods, service, and labor markets that improve economic efficiency will boost potential growth, in turn serving as important tools in the fiscal adjustment process" (p. 3).

The argument thus revolves around the concept of potential growth, that is to say, the increase in potential output that follows from so-called structural reforms induced by a government under fiscal consolidation that adopts the neoliberal policy agenda (more out of necessity than conviction). In this theoretical framework, a balanced budget, or at least a lower deficit for the general government sector reduces the domestic interest rate and hence induces firms to increase their investment for fixed capital accumulation, thus enhancing their production capacity and thereby increasing potential economic growth—notwithstanding the negative output gap that goes along with existing unemployment as a general rule in the real world and even more so as a result of a major economic crisis.

According to its advocates, this theoretical framework is supported by empirical evidence, as argued by Reinhart and Rogoff (2010) in a very controversial work that has elicited a fundamental critique notably by Herndon, Ash and Pollin (2014). According to Reinhart and Rogoff (2010), the public-debt-to-GDP ratio hinders economic growth when it is above 90%, as their database shows for a number of countries over a long period of time. This study has been used as empirical proof of the need to enter into fiscal consolidation for those countries (particularly within the euro-area) whose public sector has a debt-to-GDP ratio above 90% (notably Greece and Italy). As pointed out by Herndon et al. (2014), however, it appears that the Reinhart and Rogoff's (2010) work does not do justice to the empirical as well as methodological framework within which this investigation should be carried out, in order to be up to the scientific task of supporting the austerity policy stance adopted in several euro-area countries in the aftermath of the crisis that erupted at the end of 2009.[3]

Indeed, it is plain that the theoretical framework supporting fiscal consolidation is not confirmed by empirical evidence, insofar as it relies on a series of hypotheses that are wrong on conceptual as well as practical grounds. We will expand on this in the next section.

The core hypotheses of the mainstream view: A fundamental critique

As the reader may have noticed in the previous section, the set of arguments supporting fiscal consolidation strongly depends on a series of crucial hypotheses, many of them hidden to unsuspecting policy makers—and sometimes also to mathematical economists, who design their misleading theoretical models affected by what Caballero (2010, p. 85) names the "pretense-of-knowledge syndrome."[4]

The most striking hypothesis is that the economic system is already at full-employment equilibrium when fiscal consolidation is adopted by (or imposed upon) some government in a crisis-hit country (say Greece). If this were true, one might argue that an interest rate reduction as a result of fiscal consolidation could increase potential output as a result of firms' investment induced by lower production costs as regards both loanable funds and the wage level (see above). However, this is clearly impossible to observe when there is, as at the time of writing, a dramatically high rate of unemployment, most of which, in fact, is involuntary in Keynes's (1936) sense (see, for instance, McCombie, 1987–1988). In an under-employment situation indeed, and particularly when the unemployment rate is (close to) a double-digit figure, firms are reluctant to invest, since they fear that their newly-produced output will remain partly unsold, in light of both the situation on the labor market and the lack of effective demand (see Keynes, 1936).

Even mainstream economists who are aware that full employment is a chimera—particularly in those euro-area countries most severely hit by the crisis—as well as the government institutions and monetary authorities they advise, think that the higher unemployment rate induced by fiscal consolidation will increase firms' competitiveness via a reduction of their production costs, owing to lower wage levels in the short run. In fact, managers are inclined to increase mark-ups, and hence profit rates—rather than reducing prices—when there is a reduction in production costs. This is even more so when (as a result of a major financial crisis) a number of competing countries—such as those within the euro-area—adopt the same (austerity) policy stance. In this case, the widely-depressed labor markets across these countries allow firms in each of them, particularly large transnational corporations, to reduce the wage level more than prices—without affecting their competitiveness but recording, in fact, higher profits overall (see Mastromatteo & Rossi, 2015, pp. 345–346).

Despite their higher profitability, however, a number of firms, particularly those of a small or medium size, do not increase their investment in order to produce more—which would increase the employment level—but prefer to invest their higher profits in financial markets (thereby inflating asset prices beyond their fundamental level defined with regard to the real capital of the relevant firms). Hence, contrary to the claims of the mainstream view, potential output does not increase when firms record higher profits, even though rates of interest are lower as a result of fiscal consolidation in the public sector.[5]

This leads us to another critique of the mainstream stance: a reduction in interest rates—particularly large when the central bank carries out so-called 'quantitative easing' policy interventions—does not really increase firms' propensity to invest, because firms are, to a large extent, aware that domestic (and possibly foreign) demand on the product market is depressed by fiscal consolidation. As Keynes (1936) explained, firms determine the level of produced output in light of effective demand, that is, the demand firms expect as a result of the actual situation and their animal spirits (that is, their expectations for the relevant future): if the situation is clearly depressed—owing notably to the negative consequences of fiscal consolidation across the national economy—firms will not invest, but rather cut back on employment, thereby in fact aggravating rather than improving both the economic performance and perspectives within the country.

Indeed, a 'free-market' economy does not tend to full employment, particularly when a systemic financial crisis induced by the bursting of a credit bubble makes all agents less prone to spend in all kinds of markets. This is where state intervention is more needed to kick-start economic growth and create a positive impact on agents' expectations, as Keynes (1936) cogently explained. This is even more so as another seminal hypothesis, concerning financial market participants, does not hold in the real world theorized by an array of neoclassical authors. Resting on the concept of the idealized *homo oeconomicus*—that is an agent who is perfectly informed and thereby able to take the best possible decision at any time—this hypothesis (known as 'efficient market hypothesis' since the work of Fama (1970)) supposes that a given individual participating in financial market transactions is always and everywhere in a position to take optimal decisions considering all of the relevant information. Hence, if the general government sector of a country were to carry out a fiscal consolidation process, a perfectly-informed agent would anticipate that both the fiscal burden and interest rates will be lower, and, on this basis, increase his/her expenditure on goods and/or assets markets (as the Ricardian equivalence theorem suggests); this, in turn, would kick-start economic activity, making it recover from its previous, negative performance due to crisis factors (and a heavily indebted public sector).

In fact, as the ten-year period preceding the eruption of the global financial crisis (2008) has shown, agents, and particularly financial market participants, are neither rational nor perfectly informed. Rather, many of them adopt a herd behavior (see, for instance, Kahneman and Tversky, 1979, and Shiller, 2000). This means that their decisions to buy, or to sell, a series of financial assets are not rationally informed but in fact follow some, alleged, leader (like a 'too-big-to-fail' financial institution), which acts pro-cyclically as Minsky (1977) cogently argued in his now famous 'financial instability hypothesis': in a boom period, agents enter increasingly into more debt, in order to profit from 'asset price inflation,' only to discover later on, when the credit bubble bursts, that they are over-indebted and thus required to fire-sell their assets, provoking a debt-deflation *à la* Fisher (1933).

As regards the allegedly favorable impact on public finance of fiscal consolidation as a result of the changed behavior of financial market participants, empirical evidence across the euro-area invalidates this claim by mainstream economists: the initial euphoria that an array of these participants show when a government announces a series of austerity cuts vanishes as time goes by to be replaced by an increasing fear of recession in the country under fiscal consolidation (Nuti, 2012, pp. 143–144). This is so because a country showing a high public-debt-to-GDP ratio (higher than the benchmark argued by Reinhart and Rogoff (2010), for instance) could experience a reduction of its GDP larger than the reduction of the general government sector debt induced by fiscal consolidation. A vicious circle can thereby give rise to a perverse effect: the borrowing conditions of the government are in fact aggravated by austerity policies, as potential lenders across global financial markets fear a 'sovereign default,' and therefore increase (rather than reduce) the relevant interest-rate differential with regard to a 'risk-free' asset, such as the German government bond. To be sure, Germany has been benefiting from the euro-area crisis, particularly as regards its borrowing costs—notably for the public sector. According to an empirical study by Dany, Gropp, Littke and Schweinitz (2015), the German federal government has saved some 100 billion euros owing to the crisis, as the relevant rates of interest paid by it are lower than they would have been without this crisis. Furthermore, Germany is also benefiting from the euro-area crisis on two other fronts. On the one hand, the largely depressed labor market conditions put downward pressure on unit labor costs, which are considered the most relevant magnitude to determine if a country is competitive in the global economy: in this regard, Germany has increased its competitiveness, as its unit labor costs have been rising much less than in all other euro-area countries (Rossi, 2013). On the other hand, the quantitative easing policies carried out by the European Central Bank since 2014 have depreciated the exchange rate of the euro against all major foreign currencies, thereby making German exports cheaper for a non-euro-area importer. This indeed increases, rather than reducing, the current account imbalances existing across Euroland, as a result of the German export-oriented attitude, which has actually been the principal origin of German economic growth since the introduction of the euro in 1999 (see Cesaratto & Stirati, 2011). In this framework, it is clear that an array of countries, notably the PIIGS, are not in a position to increase their exports and thus support their economic growth, because generally speaking they are beaten by a more competitive German economy both within the euro-area and beyond it. As long as German political leaders are unwilling to allow an increase in low wages in their domestic economy—including an appropriate reform of their welfare system so that it supports poor families, including the 'working poor' who suffer in the current situation—it will be really impossible to reduce intra-euro-area imbalances through a much higher level of German imports. As a matter of fact, the structural reforms of the labor market in Germany as well as in the PIIGS—coupled with fiscal consolidation in the latter countries—elicit strong deflationary pressures, particularly as regards the wage level, which in the end aggravate the economic situation across the euro-area, even though the impact of these pressures varies depending on a series of factors that we now explore.

Winners and losers of fiscal consolidation across the euro-area

A largely ignored result of austerity policies adopted in a number of euro-area countries, particularly in the PIIGS, concerns the asymmetric distributional effects of this stance. It is indeed easy to understand and to notice in practice that income inequality increases, generally, in those countries that carry out a fiscal consolidation in the aftermath of a major crisis (see Jenkins, Brandolini, Micklewright, & Nolan, 2012, and Ball, Furceri, Leigh, & Loungani, 2013, for empirical evidence). Many long-period analyses show indeed that, in the absence of an appropriate fiscal capacity, a government cannot induce macroeconomic stabilization and economic growth (Jordà, Schularick, & Taylor, 2016). If so, then fiscal consolidation increases the risk of poverty, particularly for the most vulnerable members of society, such as children and young people (Navicke, Rastrigina, & Sutherland, 2014). The reduction of public expenditure, and the increase in value-added taxes that often accompanies it, weigh more on the low and middle-income classes, because the latter have to spend more as a proportion of their incomes for purchasing a given basket of goods and services on the marketplace, usually with no possibility to substitute some of these items with less expensive ones, and in general with a limited savings capacity that, over the long run, would provide for a 'rainy-day fund.'[6]

As regards the private sector, fiscal consolidation affects small and medium sized firms more negatively than large transnational corporations. Whilst the former are, generally speaking, domestically oriented (even more so in the PIIGS), the latter are, by definition, global businesses that can change their strategy and move (part of) their plant and equipment around the world to react to a recession hitting a particular region of the world economy, such as the euro-area or some of its member countries. The banking sector of a crisis-hit country is also more reluctant to increase its lending to private companies, in light of the more fragile balance sheets of banks within that country. Credit channels, however, operate differently according to the features of the potential borrower: big transnational corporations are certainly in a better position than small and medium-sized firms oriented to the domestic market only. The former can raise funds also on financial markets, thereby bypassing the banking sector, whilst the latter firms usually cannot do so (see Gambacorta & Marques-Ibanez, 2011). Furthermore, big firms may also be 'too big to fail,' and therefore likely to receive government support in the form of bail-out funds in the event of financial distress. As a result, their borrowing costs could be, in general, lower than those faced by smaller firms, even though the latter borrow lower amounts of money than the former, which moreover can often self-finance their projects and actually do so to some extent. In this regard, there is also a country-specific effect: a German bank is in a position to provide a cheaper credit line than a Greek bank can do—owing to the fact that Germany has a much stronger private economy than Greece, and a much less indebted public sector with respect to GDP than does the Greek government. Thus, German banks can support domestic firms—hence economic activity—much more than Greek banks can do as a result of the euro-area crisis, thereby increasing the imbalances across that area instead of reducing them over time.

These distributional effects in the relationships between firms and banks are aggravated by fiscal consolidation, because the latter weighs on (small) firms and (fragile) banks in crisis-hit countries more than it burdens the business activity of (larger) firms and (strong) banks in those countries that are relatively less affected by the euro-area crisis—a situation that increases economic divergence between these two groups of countries as time goes by.

As regards households, fiscal consolidation also has an impact that varies according to—amongst other things—the country in which they are located. In crisis-hit countries, a larger proportion of households must enter into (an increasing amount of) debt (to try) to maintain their standard of living in the aftermath of the crisis. This could also be problematic for the banking sector, particularly for domestically-oriented banks, because an increase in the relevant interest-rate differential can represent a heavier burden for those households that have to refinance (and renegotiate) mortgage loans with heavily-indebted banks—a number of which may be required to recapitalize their balance sheets as a result of the crisis. By contrast, those households that bought risk-free government bonds, and still have them in their portfolio when fiscal consolidation occurs, may experience the well-known 'wealth effect' as a result of a general 'flight to quality' across the financial markets in the euro-area and beyond it. This effect concerns mainly wealthy households, therefore the upper class, and notably those (male) individuals whose compensation lies in the top 10% of the income distribution pyramid. If this effect is unlikely to lead these households to increase their spending, particularly in the market for produced goods and services, in crisis-hit countries, it can do so, notably in real and financial asset markets, in several other countries and namely in Germany (where the real-estate market has been showing, at least since early 2013, an overheating trend with respect to residential property prices in a number of cities). This is so much so that quantitative easing policies may fuel the rapid increase in house prices, so much so that banks are keen on providing a higher volume of mortgage loans in light of both the expansionary monetary policy and the big increase in available collateral recorded as a result of the 'wealth effect.'

The overwhelming deflationary pressures induced by fiscal consolidation

As explained above, fiscal consolidation is a drag on economic activity for a number of reasons, thus impeding a country's eventual exit from crisis. Coupled with structural reforms in the labor market, this policy stance increases those deflationary pressures that exist as a result of the crisis and that a wrong-headed quantitative easing monetary policy tries to contain somewhat in vain.

Indeed, in a crisis-hit country that is also undergoing fiscal consolidation, labor market deregulation is counter-productive. Reducing public spending when private sector agents (firms and households) are also less prone to spend cannot but reduce aggregate demand in a vicious circle, because both fiscal receipts and firms' investment shrink over time as a result of a general slowdown in economic activity. Hence, higher labor market flexibility cannot but aggravate the situation, given that short-term labor agreements, increased job insecurity, and easier dismissal of workers lead to replacing the senior part of the labor force with lower-paid wage earners, whose reduced compensation leads to a drop in their consumption level, without a parallel increase in the propensity to consume by top income earners, or wealthy individuals, within the country. Furthermore, when several countries within the same currency area carry out fiscal consolidation simultaneously, the whole area is affected by mutually reinforcing recessionary effects, as intra-area trade diminishes considerably. Financial market participants all over the world then start to fear a global domino effect, implying an ever increasing number of non-performing loans in both the private and public sector of crisis-hit countries under an austerity policy stance. The vicious circle involving banks, firms, households and public sector institutions intertwined across factors and goods markets grows as time goes by, inducing mainstream-dominated government authorities to continue with (an even harsher) fiscal consolidation that can eventually create social unrest and political turmoil.

In such a scenario, the mainstream policy stance therefore leads to depression over time, for a series of mutually-reinforcing factors as explained by Morselli (2013):

1. Fiscal consolidation increases the rate of unemployment over the short run.
2. Even assuming a continuously-falling wage level, the resulting positive effect on the demand for labor is more than countered by the negative effect stemming from a lower sales level because of decreases in the purchasing power of households.
3. Firms might be led to prefer to increase their profits instead of increasing their competitiveness via a reduction in prices.

On the whole, the expansionary effects of fiscal consolidation assumed by mainstream economists are a figment of the imagination.

Conclusion

The mainstream arguments in favor of fiscal consolidation as a way to resolve the euro-area crisis are clearly flawed, on both conceptual and empirical grounds. The mirage of expansionary austerity policies should not lead us astray, particularly in light of the fact that a large part of the population involved thereby is hit hard by fiscal contraction and the induced deflationary pressures. Even though it will admittedly be very difficult to put into practice a radical alternative—mainly because of strong political resistance to any such alternatives, which go against the short-term financial interests of powerful actors and institutions across the euro-area and beyond it—it is worth trying, in order to avoid social and political unrest.

In fact, a viable and much more promising alternative to fiscal consolidation exists in economic analysis, and it has even proven helpful to kick-start the economic system that was largely depressed by the Second World War on both sides of the Atlantic Ocean. The Roosevelt New Deal supported the US economy, which recovered in the aftermath of that war, and together with the welfare system gave rise to the so-called 'Glorious Thirty' years of economic prosperity—both in the United States and across the European continent.

Indeed, there are a number of fields where public investment is necessary—both to kick-start and to support economic growth, as well as to increase the well-being of the population, and to protect the environment. These investments are likely to 'crowd-in' private investments, and to enhance the euro-area competitiveness over the long run. This is so much so that, as argued by Rossi (2012), the European Investment Bank could issue euro-bonds that would easily receive a 'triple-A' credit grade, attracting thereby those private savings, in the euro-area as well as beyond it, that at the time of writing are inflating asset prices for lack of good investment opportunities in the 'real' economy. These euro-bonds would also be helpful to make sure that the interbank market works properly across the euro-area, as they would provide good collateral for transactions on that market, especially if the European Central Bank were to include these euro-bonds in its list of eligible assets. Germany would then also benefit from the euro-area recovery, as the PIIGS would be able to import many more German goods as a result of the economic recovery induced by this expansionary policy stance at the euro-area level. This approach could even be enhanced further if German wages were increased at the bottom level of the income distribution: the increased purchasing power for the relevant households would support domestic expenditure as well as German import figures on the market for produced goods and services, thus rebalancing intra-euro-area trade in an expansionary (rather than the current austerity-induced recessionary) mood.

All in all, the mirage of expansionary fiscal consolidation cannot contribute to resolve the euro-area crisis. It actually aggravates this crisis as time goes by. An alternative does exist, and its likely results are promising. If such an alternative is not put into practice, it is because it meets with the powerful opposition of vested interests, within both creditor and debtor countries across the euro-area. This shows that economic policy decisions are actually more an issue of power relationships than of sound economic analysis. Hence, an awareness of the winners and losers of austerity policies would help direct the work of researchers analyzing the discourse on austerity and public spending.

Notes

1 In fact, the public sector's intervention within the economic system did not actually shrink as a result of this ideological stance, if one considers that, since the 1980s, the ratio between public spending and GDP has been increasing in a number of advanced economies. The neoliberal agenda, however, made the State intervention shift from the production of (public) goods and services to the distribution of income through a series of channels designed to support low and middle-income citizens who are marginalized by markets and the private sector at large. Further, owing to tax competition, both within and across national borders, the distributive role of the State since the 1990s has rather been contributing to—rather than combating—income and wealth concentration at the top of the relevant pyramid.

2 In this theoretical framework, banks are mere financial intermediaries between savers and borrowers. In other words, bank credit cannot exceed the amount of savings deposited within the banking system. There is no recognition that, actually, money is an endogenous magnitude whose amount is determined by bank credit, which means that a bank may open any credit line even though it does not have enough loanable funds, because, in fact, 'loans make deposits' (Schumpeter, 1954, pp. 1110–1117). This specific property of banks (with respect to non-bank financial institutions) has been officially recognized recently by McLeay, Radia, & Thomas (2014), among others. Since the early 1980s, it has been widely explained by heterodox economists—mostly within the post-Keynesian and monetary circuit schools (see Rochon & Rossi, 2003).
3 As Herndon et al. (2014) have pointed out, the Reinhart and Rogoff (2010) research work is flawed by selective exclusion of available data, coding errors, and inappropriate weighting of summary statistics. It is also problematic as regards the direction of causality between public debt and GDP growth, because a lower rate of economic growth may in fact originate (rather than being the result of) a higher public debt.
4 Referring to the current core of mainstream economics, Caballero (2010) explains that "it has become so mesmerized with its own internal logic that it has begun to confuse the precision it has achieved about its own world with the precision that it has about the real one" (p. 85).
5 To be sure, the actual over-capacity of production in a number of industrial branches, like the automobile and construction industries, reduces their profitability and hence hinders their propensity to invest in these economic activities.
6 The mainstream view ignores any distributional effects of fiscal consolidation, because it assumes (as in the Ricardian equivalence theorem) the existence of so-called representative agents, that is, agents who behave identically as they have the same disposable income. This is clearly a figment of the mainstream economists' imagination, which represents different human beings by a standard utility-maximizing *homo oeconomicus*.

References

Alesina, A., & Ardagna, S. (1998). Tales of fiscal adjustment. *Economic Policy, 13*(27), 487–545.

Alesina, A., & Ardagna, S. (2010). Large changes in fiscal policy: Taxes versus spending. In J. R. Brown (Ed.), *Tax policy and the economy* (Vol. 24, pp. 35–68). Chicago, IL: University of Chicago Press.

Alesina, A., & Perotti, R. (1995). Fiscal expansions and fiscal adjustments in OECD countries. *Economic Policy, 10*(21), 205–248.

Alesina, A., & Perotti, R. (1997). Fiscal adjustments in OECD countries: Composition and macroeconomic effects. *Staff Papers (International Monetary Fund), 44*(2), 210–248.

Bagnai, A. (2013). Unhappy families are all alike: Minskyan cycles, Kaldorian growth, and the Eurozone peripheral crises. In Ó. Dejuán, E. Febrero, & J. Uxó (Eds.), *Post-Keynesian views of the crisis and its remedies* (pp. 130–177). London/New York: Routledge.

Ball, L., Furceri, D., Leigh, D., & Loungani, P. (2013). *The distributional effects of fiscal consolidation*. (Working Paper No. WP/13/151). Washington, DC: International Monetary Fund. Retrieved from www.imf.org/external/pubs/ft/wp/2013/wp13151.pdf

Barro, R. J. (1974). Are government bonds net wealth? *Journal of Political Economy*, *82*(6), 1095–1117.

Barro, R. J. (1989). The Ricardian approach to budget deficits. *Journal of Economic Perspectives*, *3*(2), 37–54.

Buchanan, J. M. (1976). Barro on the Ricardian equivalence theorem. *Journal of Political Economy*, *84*(2), 337–342.

Caballero, R. J. (2010). Macroeconomics after the crisis: time to deal with the pretense-of-knowledge syndrome. *Journal of Economic Perspectives*, *24*(4), 85–102.

Cesaratto, S., & Stirati, A. (2011). Germany and the European and global crises. *International Journal of Political Economy*, *39*(4), 56–87.

Cottarelli, C., & Jaramillo, L. (2012). *Walking hand in hand: Fiscal policy and growth in advanced economies*. (Working Paper No. WP/12/137). Washington, DC: International Monetary Fund. Retrieved from www.imf.org/external/pubs/ft/wp/2012/wp12137.pdf

Dany, G., Gropp, R. E., Littke, H., & von Schweinitz, G. (2015). Germany's benefit from the Greek crisis. *Leibniz-Institute für Wirtschaftsforschung Halle IWH Online*. Retrieved from www.nachdenkseiten.de/upload/pdf/150811-studie-germanys-benefit-from-the-greek-crisis-iwa-halle-10082015_.pdf

European Central Bank (2012). The role of fiscal multipliers in the current consolidation debate. *Monthly Bulletin*, *14*(12), 82–85.

Fama, E. F. (1970). Efficient capital markets: A review of theory and empirical work. *Journal of Finance*, *25*(2), 383–417.

Fisher, I. (1933). The debt-deflation theory of great depressions. *Econometrica*, *1*(4), 337–357.

Gambacorta, L., & Marques-Ibanez, D. (2011). The bank lending channel: Lessons from the crisis. *Economic Policy*, *26*(66), 135–182.

Giavazzi, F., & Pagano, M. (1990). Can severe fiscal contractions be expansionary? Tales of two small European countries. In O. J. Blanchard & S. Fischer (Eds.), *NBER Macroeconomics Annual* (Vol. 5, pp. 75–122). Cambridge, MA: National Bureau of Economic Research.

Giavazzi, F., & Pagano, M. (1996). Non-Keynesian effects of fiscal policy changes: International evidence and the Swedish experience. *Swedish Economic Policy Review*, *3*(1), 67–103.

Herndon, T., Ash, M., & Pollin, R. (2014). Does high public debt consistently stifle economic growth? A critique of Reinhart and Rogoff. *Cambridge Journal of Economics*, *38*(2), 257–279.

Jenkins, S. P., Brandolini, A., Micklewright, J., & Nolan, B. (Eds). (2012). *The Great Recession and the distribution of household income*. Oxford/New York: Oxford University Press.

Jordà, Ò., Schularick, M., & Taylor, A. (2016). Sovereigns versus banks: Credit, crises, and consequences. *Journal of the European Economic Association*, *14*(1), 45–79.

Kahneman, D., & Tversky, A. (1979). Prospect theory: An analysis of decision under risk. *Econometrica*, *47*(2), 263–292.

Keynes, J. M. (1936). *The general theory of employment, interest and money*. London: Macmillan.

Mastromatteo, G., & Rossi, S. (2015). The economics of deflation in the euro area: A critique of fiscal austerity. *Review of Keynesian Economics*, *3*(3), 336–350.

McCombie, J. L. S. (1987–1988). Keynes and the nature of involuntary unemployment. *Journal of Post Keynesian Economics*, *10*(2), 202–215.

McLeay, M., Radia, A., & Thomas, R. (2014). Money creation in the modern economy. *Bank of England Quarterly Bulletin, 54*(1), 14–27.

Minsky, H. P. (1977). The financial instability hypothesis: An interpretation of Keynes and an alternative to 'standard' theory. *Challenge, 20*(1), 20–27.

Morselli, A. (2013, July 10). Deflazione o politiche keynesiane? *Economia e Politica*. Retrieved from www.economiaepolitica.it/index.php/primo-piano/deflazione-o-politiche-keynesiane/

Navicke, J., Rastrigina, O., & Sutherland, H. (2014). Nowcasting indicators of poverty risk in the European Union: A microsimulation approach. *Social Indicators Research, 119*(1), 101–119.

Nuti, D. M. (2012). La strategia di uscita dalla crisi dell'euro. In R. Rossanda & M. Pianta (Eds.), *La rotta d'Europa: La politica* (pp. 135–68). Rome: ManifestoLibri.

Reagan, R. (1981, January 20). 'Inaugural address.' Retrieved from https://reaganlibrary.archives.gov/archives/speeches/1981/12081a.htm

Reinhart, C., & Rogoff, K. (2010). Growth in a time of debt. *American Economic Review, 100*(2), 573–578.

Rochon, L.-P., & Rossi, S. (Eds.). (2003). *Modern theories of money: The nature and role of money in capitalist economies*. Cheltenham, UK/Northampton, MA: Edward Elgar.

Rossi, S. (2012). Replacing recession and austerity with growth and solidarity across Euroland. In M. Méaulle (Ed.). *Austerity is not the solution! Contributions to European economic policy* (pp. 33–40). Brussels: Foundation for European Progressive Studies.

Rossi, S. (2013). Financialization and monetary union in Europe: The monetary–structural causes of the euro-area crisis. *Cambridge Journal of Regions, Economy and Society, 6*(3), 381–400.

Schumpeter, J.A. (1954). *History of economic analysis*. London: George Allen & Unwin.

Seater, J. J. (1993). Ricardian equivalence. *Journal of Economic Literature, 31*(1), 142–190.

Shiller, R. J. (2000). *Irrational exuberance*. Princeton, NJ/Oxford: Princeton University Press.

13 Why should we all tighten our belts? On arguments for austerity in political discourse

Emanuele Brambilla

> Annual income twenty pounds, annual expenditure nineteen nineteen and six, result happiness.
> Annual income twenty pounds, annual expenditure twenty pounds ought and six, result misery.
>
> — Mr Micawber, *David Copperfield*

The Micawber Principle is an evocative economic theory that has become part of English-national and international language heritage (Snelling, 2009, p. 92). Despite its fame, it is actually a 'law' of personal finance rather than a fully-fledged economic theory; as such, it might appear too simple to be applied to State affairs or complex economic issues. Think of the current economic predicament derived from the 2007–2008 financial crisis: mortgage refinancing, the stock exchange, social struggles, education, technological progress, cultural values, national history and other sub-topics all find their way into crisis discourse, compound it and contribute to shaping it. As a result, when it comes to economic issues in political communication, audiences are generally denied the privilege of listening to a speaker who shares the *brevitas*, clarity and rhetorical effectiveness of David Copperfield's friend.

Yet, the second 2008 Obama–McCain presidential debate suggests that complex economic issues are not always addressed in complex terms. When Barack Obama was asked a question by audience member Teresa Finch, he answered by comparing the State budget to a family budget and the Congress to a family that has become famous for its persistently inaccurate management of financial resources.

Finch: How can we trust either of you with our money when both parties got us into this global economic crisis?

Obama: Well, look, I understand your frustration and your cynicism, because while you've been carrying out your responsibilities—most of the people here, you've got a family budget. If less money is coming in, you end up making cuts. Maybe you don't go out to dinner as much. Maybe you put off buying a new car. That's not what happens in Washington. And you're right. There is a lot of blame to go around.[1]

Obama's *Micawberian* answer to Teresa Finch shows that political discourse is certainly not averse to simplification through metaphorical language, especially in times of crisis (De Landtsheer, 2007, p. 63). After all, *economy* literally means "management/administration of a household."[2] It is and always will be about balance between income and expenditure, be it at personal 'wallet' level or regarding more complex interactive systems of production and trade of resources. Any imbalance in the economy has the potential to lead to a crisis. If an individual consistently spends more than s/he earns, s/he will inevitably meet not only poverty but also misery; similarly, if there is an imbalance in State economy, the ensuing crisis will lead to 'national misery,' resulting in failure in catering for people's needs.

The power of the argument by analogy has never been neglected in political communication (Mazzi, 2011) and the current downturn is no exception, as suggested by the above example. Since the very inception of the financial crisis, world politicians have been forced by the circumstances to deal with austerity, however unpopular this might be. In their attempts at preserving their *public positive faces* (Gruber, 1993, p. 3), they have (to differing extents) resorted to argumentative strategies of all sorts (Brambilla, 2015) to mitigate the pragmatic force of controversial arguments regarding the solution of the deficit crisis. In other words, political argumentation, understood as "the practice of justifying decisions under conditions of uncertainty" (Zarefsky, 1995, p. 43), has proved an effective discursive means to reduce the uncertainty brought along by a long-lasting recession and appease the fear triggered by the prospects of public spending cuts and tax increases.

Like all arguments, arguments for austerity are topic-related (Reisigl, 2014, p. 77), which might lead one to think that those put forward in speeches on the financial and economic crisis are more or less similar. However, cultural conventions, contextual constraints and idiosyncratic preferences also influence political argumentation (van Eemeren, Grootendorst, Snoeck, Henkemans, Blair, Johnson, Krabbe, … Zarefsky. 1996, p. 2), thereby diversifying politicians' strategies of justification and determining their relativity (van Eemeren & Grootendorst, 1992, p. 57). Against this background, the present chapter investigates the variation of arguments for austerity in political communication, with a view to providing an account of the main strategies harnessed to legitimize and/or justify the adoption of measures aimed at reducing budget deficits.

The corpus and the methodology

The study is based on *ARGO*, a multilingual corpus of political speeches on the financial and economic crisis. It is made up of 313 speeches, almost equally divided into American, British and French: 109 were delivered by Barack Obama (United States President, 2009–2017), 101 by David Cameron (Prime Minister of the United Kingdom, 2010–2016), 103 by Nicolas Sarkozy (President of the French Republic, 2007–2012) and François Hollande (President of the French Republic, 2012–2017), respectively 53 and 50. The corpus texts are *transcripts*, i.e., written texts, rather than transcriptions of oral recordings, because political texts are fundamentally written texts.

> Speeches are normally 'texts'—in the sense of materially durable products of linguistic actions [...]. Usually, they are prepared in writing, although the wording of their verbal presentation may sometimes differ considerably from the written version. They are rarely produced *ad hoc* or spontaneously, and even the sporadic *ex tempore* speeches are never improvisations out of nothing.
>
> (Reisigl, 2010, p. 243)

The transcripts of most political addresses can be found on the internet shortly after speech delivery, which shows that political texts are first written and then uttered. During the corpus construction process, the official websites of the White House, 10 Downing Street and *L'Élysée* were accessed daily in the search for freshly-delivered speeches on the economy. Relevant speech transcripts were initially chosen on the basis of the presence in the texts and/or text titles of the search terms *economic crisis*, *financial crisis*, *economy*, *economic*, *finance*, *financial*. After this first sifting, each speech was read through to assess topicality, based on which transcripts were selected or rejected. Once topicality was assessed, transcript accuracy was cross-checked with the related video, because there can be a discrepancy between the transcripts and the actually-delivered speeches (Mayaffre, 2012, p. 21). Finally, the transcripts were downloaded, corrected where necessary, and definitively inserted in the corpus folder.

ARGO is composed of 797,360 words: 292,539 make up the American sub-corpus, 180,665 the British, and 324,156 the French (respectively 194,196 and 129,960 in Sarkozy's and Hollande's text collections). Though the lower number of words in the British sub-corpus might look like lack of data homogeneity, consistency in the *number of speeches* rather than in the *number of words* has been sought. After all, homogeneity must not be understood as "approximately equal number of words"; it is a much more complex concept regarding, among other things, topicality and the contexts of speech production and reception (Bendazzoli & Sandrelli, 2009, p. 3). The considerable variation in word number among the sub-corpora is determined, first of all, by the American and French Presidents' habits of delivering dense and lengthy speeches before national audiences (Perelman & Olbrechts-Tyteca, 2008, p. 72); this has led the respective sub-corpora to 'outnumber' the British text collection, as far as the number of words is concerned. Moreover, Cameron's frequent brief interventions at the European Council and the House of Commons, together with the speaker's habit of resorting to pragmatic arguments (Perelman & Olbrechts-Tyteca, 2008, p. 358; Garssen, 2001, p. 92),[3] have determined the uniqueness of the British sub-corpus. Therefore, variation in the number of words among the sub-corpora of *ARGO* must not be seen as a shortcoming hampering the ecological validity of the study, but rather as an indicator of the fact that political argumentation takes various forms depending on cultural and contextual constraints. Speeches delivered by different speakers, from different nations, in national and international settings are, therefore, functional to assessing the relativity of argumentation.

All the speeches were delivered between 2008 and 2014 and make up a sample of the discourse on the financial and economic crisis that has monopolized political communication over the last few years, as discourse on terrorism has gradually been accompanied by a growing number of speeches on the consequences of 'economic terrorism' or 'the crime of our time' (Schechter, 2010). The 2007–2008 financial and economic crisis is largely considered the worst crisis since the Great Depression and the worst downturn since the Second World War (Schechter, 2010, p. 150), especially because it subsequently led to a broader and sustained global recession, generally referred to as *the Great Recession*. The general economic decline in world markets, which is still underway in most countries, started around the end of the first decade of the twenty-first century with the subprime mortgage crisis. It was triggered by the bursting of the United States housing bubble, i.e., the steep decline in home prices following their unjustified increase over time which reached its peak around 2006–2007 (Deflem, 2011, p. ix). During the American housing boom of the mid-2000s, financial institutions began marketing *mortgage-backed securities* (MBS), *collateralized debt obligations* (CDO) and other sophisticated derivative products at unprecedented levels. The increase in loan incentives encouraged borrowers to assume risky mortgages with an eye to quick refinancing at easier terms. However, once interest rates began to rise and housing prices started to drop in 2006–2007 in many parts of the United States, borrowers found themselves unable to refinance (Prabhakar, 2017, p. 59). In a nutshell, the US housing market went from boom to bust and large quantities of mortgage-backed securities suddenly lost value; massive defaults followed, leading millions of borrowers to contribute to the dramatic and widespread expansion of household debt.

The subprime mortgage crisis, thus, fuelled a major financial crisis (Deflem, 2011, p. ix) spreading all across the globe: the devaluation of housing-related securities jeopardized the solvency of over-leveraged banks and financial institutions in the US and Europe. The predicament became public a year later, in 2008, with the bankruptcy of Lehman Brothers, the fourth-largest investment bank in the United States. Several other major financial institutions followed in the footsteps of Lehman Brothers, triggering a significant disruption in the flow of credit to businesses and consumers and marking the onset of the Great Recession.

The total collapse of large financial institutions was prevented by the bailout of banks by national governments (Schechter, 2010, pp. 4–5). However, stock markets still dropped worldwide. The housing market was heavily affected by the financial crisis, resulting in evictions, foreclosures and prolonged unemployment. Businesses started to fail, consumer wealth declined significantly and world economic activity underwent an unprecedented and historic downturn.

Though the media have increasingly appeared to target financial speculation as the basic trigger of the 2008 financial and economic predicament, political responsibility in the lead-up to the crisis cannot be neglected either. In this respect, the causes of the Great Recession are much deeper, as the gradual destruction of the wealth of the working class (Schechter, 2010, p. 73) also stemmed from the implementation of deregulatory fiscal policies, including major revisions of the 1977 Community Reinvestment Act[4] (Nguyen & Pontell, 2011).

Despite being global plights, the housing crisis, the financial crisis and the economic crisis have given rise to an extremely articulated downturn, which has had different implications in different nations. Since the wake of the financial-economic crisis, therefore, politicians have been confronted with the task of skilfully verbalizing their endeavors to solve the predicament in their respective countries without leaking political responsibility or bothering taxpayers; this prolificacy of political discourse has provided the opportunity to assemble *ARGO*.

As regards the methodology adopted to analyze the reference corpus, a premise should be specified at the outset. This chapter stems from a broader project focusing on the analysis of political argumentation; though concerning the analysis of a corpus of texts, this project is neither a *corpus-based* nor a *corpus-driven* study.[5] Rather, it is a corpus-based study only insofar as "it is empirical, analyzing the actual patterns of use in natural texts" and "it utilizes a large and principled collection of natural texts, known as 'corpus', as the basis for analysis" (Biber, Conrad, & Reppen, 1998, p. 4). However, it cannot be considered a corpus-based study in that it does not make "extensive use of computers for analysis, using both automatic and interactive techniques" and it does not depend "on both quantitative and qualitative analytical techniques" (Biber et al., 1998, p. 4). This is because argumentation analysis is a largely qualitative research pertaining to the broader study of text pragmatics (van Eemeren et al., 1996, p. 12) and hinging on methods drawn from argumentation theory, the discipline "interested in the problems involved in the *production*, *analysis* and *evaluation* of argumentative discourse" (van Eemeren et al., 1996, p. 12, emphasis original). Particularly, the speeches have been examined through the analytical tools offered by Pragma-dialectics (van Eemeren et al., 1996, p. 274), probably the most influential argumentation theory, enabling descriptive and normative studies alike. Particular emphasis has been laid on the concept of *strategic maneuvering* (van Eemeren, 2010), according to which every act of arguing is made up of three inseparable components, namely *topical potential*, *audience demand* and *presentational devices* (van Eemeren, 2010, pp. 93–94). In simple terms, an arguer always selects the specific topic s/he wishes to address from a range of possible topics, adapts argumentation to the relevant audience and verbalizes arguments in the most strategically appropriate way, i.e., by harnessing the most effective devices at his/her disposal. Regarding topics, the interdiscursive and multi-layered nature of political communication has been taken into account in analysing *ARGO*.

> *Interdiscursivity* signifies that discourses are linked to each other in various ways. If we conceive of 'discourse' as primarily topic-related (as 'discourse on x'), we will observe that a discourse on climate change frequently refers to topics or subtopics of other discourses, such as finances or health. Discourses are open and often hybrid; new sub-topics can be created at many points.
>
> (Reisigl & Wodak, 2009, p. 90)

Interdiscursive references and sub-topics do not occur by chance but are, instead, strategically selected by speakers, in Pragma-dialectical terms. As a result, though sharing the topic of the economic crisis, *ARGO* speeches will be composed of different sub-topics, linguistically codified according to audience demand and the speaker's stylistic preferences.

Insights drawn from the Discourse-Historical Approach (Reisigl & Wodak, 2001, 2009), a branch of Critical Discourse Analysis with a strong focus on argumentation, have not been disregarded either as, like Pragma-dialectics, this chiefly descriptive methodology also enables the *content-related* reconstruction of *argument schemes* (Reisigl & Wodak, 2009, p. 114). Formally defined as "principles or rules underlying arguments that legitimize the step from premises to standpoints"[6] (Garssen, 1999, p. 225), argument schemes can be viewed as "general schemes for defending standpoints" (van Eemeren et al., 1996, p. 106) or "forms of argument that capture stereotypical patterns of human reasoning" (Walton, 2013, p. 182). Though its basic functional elements are often partially left implicit (Reisigl, 2014, p. 72; van Eemeren et al., 1996, p. 3), argumentation can always be reformulated into a structure composed of premises and conclusions. In this respect, the reconstruction of the most-frequently recurring arguments in the *ARGO* corpus has provided a descriptive account of the strategies of justification adopted by Obama, Cameron, Sarkozy and Hollande, incidentally highlighting the prominent role of arguments for austerity in their speeches.

Obama

Despite being speeches on the economic crisis, Obama's addresses often resemble more joyful types of speeches, as they are strewn with innumerable references to a prosperous future, celebrations of American values, and passionate appeals to invest in education and innovation. This comes as no surprise, because crisis discourse is not exclusively or inherently 'negative'; indeed, it is not uncommon to hear politicians prophesying a brighter future, as crisis provides them "with an opportunity to [...] present themselves as leaders, to dramatically define the situation as tragic but hopeful, and to bring out the 'resolve' of national character" (Sandaran & De Rycker, 2013, pp. 199–200).

This quotation testifies the pervasiveness of the topoi[7] of *crisis as a challenge* and *crisis as an opportunity*, whereby speakers discursively try to show the silver lining of difficult junctures. When a crisis upsets the foundations of a given system, it is generally said to have shown the weaknesses of that system, thereby providing the *challenging opportunity* to restore and possibly improve the previous order or state of affairs (Lean, Mohd Don, & Fernandez, 2013, p. 436). The recurrence of these topoi in crisis discourse is partly determined by the widespread habit of referring to the Chinese word for crisis, composed of two characters standing for 'danger' and 'opportunity.' John F. Kennedy's early reference to the Chinese pictogram, during a speech in Indianapolis in 1959,[8] acted as an imprinting for political rhetoric, and Obama has never shirked resorting to the strategies of his Democrat mentor (Zarefsky, 2014, p. 294). For instance, the following excerpt corroborates the former US President's habit of evoking a threatening socioeconomic landscape before suddenly steering discourse towards more hopeful prospects:

> But while our economy may be weakened and our confidence shaken; though we are living through difficult and uncertain times, tonight I want every American to know this: we will rebuild, we will recover, and the United States of America will emerge stronger than before.
>
> (Obama, 2009, February 24).

Over and above the topoi of *challenge* and *opportunity*, Obama's speeches feature a recurrent argument, i.e., the *argument from middle-class distress* (Brambilla, 2015, p. 306), whereby the President claims that his major aim is to rescue the middle class[9] and revive its values, namely hard work, solidarity and compassion; these values have made America what it is, but have been temporarily lost owing to the prominence rashly given to the 'bad values' of irresponsibility, speculation and selfishness. The American middle class is, thus, the target of Obama's policies; notably, most of Obama's speeches have been delivered within national borders and are, therefore, mainly directed to an American, middle-class audience. As a consequence, Obama's speeches appear to be the least 'specialist' within the whole of *ARGO*. Arguments concerning the deficit crisis are sporadically put forward and, when 'selected,' the topic is always addressed in a very simple fashion, in line with the President's answer to Teresa Finch during the 2008 debate.

Austerity arguments are, however, present in Obama's speeches as the topic is inextricably bound to the economic destiny of the country and, in particular, to the desired resurgence of the middle class. The sub-topics of education reform and innovation are generally addressed in relation to austerity in Obama's discourse, as also attested by Means (2010, p. 261); in particular, though, argumentation regarding the deficit is systematically associated with that regarding health care reform, revolving around the *Patient Protection and Affordable Care Act*, which is generally known as *Affordable Care Act* or 'Obamacare.' The reform aims at expanding coverage for the uninsured unemployed Americans by guaranteeing that they "don't go broke when they get sick," as Obama frequently asserts. It is also implemented through reform of *Medicare* and *Medicaid*, which are said to compound the deficit predicament:

> This means further reducing health care costs, including programs like *Medicare* and *Medicaid*, which are the single biggest contributor to our long-term deficit.
>
> (Obama, 2011, January 25)

Obamacare is said to be one of the keys to middle-class relief and overall economic recovery alike; it fosters deficit reduction and helps American businesses that are "saddled with rapidly increasing health care costs," to use the President's words.

The reform was signed into law in March 2010. Yet, Obama recurrently specifies that it is continually criticized and constantly risks repealing, despite its instrumental role in solving the budget deficit crisis. In this respect, argumentation in favor of deficit reduction implies the *straw man argument* (Reisigl & Wodak, 2001, p. 73),[10] whereby Obama evokes the groundless attacks of his opponents, thereby preserving his face and threatening theirs. Argumentation regarding austerity basically revolves around the claim that, despite criticism, Obamacare and the other policies promoted by the Obama administration (especially education and innovation reforms) are not compounding the deficit predicament. Even though they actually have a negative impact on the budget situation in the short term, they are part of a broader government plan to solve the deficit crisis in the long run. As previously stated, austerity is systematically addressed in a simple fashion, which sometimes provides the President with the opportunity to argue in *Micawberian* terms:

> Despite what some have claimed, *the cost of the Recovery Act is only a very small part of our current budget imbalance.* In reality, the deficit had been building dramatically over the previous eight years. We have *a structural gap between the money going out and the money coming in.*
>
> (Obama, as cited in Hechtkopf, 2009, December 8)

> If we had taken office in ordinary times, I would have liked nothing more than to start *bringing down the deficit.* But we took office amid a crisis. And our efforts to prevent a second depression have added another one trillion dollars to our national debt. That, too, is a fact. I'm absolutely convinced that was the right thing to do. *But families across the country are tightening their belts and making tough decisions. The federal government should do the same.* So tonight, I'm proposing specific steps to pay for the trillion dollars that it took to rescue the economy last year. [...] *Like any cash-strapped family, we will work within a budget to invest in what we need and sacrifice what we don't.*
>
> (Obama, 2010, January 27)

The recourse to the idiomatic expression *to tighten one's belt* bears witness to Obama's predilection for an informal register that fits in with simple argumentation and the establishment of a sympathetic interaction with the audience.

More particularly, the idiom also testifies to politicians' habit of resorting to figurative language to simplify complex political and/or socioeconomic issues (De Landtsheer, 2007, p. 63); meaning "to brace oneself against hunger or penury"—as the action "is supposed to reduce the pangs of hunger" (Partridge, 1978, p. 462)—the expression is used to evoke the sacrifices made by families, trigger a simple comparison with the government, and simplify the consequences brought about by the crisis. As American families, the harbingers of American values, are tightening their belts, everybody, including the government, should follow their example and 'moral' guidance. Obama's argument for austerity, thus, rests on a simple content-related scheme:

Premise 1: Some say that my policies compound the deficit predicament.
Premise 2: They are wrong, as the deficit predicament is serious irrespective of the impact of government policies.
Premise 3: However substantial, the impact of government policies on the deficit is negligible, as they are part of a broader plan to solve the crisis in the long term.
Premise 4: Obamacare reduces health care costs, thereby contributing to solving the deficit crisis; moreover, the economy is growing again owing to government commitment to business and innovation.
Conclusion: Therefore, I will not give up my policies so as to continue cutting the budget deficit.

Obama's argument shifts discourse from the controversial topic of public spending cuts to the more promising fields of science, education, health reform and growth, while simultaneously alluding to the nihilistic practices of unnamed opponents. Curiously, the word *austerity* does not occur in Obama's speeches, which appears like another strategy to divert the attention of the audience from potentially face-threatening or tabooed topics.

Cameron

Cameron's speeches are substantially different from Obama's. First of all, more emphasis is laid on the need to cut the deficit, pursued primarily through the reduction of public spending (Fairclough & Fairclough, 2012, p. 117). Regarding the deficit crisis, a significant difference between Obama and Cameron stands out; while the former only alludes to his Republican opponents by making reference to their obstructionist trends via the straw man argument, the latter more directly stresses the major responsibility of the former Labour government in bequeathing a disastrous debt legacy. The government's unmistakable difficulties in addressing economic issues, for which it is not to blame, are recurrently conveyed by relying on the *argument from deficit inheritance*, whereby Cameron lays the blame for the deficit crisis on the previous government. The recurrence of the argument is signalled by the verb *to inherit*, an externally caused change of state verb (Levin & Rappaport Hovav, 1995, p. 92) implying someone else's responsibility in carrying out the action denoted by the verb, as the very act of inheritance is triggered by a third party in the first place. Take the following examples:

> In Britain, we are taking the tough steps to deal with *the massive deficit that we inherited.*
>
> (Cameron, 2010, November 12)

> In Britain, cleaning up our banks and introducing a proper regulatory framework is a vital part of clearing up *the mess we inherited.*
>
> (Cameron, 2012, June 18)

> Never forget - *we inherited a deficit* bigger than Spain's. Bigger even than Greece. This has meant taking decisions no other government had dreamed of taking before.
>
> (Cameron, 2012, November 19)

The Conservative-Liberal Democrat Coalition Government is recurrently said to have inherited either a *massive deficit* or a more vivid *mess*, with occasional references to less connoted *problems*. By recurrently adopting the verb *to inherit*, the speaker presupposes and conjures up a previous, extremely negative state of affairs that has restricted the leeway and affected the actions of the present government. Cameron's utterances, thus, trigger a political implicature (van Dijk, 2005, p. 69) by implying another utterance, not visible on text surface: *The deficit is not my/our fault. The fault lies with the previous government, i.e., Labour.* Sometimes the verb *to inherit* is not present, but the political implicature highlighting the responsibility of Labour is equally evident:

> So, while the cutbacks that are coming are unavoidable now, they could have been avoided if *previously* we had spent wisely instead of showering the public sector with cash at a time when everyone else in the country was *tightening their belt.*
>
> (Cameron, 2010, June 7)

In all cases, however, the argument acts as a strategy of justification, enabling the speaker to assert the Conservative 'innocence' regarding the persistence of tough economic times. The government goodwill is attested by the recourse to the idiom *tightening their belt* with reference to *everyone else in the country*, which establishes solidarity with a considerable portion of the audience and, thus, appears to be a pillar of austerity discourse.

As regards the means adopted by the government to cut the deficit, Cameron's main strategy lies in reducing public spending. In this respect, be it for the PM's *Britishness* or not, Cameron's convictions also appear to be essentially *Micawberian*, as thrift and spending are deemed to be more important than income, at least as far as the initial task of containing the crisis is concerned: notably, saving is not merely presented as a duty but rather as the challenge issued by the economic predicament:

> *We need to do more with less.* Not just now, but permanently. It can be done.
>
> (Cameron, 2013, November 11)

Passages like the one shown above are recurrent in the British sub-corpus of *ARGO*, as they seem to serve the purpose of mitigating unpopular references to *sacrifice*, inevitably entailed by argumentation regarding the deficit crisis. Indeed, Cameron's argument for austerity is formally an *argument for thrift* (Reisigl & Wodak, 2009, p. 105), but the pragmatically detrimental consequences of evoking the idea of sacrifice are systematically pre-empted, not only by means of the argument from deficit inheritance. Spending cuts are regularly addressed by flaunting the silver lining of the predicament, i.e., the challenging nature of the aftermath of the crisis; however serious, the crisis has tested nations' abilities to survive with more modest means, which ordinary people had already been doing:

> We're in a world of unprecedented economic change, with millions of new consumers and countless innovations where *companies are starting with less investment than ever before, yet still becoming global giants within a matter of years.*
>
> (Prime Minister's Office, 2010, October 25)

The redefinition of spending standards is the challenge launched by the crisis. It is not only a challenge but a duty, as it is the prerequisite for growth:

> *Those who argue that dealing with our deficit and promoting growth are somehow alternatives are wrong.* You cannot put off the first in order to promote the second.
>
> (Cameron, 2011, January 28)

Deficit and growth are inextricably linked; consequently, the solution of the crisis depends on the government's success in reducing the deficit and promoting growth. This stance, underlying all the speeches included in the British sub-corpus, is conveyed by resorting to the following argument scheme:

Premise 1: The government has inherited a massive budget deficit.
Premise 2: The crisis has challenged and reshaped our spending standards. Even before the crisis, we were spending too much, which worsened our deficit crisis and jeopardized growth.
Premise 3: Cutting the deficit through the reduction of public spending is the government's challenge and priority, as it is essential to contain and solve the crisis.
Premise 4: The task is not easy and will require time, resilience and ingenuity.

Conclusion: Despite difficulties, the government is committed to cutting the deficit through the reduction of public spending and the promotion of growth.

Despite its pivotal role in restoring the economy and *favoring* growth, on its own the reduction of public spending with a view to cutting the deficit is not a *means* for spurring growth. The hindrance to economic recovery is, in Cameron's opinion, posed by a major *imbalance*, which also lies at the origin of the huge British debt: the imbalance between the public and the private sectors. Over the last few years, the former has 'boomed' while the latter has shrunk owing to ill-judged policies. By highlighting this major imbalance brought about, again, by the previous government, Cameron legitimizes his *rebalancing* strategy, revolving around the redistribution of resources from the public sector to the private and the launch of a 'new economic dynamism' enabled by the promotion of private-sector jobs, which are systematically described by the speaker as the prerequisite for growth.

Sarkozy

Sarkozy's speeches appear to combine Obama's predilection for argumentation from values (Walton, Reed, & Macagno, 2008, p. 321) with Cameron's more specialist arguments. A crucial similarity between Sarkozy and Cameron precisely lies in the systematic dealing with the deficit crisis. However, the topic is addressed in greater detail and also with more clarity by the former right-wing President of France; this comes as no surprise because, despite the twofold dimension of expert discourse and ideology discourse (Mayaffre, 2012, p. 53), Sarkozy's speeches remain fundamentally clear, as his argumentation resembles that of an educator (Mayaffre, 2012, p. 243). Take the following excerpts, showing the President's marked recourse to repetition and questions used as rhetorical devices:

> Le déficit est une *conséquence*. Une *conséquence* du *manque* d'investissement, du *manque* de productivité, du *manque* de compétitivité, du *manque* de travail. Une *conséquence* du *manque* de rigueur dans la gestion de la dépense. Ce qui est crucial, c'est la dépense et la nature de la dépense.
>
> (Sarkozy, 2008, December 4)
>
> [The deficit is a *consequence*. A *consequence* of *lack* of investment, of *lack* of productivity, of *lack* of competitiveness, of *lack* of employment. A *consequence* of *lack* of rigor in spending management. What is crucial is spending and the nature of spending. (author's translation)]

> Enfin, je sais parfaitement que la crise sera terminée lorsque les statistiques du chômage diminueront. Il faudra rembourser nos dettes, réduire notre déficit et notre endettement. *Mais comment peut-on le faire? On peut le faire*

> en investissant dans des dépenses d'avenir qui produiront plus de croissance et des revenus pour demain.
>
> (Sarkozy, 2009, December 1)
>
> [Finally, I know perfectly well that the crisis will come to an end when unemployment rates decrease. We will have to reimburse our debt, reduce our deficit and debt. *But how can we do it? We can do it* by investing in the spending of the future that will produce more growth and revenues for tomorrow. (author's translation)]

The clarity of Sarkozy's texts is also determined, as shown in the examples, by the speaker's recourse to the *topos of moral duty towards posterity*, shaping an extremely simple discourse regarding the deficit, as Sarkozy merely claims that investment will benefit future generations. Furthermore, comprehension of Sarkozy's argumentation regarding the deficit is also favored by the fact that the former President clarifies that there is a *bon déficit* ('good deficit') and a *mauvais déficit* ('bad deficit'). Basically, Sarkozy's plan to reduce the deficit is not different from Cameron's: cutting spending and investing in private-sector growth. However, less emphasis is laid on spending cuts, likely to be perceived as unpopular by a considerable portion of the national audience. In this respect, however clear, Sarkozy's discourse is not *Micawberian*. Argumentation in favor of austerity is systematically accompanied by comprehensive and detailed proposals to solve the deficit predicament through investment; particularly, innovation is never addressed as a topic apart but always in relation to its being the key to deficit reduction. Several policies are included in the plan contributing to the enlargement of the 'good deficit.' The most recurrent of these include the reform regarding the *crédit impôt-recherche*, systematically described by Sarkozy as the world's most favorable fiscal system for innovation (*le système fiscal [...] le plus favorable au monde pour l'innovation*). It is a tax cut on companies on the basis of their commitment to Research and Development programmes, which had been tripled by Nicolas Sarkozy.

> L'économie de la connaissance, c'est pour cela que nous avons fait le triplement du *crédit impôt-recherche*.
>
> (Sarkozy, 2009, December 1)
>
> [Growth economy, this is why we have tripled the *crédit impôt-recherche*. (author's translation)]

> Il était donc urgent de rétablir la compétitivité de nos entreprises. C'est la raison pour laquelle nous avons triplé le *crédit impôt-recherche* qui est aujourd'hui le dispositif de ce type le plus puissant dans le monde.
>
> (Sarkozy, 2010, January 6)
>
> [Restoring the competitiveness of our companies was urgent. This is why we have tripled the *crédit impôt-recherche*, the most powerful package in the world today. (author's translation)]

Another crucial measure implemented by Sarkozy's government is the reform or, rather, the abolition of the *business tax* with a view to spurring innovation.

> La France ne s'en sortira pas en investissant moins mais en investissant plus. C'est la raison pour laquelle désormais de nouveaux investissements seront exonérés de la *taxe professionnelle* qui les pénalise.
>
> (Sarkozy, 2008, September 25)
>
> [France will not overcome the crisis by investing less but by investing more. This is why new investments will now be exempted from the detrimental *business tax*. (author's translation)]

Additional measures recurrently addressed by the speaker include the support to the automobile industry, the imperative of tackling outsourcing, the need to implement a pension reform, and the creation of a *sécurité sociale professionelle* ('professional social security'), entailing the enhancement of both vocational training and unemployment benefits. Social security is also frequently dealt with by the former French President, as it has led to debt accumulation.

> Nous allons mettre en place [...] la commission réunissant le gouvernement et le Parlement pour trouver des solutions pour rembourser *la dette exceptionnelle que la sécurité sociale a accumulée pendant la crise*.
>
> (Sarkozy, 2010, January 28)
>
> [We are going to set up the commission gathering the government and the Parliament to find solutions to reimburse *the exceptional debt that the social security has accumulated during the crisis*. (author's translation)]

Broadly, Sarkozy's discourse regarding deficit reduction appears to be more 'complete' and exhaustive than Cameron's. Both macroeconomic and microeconomic issues are systematically addressed (Mayaffre, 2012, p. 47) and argumentation in favor of the adoption of austerity measures is actually replaced by a discourse whereby the deficit crisis is rebranded as an opportunity to reform, invest and nurture the 'good deficit.' However simple they might appear, Sarkozy's didactic speeches are systematically strewn with references to specific government policies, which contribute to shaping the speaker's recurrent argument for austerity.

Premise 1: The solution of the deficit crisis cannot but rely on spending cuts.
Premise 2: However, there is a 'bad deficit,' determined by public spending, and a 'good deficit,' determined by investment in research, education, innovation, and enterprise.
Premise 3: They both entail spending, but spending for the 'good deficit' will be repaid in terms of productivity and quality, thereby increasing incomes, spurring growth and benefiting posterity.

Conclusion: This is why the government is investing in research, promoting vocational training, cutting business taxes, opposing outsourcing, and reforming the social security.

This argument scheme shows that a variety of political measures are said to contribute to the main objective of deficit reduction. Among them, the *crédit impôt-recherche*, the repeal of the business tax, and the pension reform deserve particular attention not only for their recurrence but also because they are typical of several among Sarkozy's political proposals, focusing on the revision of recent, ill-judged policies implemented by governments of the left rather than on genuinely new and innovative measures. This is what Mayaffre (2012, p. 97) has labelled the *révolution conservatrice* ('conservative revolution') of Nicolas Sarkozy; this strategy pursues the main aim of political communication, i.e., gathering consensus to the detriment of political opponents, and incidentally results in a plethora of nouns and verbs with the prefix *re-* (Mayaffre, 2012, p. 147), such as *restaurer* ('restore'), *refonder* ('rebuild'), and *rehabilitation* ('restoration', 'rehabilitation').

Hollande

Despite criticism levelled by linguists and journalists at Hollande's 'sarkozysation' (Mayaffre, 2014), the speeches of the two former Presidents of the French Republic appear to be significantly different as far as argumentation is concerned. First of all, the values and ideology observed in Sarkozy's speeches give way under Hollande to a discourse governed by arguments more typical of the left, such as the *argument for the Social Conference*, whereby Hollande hopes for the active and constant cooperation between all the actors of the economy (businesses and social partners), in order to bring about a lasting solution to the crisis. One feature shared by Sarkozy and Hollande, however, lies in the expert nature of their speeches, as the topic of the deficit crisis also prompts Hollande to produce an 'accounting discourse' (Mayaffre, 2012, p. 53). Yet, whereas Sarkozy's argumentation is primarily guided by the speaker's attempt to flaunt his expertise in discussing macroeconomic problems in simple terms (Mayaffre, 2012, p. 47), Hollande's texts see a shift to increased lexical specificity in dealing, especially, with the deficit crisis:

> Nous avons perdu des parts de marché, notre *déficit commercial* dépasse 70 milliards d'euros, quand les Allemands en dégagent 150 milliards- oui, mais d'excédent.
>
> (Hollande, 2012, June 12)
>
> [We have lost market shares, our *trade deficit* exceeds 70 billion euros, while Germany is seeing a 150 billion surplus. (author's translation)]

> Le *déficit structurel* s'élève aujourd'hui à 4% du PIB, contre 3,2% en moyenne dans la zone euro et 0,8 en Allemagne, voilà la situation. [...]

> Nous sommes donc confrontés à un impératif de *rééquilibrage des comptes publics*. Je confirme, ici l'engagement pris par la France de ramener le déficit public à 3% à la fin de l'année 2013. Ce sera l'effort budgétaire le plus important depuis 30 ans.
>
> (Hollande, 2012, September 7)
>
> [The *structural deficit* has raised to 4% of the GDP, against the average 3,2% in the eurozone and 0,8% in Germany. Here is the situation. [...] Therefore, we are confronted with the imperative to *rebalance public spending*. I confirm the commitment made by France to take public spending back to 3% by the end of 2013. This is will be the most important budget effort in 30 years. (author's translation)]

The above examples testify to Hollande's habit of displaying a certain expertise in dealing with austerity. Of all *ARGO* speeches, his texts are those in which occurrences of 'structural deficit' (*déficit structurel*), 'trade deficit' (*déficit commercial*) and 'trade surplus' (*excédent commercial*) are more frequently observed. The examples above also show that Hollande's discourse is characterized by enhanced emphasis on bookkeeping, signalled by the considerable presence of numbers, which significantly contribute to bestowing credibility on the President's discourse. The imperative of *rebalancing* the economy is reiterated and is, thus, a feature that Hollande's speeches share with Cameron's. Moreover, comparison with the economic situation in Germany permeates the former French President's addresses, thereby contributing to shaping the argument scheme upon which his argument for austerity rests:

Premise 1: As regards the deficit crisis, Germany is the benchmark for analysing the situation in France.
Premise 2: In approximately ten years, our public deficit predicament has worsened. Though there are signs of recovery, we are lagging behind Germany.
Premise 3: Our structural deficit is too high, especially compared to Germany's.
Premise 4: Ten years ago the balance of trade was positive (trade surplus), but today our trade deficit is substantial, especially compared to Germany's.
Premise 5: The public debt has also increased dramatically over the last ten years.
Premise 6: Like the economic crisis, the deficit and debt crises are not over and will last long.
Conclusion: This is why we have to take steps to cut the deficit comprehensively: we must reduce public spending to solve the debt crisis and reduce the structural deficit, and we must boost growth and increase exports to bring the balance of trade back to equilibrium.

The reconstruction of Hollande's argument for austerity shows that the 'constellation of propositions' (van Eemeren et al., 1996, p. 5) put forward by the speaker in question is more substantial than that expressed or presupposed by the others. In this sense, it also attests the relativity of argumentation and the relatively complex nature of the argument at issue. As regards the more specialist nature of Hollande's texts, a few remarks are in order to put the analysis in perspective. First, no references to structural deficits can be found in Sarkozy's texts, one occurrence of *structural deficit* and one of *structural gap* are observed in the American sub-corpus, while this sub-topic is only occasionally addressed in Cameron's speeches, which indicates that it is generally considered too specialist for the heterogeneous audience of political addresses. Second, along with Hollande, Cameron is the only speaker who sometimes uses the terms *trade deficit* and *trade surplus*, but this does not mean that they are the only ones dealing with the major issue of a nation's balance of trade during the period of crisis. Sarkozy insists on the need to tackle outsourcing in order to preserve French productivity and production quality, thereby increasing the chances for exporting. Similarly, Obama recurrently deals with the balance of trade without actually naming it; he does so by dealing with outsourcing and insourcing and, also, by calling for products *made in America*. In other words, in Sarkozy's and Obama's speeches, commitment to the reduction of the trade deficit is implied in claims in favor of insourcing innovative jobs, which shows the relevance of focusing on *presentational devices*, in Pragma-dialectical terms. The fact that, at least regarding the trade deficit, Hollande and Cameron are more lexically meticulous than Obama, and Sarkozy further corroborates a tenet of argumentation theory, i.e., the usage-dependent and context-dependent relativity of all acts of arguing (van Eemeren & Grootendorst, 1992, p. 57). In simple terms, though passages drawn from the different sub-corpora deal with exactly the same sub-topic, this does not mean that they 'sound' the same way or that they are similarly perceived by audiences.

Conclusions

The analysis of argumentation for austerity in the *ARGO* corpus shows that, despite the actual complexity of the crisis and its various implications in several domains of social and political life, political communication does not refrain from resorting to simple and occasionally *Micawberian* arguments to legitimize austerity measures. In fact, these arguments appear to play an instrumental role in presenting the silver lining of the predicament by 'replacing' possible references to unpopular tax increases or severe spending cuts with themes pertaining to the more positive semantic fields of research, education, innovation and, in general, reform. The recurrence of the idiomatic expression *to tighten one's belt* in relation to ordinary families in the American and British sub-corpora further indicates the politicians' habit to resort to simple and evocative language to express solidarity with the numerous middle-class voters, hit by a crisis for which they cannot be blamed. There are no occurrences of the equivalent French expression *se serrer la ceinture* in the French sub-corpus, but (in line with the *strategic maneuvring* theory) Sarkozy and Hollande do adapt argumentation to the middle-class audience by blaming bankers and speculators, and flaunting the protection of taxpayers' money. In this respect, references to *families*, their *savings*, *sacrifice* and *resilience* run through the whole corpus.

Ordinary, middle-class voters are the emblem of thrift and economic wisdom, and institutions must follow their example to regain lost credibility.

As regards the inescapable topic of political responsibility in the lead-up to the deficit crisis, it is generally simplified and the guilt ascribed to fictional enemies, previous governments and/or opposition parties. In so doing, the speakers manage to preserve their public positive faces (PPFs) and avoid direct face-threatening acts against other politicians, while simultaneously threatening their opponents' PPFs (Gruber, 1993, pp. 3–4).

More broadly, although the analyzed speeches share the same topic, the arguments put forward by Obama, Cameron, Sarkozy and Hollande rest on very different premises and are verbalized by means of different presentational devices. In line with the theory of *strategic maneuvering*, the arguments for austerity identified in *ARGO* appear to be determined by the speakers' thematic and stylistic choices, adapted to audience demands and influenced by cultural and contextual constraints. In simpler words, although argumentation is topic-related, austerity arguments have heterogeneous implementations; therefore, they contribute to shaping a complex discourse, which calls for further analyses to examine the argumentative practices of justification adopted by politicians in times of crisis.

Notes

1 The excerpt is drawn from the *CNN* website (http://edition.cnn.com/). The complete transcript was retrieved from http://edition.cnn.com/2008/POLITICS/10/07/presidential.debate.transcript/

2 The word derives from the Ancient Greek compound term οἰκονομία, composed of οἶκος ('house') and νόμος ('law'), from νέμω ('to distribute,' 'to share,' 'to allocate,' 'to assign'). *Online Etymology Dictionary*, www.etymonline.com/index.php?term=economy

3 In *pragmatic* or *instrumental* argumentation, the (un)desirability of a particular action is justified by referring to the (un)desirability of the consequences. Pragmatic arguments are, thus, based on a causal relation (Garssen, 2001, p. 92) and their linguistic implementations often rely on relatively few lexical items.

4 "The Community Reinvestment Act is intended to encourage depository institutions to help meet the credit needs of the communities in which they operate, including low- and moderate-income neighborhoods, consistent with safe and sound operations. It was enacted by the Congress in 1977 (12 USC 2901) and is implemented by Regulation BB (12 CFR 228). The regulation was substantially revised in May 1995 and updated again in August 2005." *Board of Governors of the Federal Reserve System*, Retrieved from www.federalreserve.gov/communitydev/cra_about.htm

5 *Corpus-based* investigations use corpora as sources of examples, to check research intuition or to examine the frequency and/or plausibility of the language contained within a smaller data set. *Corpus-driven* analyses proceed in a more inductive way—the corpus itself is the data and the patterns in it are noted as a way of expressing regularities and exceptions in language (Baker, 2006, p. 16).

6 Argumentation is composed of at least three basic functional elements, namely "argument, conclusion rule, claim" (Reisigl, 2014, p. 72). These central elements

of argumentation have different denominations in different argumentation theories (Crevatin, 1998, p. xv); for instance, while Reisigl (2014) and Kienpointner (2005) opt for the term *claim*, Pragma-dialecticians prefer to use *standpoint*. In adopting *standpoint*, Pragma-dialecticians acknowledge its manifold synonyms: "Other virtual synonyms of the term *standpoint*, used by various authors, are *view*, *viewpoint*, *point of view*, *claim*, *thesis*, etc." (van Eemeren et al., 1996, p. 2).

7 "*Topoi* [singular: topos] can be described as parts of argumentation which belong to the required premises. They [...] connect the argument(s) with the conclusion, the claim" (Reisigl & Wodak, 2009, p. 110).

8 Kennedy's speech, entitled "Remarks at the Convocation of the United Negro College Fund" and delivered on April 12, 1959, was retrieved from *John F. Kennedy—Presidential Library and Museum* www.jfklibrary.org/Research/Research-Aids/JFK-Speeches/Indianapolis-IN_19590412.aspx

9 However vague and unspecific, the term *middle class* is recurrently employed in the American sub-corpus of *ARGO* and is, thus, also used to describe Obama's argumentation patterns.

10 The argumentative strategy in question consists in "*twisting somebody's words*, [...] presenting a distorted picture of the antagonist's standpoint in order to be able to refute [it] more easily and to make it less tenable" (Reisigl & Wodak, 2001, p. 73).

References

Baker, P. (2006). *Using corpora in Discourse Analysis*. London: Continuum.

Bendazzoli, C., & Sandrelli, A. (2009). Corpus-based interpreting studies: Early work and future prospects. *Revista Tradumàtica,* 7. Retrieved from: webs2002.uab.es/tradumatica/revista/num7/articles/08/08art.htm

Biber, D., Conrad, S., & Reppen, R. (1998). *Corpus linguistics: Investigating language structure and use*. Cambridge, UK: Cambridge University Press.

Brambilla, E. (2015). Argumentative equivalence as the reproduction of strategic maneuvering in interpreted texts. *Journal of Argumentation in Context*, *4*(3), 299–316.

Cameron, D. (2010, June 7). Prime Minister's speech on the economy. [speech] Retrieved from www.gov.uk/government/speeches/prime-ministers-speech-on-the-economy

Cameron, D. (2010, November 12). Speech: PM press conference at G20. [speech] Retrieved from www.gov.uk/government/speeches/pm-press-conference-at-g20

Cameron, D. (2011). Speech to World Economic Forum Annual Meeting. *New Statesman* [news magazine]. Retrieved from www.newstatesman.com/economy/2011/01/europe-world-growth-values

Cameron, D. (2012, June 18). Prime Minister's speech at Mexico G20. [speech] Retrieved from www.gov.uk/government/speeches/prime-ministers-speech-at-mexico-g20

Cameron, D. (2012, November 19). [speech] Retrieved from www.gov.uk/government/speeches/prime-ministers-speech-to-cbi

Cameron, D. (2013, November 11). Lord Mayor's Banquet 2013: Prime Minister's speech. Retrieved from www.gov.uk/government/speeches/lord-mayors-banquet-2013-prime-ministers-speech

Crevatin, F. (1998). Prefazione. In C. Marzocchi (Ed.), *Interpretare il discorso argomentativo: Teoria, aspetti e problemi* (pp. vii–xvii). Trieste: Scuola superiore di lingue moderne per interpreti e traduttori.

Deflem, M. (2011). Introduction: Criminological perspectives on the crisis. In M. Deflem (Ed.), *Economic crisis and crime* (pp. ix–xii). Bingley: Emerald Publishing.

De Landtsheer, C. (2007). Crisis style or radical rhetoric? The speech by Dyab Abou Jahjah, leader of the Arab European League. In C. Hart & D. Lukeš (Eds.), *Cognitive linguistics in Critical Discourse Analysis* (pp. 57–80). Newcastle, UK: Cambridge Scholars Publishing.

Fairclough, I., & Fairclough, N. (2012). *Political Discourse Analysis. A method for advanced students*. London/New York: Routledge.

Garssen, B. (1999). The nature of symptomatic argumentation. In F. H. van Eemeren, R. Grootendorst, J. A. Blair, & C. A. Willard (Eds.), *Proceedings of the Fourth International Conference of the International Society for the Study of Argumentation* (pp. 225–227). Amsterdam, Netherlands: SICSAT.

Garssen, B. (2001). Argument schemes. In F. H. van Eemeren (Ed.), *Crucial concepts in Argumentation Theory* (pp. 81–99). Amsterdam, Netherlands: Amsterdam University Press.

Gruber, H. (1993). Political language and textual vagueness. *Pragmatics, 3*(1), 1–28.

Hechtkopf, K. (2009, December 8). Text: Obama's speech on jobs. *CBS* [news portal] Retrieved from www.cbsnews.com/news/text-obamas-speech-on-jobs

Hollande, F. (2012, June 12). Déclaration de M. François Hollande, Président de la République, sur le rôle du Conseil économique, social et environnemental et sur les défis et priorités de son quinquennat, à Paris le 12 juin 2012. Retrieved from http://discours.vie-publique.fr/notices/127001131.html

Hollande, F. (2012, September 7). Déclaration de M. François Hollande, Président de la République, sur l'état des finances publiques, le rétablissement de l'équilibre budgétaire et sur le rôle de la Cour des Comptes, à Paris le 7 septembre 2012. Retrieved from http://discours.vie-publique.fr/notices/127001634.html

Kienpointner, M. (2005). Racist manipulation within Austrian, German, Dutch, French and Italian right-wing populism. In L. de Saussure & P. Schulz (Eds.), *Manipulation and ideologies in the twentieth century* (pp. 213–235). Amsterdam, Netherlands/Philadelphia: John Benjamins.

Lean, M. L., Mohd Don, Z., & Fernandez, P. R. (2013). Polarization in the media representation of terrorism crises: Transitivity and lexical choices in Malaysia's leading English dailies. In A. De Rycker & Z. Mohd Don (Eds.), *Discourse and crisis: Critical perspective.* (pp. 435–461). Amsterdam, Netherlands/Philadelphia: John Benjamins.

Levin, B., & Hovav, M. R. (1995). *Unaccusativity: At the syntax-lexical semantics interface.* Cambridge. MA: MIT Press.

Mayaffre, D. (2012). *Nicolas Sarkozy: Mesure et démesure du discours (2007–2012).* Paris: SciencesPo. Les Presses.

Mayaffre, D. (2014, January 13). Hollande se sarkozyse. *Interview for Nice-Matin.* Retrieved from http://archives.nicematin.com/societe/damon-mayaffre-hollande-se-sarkozyse.1583056.html

Mazzi, D. (2011). 'Palmerston bustles around with the foreign policy of this powerful nation, like a furious and old drunkard…': On the discursive formulation of argument by analogy in history. In F. H. van Eemeren, B. Garssen, D. Godden, & G. Mitchell (Eds.), *Proceedings of the Seventh International Conference for the Study of Argumentation* (pp. 1221–1233). Amsterdam, Netherlands: SICSAT.

Means, A. (2010). Securing the corporate state: Education, economism, and crisis in the Age of Obama. In K. J. Saltman & D. A. Gabbard (Eds.), *Education as enforcement: The militarization and corporatization of schools* (2nd ed., pp. 261–273). London/New York: Routledge.

Nguyen, T. H., & Pontell, H. N. (2011). Fraud and inequality in the subprime mortgage crisis. In M. Deflem (Ed.), *Economic crisis and crime* (pp. 3–24). Bingley: Emerald Publishing.
Obama, B. (2009, February 24). Obama speech to Congress focuses on economy. *CNN* [news portal]. Retrieved from http://edition.cnn.com/2009/POLITICS/02/24/sotn.obama.transcript
Obama, B. (2010, January 27). Text: Obama's State of the Union Address. *The New York Times* [online newspaper] Retrieved from www.nytimes.com/2010/01/28/us/politics/28obama.text.html
Obama, B. (2011, January 25). Transcript: Obama's State of the Union Address. *NPR* [news portal]. Retrieved from www.npr.org/2011/01/26/133224933/transcript-obamas-state-of-union-address
Partridge, E. (1978). *A dictionary of clichés* (5th ed.). London/New York: Routledge.
Perelman, C., & Olbrechts-Tyteca, L. (2008). *Traité de l'argumentation: La nouvelle rhétorique.* (6ème édition). Bruxelles: Éditions de l'Université de Bruxelles.
Prabhakar, A. C. (2017). *The current global recession: A theoretical and empirical investigation into developed and BRICS economies.* Bingley: Emerald.
Prime Minister's Office (2010, October 25). Creating a 'new economic dynamism.' Retrieved from www.gov.uk/government/news/creating-a-new-economic-dynamism
Reisigl, M. (2010). Rhetoric of political speeches. In R. Wodak & V. Koller (Eds.), *Handbook of communication in the public sphere* (pp. 243–269). Berlin/New York: de Gruyter Mouton.
Reisigl, M. (2014). Argumentation analysis and the Discourse-Historical Approach: A methodological framework. In C. Hart & P. Cap (Eds.), *Contemporary Critical Discourse Studies* (pp. 67–96). London/New York: Bloomsbury.
Reisigl, M., & Wodak, R. (2001). *Discourse and discrimination: Rhetorics of racism and anti-semitism.* London/New York: Routledge.
Reisigl, M., & Wodak, R. (2009). The discourse-historical approach (DHA). In R. Wodak & M. Meyer (Eds.), *Methods of Critical Discourse Analysis* (pp. 87–121). London: SAGE Publications.
Sandaran, S. C., & De Rycker, A. (2013). The political use of a national crisis: Bush's legitimation of the USA Freedom Corps in the wake of September 11. In A. De Rycker & Z. Mohd Don (Eds.), *Discourse and crisis: Critical perspectives* (pp. 187–214). Amsterdam, Netherlands/Philadelphia: John Benjamins.
Sarkozy, N. (2008, September 25). Le discours de Nicolas Sarkozy à Toulon. *Le Monde* [online newspaper]. Retrieved from www.lemonde.fr/politique/article/2008/09/25/le-discours-de-nicolas-sarkozy-a-toulon_1099795_823448.html
Sarkozy, N. (2008, November 4). Déclaration de M. Nicolas Sarkozy, Président de la République, sur le plan de relance de l'économie française, à Douai le 4 décembre 2008. *viepublique.fr* [news portal] Retrieved from http://discours.vie-publique.fr/notices/087003839.html
Sarkozy, N. (2009, December 1). Déclaration de M. Nicolas Sarkozy, Président de la République, sur la politique menée face à la crise économique et financière, à Toulon le 1er décembre 2009. *viepublique.fr* [news portal] Retrieved from http://discours.vie-publique.fr/notices/097003488.html
Sarkozy, N. (2010, January 6). Déclaration de M. Nicolas Sarkozy, Président de la République, sur la politique mise en oeuvre face à la crise et sur les réformes engagées en 2009, à Cholet le 6 janvier 2010. *viepublique.fr* [news portal] Retrieved from http://discours.vie-publique.fr/notices/107000030.html

Sarkozy, N. (2010, January 28). Déclaration de M. Nicolas Sarkozy, Président de la République, sur les politiques à mettre en oeuvre pour rétablir les finances publiques, à Paris le 28 janvier 2010. *viepublique.fr* [news portal] Retrieved from http://discours.vie-publique.fr/notices/107000263.html

Schechter, D. (2010). *The crime of our time: Why Wall Street is not too big to jail.* New York: The Disinformation Company.

Snelling, D. (2009). The interpreter's general knowledge. *The Interpreters' Newsletter, 14*, 91–98.

van Dijk, T. A. (2005). War rhetoric of a little ally: Political implicatures and Aznar's legitimization of the war in Iraq. *Journal of Language and Politics, 4*(1), 65–92.

van Eemeren, F. H. (2010). *Strategic maneuvering in argumentative discourse*. Amsterdam. Netherlands/Philadelphia: John Benjamins.

van Eemeren, F. H., & Grootendorst, R. (1992). *Argumentation, communication and fallacies: A Pragma-Dialectical perspective.* Mahwah, NJ: Lawrence Erlbaum Associates.

van Eemeren, F. H., Grootendorst, R., Snoeck Henkemans, F., Blair, J. A., Johnson, R. H., Krabbe, E. C. W., … Zarefsky, D. (Eds.). (1996). *Fundamentals of Argumentation Theory: A handbook of historical backgrounds and contemporary developments*. London/New York: Routledge.

Walton, D. (2013). *Methods of argumentation*. New York: Cambridge University Press.

Walton, D., Reed, C., & Macagno, F. (2008). *Argumentation schemes*. Cambridge. UK: Cambridge University Press.

Zarefsky, D. (1995). Argumentation in the tradition of speech communication studies. In F. H. van Eemeren, R. Grootendorst, J. A. Blair, & C. A. Willard (Eds.), *Perspectives and approaches. Proceedings of the Third International Conference on Argumentation:* (Vol. 1, pp. 32–49). Amsterdam, Netherlands: SICSAT.

Zarefsky, D. (2014). *Political argumentation in the United States*. Amsterdam, Netherlands/Philadelphia: John Benjamins.

Part VI

Responses to 'crisis'

In this final part, we examine public debate around austerity, viewed as a response to crisis, and we see two very different responses: the first reinforces a prevailing ideology; the second challenges the status quo.

In Chapter 14, Alina Bârgăoanu and Loredanu Radu analyze several official statements by former Romanian President Traian Băsescu and the then Governor of Romania's National Bank, each of which signals that country's embrace of austerity policies. In doing so, they point to the highly situated nature of austerity discourses. They explain, for example, that there was no substantive opposition to, or backlash against, the implementation of austerity measures in Romania between 2009 and 2011, because those measures had been successfully framed by Romanian political and economic elites as the common sense solution to financial crisis, within a pro-Europeanization narrative. Bârgăoanu and Radu also demonstrate that, although both sets of statements render crisis inevitable and austerity legitimate, each relies on variations on the dominant (non-systemic, moralistic) theme. Moreover, the pro-austerity discourse evident in these statements consolidated its primacy by tapping into several distinctively Romanian sensitivities (including an entrenched suspicion of State agents and the perceived desirability of EU membership).

In contrast, Piedad Fernández Toledo and Virginia Villaplana-Ruiz (Chapter 15) describe public opposition to Spanish austerity measures, within both the 15-M movement and political groups that emerged from it, as well as on social media. Their focus is on the satirical cartoons of Andrés Rábago (published in *El País* newspaper under the pseudonym 'El Roto'), which have played a prominent role in critiquing austerity in Spain. Like Bârgăoanu and Radu, Toledo and Villaplana-Ruiz illustrate the context-dependent nature of austerity discourses, in particular its diachronic variation in relation to key political events, and a recognizable alignment between specific discourses and communication channels.

As we have seen elsewhere in this book, these chapters model the application of two important discourse analytic approaches to the important issue of austerity—and we suggest that both approaches can be just as readily directed to other economic questions.

On the one hand, Bârgăoanu and Radu use narrative analysis to identify the key political and economic supports for Romania's austerity measures (we have also seen narrative analysis employed in Chapter 2). This approach proceeds on the understanding that narratives can have considerable explanatory and persuasive power, particularly when they correspond to lived experience, but that they are not always rational or accurate; nor are they necessarily recounted overtly, but may need to be reconstructed from discursive fragments. Nevertheless, it is possible to identify replicated patterns in how reality is discursively organized and, thus, endowed with meaning.

On the other hand, Toledo and Villaplana-Ruiz adopt a multimodal approach, considering both the written and visual elements of El Roto's cartoons. Multimodal discourse analysis (often referred to as MMDA) is a highly complex but particularly valuable way of analyzing contemporary meaning-making, given that so much of the communication we encounter relies not only on speech or writing, but also on image, design (e.g., colors, layout, font), music, sound, gesture, gaze, and so on—and each of these modes have their own affordances, or meaning-making possibilities. Within the field of economics, for example, tables, graphs and other diagrams can often be integral to meaning, and therefore invite close consideration.

14 The austerity discourse of the Romanian economic-political elites

Neoliberal or (pseudo)European?

Alina Bârgăoanu and Loredana Radu

The pursuit of austerity

In the context of the 2007–2008 crisis, Europe's economic-political elites grew obsessed with austerity (Stigltiz 2016, as cited in Hackwell, 2016). 'Austerity' became the new buzzword, a legitimate ideology, and a panacea to cure the effects of the turmoil. José Manuel Barroso—the then President of the European Commission—publicly defended Europe's move towards austerity, by stating that "without addressing this issue [of austerity], there will be no confidence, and without confidence, no growth" (as cited in Erlanger & Castlejune, 2010, p. 1). In the same vein, Jean-Claude Trichet—the then President of the European Central Bank—declared: "The idea that austerity could trigger stagnation is incorrect, because confidence-inspiring policies will foster and not hamper economic recovery" (as cited in Clarke & Newman, 2012, p. 301). A sort of 'magical thinking' flourished, centered on the 'alchemy of austerity,' which "might turn disaster into triumph—the triumph being a new neo-liberal settlement" (Clarke & Newman, 2012, p. 302).

This chapter seeks to shed light on the distorting mechanisms underlying austerity discourses, with a view to adding to the intriguing question as to why capitalism in general, or its contemporary manifestation known as neoliberalism, have been left untouched by the economic and political turmoil brought about by the Great Recession (see Paul Krugman's influential characterization of the austerity measures and the ensuing "structural reforms" as "a strange triumph of failed ideas" in 2010, and Colin Crouch's flagship book *The Strange Non-Death of Neoliberalism*, published 2011). We will contribute to this debate by looking at Romania, an austerity champion alongside Estonia, Bulgaria, Latvia, and Lithuania, the group of Eastern European Countries that Mark Blyth (2013) calls the "REBLL Alliance" (p. 1). We will support our claims by means of qualitative research, which consists of narrative analysis of public statements made by the economic-political elites in Romania when the austerity measures were decided, publicly announced and implemented (2009–2011).

In 2010, the Romanian government implemented a set of harsh austerity measures, which would have made one expect the emergence of a strong anti-austerity discourse and an equally strong anti-austerity political movement.

That did not materialize and, in this context, this chapter claims that the pro-austerity discourse in Romania manufactured the appearance of common sense by promoting some very simple narratives, such as the pro-Europeanization narrative. This simplification, coupled with the device of exceptionalizing the subjects of the austerity measures ('the people,' 'the political class'), has been powerful in blocking ideological interrogations having to do with broader topics such as: solidarity, inequality, poverty, polarization, progressive taxation, the welfare state, disenfranchisement of citizens, financialization of societies, center/periphery relations in the EU, and the exclusion and marginality of a country such as Romania both from and within the EU.

Austerity is such a seductive idea (Blyth, 2013) because it entertains this strong link with common sense: when one lives beyond one's means and debt piles up, it makes sense to cut spending. This commonsensical approach is strengthened by references to intellectual or moral failures: one ended up in over-indebtedness because one did not properly judge the consequences of one's economic actions (intellectual failure) or because one was greedy, lazy, profligate (moral failure). These failures (especially the latter) provide a strong opposition to highly-esteemed intellectual and moral traits: thrift, discipline, rigor, calculation, strain, and delayed gratification.

However, the concept of austerity, at least the way in which it has been understood and applied in a European context, can be questioned at several levels. First, the problem with these easy-to-understand references to personal life is exactly this: personal life is hardly a proxy for the economic life, especially in an interdependent world, involving interdependence between economies, continents, markets, debtors and creditors, and private and public institutions. Second, this problem is compounded by the fact that austerity, just like anything else, is context-dependent: what could make sense during one business cycle of capitalist economies could prove utterly disastrous during another. So, avoiding procyclical austerity policies should be a mantra of crisis economists. Third, in order to prove its viability as a solution, austerity should address a properly-identified problem. Debt is definitely a problem of our neoliberal capitalist societies. But whose debt are we talking about, and how have the states, economies, and citizens ended up with so much debt in the first place? The crisis that started in 2008—and whose effects are still deeply felt—created at least that consensus: it was a "failure of the operation of the private financial institutions, and led to a huge demand for reinstating some of the state regulations, particularly of the financial markets" (Sen, 2015). How a crisis originating in the failure of private institutions came to be seen as people and states 'living beyond their means,' with austerity as the natural answer or 'cure,' is still a fascinating question.

It is difficult to talk about a unified pro-austerity camp in the scholarly literature. In fact, with few exceptions (Alesina & Ardagna, 2009; Biggs, Hassett, & Jensen, 2010; possibly Reinhardt & Rogoff, 2014; Niall Ferguson, 2015), the pro-austerity camp is filled with policy-makers, politicians, and financial leaders, be they central bankers or heads of international financial institutions such as the International Monetary Fund (IMF). The opposite camp benefits from much more numerous ranks, among which Nobel-prize winners figure prominently: Joseph Stiglitz (2014) sees austerity as "an utter and unmitigated disaster," Amartya Sen (2015) compares it to "rat poison," while Paul Krugman (2015) talks about "the austerity delusion." Mark Blyth (2013) considers austerity a "dangerous, but seductive idea" (p. 2), an "ideology immune to facts and basic empirical refutation" (p. 226). Even Carmen Reinhart and Kenneth Rogoff (2014), associated with pro-austerity thinking as a result of their work on the famous 90% threshold, over which debt arguably becomes unsustainable, came up with more nuanced positions, underlining that "output remains well below its pre-crisis peak in ten of the twelve crisis countries. The gap with potential output is even greater" (pp. 10–11).

Not all policy-makers, no matter how close they may have been at some point to austerity- or neoliberalism-inspired measures, share the same view. Larry Summers (2012), the Secretary of the Treasury during the Clinton administration, underlined that austerity efforts are counterproductive to growth. Not to mention the second thoughts of the IMF, one of the institutions pertaining to the Troika and responsible for advocating the imposition of austerity measures on Greece, across the whole South of the Eurozone, and in Central and Eastern Europe: "we failed to realise the damage austerity would do to Greece [...] Market confidence was not restored, the banking system lost 30% of its deposits and the economy encountered a much deeper than expected recession with exceptionally high unemployment" (IMF Report 2013, as cited in Elliott, Inman, & Smith, 2013, p. 4). Interestingly, no such second thoughts were expressed in relation to the austerity imposed on Central Eastern European (CEE) states.

Substance and timeline of the austerity measures implemented in Romania

In late 2009 and predominantly in 2010, CEE (the so-called 'new member states') became the new bridgehead of the crisis, with the IMF economists labeling the problems of the European Union periphery as 'particularly acute' (IMF, 2011, p. xv). The public debate on debt loomed. While relevant for understanding the causes of the whole turmoil, the label 'debt' soon oversimplified what ought to have been a very complex, technical analysis. In Romania and other Eastern European countries, perhaps the most relevant oversimplification stemmed from the fact that many spoke about public and private debt indiscriminately. Through an intensive ideological rewriting, the financial crisis was transformed into a fiscal crisis centered on government debt (Clarke & Newman, 2012).

It is difficult to agree on a zero point in the recent history of Romania which could be relevant for our inquiry into austerity discourse. In the 2000s, Romania, along other CEE states, was dubbed the "Central European tigers" (Kalan & Durlik, 2015, p. 8). After 2000, it entered a path of steady economic growth as measured by the GDP (5.7% in 2001, 5.1% 2002, 5.2% 2003, and 8.5% 2004). It became a member of the EU, a laggard, together with Bulgaria, in the process of eastward enlargement that started in 2004. Between 2004 and 2008, the country experienced an average annual increase in GDP of 6.8%; most of that growth was generated either by investment in non-marketable sectors (for example, construction) or by consumption of durable goods, mostly imported (Stoiciu, 2012). Throughout that period, Romania also experienced an increase in its current account deficit, which peaked at 13.6% of the GDP in 2007. Indebtedness in the private sector also grew because of the loans incurred in order to finance consumption and investments. From the end of 2008 until 2011, public debt increased by 150% of the GDP, from 13.4% to 33.3% (Stoiciu, 2012, p. 2).

The growth model on which Romania developed during those years, is characterized by Mark Blyth (2013) in the following terms: "a unique growth model based on massive foreign investment, even more massive foreign borrowing, and economic institutions that could only be described as open to money coming in and people going out" (p. 218). The characteristics of this unique growth model were "its high degree of dependence on transnational capital flows, its tendency to develop large account deficits and its chronically weak export performance" (Blyth, 2013, p. 218). In 2009, 73% to 95% of the direct foreign investments in CEE were done by countries in the Euro area (Isărescu, 2009, p. 14). Investors in the Euro area owned most of the bank assets in the CEE, which made the latter extremely vulnerable to financial shocks (Onaran, 2011).

So, between 2004 and 2008, there was GDP growth in the CEE, but with massive foreign investment, massive borrowing, and foreign ownership of the banking sector, consumption, expanding credit, and a housing bubble. Notably, however, we can hardly speak about skyrocketing governmental debt between 2006 and 2008 in Romania. As Figure 14.1 below indicates, the country was

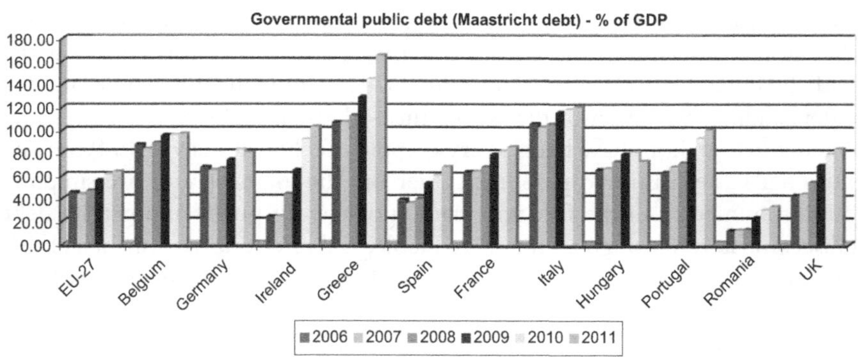

Figure 14.1 Public debit in Romania and in other Member States, as well as in EU-27
Source: Eurostat, own calculations

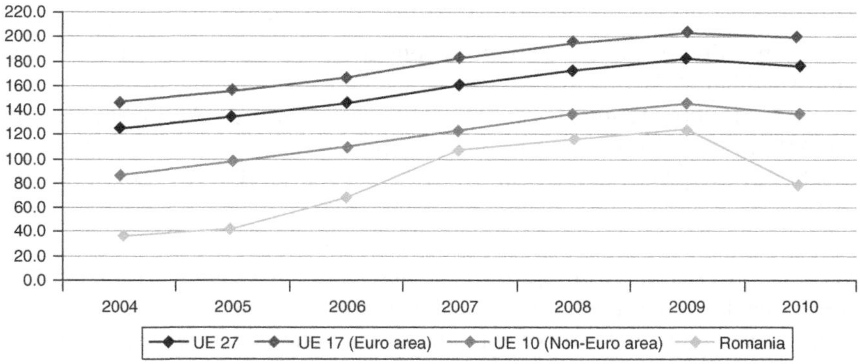

Figure 14.2 Evolution of the private debt in EU-27, EU-17, EU-10, and Romania between 2006 and 2010 (% of GDP)

Source: Eurostat, own calculations

one of the EU member states with a rather modest governmental debt (a point to which we will come back in the end of this section).

What happened afterwards? The 2009 "credit crunch" or "the sharp drop in private capital inflows," as Dominique Strauss-Kahn, the then IMF managing director, called it (as cited in Evans-Pritchard, 2009, p. 9), deprived Romania of its most important capital source: if in 2009 the ratio of the private credit to GDP was 123.3%, in 2010, it dropped to 77.7% (see Figure 14.2 below). This problem was compounded by the fact that the global economic crisis "led investors to sell the currencies of smaller countries in a flight to dollars, euros and the Japanese yen," creating a 'hole' in the country's finance (Jolly, 2009, pp. 6–8).

In the first eight months of 2009, as a result of the global turmoil and that in the Eurozone, the exports of Romania fell by 19.1% and imports by 36.6% respectively, compared to the same period in 2008. The housing bubble burst that same year. The exchange rate depreciated by more than 15% against the euro between October 2008 and May 2009. And the period between January and August 2009 saw a steep increase of the government bonds long-term interest rate, from 7% to 11.4%. Given the exposure of multinational banks in CEE states, towards the end of 2008, the Austrian government and the representatives of those multinational banks held informal discussions in Vienna known by the name of "the European Bank Coordination Initiative" (or "the Vienna Initiative"), which soon took the shape of agreements between the Western banks with exposure to CEE, the Troika (IMF, the European Commission and the European Central Bank), and Romania, Hungary and Latvia (De Haas, Korniyenko, Pivovarsky, & Loukoianova, 2012). According to Blyth (2013), the agreements committed Western European banks to keeping their funds in their Eastern European banks if these governments committed to austerity to stabilize local banks' balance sheets: "it was all about saving the banks, and the bill for doing so, in the form of austerity, high interest rates, unemployment and the rest, was dumped once again on the public sector balance sheet in the states concerned" (p. 221).

In March 2009, Romania signed a 24-month Stand-By Arrangement with the IMF for a total amount of EUR 12.95 billion. The total financing package, which also included money from the EU and the World Bank, amounted to EUR 19.95 billion. Most of the money from the IMF went to the National Bank, to help it strengthen its foreign currency reserves and defend the EUR/RON exchange rate, which was under pressure due to capital withdrawals by foreign banks and other international investors (www.romania-insider.com/romania-wraps-up-its-business-with-the-imf/). The financial package was agreed upon based on the commitment by the Romanian authorities to limit the budget deficit to 5.1% in 2009 and further to 3% in 2011. In order to meet this target, the financial package included some harsh austerity provisions, such as cutting wages in the public sector by 25% and reducing pensions by 5%.

There was no implementation of these austerity measures in 2009 due to the Presidential elections in December that year. In May 2010, the incumbent President, Traian Băsescu, announced the austerity measures to which the Romanian authorities had committed almost a year previously: wages of government employees were cut by 25%, social security benefits by 15%, VAT increased by 5% from 19% to 24%; 78,700 jobs were terminated (21% of the total jobs terminated in EU countries); out of the total jobs cut, 60,610 were government positions, making for 54.64% of the total government positions terminated in the entire EU (Stoiciu, 2012). Pensions were not cut due to the decision of the Constitutional Court, but they were frozen. However, the retirement age was elevated to 65 years in the case of men and to 60 years in the case of women; the Social Dialogue Code was passed, establishing new criteria for registering new unions and eliminating the national collective agreements. In 2011, 67 hospitals were shut down. The same year, there were changes in the legislation regarding the labor market; the New Labor Code was voted and privatization of major state companies started.

At the beginning of 2012, a draft bill to change the health care system, including the emergency system, was put up for public debate. This bill was heavily criticized in the public sphere by a charismatic, highly esteemed professional, doctor Raed Arafat, the architect of the emergency health care system in Romania. This criticism sparked massive protests between January and February 2012. A new government formed by social democrats, liberals and conservatives and headed by Victor Ponta came to power. Immediately after coming to power, the Ponta cabinet raised public employees' salaries by 25% and reached an agreement with the IMF for the privatizations of six state companies.

Between 2010 and 2011, Romania was subject to a complete set of austerity measures: wages cuts in both the public and the private sector; termination of jobs in both the public and the private sector (in 2009, the private sector was the first to experience layoffs, with 315,000 jobs terminated mainly in the construction and retail trade sectors); freezing of public pensions; tax increases, but only on regressive taxes (VAT); deregulation of social and labor rights; privatization of strategic state assets (energy and transport); cuts of social services; health spending cuts; hospital shutdowns; deregulation of the health sector and attempts at its privatization; and state downsizing. Not to mention the external devaluation (the depreciation of the exchange rate), which added to the internal devaluation created by means of austerity. In a nutshell, austerity measures—amongst the harshest in the entire EU—have accomplished in Romania exactly this: foreign capital and the government switching places as main debtor. The government debt, which, as we have already underlined, was at modest levels in 2007 compared both to the EU average and to other EU member states, experienced the opposite trend: from the smallest debtor in 2007 (16.43%) to the main debtor in 2013 (30.54%).

Austerity in the discourse of Romanian economic-political elites

The discursive construction of austerity

As discussed in the previous section, austerity has been first and foremost legitimated through discursive strategies. Highly specialized voices—such as those belonging to Noble-prize economists—made it clear that harsh austerity will only give a final blow to the last chances to stabilize markets, making recovery more lengthy, costly, and complicated (Stiglitz, 2012 ; Krugman, 2008). However, not only did European leaders undertake intensive efforts to convince everybody about the desirability and necessity of 'belt-tightening' measures, but they also postulated that austerity was the only way out of crisis. The 'alchemy of austerity' gave birth to the symbolic halo of the crisis, which shaped reality by injecting meaning and substance into facts and events.

Especially in critical contexts, the discursive construction of reality overshadows the relative objectivity of events, decisions, and actions. Uncorrelated data, competing explanations, overwhelming amounts of information, and the multitude of actors involved in any crisis create confusion. This is where stories or narratives intervene, as they help us cope with uncertainty (Godart & White, 2010) and give meaning to seemingly meaningless situations: "Narratives are analytic constructs that unify a number of past or contemporaneous actions and happenings [...] into a coherent relational whole" (Griffin, 1993, p. 1097), which creates consistency, identifying explanations and arguments for any given event. To Polkinghorne (1998), "a narrative is a meaning structure that organizes events and human actions into a whole" (p. 18). Narratives owe their importance to their capacity to "give external expression to assumed representations of individual, internal representations of phenomena—events, thoughts and feelings" (Squire, Andrews, & Tamboukou, 2013, p. 7). Narratives help scholars read between the lines of the social world (Somers, 1994; Andrews, 2007).

The discursive construction of reality eludes chronology or cause and effect flows. Narratives can be constructed in a rather irrational manner. Depending on the preferences of the discourse owner, the rationality or the cause and effect chain is pushed aside, giving place to ad-hoc associations and combinations of origins, causes, events, outcomes, and actors. Their logic and causality can be reinvented and twisted, depending on specific interests and social relations: "Stories are primarily relational rather than temporal, which means we need to link everyday narratives to social relations" (Seabrooke & Thomsen, 2016, p. 252). However, narratives are not constructed in a vacuum. People's predispositions, concerns, and vulnerabilities form the fertile 'soil' in which narratives are seeded: "The main source of legitimation is from telling a causal story that resonates with pre-existing experiences and values" (Stanley, 2014, p. 912). In the case of the recent crisis, austerity discourse has been anchored in the generalized panic of those who realized that they could no longer pay off their mortgage. But the locus of action suffered a subtle twist from the financial sector (i.e., banks) to fiscal overspending (i.e., public deficit), thus "reflecting wider societal experiences of perceived overspending and related feelings of guilt concerning pre-2008 excessive consumption and financialisation" (Stanley, 2014, p. 897).

How people make sense of the crisis has a stake in the rise and fall of political ideas and regimes. To Žižek (2009), the outcome of the crisis "depends on how it comes to be symbolized, on what ideological interpretation or story imposes itself and determines the general perception of the crisis" (p. 18). Jessop (2002) believes that crises create the space for competing "strategic interventions to significantly redirect the course of events as well as for attempts to 'muddle through'" (pp. 6–7). Furthermore, which strategies prevail partly depends upon 'discursive struggles,' where different narratives of the causes and effects of the crisis, including economic and political scenarios for possible future states of affairs and systems collide (Jessop, 2002, pp. 92–94). "Getting people to accept a particular narrative of the crisis, to see it in a certain way, is generally a political concern precisely because it gives people a reason for favoring or accepting certain lines of action and policies rather than others" (Fairclough & Fairclough, 2012, p. 4). In a nutshell, the success of a certain type or category of narratives can give us important hints on the outcome of crisis in terms of prevailing ideology—whether, for example, market fundamentalism, populism of any kind, or a more aggressive form of neo-liberalism will prevail.

Understanding the way in which political-economic elites make sense of austerity is perhaps more important than the dynamics of the crisis itself because the entire 'itinerary' of the crisis has been markedly 'drawn' by (public) austerity-centered policies all over Europe. Since Romania was one of the 'champions of austerity' in Europe, we are interested to see how political-economic elites in Romania built their arguments about austerity, what was the substance of their discourse, and what were the main constitutive elements of their discursive strategies.

Research objectives and methodology

The goal of our research is two-fold. First, we seek to uncover the key narratives of the (pro)austerity discourse, as employed by the promoters of the belt-tightening measures. Second, we aim to understand whether and how the (pro) austerity discourse has been linked to, or even derived from, a pro-European positioning of the relevant actors.

Our analysis builds on the typology of the crisis narratives as proposed by Isabela Fairclough and Norman Fairclough (2012, pp. 6–7), who argue that there are four main narratives explaining the global economic crisis starting in 2007: two systemic and two non-systemic. Systemic variants have two main variants: "those who attribute the crisis to the form of capitalism which has been dominant especially in the United States and Britain for the past 30 years or so—neo-liberalism; and those which attribute it to the nature of capitalism as such, not just a particular form of it" (pp. 6–7). Non-systemic accounts also have two main variants: those that attribute the origins and causes of the crisis to peripheral attributes of the economic system (rather than to the system as such), and those that attribute them to intellectual or moral failures of people. According to Fairclough and Fairclough, the first of these variants can be further divided into two types of account: 'market fundamentalism accounts,' which blame state attempts to regulate or control the market (too much regulation and interference of the State in economic life), and 'regulationist accounts,' which blame inadequate regulation either at a national or at a global level. The second of these variants, on the other hand, may focus upon either people's failure to understand or consider the consequences of their actions (intellectual failures), or their selfishness, recklessness and greed (moral failures) (pp. 6–7).

Our research reveals the main pro-austerity narratives pertaining to the political (i.e., focusing on President Băsescu) and economic (i.e., focusing on Governor Isărescu) discourse in Romania. We have analyzed press statements and other official declarations and presentations made by the President of Romania during the time in which the austerity measures were decided, announced and implemented (2009–2011). Official statements made by the Governor of the National Bank of Romania during the same period of time are also investigated. All statements were made in Romanian and the analysis is based on the authors' own translations.

Findings

Austerity in political discourse

We investigate the main austerity narratives identified in the discourse of President Traian Băsescu in 2010 and 2011. As anticipated, all accounts of the austerity-centered policies are non-systemic, being linked to moral considerations, under the shape of either the 'duty' of Romanian politicians and ordinary citizens to 'save the country and its future,' or to Romanians' moral obligation to subscribe to European norms and values. In order to illustrate this call for solidarity, we can look at the following statement made by President Băsescu in May 2010, when austerity measures were announced:

> I am counting on the solidarity of politicians in the governmental area at least. The alternative to this program aimed at boosting confidence in Romania [austerity] is to immediately increase taxes as a solution to bring money into the budget.

Looking across our whole corpus, we identified three types of operationalization of *non-systemic accounts of austerity*. In short, the first—*Austerity is a European solution!*—captures all austerity stories that are built on the triumphant narratives (i.e., narratives capable of being told) of Europeanization. The resulting logic is that Romanians must comply with austerity so as to prove they are good Europeans. The second—*The obese state shall be put on a diet!*—although an extension of the European/modernization narrative, is more focused on the Romanian public administration and state as a big and obscure spender that needs to be reformed. The third—*No Austerity for Banks!*—portrays the banks and the private sector in general as entities which must be saved by all means.

'Austerity is a European solution!'

In many of his speeches, President Băsescu presented austerity as a European solution to Romania's structural problems. In his logic, severe austerity will generate sustainable development, through increased competitiveness and structural reforms aimed at making everything more efficient for a better and ever prosperous life inside the EU.

> We cannot keep our competitiveness at a European level if we don't rapidly implement programs for restructuring our own national economies, our own expenses. So, a high-performing Europe can only be imagined with programs aimed at creating efficient measures for each of us and, also, for all of us.
>
> (Băsescu, 2010)

> I opt to go further with Europe. Only together can we face the processes of globalization. And, at the same time, I would say that everybody would understand what I really mean, we are faced with an existential choice: what are we going to leave to our children—a house or a piece of debt?
>
> (Băsescu, 2011)

By going through the statements made by President Băsescu, the word 'austerity' is absent or we might as well say that it is disguised in various 'pro-European' statements, such as: 'maintain/increase competitiveness,' 'high-performing

Europe,' 'respect the European criteria,' 'restructuring measures,' 'prosperous and stable European Union.'

> Europe is at the epicenter of the economic crisis. There is plenty of uncertainty, we are facing a situation in which, in order to become competitive, all states or—in order to avoid any vanity—most of the member states need to implement coherent financial and economic restructuring measures, especially by paying attention to budgetary expenses.
>
> (Băsescu, 2011)

> ...one of the main causes for this crisis has been the deliberate overshadowing of the Stability and Growth Pact, which targeted a structural deficit of 5%, with the explicit recommendation to aim for surplus in order to ensure a prosperous and stable European Union.
>
> (Băsescu, 2011)

Moreover, Romanians are often narrated as 'quasi' Europeans who, through extreme austerity, could become reference models to citizens in well-established democracies:

> I know we will need to take into account solutions to improve the standard of living, but for now we haven't reached our main goal—to regain stability—and the [austerity] measures that we implemented are only now starting to be implemented in other Member-States.
>
> (Băsescu, 2011)

> Today, the necessity to spend responsibly becomes the supreme commandment of all member states in the EU.
>
> (Băsescu, 2011)

In some instances, the accountability for austerity measures is completely outsourced to the EU, as it is in the case below:

> Thus, I do not advance to the Romanians a future full of austerity. If we enter into this treaty, Romania will become more attractive for investments...
>
> (Băsescu, 2010)

As already mentioned, the objective cause-effect relationship is not relevant for discourses, because narratives are relational and not temporal. In his speeches, the President invents a new logic of austerity, in which budgetary cuts in Romania are seen as leading or contributing to a crisis-proof Europe, where all citizens could eventually benefit from stability and prosperity. We might infer that the President sought to capitalize on Romanians' traditional Euro-enthusiasm, even Europhilia (Radu, 2016; Radu & Bârgăoanu, 2015), when linking pro-austerity discourse with the pro-European narrative.

"The obese state shall be put on a diet!"

The need to reform and reorganize the State is another narrative in the presidential discourse on austerity, with a strong connection to the previous, European narrative. The European Union is seen as the trigger for the modernization of Romania and the Romanian state.

> We can see two main national goals, these meaning objectives that each Member-State must assume: fiscal consolidation and structural reforms. I want you to know that these goals are not for Romania only. Most states in the European Union need to undergo a rigid process of fiscal consolidation and structural reforms.
>
> (Băsescu, 2010)

Narrated in the same non-systemic logic, austerity (meaning cuts) is framed as a universal solution for all kinds of problems, from education, to healthcare, sound public administration, and so on.

> ...reforming the state [...] means not only constitutional reform, but also reforming the institutions, reducing the bureaucracy, de-centralization, and the reduction of the useless adminstrative structures in the Romanian state. These are the measures that should be implemented for these goals to be achieved.
>
> (Băsescu, 2010)

The vital character of 'structural reforms' or 'state modernization' is most often made operational by means of blaming strategies. The President performs what Žižek (2012) has called the 'cheap moralization' of the austerity logic (p. 16), by indicating the intellectual and moral failures of both decision-makers and ordinary people, their fault in making the crisis happen and, at the same time, their ultimate accountability as final recipients of the crisis-tackling measures. Some relevant remarks can be found in the excerpts below:

> We make some basic calculations and we know where we are: 62% of the state budget. We then ask ourselves how we could reallocate sufficient funds for schools, hospitals, the Army or the Police? [*Intellectual failure—decision-makers misallocated the resources*].
>
> (Băsescu, 2010)

> In Romania we currently have 16 welfare programs, most of them implemented before the elections [*politicians' moral failure, out of corruption and self-interest*]—starting with the granting of diapers and ending with the minimum guaranteed wage. These work so independently, that there are persons who cumulate 4–5 such social subsidies from various programs, so that they find it more convenient to stay at home [*moral failure – lazy*

> *people*] than finding a job. The 16 social programs will be reanalyzed so that they attain their targets and not encourage people to earn money without going to work [*moral failure – lazy people*]. Furthermore, as regards the solutions that will be implemented, we are also thinking about those exceptions that have eroded the credibility of the governmental measures aimed at reducing exaggerated benefits [*intellectual failure – the design of social benefits was wrong],* as well as illegal. incomes [*moral failure – corruption, criminal behavior*].
>
> (Băsescu, 2010)

> In the first place, we speak about reducing by 25% the salaries for the entire budgetary staff in Romania, and, till the end of the year, the managers in these public institutions are obliged to make the correct selection, to choose the best from the best, and not the political clientele. [*Moral failure – people were irresponsible or self-interested*].
>
> (Băsescu, 2010)

'The obese state,' with its lazy and incompetent staff, with its corruption and lack of transparency, needs to be 'put on a diet' through targeted reforms (meaning austerity).

> I want you to understand that, if we had chosen taxes increases in extremely sensitive areas—VAT and the flat income tax—the budgetary apparatus would have transferred on the shoulders of the real economy the pressure for ensuring its own subsistence. [*Moral failure – the obese, greedy, state*].
>
> (Băsescu, 2010)

As illustrated in the statements above, the welfare state and its attributes are put under severe scrutiny and downsizing, in the context where it was not the public debt, but the problems originating in the financial and banking sector that triggered the crisis in Romania. These non-systemic accounts of austerity were designed to match the pre-existing fears, inclinations, and biases of the electoral, political and social pool that brought President Băsescu to power in the first place in 2004: mistrust in oversized state institutions; mistrust in an inefficient, overly bureaucratic, even corrupt public administration; fear of not being accepted as Europeans or of being abandoned by the EU and the West. According to President Băsescu, for all of these fears, inclinations and biases, there is one cure only: austerity. This finding is in line with Amartya Sen's (2015) analysis of the thinking to which many austerity implementers in Europe have subscribed:

> There was an odd confusion in policy thinking between the real need for institutional reform in Europe and the imagined need for austerity—two quite different things. [...] But the real (and strong) case for institutional reform has to be distinguished from an imagined case for indiscriminate

> austerity, which does not do anything to change a system while hugely inflicting pain.

Austerity and structural reforms made up a toxic "chemical compound" that "did not serve the cause of reform at all" (Sen, 2015).

'No austerity for banks'

The strategy to avoid any larger interrogations regarding the origins of the crisis and austerity measures is apparent when the President approaches the role of the private sector, more specifically, of banks, in economic life.

> For any bank that might find itself in difficulties, funding solutions for the capitalization of the banks are to be found in almost any Member-State. So, the EU has thought of measures so that no important bank in the national banking systems will face difficulties. And whenever necessary, states will intervene, as states have access to funding sources made available by the EU.
>
> Băsescu, 2011)

Building on the citizens' concern over their ability to pay off their loans, the President reassures the public that no bank will be left aside. In this way, narratives of austerity reach the public, because they resonate with a very deep and tangible anxiety of any indebted citizen.

> Thus, good quality capital is currently being injected in the European banking system... So, our deep concern has received a positive resolution on behalf of the Member States...
>
> (Băsescu, 2011)

As mentioned above, Romania experienced—at least at the beginning of the turmoil—a financial and banking crisis, generated by a severe contraction of lending, the withdrawal of credit lines by the Western banks in order to provide for the problems back home, and investors' flight to dollars, euros and the yen. Yet, it is precisely this topic—which, in our view, constitutes the core of the whole debate on crisis and austerity—that is continuously avoided in the President's austerity discourse. The European narratives are visible and are largely used in order to legitimize the massive bailouts of the banks active in Romania. This European stance contributes to building arguments that take for granted the need to recapitalize the banks, even by harsh austerity:

> Our request is that, in the process of capitalization of the banks that work in Romania—and I believe that this is valid for the entire Euro area—that a condition be taken into account that all banks maintain their exposure in the countries out of the euro-area.
>
> (Băsescu, 2011)

In a nutshell, the presidential discourse on austerity is built around three central ideas. First, austerity is not an option, but a European obligation. Second, the obese state must be reformed through tough cuts. Last, but not least, the need to save the banks is self-evident, is a fact that is closed to any public negotiation.

Austerity in economic discourse

As regards the discourse of the Romanian economic elites—particularly the Governor of the National Bank of Romania, Mugur Isărescu—we could identify three narrative patterns pertaining to non-systemic argumentation. The first concerns "the confidence-restoring role of the international agreements." This is the dominant narrative in the discourse of the economic elites managing the central bank in Romania, who narrate that stand-by agreements with the IMF and the EU played the most important role in the confidence-restoring game:

> In this context, the agreements with the IMF and EU have provided the Romanian economy with two key elements: bridging the funding gap and restoring credibility.
>
> (Isărescu, 2009)

> The import of credibility from EU and IMF has prevented some of the private funding from slowing down or terminating. The measures included in these agreements have ensured the funding of the Romanian economy.
>
> (Isărescu, 2009)

The second type of narrative is centered on the message that "budgetary cuts are not enough, though necessary," which emphasizes the need for budgetary discipline, while viewing it is as only a first step towards economic recovery.

> Other adjustments, such as the lowering of public expenses, including salaries cuts…though necessary, would have borne the stigma of low credibility.
>
> (Isărescu, 2009).

The Governor of the Romanian Central Bank highlights the timing and desirability of the austerity policies implemented in 2010:

> The mix of policies implemented in 2009 and 2010 is coherent and compatible with the new challenge [i.e., the crisis].
>
> (Isărescu, 2010)

The last cluster of narrative accounts—"the crisis would have taken place anyway in Romania"—triggers some systemic explanations (e.g., Romania's growth model is based on foreign capital-fueled consumption), even though it remains essentially non-systemic in the sense that it highlights only people's excessive indebtedness.

> We can thus state that the causes of a fully fledged Romanian [...] were accumulating. The outburst of the global financial crisis did not do anything but accelerate the outburst of the Romanian crisis.
>
> (Isărescu, 2010)

> The attempts to accelerate the increase in the living standard through procyclical policies do not yield results. In the medium term, the improvement of the standard of living depends upon policy consistency.
>
> (Isărescu, 2010)

The only distinctive feature of Romania's economic discourse has to do with the scarcity of Europeanization accounts. The EU is brought into Romania's austerity story most often in relation to the IMF (i.e., the EU-IMF agreement as a vehicle to restore credibility). In Isărescu's approach to austerity, Băsescu's pro-European stance is replaced by macroeconomic and apparently technical arguments. As in Băsescu's statements, however, the term 'austerity' is avoided altogether and replaced by subtler verbal constructions, such as "mix of policies implemented in 2009 and 2010."

The apparently technical or economic discourse is consistent with and complementary to the presidential discourse on austerity. Both types of discourse—political and economic—contribute to creating a 'smooth' and apparently flawless logic, which places the roots of the crisis under the auspices of a sort of fatality, or accumulation of unavoidable causes over time, while legitimizing austerity from a pro-European, pro-Western, pro-modernization stance. Systemic arguments are quasi-invisible. Instead, the 'people' are blamed for bringing on the crisis in the first place; hence, they need to accept the crisis-resolution (austerity) measures. The people to blame are, first, politicians, who committed intellectual failure (by not understanding or considering the consequences of increasing the country's debt) and/or moral failure (by being corrupt, greedy or irresponsible); and, second, citizens, who also committed intellectual failure (by not understanding or considering the consequences of taking loans) and/or moral failure (by being greedy, overspending, lazy, or dependent on the welfare state).

Conclusions

This chapter has claimed that the pro-austerity discourse of the Romanian economic-political elites tried to legitimize itself by resorting to commonsensical, simplified and unquestionable pro-Europeanization narratives (see Radu & Bârgăoanu, 2015; Radu, 2016). These narratives resonated, just like the theory predicted (i.e., Seabrooke & Thomsen, 2016; Žižek, 2009; Jessop, 2002) with social concerns, and vulnerabilities. Systemic, more complex explanations were left aside by exceptionalizing and blaming the (resisting) subjects of the austerity measures for their intellectual or moral failures. The manufacturing of the appearance of common sense, desirability and necessity (Europeanization, modernization, prosperity) and the blaming strategies were equally powerful in blocking systemic explanations that would have put capitalism, neoliberalism, and even some Europeanization processes under a question mark.

Responsibility for the austerity measures in Romania has been attributed either to an abstract 'EU' (Western institutions, in general) or to people, be they citizens, politicians. or the whole political class. This pattern is in line with Fairclough and Fairclough's finding that elites favor non-systemic explanations, which is far more than a theoretical argument, since non-systemic explanations drive non-systemic measures (in our case, austerity). The public debate focused on whether or not the government (the 'Băsescu regime') outdid what the foreign lenders asked in exchange for their financial package; on whether austerity was imposed by those foreign lenders or the choice of the Romanian authorities; on whether President Băsescu implemented austerity 'out of hate' or 'disdain' for his own people, especially for people outside his constituency (pensioners, public employees, people living on welfare benefits); on whether the austerity measures created the premises for the resulting economic growth; on whether or not people (citizens and politicians) are indeed greedy, lazy, corrupt, or dependent on the welfare state; and on whether the new government, coming from a different political family (the left), reversed (some of) the austerity measures and thus resumed growth. The 'best' argument that was able to enter the public debate was that austerity was necessary, unavoidable, although misguided and poorly designed. In this context, it is almost ironic that even the IMF's then managing director Dominique Strauss Kahn protested that, in the case of Romania, the government should have taxed the wealthy instead of pursuing austerity measures (Blyth, 2013, p. 222).

The battle for interpretation over the necessity, desirability, and rightness of austerity far exceeds the term of one President and one government. It took place against, and then reinforced, a discursive landscape characterized by the political battle between the 'right' and the 'left'. This is also a discursive battle, however, in which the former camp (the right—in fact, neoliberalism) tries to sell itself as modern, European and cosmopolitan, while depicting the latter (the left) as un-modern, un-European, rural, backward and dependent on the welfare state. The pro-austerity discourse resonated with some predispositions, concerns, and vulnerabilities of the Romanian public: mistrust in state institutions, anger and frustration with the corruption of public administration, expectations of prosperity brought about by European Union membership, and fear of being failed Europeans (see Radu & Bârgăoanu, 2015; Radu, 2016). Together, these vulnerabilities and austerity narratives were powerful in leaving outside public discourse many important, broader topics including: solidarity, inequality, poverty, polarization, progressive taxation, the welfare state, disenfranchisement of citizens, financialization, income distribution, center-periphery or East-West divide in the EU, and the exclusion from and marginality within the EU of countries such as Romania.

References

Alesina, A., & Ardagna, S. (2009). *Large changes in fiscal policy: Taxes versus spending*. (Working Paper No. 15438). Washington, DC: NBER. Retrieved from www.nber.org/papers/w15438

Andrews, M. (2007). *Shaping history: Narratives of political change*. Cambridge, UK: Cambridge University Press.

Arpad, T. (2014). Romania's austerity policies in the European Context. *The Romanian Journal of Society and Politics, 9*(1), 25–41.

Băsescu, T. (2010, 2011). Articles and news retrieved from hotnews.ro and ziare.com

Biggs, A., Hassett, K., & Jensen, M. (2010). *A guide for deficit reduction in the United States based on historical consolidations that worked*. (AEI Economic Policy Working Paper No. 2010–04). Washington, DC: American Enterprise Institute. Retrieved from www.aei.org/paper/100179

Blyth, M. (2013). *Austerity: The history of a dangerous idea*. New York: Oxford University Press.

Clarke, J., & Newman, J. (2012). The alchemy of austerity. *Critical Social Policy, 32*(3), 299–319.

De Haas, R., Korniyenko, Y., Loukoianova, E., & Pivovarsky, A. (2012). *Foreign banks and the Vienna Initiative: Turning sinners into saints?* IMF Working Paper No. 12/117. Washington, DC: International Monetary Fund. Retrieved from www.imf.org/external/pubs/ft/wp/2012/wp12117.pdf.

Elliott, L., Inman, Ph., & Smith, H. (2013, June 5). IMF admits: We failed to realise the damage austerity would do to Greece. *The Guardian*. Retrieved from www.theguardian.com/business/2013/jun/05/imf-underestimated-damage-austerity-would-do-to-greece.

Erlanger, S., & Castlejune, S. (2010, June 22). Barroso defends Europe's move toward austerity. *The New York Times*. Retrieved from www.nytimes.com/2010/06/22/world/europe/22europe.html.

Evans-Pritchard, A. (2009). IMF rescues Romania with €20bn aid while Serbia handed €4bn. *The Telegraph*. Retrieved from www.telegraph.co.uk/finance/economics/5051495/IMF-rescues-Romania-with-20bn-aid-while-Serbia-handed-4bn.html.

Fairclough, I., & Fairclough, N. (2012). *Political Discourse Analysis: A methods for advanced students*. London: Routledge.

Ferguson, N. (2015). The UK Labour party should blame Keynes for their election defeat. *Financial Times*. Retrieved from www.ft.com/content/9dd9c7ee-f71c-11e4-99aa-00144feab7de

Godart F. C., & White, H. C. (2010). Switching under uncertainity: The coming and becoming of meanings. *Poetics, 38*(6), 567–586.

Griffin, L. J. (1993). Narrative, event-structure analysis and causal interpretation in historical sociology. *American Journal of Sociology, 98*(5), 1094–1133.

Hackwell, R., (2016, October 6). Austerity obsession is pushing EU into crisis warns Stiglitz. Retrieved from www.euronews.com/2016/10/06/obsession-with-austerity-pushing-eu-into-crisis-warns-stiglitz

International Monetary Fund. (2011). *Global Financial Stability Review*. Washington, DC: International Monetary Fund.

Isărescu, M. (2009). Finanțarea dezechilibrului extern și ajustarea macroeconomică în condițiile crizei financiare. *Cazul României*. Retrieved from www.bnr.ro/Studii,-analize,-puncte-de-vedere-4009.aspx

Isărescu, M. (2010). Measuring the anti-cyclical character of the fiscal policy. Retrieved from http://www.bnr.ro/Prezentari-si-interviuri--1332.aspx?fld_issue_year=2010

Jessop, B. (2002) *The future of the Capitalist State*. Cambridge. UK: Polity Press.

Jolly. D. (2009, March 26). IMF announces financial rescue plan for Romania. *The New York Times*. Retrieved from www.nytimes.com/2009/03/26/business/worldbusiness/26romania.html?_r=0

Kalan, D., & Durlik, M. (2015, October 20). Central Europe's limping tigers: Hungary's unorthodox policy vs. Romanian austerity. *Foreign Affairs*. Retrieved from www.foreignaffairs.com/articles/hungary/2015-10-20/central-europes-limping-tigers

Krugman, P. (2008). *The return of Depression economics and the crisis of 2008*. NewYork/London: W.W. Norton & Company, Inc.

Krugman, P. (2015, April 29). The case for cuts was a lie. Why does Britain still believe it? The austerity delusion. *The Guardian*. Retrieved from www.theguardian.com/business/ng-interactive/2015/apr/29/the-austerity-delusion

Onaran, Ö. (2011). From transition crisis to the global crisis: Twenty years of capitalism and labour in the Central and Eastern EU new member states. *Capital & Class, 35*(2), 213–231.

Polkinghorne, D. E. (1998). *Narrative knowing and the human sciences*. Albany, NY: State of New York University Press.

Radu, L. (2016). Unconditional trust? Public opinion towards the EU in Romania. *Journal of Media Research, 1*(24), 60–79.

Radu, L., & Bârgăoanu, A. (2015). Advocates or challengers of Europeanization? An inquiry into the discourse of the Romanian elites on the European Union in the context of EU elections 2014. *Transylvanian Review of Administrative Sciences, 2015*(46E), 162–177.

Reinhardt, C., & Rogoff, K. (2014). *Recovery from financial crises: Evidence from 100 episodes*. (Working Paper No. 19823). Washington, DC: NBER. Retrieved from www.nber.org/papers/w19823

Seabrooke, L., & Thomsen, R. R. (2016). Making sense of austerity: Everyday narratives in Denmark and the United Kingdom. *Politics, 36*(3) 250–261

Sen, A. (2015, June 4). The economic consequences of austerity. *New Statesman*. Retrieved from www.newstatesman.com/politics/2015/06/amartya-sen-economic-consequences-austerity

Squire, C., Andrews, M., & Tamboukou, M. (2013). Introduction: What is narrative research? In M. Andrews, C. Squire, & M. Tamboukou (Eds.). *Doing narrative research* (2nd ed., pp. 1–26). London: Sage Publications.

Somers, M. R. (1994). The narrative constitution of identity: A relational and network approach. *Theory and Society, 23*(5), 605–649.

Stanley, L. (2014). 'We're reaping what we sowed': Everyday crisis narratives and acquiescence to the age of austerity. *New Political Economy, 19*(6), 895–917.

Stiglitz, J. (2012). Austerity – Europe's man-made disaster. *Social Europe Journal*. Retrieved from www.socialeurope.eu/austerity-europes-man-made-disasterStiglitz, J. E. (2014, October 2). Austerity has been an utter disaster for the eurozone 2014. *The Guardian*. Retrieved from www.theguardian.com/business/2014/oct/01/austerity-eurozone-disaster-joseph-stiglitz

Stoiciu, V. (2012). *Austerity and structural reforms in Romania: Severe measures, questionable economic results and negative social consequences*. Berlin: Friedrich-Ebert-Stiftung. Retrieved from http://library.fes.de/pdf-files/id-moe/09310.pdf

Summers, L. (2012, April 30). Growth not austerity is best remedy for Europe. *Financial Times*. Retrieved from www.ft.com/content/dbb65da8-9062-11e1-8adc-00144feab49a

Žižek, S. (2009). *First as tragedy, then as farce*. London: Verso.

Žižek, S. (2012, April 24). Occupy Wall Street: What is to be done next? *The Guardian*. Retrieved from www.theguardian.com/commentisfree/cifamerica/2012/apr/24/occupy-wall-street-what-is-to-be-done-next

15 An analysis of El Roto's newspaper cartoons discourse as social indictment against Spanish austerity policies

Piedad Fernández Toledo and Virginia Villaplana-Ruiz[1]

From the start of the economic crisis in 2008, there was a shift in the Spanish social landscape, with growing opposition to the government's austerity measures. The opposition reached a peak in 2011 with the rise of the 15-M movement, and from then on people have kept claiming for citizens' rights in the streets and organizing themselves in social movements, such as *Indignados*, *Real Democracy*, or even political parties, like *Podemos*.

Within this panorama, some professional voices from the mainstream media have increased their popularity as social conveyors of outrage and protest, in contrast to the more common trend, among these same traditional media, of adopting austerity policies (Fouce, Álvarez-Peralta, & Peña-Marín, 2016). Contest against imposed austerity has also found its natural space in the digital media and social networks, and in parallel to those newspaper voices—mainly from cartoons and opinion columns—new digital newspapers, such as *Infolibre*, *El Diario*, or *Huffington Post*, have developed in Spain, the same as in other countries, offering a fresh and more independent view on current issues, and more especially on sociopolitical ones.

But the arena where the real discursive revolution is taking place is social media (Pedro Carañana 2016). In this sense, Álvarez-Peralta (2014) shows how the main traditional Spanish newspapers, such as *El País*, have framed the "natural disaster metaphor" through their narratives on the economic crisis, whereas "having a look at the hegemonic narratives in the Twitter digital agora, we find a very different kind of constructions, much closer to the alternative discourses from minor journals, criticizing the bailout politics" (Álvarez-Peralta, 2014, p. 144).

The potential of the newspaper political cartoon genre for stirring social awareness has remained highly unexplored apart from a few exceptions (see, for example, Sani, Abdullah, Abdullah, & Ali, 2012), possibly because of their complex discursive nature (El Refaie & Hörschelmann, 2010). As Domínguez and Mateu (2014) state: "Cartoons are a useful tool for the analysis of social reality, reflected in their use of visual language and an aphoristic and judgemental phrase" (p. 187). The specific role newspaper cartoon narratives have played in the depiction of the Spanish crisis—and, in particular, on the effect of austerity policies in society—has not been examined, to our knowledge, except for our own previous approaches to El Roto's work (Fernández Toledo & Villanueva, 2012), despite some of those cartoonists (i.e., Mora and El Roto) suddenly jumping from mainstream newspapers (*El País* in the case of El Roto) to social media, becoming popular in the latter while keeping their activity in the former.

In this chapter, we illustrate how El Roto's cartoons have regularly conveyed social messages in the form of prototypical frames that have helped to raise awareness of inequalities derived from the economic policies implemented in the past years. That regularity leads us to regard El Roto as an opinion leader, more than many other cartoonists who have also contributed to this cause. His personal and professional commitment to the indictment of abusive political practices is a good example of this contribution to liven up public contest against austerity measures.

In the present chapter, we focus on the social imaginaries created by El Roto during the period comprising the past general elections and the two polls that took place between December 20, 2015 and June 26, 2016. In both cases, and contrary to what had been the political trend up to that point, there was no voting majority for any party. The present political landscape, after an endless negotiation process during which continuous political confrontation and constant party corruption indictments took place, consists of a more than ever varied composition in the Spanish Parliament, with a minority ruling right wing Popular Party and a strong opposition made of many newer and older groups. These include: the socialist party, *Unidad Popular;* the brand new *Podemos* party, born from the 15-M movements; the recently born green party, *Equo*; the left wing *Izquierda Unida* (IU); and the new party *Ciudadanos*. Most of them were formed by the amalgamation of outraged movements and many other previously existing smaller parties.

If the double election period was full of tension, so too has been the period following it, during which many previous ministers have been indicted, and some of them, together with former bankers and economic advisors, are now in prison because of their corrupt practices. Using discourse and genre analytic tools we have looked into the combination of iconic and linguistic contesting narratives in El Roto's cartoons, focusing on four frames or imaginaries (Castoriadis, 1997) identified in his daily output for the period selected: the loss of social rights and welfare as a consequence of austerity measures; the representation of capitalism and neoliberal policies; the growing social awareness among the Spanish population; and, lastly, the past complex general election process as a social scenario on which the former frames seemed to have been emphasized.

In the rest of the chapter, we briefly describe the Spanish economic context since the start of the economic crisis in 2008, and the way society reacted against the austerity measures gradually implemented. We then pinpoint the role of Andrés Rábago (i.e., "El Roto" in *El País* newspaper) as a leading voice in the contest against those policies. Third, we describe the results of our ongoing project (Fernández Toledo & Villaplana-Ruiz, 2016) consisting of a both multimodal (Archer & Breuer, 2015) and a multi-perspective (Bhatia, 2002) approach to the analysis of El Roto's newspaper political cartoons. Multimodality mainly refers here to the fact that there are two codes interplaying in the cartoon genre, i.e., the visual and the written one, which permits a high expressive potentiality that El Roto masterfully uses to produce a powerful effect on the reader. Besides, the fact that cartoons involve the co-existence of highly symbolic artistic design with rhetorically charged written discourse makes it necessary to adopt a multimodal analysis in order to correctly interpret and value them (O'Toole, 2015).

The analytical approach to cartoons also needs to be a multi-perspective one (Bhatia, 2002), so these are described not only as visual/written discourse, but also as instances of a professional discourse genre—i.e., Journalism—in which opinion creation is a key activity and, as such, highly valued as a complex professional skill. Lastly, they also need to be interpreted as contextually-situated discourse in a given sociocultural reality and at a given point in time.

Thus, from a textual perspective, we have gathered a sample of cartoons in the period around the past general elections, seeking for regular patterns in both the visual code and the short written statements. These patterns, repeated throughout time, conform archetypical characters and/or situations that need to be 'translated' from the sociocognitive angle in order to ascertain their functionality as reflecting the actions, social values or actors they symbolize in the cartoon genre. From a sociocritical perspective, we have sought to relate El Roto's critical position against austerity measures to the way the message is conveyed through an assortment of prototypical frames—imaginaries. Readers identify these imaginaries and interpret the cartoon messages in relation to them, with the help of their previous knowledge of sociopolitical current affairs.

The Spanish economic crisis and its consequences

The European economic crisis derived from the implementation of austerity measures (Moreno, 2012) in many of the member states (Van Gool & Pearson, 2014). In Spain, social and economic inequalities (Rodríguez, Aguilar, & Alfama, 2014) were reflected since 2007 in policies related to health (Bacigalupe, Martín, Font, González-Rábago, & Bergantiños, 2016) and to other areas such as housing, employment or vulnerable group support. The crisis affected especially the health system and led to more inequality in this respect (Segura, 2014).

In 2008, job cuts started and both the employment rates and the rate of GDP growth decreased. More specifically, between October 2007 and October 2008 the rate of unemployment rose in Spain from 8.6% to 13.9%. During the same period employment rates decreased from 54% to 51.8% and the rate of GDP growth plummeted from 3.6% to 0.9%. As a consequence, the poverty rate in Spain rose to 19.5% in 2009, reaching 20.8% in 2010. According to the 2017 Labor Force Survey (INE, 2017), the number of people unemployed in the last term of 2016 in Spain was 4,237,800, with an unemployment rate of 18.63%.

Due to this crisis, the welfare state has become gradually fragmented. In this sense, we can speak of a move from coordinated to liberal market economies

(Hall & Soskice, 2001), the latter being fluent labor markets with greater capital mobility which, in turn, foster competitive labor relations based on prices, and lead to market oriented business models. So, while coordinated market economies foster longer and more rigid contracts at sectoral levels, liberal market economies lead to more flexible and dynamic labor markets, with higher rotation. Consequently, economic precarity in a neoliberal context clearly adjusts to the liberal market economy type.

In the case of Spain, 'crisis' has become equivalent to budget reductions and government authoritarianism leaving a trail of unemployment, wage reductions or freezing, precarity, cutbacks, evictions, loss of rights, low employment expectations, worsening of living conditions and, as a consequence, social fragmentation. At the same time, there has been a spread of national identity related attitudes leading to a rise of racist, intolerant or xenophobic social behavior over and across Europe.

Spanish social reactions against austerity

The Spanish 15-M movement that arose in 2011 roughly drew two main discourse lines: on the one hand, an attempt to join forces against capitalism and the social consequences of its implementation; on the other, the search for a new institutional frame, by dismantling capitalist society's naturalized day to day experiences through a new language. Within the former line, open democracy mechanisms have been sought after (e.g., binding referendums, Democracy 4.0, or campaigns against financial market deregulation and speculation, media misrepresentation, institutionalized corruption, and the interdependence of financial and political elites).

Within the latter, a reaction against hegemonic discourses that have favored social division has taken place over the last decade, in addition to the search for ways of enhancing social change through collective action. These actions have stemmed from civil disobedience practices that used space appropriation as a tool—with capital city open air squares becoming a reflection of the Greek space for debate (i.e., the 'agora').

Health and education, as key foundations of the welfare state, were the two referents for social mobilization against the crisis and its austerity effects. This mobilization surpassed the strict labor right defence (which had been traditionally represented by the main state-based trade unions) to become the stronghold of the call for basic public rights, thus gathering together both workers and lay people in the defence of the same social goals (Dardot & Laval, 2013). The different 'marea' (tide) movements—with the green tide representing education and white the public health system—came out as a political action lab, in which the (not too easy) alliances between professionals and users have extended beyond these two mainly institutionalized factors: first, by surpassing the limits of the wage struggle and linking it to the public service defence; and, second, by joining against the dismantling of the welfare state.

According to Holloway (2010), the above-mentioned process can be considered "ruptures of everyday life," as a kind of mobilization lab aiming at the common wealth, i.e., everyday activism practices are taking on both the ends and the means to achieve these. In this sense, Slavoj Žižek and Alexis Tsipras regard the neoliberalism-driven financial and economic crisis that arose in 2008 as an opportunity to implement democratic reforms, and even to rewrite history (Žižek & Tsipras, 2014).

El Roto's cartoon discourse against austerity

Andrés Rábago has consistently defended fairer democratic ways and practices through his cartoons for *El País* as "El Roto." A cartoonist traditionally followed by certain newsreader generations—who mostly grew up in the Spanish post-war, if not before—suddenly became an opinion leader for 2.0 generations who defend a new state of things and communicate through alternative online platforms like *Democracy Now* (2011) in order to share information and claim their rights.

El Roto's daily cartoon output is kept and updated both in Andrés Rábago's personal homepage (www.elroto-rabago.com/ops.html), and in the *El País* Opinion subsection 'cartoons' for the newspaper digital version (https://elpais.com/tag/c/0e38dfc9210dd08fb05b8226dd54b018), which also contains the work of other cartoonists working for *El País*, such as Forges and Ros.

In addition, El Roto has used Facebook to spread his output, reaching 32.457 'likes' in his own page and 32,710 followers at the moment of writing this chapter. There is also a fan page (www.facebook.com/El.Roto.fans/) aimed at gathering all El Roto's cartoons published in the past years and to provide a space for his readers' participation via posts. In 2017, each cartoon publication was being followed by an average of eight posts. Similarly, the average number of likes for each of the cartoons is 500. A special section in *El País*'s online publication from 2016 entitled "Viñetas para el 15-M"[2] recalls both El Roto's and Forges' commitment to the 15-M cause.

The integration of visual and written discourse to reinforce the satirical effect is possibly what makes El Roto's cartoons so powerful (Carabaño Aguado, 2008). Visually, satire is obtained through iconicity, conveyed through the use of apparently simple images which nevertheless carry a strong symbolic effect (e.g., animals representing qualities, or an intelligent use of metonymy), or through the inclusion of well-known scenarios symbolizing historical events or social movements (e.g., Plaza del Sol as symbol of the 15-M movement), or institutions (e.g., the Spanish Parliament front door for the government, or the World Trade headquarters representing neoliberal power).

Parody plays an important role in the depiction of prototypical characters, such as politicians, bankers or economists. Other times, however, the different protagonists are represented through symbols, such as buildings, places or animals, as explained above. The instantiation of meaning becomes a complex guessing game for the reader, who commonly needs to draw upon previous knowledge of diverse kinds—historical, cultural, social or political, just to name some possibilities.

The use of contrast is another typical and powerful element in El Roto's idiolect, both visually (through the interplay of color for marked information and black and white for context, or the inclusion of opposing characters or realities), and textually (most often through antithesis, but also through the contrast between implied referents and explicit visual and/or written information). Written discourse is apparently simple but rhetorically complex, through the use of irony, synecdoche (i.e., the use of the part to represent the whole), antithesis or hyperbole, as shown in previous research (Fernández Toledo & Villanueva, 2012).

El Roto's cartoon textual patterns regarding both visual and written discourse—as identified in a previous work by Fernández Toledo and Villanueva (2012)—are confirmed in the present study; these patterns have been interpreted from a cognitive-functional angle against the immediate context of media opinion creation practices, following Paltridge's (1995) model for genre analysis, which looks both at the interactional frame (based on the immediate context of situation) and the cognitive-conceptual one (having to do with professional culture and institutionalized discourse practices and conventions). Lastly, we have interpreted from a sociocritical perspective the overall message conveyed in each cartoon and achieved through various means, with the aim of disclosing the underlying ideological positioning of El Roto, who in his professional role of opinion creator encourages newsreaders to react against austerity and foster dissension and public action through his blended cartoon discourse.

The sample for this work consisted of 132 cartoons selected during four different periods ranging from December 2015 to June 2016. We used as selection criteria the direct relationship between the message conveyed and the present Spanish austerity situation. The periods were chosen around four critical events:

- the ***first general elections poll***, which took place on December 20, 2015; this period ranges between November 29 and December 27, 2015 (i.e., three weeks before the polls and the week following them);
- the period of ***party negotiations*** to form a national government, starting the day after the poll (December 21, 2015) and ending on April 23, 2016, which was the deadline for—failed—efforts by the party to form a government;
- the ***15-M's fifth anniversary***, coinciding with the time between the first and second polls (i.e., three weeks before and one week following May 15);
- the period around the ***second poll*** on June 26, 2016, which includes three weeks before the second elections and one further week after them.

As can be seen in Table 15.1 below, except for the first period—i.e., the first general elections poll—in which the thematic focus of cartoons was more varied, austerity and derived issues are the focus of more than two thirds of all cartoons issued.

Table 15.1 Percentage of austerity-related cartoons and subtopic distribution for each period

PERIODS→ *Total cartoon number and austerity –related selection size (N)* ***SUBTOPICS***	**1st elections** *Total: 33;* **N= 12 (36.33%)**	**Party negotiations** *Total: 72;* **N= 55 (76.39%)**	**15th May anniversary** *Total: 31;* **N= 22 (70.9%)**	**2nd elections** *Total: 33;* **N= 28 (84.84%)**
Austerity and its victims	3 (9%)	**9 (12.5%)**	**8 (25.8%)**	—
Neoliberalism depicted	—	**30 (41.6%)**	7 (22.5%)	5 (15.2%)
People's awareness	—	1 (1.4%)	4 (12.9%)	**10 (30.3%)**
Elections	**9 (27.3%)**	4 (5.6%)	3 (9.7%)	**13 (39.4%)**

We identified four main subtopics related to austerity, which lead to the corresponding imaginaries that will be further described later in this chapter, i.e., 'austerity and its victims,' 'neoliberalism depicted,' 'people's awareness,' and 'elections.'

These four subtopics show an uneven distribution for each stage or period. In addition, sometimes two or more subtopics may coincide in one cartoon, for example citizens may be shown as critically pointing to corruption practices and how these affect election processes. Furthermore, all cartoons under each of the subtopics clearly include either neoliberal or austerity aspects elements, or even both. However, textual analysis of both visual and written codes permits identification of one of the subtopics as the focal point for each cartoon instance.

Thus, austerity-related cartoons in the first period represent more than one-third (36.33%) of the total output, and are mostly related to the elections as part of the neoliberal system. In the second period—i.e., failed party negotiations—they amount to more than two-thirds of the total drawings (76.39%) and witness the political stagnation during the process when a ruling coalition was being sought by the parties, together with the rise of new political groups stemming from 15-M and their presence in this scenario. In parallel, the new meaning of austerity as 'capitalism-driven poverty' is shown in many cartoons that depict the different areas and social victims directly affected; the citizenry is also portrayed in some instances as becoming aware of their own situation from a critical stance. The 15-M period also includes quite a large number of cartoons devoted to austerity-related issues (70.9% of the sample), with a split between those depicting the austerity side and those portraying the neoliberal ruling class that has fostered the present situation, and just some instances presenting people's awareness or directly related to elections. This last subtopic is the main protagonist in the final period around the second election, during which the number of cartoons devoted to the election process itself surpasses that for the previous stages (rising to 84.84% within the sample); citizenry awareness is nearly as present in this period as the election subtopic, with some instances where neoliberalism continues to be depicted.

We will next review the different imaginaries created in relation to each subtopic, and will show in more detail how El Roto shapes them in the cartoons published along the four periods in our study.

Spanish austerity and its victims

The lack of rights and the diminishment of the welfare state are portrayed in El Roto's depiction of different austerity victims: children and education, citizens in the street, welfare, art and culture. Poverty is part of the landscape in most cartoons in this category, and is presented both visually and in written form, with humble home settings symbolizing underdevelopment. Symbolism and intertextuality are very much present, as a way to denounce scarcity and the perpetuation of austerity. For example, clear connotations of dark Spanish post-war times can be recognized in some of these images. The clearest example of this is the January 13 cartoon (see Figure 15.1 above), which could be considered an allegory of austerity itself. In it, an old mourning mother is pressing her hand on an adult son's head while telling him he will not be able to grow this year, either. The son, scarcely dressed and looking downwards, may represent the economic stagnation of a whole nation, while the mother, all dressed in black like a post-war widow, might well represent Europe, even though to Spanish eyes she mainly resembles the dark post-war Spanish scarcity era. The son's lack of clothes and the scarce use of color are very symbolic too, as a sign of scarcity itself.

Metaphor also serves to create powerful images in many cartoons like the one just described. Another striking example is the image of the shark-shaped image of a plane about to destroy the New York World Trade Center towers in a February 25 cartoon (El Roto, 2016, February 25): a sign on top of the towers, with 'ART' written on it, helps to establish the connection between the terrorist attacks and the destruction of art in Spain through neoliberal cutback policies.

We can also observe a clear ironic effect in the depiction of advertising and marketing practices that appeal to citizens, either attracted by colorful shop windows in the street, or led by the social mobility illusion as they just move up and down department store escalators dressed in bright colors and holding shopping bags (El Roto, 2015, December 16). Thus, consumption is presented as both the new space for leisure and an ally for self-deception, in contrast to an alternative model of leisure as 'culture consumption' and 'participative creation.' To complement the social scenery and in contrast with this idea of 'illusion,' lack of solidarity and citizen alienation are recurrent images across the four time periods. A good example is the May 14 cartoon (El Roto, 2016, May 14),

Figure 15.1 Austerity and its victims (cartoon published in *El País* on January 13, 2016)
Source: El Roto (2016, January 13)

through which El Roto directly criticizes the fact that a good part of society is blunt by comfort and routine, just one day before the 15-M anniversary. A young bearded man, prototype of the young intellectual, claims to be in solidarity just because he thinks it. Irony comes from the contrast between doing and just thinking, between present spirituality and solidarity itself as terms emptied of meaning when there is no actual commitment prompting people to actively take part.

Neoliberalism in El Roto's cartoon discourse

The opposing link between austerity and neoliberalism is implied in many cartoons, at a time when neoliberal discourse is also the focus of many academic works (Holborow, 2015).

The fact that the economy gradually became the focus of a legitimated discourse has been a common message in many of El Roto's cartoons up to the present, and is the more consistent imaginary in the sample studied. El Roto shows by different means how the marketing dictatorship is ruling everybody's lives through fraud and deception, as in his February 20, 2016 cartoon (El Roto, 2016, February 20), whose protagonist might well be the former economy minister Rodrigo Rato, responsible at the time of bank system restructuring. The character is boasting at the way he has been able to avoid prison thanks to the amount of money he had previously stolen. A pun is made with the Spanish word 'banquillo,' meaning both the Spanish diminutive for 'bank' (i.e., people's money administered and stolen) and the culprit's dock at the Court.

In a similar vein, economic power and theocracy are made equal by means of hybridization in the May 24, 2016 cartoon (El Roto, 2016, May 24). In it, the biblical prophet Moses is depicted showing supply and demand tables (rather than the traditional stone tablets containing the Ten Commandments). If we look more closely at it, an implicit parallelism can be established between the strong faith that made Hebrew people follow Moses and the way in which citizens are led by economic 'cash flow,' an idea which is more openly conveyed in other cartoons by El Roto. The use of an English word ('cash flow' for 'flujo monetario') introduces a marked link to capitalism and its US origins. Other marked elements are the red colored money bag—red normally points to the information focus in El Roto's cartoons—or the fact that Moses' tunic has turned into a black suit even though his long beard and the golden halo still remain. The character is looking front, as if addressing the readers, or 'followers.' The Ten Commandments may be summarized in one—cash flow—as the only text in the cartoon and the only thing that matters nowadays.

Furthermore, the fierce market driven manipulation of nature and people's lives to achieve economic benefits at all costs is also reflected in many cartoons. A very expressive example is the cartoon from March 5, 2016 (El Roto, 2016, March 5), in which a sunflower is fighting to keep its natural movement against the one being imposed by the market. In many other instances, nature and society's subjugation by the market are denounced as well.

Another recurrent topic in all periods is corruption and the way in which it has become widespread. Not only are the government (El Roto, 2016, March 14) and the administration (El Roto, 2016, January 15) portrayed as corrupted, but also the citizenry that wants to benefit from this new state of affairs (El Roto, 2016, April 29). Many cartoons depict the collusion of political and economic powers to destroy the welfare state, to the point that social determinism is imposed on the working class, as openly shown in the February 18, 2016 cartoon (El Roto, 2016, February 18). Meanwhile, the different government representatives keep holding their chairs in a kind of stagnation state, as reflected in the February 16 cartoon caption (El Roto, 2016, February 16). The caption wording is nearly identical to Augusto Monterroso's short story—actually the shortest one ever written—: "When he woke up, the dinosaur was still there." This use of intertextuality helps to instantiate cultural and/or social phenomena and is akin to El Roto's style, as a resource that provides strength to the message conveyed.

The role of the media acting as a support for economic power is another recurrent message which appears, among others, in the January 5, 2016 cartoon about overt manipulation (El Roto, 2016, January 5). This message coincides with the claim by Fouce, Álvarez-Peralta and Peña-Marín (2016) in an *Open Democracy* report, about the role of Spanish media which are "acting as megaphones for established powers supporting austerity measures and politics."

A considerable number of cartoons reflect the values of the neoliberal ruling class and its cynical attitude towards its own practices and the austerity they are imposing on others. Economic power is overwhelmingly illustrated as manipulating and deceiving weak social groups especially, as in the May 11 cartoon (El Roto, 2016, May 11), which shows a technocrat offering a homeless child a website, rather than a home, as a place to stay. Archetypes are created through the portrayal of the varied social agents to blame for corruption and abusive practices. These agents appear under different categories but share a common ideology and objective: to benefit themselves at the expense of the economically fragile, just ignoring them. They are often displayed in an overtly cynical stance towards their own practices and values.

Really stunning messages and imaginaries are often conveyed, like the one published on January 27 in which the protagonists are purposefully ignoring basic human rights, in this case those of immigrants who die when trying to reach Spain's coasts (El Roto, 2016, January 27). The effect is achieved through a powerful use of visual ellipsis combined with contrast: the scarce text offers the cue to complete the information implied but not seen in the picture—dead immigrants in the sea—and to understand who the characters are talking about. There is no pronoun, just a mention of "their old-fashioned expectations of having a job, a house or food"—so there is a double contrast on the one hand between the apparently quiet sunset on a boat and the hidden and dreadful reality down in the water, and on the other between the implied reality and the men's cynical and cold attitude towards immigration as expressed in the text, which increases the shocking effect.

The neoliberal imaginary is also created through recurrent visual elements: luxurious settings and clothes, blonde hairstyles, and the fact that wealthy individuals are depicted sitting comfortably and holding cups while deciding how to rule the work, which sharply contrast with the humble settings described under the previous subtopic, with austerity victims as the focus.

Another very illustrative example is the cartoon portraying a wealthy young couple talking about the rights of the poor as something not to care about, while holding their cups at an evening party (El Roto, 2016, February 4). The contrast between upper class physical (visual) and ideological (textual) attributes and lower class austerity problems (implied by the text) serves to denounce the young couple's absolute lack of solidarity.

The cartoon issued on March 19, 2016 (see Figure 15.2 above) possibly best summarizes the core capitalist philosophy, based on people's domination. A technocrat is facing the reader—as in many other similar cartoons—as his statement reads "the devaluation of consciousness diminishes production costs" (El Roto, 2016, March 19).

Figure 15.2 The devaluation of consciousness diminishes production costs (cartoon published in *El País* on March 19, 2016)

Source: El Roto (2016, March 19)

Other cartoons point to the different ways this devaluation is being achieved, including the spread of illiteracy (El Roto, 2016, January 9), or the subtle introduction of a state of fear, as the July 1 cartoon (El Roto, 2016, July 1) suggests through an extremely satiric imaginary linking death and power, and which could be visually related to Dark Ages pictorial aesthetics. People's fear and ignorance are thus identified as foundations for the neoliberal system.

From social movement dissension to pervasive people awareness

Even though this third thematic subgroup of cartoons is visually quite similar to the first one about austerity and its victims, some qualitative differences can be established which have to do with the victims' own attitudes and discourse. At the same time, and in contrast with the aforementioned neoliberal archetypes, the protagonists in this subgroup appear as contesting the austerity policies imposed by the former. They are mostly depicted as ordinary people, who are either thinking aloud in isolation or holding a casual conversation in any street. There is only one depiction of protesters in the present sample, in contrast with previous years in which this prototypical character was more frequent across cartoons. In this instance, a young couple is denouncing their loss of rights, shouting as they walk in the midst of flags to reject the charity state that is being imposed on Spanish society—evoking a return to Spanish civil post-war charity times (El Roto, 2016, January 29).

Monologue is more frequent in this 'awareness' subgroup, and social impoverishment is often reported through the characters' 'thinking out loud' about their own situation. By paying attention to their bodily gestures and appearance, we can see that they do not look frontwards, as many neoliberal characters do, in a contemptuous way; rather, they are presented as looking down or aside, as if worried or thoughtful, like the unemployed man who complains about the loss of rights hidden under the euphemistic label 'job creation policies' (El Roto, 2016, February 2).

The social class discourse and philosophy that can be identified across the first subgroup on austerity victims, becomes more explicit in this category which constitutes a twist from sadness and desperation to reaction and contestation. Indeed, the first steps for reacting against austerity policies are for citizens to become aware of the manipulation exerted upon them and to openly acknowledge this state: only then may changes occur. This idea is overwhelmingly widespread in many of the cartoons in this series, with different archetypal characters, like the unemployed (already noted above), the woman sitting at home and acknowledging being 'changed' by TV (El Roto, 2016, February 14), or the female textile factory worker (see Figure 15.3 below).

The value of education as a legitimate tool for future generations to overcome the present state of ignorance and fear is the focus of a cartoon published on December 15, 2015, presenting children as having the power for change (symbolized by the green color in their green caps and clothes meaning hope), but also as a menace to the system, as their conversation suggests: they need to hide in order to read safely without alarming their parents, who are thus part of the system themselves (El Roto, 2015, December 15).

Dissension is also shaped through victims pointing to the corrupt practices of those who own the money (El Roto, 2016, March 2), or a female student who complains about an education system that just teaches submission (El Roto, 2016, June 10).

It is somehow significant that these latest examples appeared in May and June, just before the second poll that took place on June 20. El Roto seems to be trying to make people react by conveying the idea of gradual citizen awareness and empowerment, in relation to cutbacks and their different sceneries—culture, health, education, jobs—perhaps aiming for people's reactions to be reflected in the election results as well.

A powerful image used recurrently with an intertextual—and varying—effect is the concept of fear, as it appears in the different subgroups described

Figure 15.3 Female worker complaining about the loss of labor rights (cartoon published in *El País* on May 17, 2016)

Source: El Roto (2016, May 17)

up to this point. Thus, in the cartoon issued on June 18 (El Roto, 2016, June 18)—just two days before the second poll—we can see a humble, middle-aged woman who regrets the way "we have been moved from a welfare state to a panic one without notice." In contrast to this cartoon, which could be aimed at stirring people's reactions, the previously mentioned July 1 cartoon (El Roto, 2016, July 1) presents fear from a neoliberal perspective, as the way to maintain the status quo—here translated as more votes for the conservative party as compared with the first poll results—in what may seem an absurd contradiction: people keep voting for the same parties led by their fear of change, despite having suffered from cutbacks, evictions or repressive laws brought about by absolute majority governments biased towards liaising with economic forces.

Even more noteworthy is the fact that the protagonists in both cartoons—as never before in El Roto's cartoons, to our knowledge—are demonstrably aware of the role they are playing in a time of economic and political crisis. There may be two reasons for this: his depiction of the situation gets gradually more radical in order to foster reaction; or else he is trying to find an explanation himself for the disappointing outcome yielded after the second poll.

Elections

Cartoons overtly focusing on elections are logically more present during the two election periods in our sample, with 9 and 13 instances corresponding to the first and second polls, respectively (see Table 15.1 above). It is difficult to detach the subgroup 'elections' from the previous one on 'citizenry awareness,' to the extent that we could consider the former as part of the latter, with a clear reference to the election system.

In many instances, elections may be depicted as show business (El Roto, 2015, December 14); other times we find young candidates as potentially corrupt (El Roto, 2016, February 6); or we could find predatory animals hidden under smartly dressed candidates (El Roto, 2015, December 13).

Overall, we can check the extent to which El Roto is skeptical about the likelihood of social change through elections—this view becoming more evident during the second poll period, but also present in the first. The December 17 cartoon (El Roto, 2015, December 17)—published three days before the first poll—shows a voter looking to the front in a doubtful manner and stating that whatever he votes he will be wrong, as he holds three differently-colored ballots in is hand.

In the same vein, the day before the second poll—another critical day as to influence readers—a citizen in the street (i.e., someone contesting the status quo) considers voting a pointless action as the market system will be the one to rule anyway (El Roto, 2016, June 25).

Just after the second election El Roto's stance gets even clearer, as the character in the June 28 cartoon—archetype of the critical, committed citizen possibly taking part in the pride day parade which was taking place some days later—complains about the contradictory situation by which what was supposed to be outdated has rejuvenated, while what apparently was brand new has suddenly grown old (see Figure 15.4 below).

The social contradiction after the elections is thus expressed in this cartoon, which reflects more than any other El Roto's disappointment at the elections results, yielding a striking support to the conservative party after years of repressive policies and austerity imposition, while the brand new options would not achieve the expected outcome. The cartoon issued on the following day (El Roto, 2016, June 29) insists on the idea of disappointment (and possibly the cartoonist's annoyance), as overtly expressed by a 2.0 youngster who still cannot understand the gap between the real world and that of the social networks—which he had actually believed to be the real one. This paradox perfectly reflects the sociotechnological gap regarding elections and forecasts, as the support for the promising young 15-M-related parties and their left-wing allies, which had been especially high and active in the social networks, did not seem to be reflected in Spanish society as a whole.

Figure 15.4 Post-election disappointment (cartoon published in *El País* on June 28, 2016)

Source: El Roto (2016, June 29)

Conclusions

The fostering of critical consciousness in El Roto's cartoons

We have described through this chapter how El Roto has created clear imaginaries throughout time, not only to denounce the social situation brought about by the austerity measures imposed by the ruling elites, but also to raise people's consciousness. In the sense that cartoons are categorized as part of the reporting genres—and, more specifically, opinion subgenres—El Roto's output shows a clear political stance and a moral commitment to current Spanish issues and problems, especially those related to the imposition of austerity for the sample discussed.

The analysis of this sample confirms our earlier works about El Roto's output and the critical role of his cartoons to raise popular consciousness. It clearly shows that the apparent role of 'observer' in El Roto's cartoons is, in most cases, actually that of 'indicter' (Swain, 2012). The generalization of austerity and poverty, together with the lack of rights and the diminishment of the welfare state, are conveyed through different archetypes and abstract messages. Over time, these are contrasted with the frivolous defence of capitalist measures by those who take advantage of capitalism: different professional and social profiles—i.e., bankers and politicians—as archetypes of capitalism who even boast at their wealth accumulation and lack of solidarity.

Corruption is topicalized mainly by the depiction of those archetypes, complemented with conceptual elements or ideas which appear with varying degrees of explicitness across the 'neoliberalism' subgroup: the market economy as a legitimized discourse; the merging of political and economic powers to destroy the welfare state; social determinism; and governments' impunity and stagnation.

We have also checked how the system is overtly indicted by its victims, who are portrayed as immigrants, artists, protesters, unemployed, retired and health service workers, among others, and often depicted in streets or in humble settings, as the legitimate spaces from which socioeconomic policies have been contested.

At the same time, as could be seen, a parallelism is established over time among the referents of the different three subtopics (austerity victims, neoliberalism, awareness), so the same reality is looked at both from the views of those who impose austerity to benefit themselves, and from people who suffer their abusive practices, i.e., economically weak social classes and groups.

Multimodality is masterfully exploited by El Roto to point to these social paradoxes conveying a sense of the absurd, boosted in such a way that the initial shocking effect achieved through apparent parody turns into something sourer—a kind of frustration—once the verbal and visual pieces are put and interpreted together at a deeper level and, what is more, once the different imaginaries (related to the subtopics identified) are interrelated.

By focusing on the period chosen, we could specifically track the way political campaigns and elections determined El Roto's agenda, influencing not only his choice of topics but also his critical stance towards the whole process as part of a corrupt system, notwithstanding his seemingly increasing attempts to stir consciousness among the population as the whole election process turns more complex and lengthy.

Finally, this study contributes to highlight the special role cartoonists such as El Roto are currently playing as opinion leaders. The ability to synthesize social ideas and values in a combination of high artistic and satiric effect is possibly the reason El Roto's cartoons are so successful in the echoing and fostering of contestation among an outraged Spanish population.

Notes

1 We wish to express our gratitude to our reviewers for their constructive and enriching comments on our first draft.

2 The protests that gave rise to the movement of the 15-M had their impact in several vignettes that El Roto and Forges published: https://elpais.com/elpais/2015/05/15/album/1431680930_609813.html?id_externo_rsoc=FB_CM#1431680930_609813_1431688071

References

Carabaño Aguado, I. (2008). *Llorar es sonreír despacio: El impacto en las viñetas de El Roto.* Madrid: CTO Editorial.

Álvarez-Peralta, M. (2014). Hegemonías discursivas en el relato transmediático de la crisis: Narrativas digitales *vs* periodísticas. *CIC—Cuadernos de Información y Comunicación, 19*, 125–144.

Archer, A., & Breuer, E. (2015). *Multimodality in writing: The state of the art in theory, methodology and pedagogy.* Leiden: Brill.

Bacigalupe, A., Martín, U., Font, R., González-Rábago, Y., & Bergantiños, N. (2016). Austeridad y privatización sanitaria en época de crisis: ¿Existen diferencias entre las comunidades autónomas? *Gaceta Sanitaria, 30*(1), 47–51 Retrieved from www.gacetasanitaria.org/es/austeridad-privatizacion-sanitaria-epoca-crisis/articulo/S0213911115002071/

Bhatia, V. (2002). Applied genre analysis: A multiperspective model. *Ibérica, 4*, 3–19.

Carañana, J. P. (2016, June 16). Anti-austerity forces and the digital media in Spain. *Open Democracy.* Retrieved from www.opendemocracy.net/uk/joan-pedro/anti-austerity-forces-and-digital-media-in-spain

Castoriadis, C. (1997). *The imaginary institution of society.* (K. Blamey, Trans.). Cambridge, MA: MIT Press.

Dardot, P., & Laval, C. (2013). *La nueva razón del mundo: Ensayo sobre la sociedad neoliberal.* Barcelona: Editorial Gedisa.

Democracy Now (2011, May 25). #SpanishRevolution—Instaling Democracy 2.0. Retrieved from https://barcelonaentransicio.wordpress.com/2011/05/25/spanish revolution-instaling-democracy-2-0/

Domínguez, M., & Mateu, A. (2014). Are the winds of change blowing in Spain? Cartoonists' critical analysis of King Juan Carlos' elephant-hunting trip. *Journalism Studies, 15*(2), 187–203.

El Refaie, E., & Hörschelmann, K. (2010). Young people's readings of a political cartoon and the concept of multimodal literacy. *Discourse: Studies in the Cultural Politics of Education, 31*(2), 195–207.

El Roto. (2015, December 13). Elections may be depicted candidates as predatory animals. *El País.* Retrieved from https://elpais.com/elpais/2015/12/11/vinetas/1449847369_472673.html

El Roto. (2015, December 14). Elections may be depicted as a show business. *El País.* Retrieved from https://elpais.com/elpais/2015/12/11/vinetas/1449852170_002304.html

El Roto. (2015, December 15). From social movement dissension to pervasive people awareness. *El País.* Retrieved from http://elpais.com/elpais/2015/12/14/vinetas/1450112236_014357.html

El Roto. (2015, December 16). Advertising and marketing practices that appeal to citizens. *El País.* Retrieved from https://elpais.com/elpais/2015/12/15/vinetas/1450201348_713759.html

El Roto. (2015, December 17). The first poll period. *El País.* Retrieved from https://elpais.com/elpais/2015/12/16/vinetas/1450288195_713301.html

El Roto. (2016, January 5). The role of the media. *El País*. Retrieved from https://elpais.com/elpais/2016/01/04/vinetas/1451911204_017527.html

El Roto. (2016, January 9). Neoliberalism depicted. *El País*. Retrieved from https://elpais.com/elpais/2016/01/08/vinetas/1452248719_781095.html

El Roto. (2016, January 13). Austerity and its victims. *El País*. Retrieved from http://elpais.com/elpais/2016/01/12/vinetas/1452612035_826268.html

El Roto. (2016, January 15). The administration. *El País*. Retrieved from https://elpais.com/elpais/2016/01/14/vinetas/1452789297_400779.html

El Roto (2016, January 27). Immigrants, work and dignity. *El País*. Retrieved from https://elpais.com/elpais/2016/01/26/vinetas/1453803737_633488.html

El Roto. (2016, January 29). Spanish civil post-war charity times. *El País*. Retrieved from https://elpais.com/elpais/2016/01/28/vinetas/1453976792_471376.html

El Roto. (2016, February 2). Economy and job creation policies. *El País*. Retrieved from https://elpais.com/elpais/2016/02/01/vinetas/1454351755_945462.html

El Roto. (2016, February 4). Irony and lower class austerity problems. *El País*. Retrieved from https://elpais.com/elpais/2016/02/03/vinetas/1454496024_033603.html

El Roto. (2016, February 6). Elections may be depicted candidates as potentially corrupt. *El País*. Retrieved from https://elpais.com/elpais/2016/02/05/vinetas/1454692836_802553.html

El Roto. (2016, February 14). Economy and social archetypal characters. *El País*. Retrieved from https://elpais.com/elpais/2016/02/13/vinetas/1455380537_328023.html

El Roto. (2016, February 16). Economy and short-story. *El País*. Retrieved from https://elpais.com/elpais/2016/01/15/vinetas/1452871438_996937.html

El Roto. (2016, February 18). The collusion of political and economic powers to destroy the welfare state. *El País*. Retrieved from https://elpais.com/elpais/2016/02/17/vinetas/1455727979_072418.html

El Roto. (2016, February 20). People's money administered and stolen. *El País*. Retrieved from https://elpais.com/elpais/2016/02/19/vinetas/1455895624_463933.html

El Roto. (2016, February 25). New York WTC towers. *El País*. Retrieved from https://elpais.com/elpais/2016/02/24/vinetas/1456339496_403715.html

El Roto. (2016, March 2). Economy and social archetypal characters. *El País*, Spain. Retrieved from https://elpais.com/elpais/2016/03/01/vinetas/1456857932_798572.html

El Roto. (2016, March 5). A sunflower is fighting to keep its natural movement against the one being imposed by the market. *El País*. Retrieved from https://elpais.com/elpais/2016/03/04/vinetas/1457111271_230436.html

El Roto. (2016, March 14). Corruption and the way it has become widespread. *El País*. Retrieved from https://elpais.com/elpais/2016/03/13/vinetas/1457885083_436662.html

El Roto. (2016, March 19). The devaluation of consciousness diminishes production costs. *El País*. Retrieved from https://elpais.com/elpais/2016/03/18/vinetas/1458312585_727315.html

El Roto. (2016, April 29). Economy and new state of affairs. *El País*. Retrieved from https://elpais.com/elpais/2016/04/28/inenglish/1461839247_478989.html

El Roto. (2016, May 11). A technocrat offering a homeless child a place in cyberspace. *El País*. Retrieved from https://elpais.com/elpais/2016/05/11/inenglish/1462961411_763052.html

El Roto. (2016, May 14). A young bearded man, prototype of the young intellectual, claims to be solidarity just because he thinks it. *El País*. Retrieved from https://elpais.com/elpais/2016/05/13/opinion/1463163025_790452.html

El Roto. (2016, May 17). Economy and social archetypal characters. *El País*. Retrieved from https://elpais.com/elpais/2016/05/17/inenglish/1463476707_883672.html

El Roto. (2016, May 24). The way citizens are led by the economic 'cash flow.' *El País*. Retrieved from https://elpais.com/elpais/2016/05/23/opinion/1464025627_708618.html?rel=cx_articulo#cxrecs

El Roto. (2016, June 10). Education and submission. *El País*. Retrieved from https://elpais.com/elpais/2016/06/09/opinion/1465463910_534016.html

El Roto. (2016, June 18). We have been moved from a welfare state to a panic one without notice. *El País*. Retrieved from https://elpais.com/elpais/2016/06/17/opinion/1466180943_531254.html

El Roto (2016, June 25). The second poll period. *El País*. Retrieved from https://elpais.com/elpais/2016/06/24/opinion/1466784271_197101.html

El Roto. (2016, June 29). *El País*. Retrieved from https://elpais.com/elpais/2016/06/28/opinion/1467123498_006196.html

El Roto. (2016, July 1). Neoliberal system and Dark Ages pictorial aesthetics. *El País*. Retrieved from https://elpais.com/elpais/2016/06/30/opinion/1467299452_749287.html

Fernández Toledo, P., & Villanueva, J. C. (2012). El Roto ante la Ola de Cambio: Tomando la calle desde las viñetas. In P. Fernández Toledo & G. F. Rodríguez (Eds.), *Del yo al nostros: Los discursos y la communicación en la colectividad digital* (pp. 53–83). Saabrücken: Lambert Academic Publishing.

Fernández Toledo, P., & Villaplana-Ruiz, V. (2016, June 19). El Roto and graphic humour as a generator of alternative public opinion in Spain. *Open Democracy*. Retrieved from www.opendemocracy.net/uk/austerity-media/piedad-fern-ndez-toledo-virginia-villaplana-ruiz/el-roto-and-graphic-humour-as-ge

Fouce, H. Álvarez-Peralta, M., & Peña Marín, C. (2016, July 7) Stolen debates: The financial crisis and Spanish media. Open Democracy UK. Retrieved from www.opendemocracy.net/uk/austerity-media/h-ctor-fouce-miguel-lvarez-peralta-cristina-pe-amar-n/stolen-debates-financial-cr

Hall, P., & Soskice, D. (Eds.). (2001). *Varieties of capitalism: The institutional foundations of comparative advantage*. Oxford: Oxford University Press.

Holborow, M. (2015). *Language and neoliberalism*. London: Routledge.

Holloway, J. (2010). *Crack capitalism*. London: Pluto Press.

Moreno, L. (2012). *La Europa asocial. ¿Caminamos hacia un individualismo posesivo?* Barcelona: Ediciones Península.

O'Toole, M. (2015). Word pictures and painted narrative: The systemic-functional model relating the analysis of pictorial discourse, verbal discourse and narrative form. In A. Archer & E. Breuer (Eds.), *Multimodality in writing: The state of the art in theory, methodology and pedagogy* (pp. 65–83). Leiden: Brill.

Paltridge, B. (1995). Working with genre: A pragmatic perspective. *Journal of Pragmatics, 24*(4), 393–406.

Rodríguez, G., Aguilar, M., & Alfama, E. (2014). *Estado de bienestar en España: Transformaciones y tendencias de cambio en el marco de la Unión Europea: VII Informe sobre exclusión y desarrollo social en España*. Madrid: Fundación Foessa. Retrieved from: www.foessa2014.es/informe/uploaded/descargas/VII_INFORME.pdf

Sani, I., Abdullah, M.H., Abdullah, F.S., & Ali, A.M. (2012). Political cartoons as a vehicle of setting social agenda: The newspaper example. *Asian Social Science, 8*(6), 156–164.

Segura A. (2014). Recortes, austeridad y salud: Informe SESPAS 2014. *Gaceta Sanitaria, 28*(S1), 7–11. Retrieved from: www.gacetasanitaria.org/es/recortes-austeridad-salud-informe-sespas/articulo/S0213911114000508/%2011

Swain, E. (2012). Analysing evaluation in political cartoons. *Discourse, Context & Media, 1*(2), 82–94.

Van Gool, K., & Pearson, M. (2014). *Health, austerity and economic crisis: Assessing the short-term impact in OECD countries*. (OECD Health Working Paper No. 76). Paris: OECD. Retrieved from http://dx.doi.org/10.1787/5jxx71lt1zg6-en

Žižek, S, & Tsipras, A. (2014). La destrucción de Grecia: Un modelo europeo. ¿Merece Europa un porvenir así? In S. Horvat & S. Žižek (Eds.). *El sur pide la palabra: El futuro de una Europa en crisis* (pp. 8–29). Madrid: El lince.

Conclusion

Kate Power, Tanweer Ali and Eva Lebdušková

The denouement of early twenty-first century austerity has been well-documented in the decade since the 2008 global financial crisis (see, for example, Blyth, 2013; Jessop, 2016; Karyotis & Gerodimos, 2015; Krugman, 2013; Varoufakis, 2018). In the immediate aftermath of the crisis, governments around the developed world coordinated policy moves to stimulate economic activity and avert a depression. In subsequent years, however, a perceived need to control government debt became the dominant narrative on economic policy. Cuts to public expenditure, or austerity, were widely viewed as necessary to avert disaster on both sides of the Atlantic—and few mainstream public players offered a coherent alternative policy prescription. These developments occurred in the context of—and can be viewed as evidence of—pervasive neoliberalizing processes, in which multiple, highly situated forms of neoliberalism had colonized (and continue to colonize) diverse historical, geographical, institutional, and subjective locations.

Rooted in an appreciation of the complexities of neoliberalization, this edited volume examines manifestations of the post-crisis era's most influential public discourses—namely, discourses of austerity—as these have played out in media, policy, and academic settings across Europe and in the Americas. More specifically, it empirically and theoretically analyzes arguments in favor of austerity; and, using both European and American case studies involving diverse texts—ranging from political speeches to newspapers articles, and from academic blogs to cartoons—, it explains the sociopolitical, economic, and ideological drivers behind the austerity juggernaut, as well as the ways in which notions of 'crisis' and various metaphors and other rhetorical devices have been recruited to its cause. In doing so, this volume models the use of several leading discourse analytic methods. It also argues that approaching issues such as austerity armed with both an appreciation of the role of discourse(s) in the construction (i.e., realization) of social phenomena, and an understanding (theoretical and empirical) of the underlying economics, builds the kind of critical literacy needed to hold economic (and other) powers accountable, and, in doing so, to counter economic (and other) injustices. Indeed, we believe this kind of interdisciplinary* literacy is essential not only for scholars but, even more importantly, for everyday citizens who routinely encounter and must therefore navigate a constant barrage of political, economic, and other 'spin.'

In concluding this volume, we will now briefly revisit some of the key findings presented by our contributors about austerity discourses, and we will comment on both discourse analysis as research method and on interdisciplinarity*: its significance and the potential we see for further collaboration between discourse analysis and economics.

Findings

As several of our contributors have noted, it is important to recognize the highly situated nature of austerity policies (and discourses), and to avoid conflating geographical (and textual) differences in the quest for a single grand narrative. In all of their diversity, however, the studies presented here do point to several forces common to twenty-first century austerity as it has played out across geographical boundaries. In particular, looking at the drivers behind austerity policies, we can see that—their repeated depiction as a purely economic policy response to financial crisis notwithstanding—austerity programs throughout Europe and in the Americas arguably had much broader aspirations: to eviscerate emerging critique of the neoliberal paradigm; to extend the capitalization of social life; to transfer political power from the State to private interests; to strengthen the domination of the market over social and economic life; and to consolidate wealth within concentrated capital.

We can also see patterns in the discursive representation of, and argumentation for, austerity across the diverse text-types and contexts addressed in this volume. First, several of our contributors corroborate previously documented observations that there is more than one way of construing (i.e., representing) economic phenomena. Setting the discursive agenda—that is, gaining the upper hand by discursively framing a situation in ways that will persuade and be taken up by others—is a well-known and widely-used strategic move in policy (and other) contests. Recognizing this move and countering it when made disingenuously is, therefore, central to participating effectively in public debate. For example, both the 2008 financial crisis and austerity as the preferred policy response to it were successfully "'framed' in various ways" (Fairclough, 2016, p. 69; see also Basu, Schifferes, & Knowles, 2018; Kelsey, Mueller, Whittle, & KhosraviNik, 2017)—which in turn facilitated the widespread adoption of austerity measures. That is, the crisis was construed largely in moral terms by political and economic leaders, as well as the mainstream media, with governments and populations repeatedly blamed for moral failure (e.g., excessive spending) and/or ineptitude (e.g., mismanagement of funds); but the accrual of inordinate debt by the banks was substantially elided in public discussion.

Second, and relatedly, the key terms and arguments upon which austerity discourses are premised are themselves subject to permutation—and because such shifts in meaning, prominence, and power are seldom announced, close attention is needed to recognize when, how, and why they occur. The word 'austerity,' for example, has meant quite different things in different contexts: in early twenty-first century Romania, it was widely embraced as representing *Europeanization*, *Westernization*, and *modernization*. Parliamentary debates in the UK, by contrast, traded on earlier, positive, post-war resonances of the term.

Third, while technical arguments in favor of twenty-first century austerity policies have been limited in number (and have repeatedly relied on flawed hypotheses concerning the restoration of confidence and growth), non-technical arguments have been more varied. The latter draw heavily on metaphors involving mechanics (e.g., tools, containers, warfare), wellbeing (e.g., the body, medicine, diet, religion), and the environment (e.g., physical entities, natural forces, disasters). The chief of these metaphors reductionistically likens national and international economies to households, and economic policy to house-keeping, disregarding not only the basic fallacy of composition involved in assuming that the logic that applies to an individual must also apply to the collective (i.e., the whole economy), but also the fact that governments have financial and policy options not available to the average family. Because of its pervasiveness and popular appeal, this misleading metaphor must repeatedly be challenged, wherever it is used.

Fourth, both technical and non-technical arguments in favor of austerity policies tend to be predicated upon and situated within a limited set of narratives (e.g., crime and punishment, excess and retrenchment, dissatisfaction with the State, pro-Europeanization), in terms of which austerity appears to make sense, and is thereby legitimated. Pro-austerity policies are not always accompanied by pro-austerity discourse, however; and it is important to recognize that discursive silences can be just as powerful as—potentially even more so than—explicit mentions and/or arguments (cf. Jaworski, 1993; Dimitrov, 2018; Schröter, 2013; Schröter & Taylor, 2018). Understanding the relationships between discourse, history, and economics is critical in this regard, which is one reason we are arguing for greater interdisciplinary* collaboration between economists and discourse analysts.

Discourse analytic methods

The focus of this volume has been austerity discourses, rather than austerity policies per se. As Hart and Cap (2014) observe, "the dialectical relationship between discourse and social reality is quite evidently complex," with scholars in this field tending to work "at different locations on the continuum that links the 'micro' (the linguistic) with the 'macro' (the social)" (p. 2; see also Lemke, 1995). This volume was designed as a selective 'tasting menu' of leading discourse analytic methods, and we have contributors drawing on approaches from various points along that continuum. At the 'macro' end, this volume includes social semiotics (Chapter 1), the Discourse Historical Approach (Chapters 4 and 13), new rhetorical analysis (Chapter 6), Cultural Political Economy (Chapter 7), post-structural discourse analysis (Chapter 8), and narrative analysis (Chapter 14). At the 'micro' end, paying closer attention to fine-grained linguistic and paralinguistic details, this volume features Corpus Linguistics (Chapters 3 and 11), Systemic Functional Linguistics (Chapters 5 and 10), Cognitive Metaphor Theory (Chapters 9 and 11), and Multi-Modal Analysis (Chapter 15). As the foregoing list indicates, this volume also demonstrates that different discourse analytic methods can be fruitfully combined.

With the possible exception of rhetorical analysis, which tends to rely on categories and terms drawn from classical rhetoric, each of these approaches deals explicitly with 'discourse'—and we noted in the introduction to this volume that the polysemy of that term can give rise to considerable confusion. An essential first step in any discourse analysis, therefore, is to adopt a clear working definition of 'discourse' (or of 'rhetoric,' which is a similarly slippery term). In this volume, we follow Fairclough (1995) in conceptualizing *discourse* (count noun) as "the language used in representing a given social practice from a particular point of view" (p. 56), with the plural form signifying the multiple perspectives from which austerity can be conceptualized and addressed.

We would like to mention here, however, that although 'discourse' is the more common term the linguistic and argumentative patterns used to justify and promote austerity policies can also be viewed as 'interpretative repertoires'—that is, as "recurrently used systems of terms for characterizing and evaluating actions, events, or other phenomena" (Potter & Wetherell, 1987, p. 149), or "culturally familiar and habitual line[s] of argument comprised from recognisable themes, common places and tropes (doxa)" (Wetherell, 1988, p. 400). Other interpretative repertoires (not related to austerity), for example, include: the apocalyptic framing often used to sustain global warming discourse (Foust & O'Shannon Murphy, 2009); blaming and justificatory repertoires in non-Maori doctors' explanations of Maori health problems and levels of medical care (McCreanor & Nairn, 2002); contrasting depictions of feminists in young men's negotiations of their own masculinity (Edley, 2001); "empiricist" and "contingent" repertoires in scientists' accounts of their own and other scholars' research (McKinlay & Potter, 1987, p. 445); and oppositional "realist" and "game" repertoires used by journalists to disassociate themselves from public relations professionals (Francoeur, 2016, p. 64).

The terms 'discourse' and 'interpretative repertoires' are sometimes used interchangeably, with 'discourse' tending to be used "in the context of research which adopts more of a Foucauldian perspective .... centrally concerned with the operation of power, and tend[ing], if anything, towards a view of people as *subjectified*"; by contrast, 'interpretative repertoires' is more often the choice of "those who want to place more emphasis upon human *agency* within the flexible deployment of language" (Edley, 2001, p. 202, emphasis original). In this volume, we have chosen to use the term 'discourse(s)'—with the plural form signifying the multiple perspectives from which austerity can be conceptualized and addressed—because we view public debate around austerity as intrinsically related to power and its exertion. However, we mention the term 'interpretative repertoires' here, first, to alert non-linguist readers to the similarity (even synonymity) of these terms; and, second, to highlight its usefulness for readers who might wish to work with "less monolithic … smaller and more fragmented" language use (Edley, 2001, p. 202).

Interdisciplinarity*

As we explained in the introduction to this volume, we understand interdisciplinarity* in terms of scholars from different disciplines working together on a common set of research questions and sharing perspectives, theories and methods drawn from each discipline, with a view to (1) making new knowledge that transcends the affordances of any single discipline (Cheng et al., 2009), and (2) opening a space for the mutual enrichment and development of participating disciplines. In this volume, for example, we have shown that linguistic sensibilities are valuable for recognizing, systematically documenting, and describing how economic language is used; and economic consciousness is needed to make robust sense of such language use in (often unstable and evolving) contexts. Our firm belief here is that working collaboratively across both discourse analysis and economics is the best way to gain a holistic understanding of contemporary austerity and the discourses with which it has been both promoted and contested. We have therefore sought both to practice and to model that collaboration.

Clearly, our subject matter is fundamentally economic and the basic economic approach is Keynesian—insofar as it accepts that the policy of austerity is ineffective in terms of its stated goals—but our contributors represent different schools of thought. Most have backgrounds in linguistics and the approaches they use are chiefly discourse analytic, not only because these tools have been largely overlooked within the field of economics, but also because, as Rudyard Kipling (1923) once said, "Words are, of course, the most powerful drug used by mankind." We must come to grips with how they are used.

We believe that the volume has value for both economists and discourse analysts. Key 'take-homes' for economists are that: (1) discourse can be treated as a form of data, with different text types (e.g., political, policy, academic, media) being salient for different discourse-related research questions; (2) discourse analysis can be more or less linguistic in nature, with different approaches focusing on context, content, language use, and multi-modality; (3) close linguistic analysis can focus on different features of language (e.g., narrative, metaphor, representation), but must always be situated contextually; and (4) the possibilities for economics to make meaningful use of discourse analytic tools include generating (economics-related) discourse analytic research questions, identifying salient (economics-related) discursive data, and providing (economics-related) contextual and theoretical insights.

Similarly, we suggest a number of key 'take-homes' for discourse analysts: (1) the fundamental difference in approach between the proponents of austerity, basing the larger economy on a set of assumptions founded in classical microeconomics, and their opponents, deriving their ideas of a macroeconomy from the work of John Maynard Keynes and his followers; (2) the nature of modern money and its creation within the financial system of a developed economy, including an appreciation of the different views held by different schools of thought; and (3) the basics of national accounting, including the components of Gross Domestic Product (and alternative measures) and public sector debt.

Further collaboration

Whilst a great deal of research has already been undertaken on the discourses of austerity—and we hope this volume will prove to be a valuable contribution to this work—there remains considerable scope for further research across several disciplines: this effort is yet in its early days. For example, most of the contributions in this book have focused on the public discussion of austerity, with several authors looking at the speeches and pronouncements of experts. A closer look at the language of academic papers and conference proceedings would shed light on the formation of ideas and thoughts beneath the surface of public debate. The examination of economic models would also provide interesting insights into the thought structures and moral assumptions behind austerity. Furthermore, we believe that a study of the ways in which textbooks disseminate ideas on public finance would provide valuable insights into both the training of the economics profession and the formation of received wisdom amongst mainstream economists.

Related to this last point, we see the need for further research exploring the linkage between austerity and other basic economic questions, as well as broader social issues. A full study of the views of the nature of money underpinning the arguments for and against austerity has yet to be done. Similarly, it would be enlightening to have a greater understanding of the labor market models associated with overall economic positions that support austerity—and the related moral premises. In our introduction, we briefly touched upon the gender aspects of the impact of austerity on women. There is further work to be done on the ways in which language and discourse shape thinking about the underlying economics of austerity—and the policies that impact men and women differently and with varying degrees of intensity. We would also be interested to see whether, and if so how, austerity is represented in text types explicitly directed to women, such as women's magazines—or whether this represents an area of discursive silence in such texts, and what such a silence might add to our understanding of both genre expectations and gender relations. Similarly, although we have seen references to the way southern European countries have been treated discursively, with the application of the collective term 'PIIGS,' a more detailed analysis of the ways in which ethnic and class prejudices and stereotypes enter into the public discussion of austerity would be a welcome addition to our knowledge of the phenomenon.

In terms of the resources available for further linguistic examination of austerity, we believe there is scope for economies of scale in terms of corpus building. Many of the contributors to this volume have created corpora to assist in their analysis. We would welcome efforts to create larger corpora assembling more extensive samples of austerity discourses, drawing on a more expansive array of text types, which could be made widely available to researchers. Such a resource would enable more generalizable research, while helping to avoid duplication of efforts as regards the time-consuming business of corpus building. Such efforts would also foster interdisciplinarity*, facilitating collaboration across disciplinary, institutional, and geographical boundaries.

Another angle for future research involves the media. Although several scholars (including in this volume) have studied the representation of austerity in the media—and we acknowledge in particular the recent volume edited by Basu et al. (2018)—there remains much to learn: what influences journalists to cover austerity as they do? Do particular forms of economic education contribute to reporting on austerity? What relationship, if any, exists between a media outlet's stance on austerity and its ownership structure? How do austerity discourses compare across mainstream, alternative, and social media? Such research would shed light on the ways in which power is used to buttress ideology, and contribute to our overall understanding of the role of media ownership in politics.

Of course, we also hope that both economists and linguists will explore further approaches to interdisciplinarity*—of which the model we have adopted in this volume is just one. We consider the main strength of this model to be that it pushes interdisciplinary collaboration between economists and linguists further than much previous work has done, ensuring disciplinary rigor with respect to both fields, while remaining manageable for individual contributors with little or no institutional support for cross-disciplinary collaboration. Its main limitation—which is common to interdisciplinary work of all kinds—was that a lack of familiarity with each other's "training, aptitudes and ways of viewing and interrogating the world" (Marzano Carss, & Bell, 2006, p. 194) meant some contributors found it difficult to make substantive comments on work from other disciplines. We responded to this challenge by incorporating additional rounds of peer review, so that the final versions of all chapters benefited from both disciplinary perspectives. We would like to acknowledge all of our fearless contributors in this regard: we asked them to work well beyond their disciplinary comfort zones and we recognize that not all scholars might be so willing to venture into unknown territories.

Nevertheless, we do hope that other economists and discourse analysts will work together, along these or other interdisciplinary* lines, because we see tremendous potential in this kind of scholarship. There remains considerable room yet for economists and discourse analysts not only to study other economic discourses (i.e., those not directly related to austerity) in the service of fairer markets, but also to study the possibly less overt, but still important economic dimensions of other public discourses and debates (i.e., those not directly related to economics), in the service of fairer institutions. Finally, we believe that both economists and discourse analysts should seek to equip students, as well as non-scholarly communities, with an interdisciplinary* perspective and the critical literacy it affords, in the service of a fairer world.

References

Basu, L., Schifferes, S., & Knowles, S. (Eds.). (2018). *The media and austerity: Comparative perspectives*. London: Routledge.

Blyth, M. (2013). *Austerity: The history of a dangerous idea*. New York: Oxford University Press.

Cheng, J. L. C., Henisz, W. J., Roth, K., & Swaminathan, A. (2009). From the Editors: Advancing interdisciplinary research in the field of international business: Prospects, issues and challenges. *Journal of International Business Studies, 40*(1), 1070–1074. doi:10.1057/jibs.2009.41

Dimitrov, R. (2018). *Strategic silence: Public relations and indirect communication*. London: Routledge.

Edley, N. (2001). Analysing masculinity: Interpretative repertoires, ideological dilemmas and subject positions. In M. Wetherell, S. Taylor, & S. J. Yates (Eds.), *Discourse as data: A guide for analysis* (pp. 189–228). London: Sage and The Open University Press.

Fairclough, I. (2016). Evaluating policy as argument: The public debate over the first UK austerity budget. *Critical Discourse Studies, 13*(1), 57–77.

Foust, C. R., & O'Shannon Murphy, W. (2009). Revealing and reframing apocalyptic tragedy in global warming discourse. *Environmental Communication, 3*(2), 151–167.

Francoeur, C. (2016). Maintaining the boundaries: The interpretative repertoires journalists use to differentiate themselves from the public relations industry. *Brazilian Journalism Research, 12*(3), 56–73.

Hart, C., & Cap, P. (Eds.). (2014). *Contemporary Critical Discourse Studies*. London/New York: Bloomsbury.

Jaworski, A. (1993). *The power of silence: Social and pragmatic perspectives*. Newbury Park: Sage.

Jessop, R. D. (2016). The heartlands of neoliberalism and the rise of the austerity state. In S. Springer, K. Birch, & J. McLeavy (Eds.), *The handbook of neoliberalism* (pp. 410–421). London: Routledge.

Karyotis, G., & Gerodimos, R. (Eds.). (2015). *The politics of extreme austerity: Greece in the Eurozone crisis*. Houndmills, Basingstoke, UK: Palgrave Macmillan.

Kelsey, D., Mueller, F., Whittle, A., & KhosraviNik, M. (2017). *The discourse of financial crisis and austerity: Critical analyses of business and economics across disciplines*. London: Routledge.

Kipling, R. (1923, February 14). "Surgeons and the Soul" [Speech to the Royal College of Surgeons, Lincoln's Inn] in *A Book of Words*. Retrieved from www.kiplingsociety.co.uk/rg_words_twentythree.htm

Krugman, P. (2013). *End this depression now!* New York: W.W. Norton & Company, Inc.

Lemke, J. (1995). *Textual politics: Discourse and social dynamics*. London: Taylor & Francis.

Marzano, M., Carss, D. N., & Bell, S. (2006). Working to make interdisciplinarity work: Investing in communication and interpersonal relationships. *Journal of Agricultural Economics, 57*(2), 185–197.

McCreanor, T., & Nairn, R. (2002). Tauiwi general practitioners' talk about Maori health: Interpretative repertoires. *The New Zealand Medical Journal*, 115(1167).

McKinlay, A., & Potter, J. (1987). Model discourse: Interpretative repertoires in scientists' conference talk. *Social Studies of Science, 17*, 443–463.

Potter, J., & Wetherell, M. (1987). *Discourse and Social Psychology*. London: Sage.

Schröter, M. (2013). *Silence and concealment in political discourse*. Amsterdam, Netherlands: John Benjamins.

Schröter, M., & Taylor, C. (Eds.). (2018). *Exploring silence and absence in discourse: Empirical approaches*. Houndmills, Basingstoke, UK: Palgrave Macmillan.
Varoufakis, Y. (2018). *Austerity: Vintage minis*. London: Vintage Classics.
Wetherell, M. (1988). Positioning and interpretative repertoires: Conversation analysis and post-structuralism in dialogue. *Discourse & Society, 9*(3), 387–412.

Index

Note: **bold** page numbers indicate figures, *italic* numbers indicate tables.